CONFEDERATES
IN THE ATTIC

Also by
TONY HORWITZ

Baghdad Without a Map
One for the Road

CONFEDERATES
IN THE ATTIC

Dispatches from the
Unfinished Civil War

TONY HORWITZ

Pantheon Books   NEW YORK

Chapter 5 of this work was originally published in a
different form in *The New Yorker.*

Grateful acknowledgment is made to Random House, Inc., for
permission to reprint an excerpt from *Intruder in the Dust* by
William Faulkner. Copyright © 1948 by Random House, Inc.
Reprinted by permission of Random House, Inc.

Library of Congress Cataloging-in-Publication Data

Horwitz, Tony, 1958–
Confederates in the attic : dispatches from the unfinished
Civil War / Tony Horwitz.
p.   cm
ISBN 0–679–43978–1
1. United States—History—Civil War, 1861–1865—Influence.
2. Horwitz, Tony, 1958–   —Journeys—Southern States.   I. Title.
E468.9.H78   1998
973.7—dc21   97-26759
CIP

Random House Web Address: http://www.randomhouse.com

Book design by M. Kristen Bearse

Printed in the United States of America

First Edition

2 4 6 8 9 7 5 3 1

*To my father
who gave me the passion,
and to my mother
who gave me the paint*

Southerners are very strange about that war.

—SHELBY FOOTE

CONTENTS

CONFEDERATES
IN THE ATTIC

1

CONFEDERATES
IN THE ATTIC

*There never will be anything more interesting
in America than that Civil War never.*
—GERTRUDE STEIN

In 1965, a century after Appomattox, the Civil War began for me at a musty apartment in New Haven, Connecticut. My great-grandfather held a magnifying glass to his spectacles and studied an enormous book spread open on the rug. Peering over his shoulder, I saw pen-and-ink soldiers hurtling up at me with bayonets.

I was six, Poppa Isaac 101. Egg-bald, barely five feet tall, Poppa Isaac lived so frugally that he sliced cigarettes in half before smoking them. An elderly relative later told me that Poppa Isaac bought the book of Civil War sketches soon after emigrating to America in 1882. He often shared it with his children and grandchildren before I came along.

Years later, I realized what was odd about this one vivid memory of my great-grandfather. Isaac Moses Perski fled Czarist Russia as a teenaged draft dodger—in Yiddish, a *shirker*—and arrived at Ellis Island without money or English or family. He worked at a Lower East Side sweatshop and lived literally on peanuts, which were cheap, filling and nutritious. Why, I wondered, had this thrifty refugee chosen as one of his first purchases in America a book written in a language he could barely understand, about a war in a land he barely knew, a book that he kept poring over until his death at 102?

By the time Poppa Isaac died, my father had begun reading aloud to me each night from a ten-volume collection called *The Photographic History of the Civil War*. Published in 1911, the volumes' ripe prose sounded as foreign to me as the captions of my great-grandfather's book must have seemed to him. So, like Poppa Isaac, I lost myself in the pictures: sepia men leading sepia horses across cornfields and creeks; jaunty volunteers, their faces framed by squished caps and fire-hazard beards; barefoot Confederates sprawled in trench mud, eyes open, limbs twisted like licorice. For me, the fantastical creatures of Maurice Sendak held little magic compared to the man-boys of Mathew Brady who stared back across the century separating their lives from mine.

Before long, I began to read aloud with my father, chanting the strange and wondrous rivers—Shenandoah, Rappahannock, Chickahominy—and wrapping my tongue around the risible names of rebel generals: Braxton Bragg, Jubal Early, John Sappington Marmaduke, William "Extra Billy" Smith, Pierre Gustave Toutant Beauregard. I learned about palindromes from the Southern sea captain Raphael Semmes. And I began to match Brady's still-deaths with the curt stutter of farm roads and rocks that formed the photographer's backdrop: Mule Shoe, Slaughter Pen, Bloody Lane, Devil's Den.

In third grade, I penciled a highly derivative Civil War history of my own—"The war was started when after all the states had seceded," it began—and embarked on an ambitious art project, painting the walls of our attic with a lurid narrative of the conflict. Preferring underdogs, I posted a life-sized Johnny Reb by the bathroom door. A pharaonic frieze of rebel soldiers at Antietam stretched from the stairs to the attic window. Albert Sidney Johnston's death at Shiloh splashed across an entire wall. General Pickett and his men charged bravely into the eaves.

I'd reached the summer of 1863 and run out of wall. But standing in the middle of the attic, I could whirl and whirl and make myself dizzy with my own cyclorama. The attic became my bedroom and the murals inhabited my boyhood dreaming. And each morning I woke to a comforting sound: my father bounding up the attic steps, blowing a mock bugle call through his fingers and shouting, "General, the troops await your command!"

TWENTY-FIVE YEARS LATER, the murals were still there and so was my boyhood obsession. I'd just returned to America after nine years abroad and moved to an old house in the foothills of the Blue Ridge Mountains. My Australian wife chose the spot; the fields and cows and crooked fences fit Geraldine's image of outback America. For me, the place stirred something else. I stared at a brick church still bullet-scarred from a Civil War skirmish. In the lumpy village graveyard, I found Confederates and Yankees buried side by side, some of them kin to each other. Within an hour of our new home lay several of the battlegrounds I'd painted as a child, and to which I now dragged Geraldine on weekend drives.

At a picnic soon after our arrival, I overheard a neighbor ask Geraldine how she liked Virginia. "Fine," she sighed. "Except that my husband's become a Civil War bore."

I'd always been one, of course, but my obsession had lain dormant for several decades. With adolescence had come other passions, and I'd stuffed my toy musket, plastic rebel soldiers and Lincoln Logs into a closet reserved for boyish things. A Day-Glo poster of Jimi Hendrix supplanted Johnny Reb. Pickett's Charge and Antietam Creek vanished behind dart boards, Star Trek posters and steep drifts of teenage clutter.

But a curious thing had happened while I'd lived abroad. Millions of Americans caught my childhood bug. Ken Burns's TV documentary on the Civil War riveted the nation for weeks. *Glory* and *Gettysburg* played to packed movie houses. The number of books on the Civil War passed 60,000; a bibliography of works on Gettysburg alone ran to 277 pages.

On the face of it, this fad seemed out of character for America. Like most returning expatriates, I found my native country new and strange, and few things felt stranger than America's amnesia about its past. During the previous decade, I'd worked as a foreign correspondent in lands where memories were elephantine: Bosnia, Iraq,

Northern Ireland, Aboriginal Australia. Serbs spoke bitterly of their defeat by Muslim armies at Kosovo as though the battle had occurred yesterday, not in 1389. Protestants in Belfast referred fondly to "King Billy" as if he were a family friend rather than the English monarch who led Orangemen to victory in 1690.

Returning to America, I found the background I lacked wasn't historical, it was pop-cultural. People kept referring to TV shows I'd missed while abroad, or to athletes and music stars I'd never seen perform. In the newspaper, I read a government survey showing that 93 percent of American students couldn't identify "an important event" in Philadelphia in 1776. Most parents also flunked; 73 percent of adults didn't know what event "D-Day" referred to.

Yet Americans remained obsessed with the Civil War. Nor was this passion confined to books and movies. Fights kept erupting over displays of the rebel flag, over the relevancy of states' rights, over a statue of Arthur Ashe slated to go up beside Robert E. Lee and Stonewall Jackson in Richmond. Soon after my return, the Walt Disney Company unveiled plans for a Civil War theme park beside the Manassas battlefield. This provoked howls of protest that Disney would vulgarize history and sully the nation's "hallowed ground." It seemed as though the black-and-white photographs I'd studied as a child had blurred together, forming a Rorschach blot in which Americans now saw all sorts of unresolved strife: over race, sovereignty, the sanctity of historic landscapes, and who should interpret the past.

THEN, EARLY ONE MORNING, the Civil War crashed into my bedroom. A loud popping noise crackled just outside our window. "Is that what I think it is?" Geraldine asked, bolting awake. We'd sometimes heard gunfire while working in the Middle East, but it was the last sound we expected here, in a hamlet of 250 where bleating sheep had been our reveille for the past six months.

I went to the window and saw men in gray uniforms firing muskets on the road in front of our house. Then a woman popped up from behind a stone wall and yelled "Cut!" The firing stopped and the Confederates collapsed in our yard. I brewed a pot of coffee, gathered some mugs and went outside. It turned out that our village had been chosen as the set for a TV documentary on Fredericksburg, an 1862 battle fought partly along eighteenth-century streets that resembled ours.

But the men weren't actors, at least not professionals, and they performed in the film shoot for little or no pay. "We do this sort of thing most weekends anyway," said a lean rebel with gunpowder smudges on his face and the felicitous name of Troy Cool.

In the local paper, I'd often read about Civil War reenactors who staged mock battles with smoke bombs and reproduction muskets. It was a popular hobby in our part of Virginia. But when I asked about this, Troy Cool frowned. "We're hardcores," he said.

Between gulps of coffee—which the men insisted on drinking from their own tin cups rather than our ceramic mugs—Cool and his comrades explained the distinction. Hardcores didn't just dress up and shoot blanks. They sought absolute fidelity to the 1860s: its homespun clothing, antique speech patterns, sparse diet and simple utensils. Adhered to properly, this fundamentalism produced a time-travel high, or what hardcores called a "period rush."

"Look at these buttons," one soldier said, fingering his gray wool jacket. "I soaked them overnight in a saucer filled with urine." Uric acid oxidized the brass, giving it the patina of buttons from the 1860s. "My wife woke up this morning, sniffed the air and said, 'Tim, you've been peeing on your buttons again.'"

In the field, hardcores ate only foods that Civil War soldiers consumed, such as hardtack and salt pork. And they limited their speech to mid-nineteenth-century dialect and topics. "You don't talk about Monday Night football," Tim explained. "You curse Abe Lincoln or say things like, 'I wonder how Becky's getting on back at the farm.'"

One hardcore took this Method acting to a bizarre extreme. His name was Robert Lee Hodge and the soldiers pointed him out as he ambled toward us. Hodge looked as though he'd stepped from a Civil War tintype: tall, rail-thin, with a long pointed beard and a butternut uniform so frayed and filthy that it clung to his lank frame like rags to a scarecrow.

As he drew near, Troy Cool called out, "Rob, do the bloat!" Hodge clutched his stomach and crumpled to the ground. His belly swelled grotesquely, his hands curled, his cheeks puffed out, his mouth contorted in a rictus of pain and astonishment. It was a flawless counterfeit of the bloated corpses photographed at Antietam and Gettysburg that I'd so often stared at as a child.

Hodge leapt to his feet and smiled. "It's an ice-breaker at parties," he said.

For Robert Lee Hodge, it was also a way of life. As the Marlon Brando of battlefield bloating, he was often hired for Civil War movies. He also posed—dead and alive—for painters and photographers who reproduced Civil War subjects and techniques. "I go to the National Archives a lot to look at their Civil War photographs," he said. "You can see much more detail in the original pictures than you can in books."

A crowd of blue-clad soldiers formed down the road. It was time for the battle to resume. Hodge reached in his haversack and handed me a business card. "You should come out with us sometime," he said, his brown eyes boring into mine with evangelical fervor, "and see what a period rush feels like." Then he loped off to join the other rebels crouched behind a stone wall.

I watched the men fight for a while, then went back inside and built a fire. I pulled down Poppa Isaac's book from the shelf. The tome was so creased with age that the title had rubbed off its spine and the pages discharged a puff of yellowed paper-dust each time I opened the massive cover. Searching for pictures of Fredericksburg, I quickly became lost in the Civil War, as I'd been so often since our return to America.

Geraldine came in with a cup of coffee. She'd chatted with a few of the men, too. "It's strange," she said, "but they seemed like ordinary guys." One worked as a Bell Atlantic salesman, another as a forklift operator. Even Robert Lee Hodge had seemed, well, normal. During the week, he waited on tables and sometimes freelanced articles for Civil War magazines. I'd once worked as a waiter, and at twenty-eight, which was Hodge's age, I'd been a freelancer, too, although writing about more recent wars.

Then again, I'd never spent weekends grubbing around the woods in urine-soaked clothes, gnawing on salt pork and bloating in the road. Not that my own behavior was altogether explicable, sitting here in a crooked house in the hills of Virginia, poring over sketches of long-dead Confederates. I was born seven years after the last rebel soldier, Pleasant Crump, died at home in Lincoln, Alabama. I was raised in Maryland, a border state in the Civil War that now belonged to the "Mid-Atlantic States," a sort of regionless buffer between North and South. Nor did I have blood ties to the War. My forebears were digging potatoes and studying Torah between Minsk and Pinsk when Pleasant Crump trudged through Virginia with the 10th Alabama.

I took out the card Robert Lee Hodge had given me. It was colored Confederate gray; the phone number ended in 1865. Muskets crackled outside and shrieks of mock pain filled the air. Why did this war still obsess so many Americans 130 years after Appomattox? I returned to Poppa Isaac's book. What did that war have to do with him, or with me?

A FEW WEEKS LATER I gave Rob Hodge a call. He seemed unsurprised to hear from me and renewed his offer to take me out in the field. Hodge's unit, the Southern Guard, was about to hold a drill to keep its skills sharp during the long winter layoff (battle reenactments, like real Civil War combat, clustered between spring and fall). "It'll be forty-eight hours of hardcore marching," he said. "Wanna come?"

Hodge gave me the number for the Guardsman hosting the event, a Virginia farmer named Robert Young. I called for directions and also asked what to bring. "I've got a sleeping bag," I told him. The voice on the other end went silent. "Or some blankets," I added.

"You'll be issued a bedroll and other kit as needed," Young said. "Bring food, but nothing modern. Absolutely no plastic." He suggested I arrive early so he could check out my gear.

I donned an old-fashioned pair of one-piece long johns known as a union suit (which sounded Civil War–ish), a pair of faded button-fly jeans, muddy work boots, and a rough cotton shirt a hippie girlfriend had given me years before. Ignorant of nineteenth-century food packaging, I tossed a hunk of cheese and a few apples into a leather shoulder bag, along with a rusty canteen and camping knife.

Surely the others would share their grub. I imagined the Guardsmen gathered round a crackling bonfire, talking about the homefront while slicing potatoes into a bubbling Irish stew.

Two young Confederates stood guard at the entrance to the drill site, a 400-acre farm in the bucolic horse country of the Virginia Piedmont. One was my host, Robert Young. He welcomed me with a curt nod and a full-body frisk for twentieth-century contraband. The apples had to go; they were shiny Granny Smiths, nothing like the mottled fruit of the 1860s. The knife and canteen and shoulder bag also were deemed too pristine, as was my entire wardrobe. Even the union suit was wrong; long johns in the 1860s were two-piece, not one.

In exchange, Young tossed me scratchy wool trousers, a filthy shirt, hobnailed boots, a jacket tailored for a Confederate midget, and wool socks that smelled as though they hadn't been washed since Second Manassas. Then he reached for my tortoiseshell glasses. "The frames are modern," he explained, handing me a pair of wire-rimmed spectacles with tiny, weak lenses. Finally, he slung a thin blanket over my shoulder. "We'll probably be spooning tonight," he said.

Spooning? His manner didn't invite questions. I was a soldier now; mine was not to question why. So half-blind and hobbled by the ill-fitting brogans—boots weren't always molded to right and left in the Civil War—I trailed the two men to a cramped farm building behind the inviting antebellum mansion I'd seen from the road. We sat shivering inside, waiting for the others. Unsure about the ground rules for conversation, I asked my host, "How did you become a reenactor?"

He grimaced. I'd forgotten that the "R word" was distasteful to hardcores. "We're living historians," he said, "or historical interpreters if you like." The Southern Guard had formed the year before as a schismatic faction, breaking off from a unit that had too many "farbs," he said.

"Farb" was the worst insult in the hardcore vocabulary. It referred to reenactors who approached the past with a lack of verisimilitude. The word's etymology was obscure; Young guessed that "farb" was short for "far-be-it-from-authentic," or possibly a respelling of "barf."

Violations serious enough to earn the slur included wearing a wrist-watch, smoking cigarettes, smearing oneself with sunblock or insect repellent—or, worst of all, fake blood. Farb was also a fungible word; it could become an adjective (farby), a verb (as in, "don't farb out on me"), an adverb (farbily) and a heretical school of thought (Farbism or Farbiness).

The Southern Guard remained vigilant against even accidental Farbiness; it had formed an "authenticity committee" to research subjects such as underwear buttons and 1860s dye to make sure that Guardsmen attired themselves exactly as soldiers did. "Sometimes after weekends like this, it takes me three or four days to come back to so-called reality," Young said. "That's the ultimate."

As we talked, other Guardsmen trickled in, announcing themselves with a clatter of hobnailed boots on the path outside. Rob Hodge arrived and greeted his comrades with a pained grin. A few days before, he'd been dragged by a horse while playing Nathan Bedford Forrest in a cable show about the rebel cavalryman. The accident had left Rob with three cracked ribs, a broken toe and a hematoma on his tibia. "I wanted to go on a march down in Louisiana," Rob told his mates, "but the doctor said it would mess up my leg so bad that it might even have to be amputated."

"Super hardcore!" the others shouted in unison. If farb was the worst insult a Guardsman could bestow, super hardcore was the highest plaudit, signifying an unusually bold stab at recapturing the Civil War.

Many of the Guardsmen lived outside Virginia and hadn't seen their comrades since the previous year's campaign. As the room filled with twenty or so men, greeting each other with hugs and shouts, it became obvious that there would be little attempt to maintain period dialogue. Instead, the gathering took on a peculiar cast: part frat party, part fashion show, part Weight Watchers' meeting.

"Yo, look at Joel!" someone shouted as a tall, wasp-waisted Guardsman arrived. Joel Bohy twirled at the center of the room and slid off his gray jacket like a catwalk model. Then, reaching into his hip-hugging trousers, he raised his cotton shirt.

"Check out those abs!"

"Mmmm."

"Awesome jacket. What's the cut?"

"Type one, early to mid '62, with piping," Joel said. "Cotton and wool jean. Stitched it myself."

"Way cool!"

Rob Hodge inspected the needlework, obviously impressed. He turned to me and said, "We're all GQ fashion snobs when it comes to Civil War gear."

"CQ," Joel corrected. "Confederate Quarterly." The two men embraced, and Rob said approvingly, "You've dropped some weight." Joel smiled. "Fifteen pounds just in the last two months. I had a pizza yesterday but nothing at all today."

Losing weight was a hardcore obsession, part of the never-ending quest for authenticity. "If you look at pension records, you realize that very few Civil War soldiers weighed more than a hundred thirty-five pounds," Rob explained. Southern soldiers were especially lean. So it was every Guardsman's dream to drop a few pants' sizes and achieve the gaunt, hollow-eyed look of underfed Confederates.

Rob had lost thirty-five pounds over the past year, leaving little or no meat on his six-foot-two frame. Joel, a construction worker, had dropped eighty-five pounds, losing what he called his "keg legs" and slimming his beer-bellied waist from forty inches to thirty. "The Civil War's over, but the Battle of the Bulge never ends," he quipped, offering Rob a Pritikin recipe for skinless breast of chicken.

Unfortunately, there was no food—diet or otherwise—in sight. Instead, the Guardsmen puffed at corncob pipes or chewed tobacco, interspersed with swigs from antique jugs filled with Miller Lite and rimmed with bits of each other's burley. Eavesdropping on the chat—about grooming, sewing, hip size, honed biceps—I couldn't help wondering if I'd stumbled on a curious gay subculture in the Piedmont of Virginia.

"I've got a killer recipe for ratatouille. Hardly any oil. Got to drop another five pounds before posing for that painter again. He loves small waists on Confederates."

"Do you think we should recruit that newbie who came to the picket post? He looks real good, tall and slim."

"Ask him, 'Have you got a Richmond depot jacket? Do you sew?' A lot of guys look good at first but they don't know a thing about jackets and shoes."

The sleeping arrangements did little to allay my suspicions. As we hiked to our bivouac spot in a moonlit orchard, my breath clouded in the frigid night air. The thin wool blanket I'd been issued seemed woefully inadequate, and I wondered aloud how we'd avoid waking up resembling one of Rob Hodge's impressions of the Confederate dead. "Spooning," Joel said. "Same as they did in the War."

The Guardsmen stacked their muskets and unfurled ground cloths. "Sardine time," Joel said, flopping to the ground and pulling his blanket and coat over his chest. One by one the others lay down as well, packed close, as if on a slave ship. Feeling awkward, I shuffled to the end of the clump, lying a few feet from the nearest man.

"Spoon right!" someone shouted. Each man rolled onto his side and clutched the man beside him. Following suit, I snuggled my neighbor. A few bodies down, a man wedged between Joel and Rob began griping. "You guys are so skinny you don't give off any heat. You're just sucking it out of me!"

After fifteen minutes, someone shouted "spoon left!" and the pack rolled over. Now my back was warm but my front was exposed to the chill air. I was in the "anchor" position, my neighbor explained, the coldest spot in a Civil War spoon.

Famished and half-frozen, I began fantasizing about the campfire stew I'd naively looked forward to. Somewhere in the distance a horse snorted. Then one of the soldiers let loose a titanic fart. "You farb," his neighbor shouted. "Gas didn't come in until World War One!"

This prompted a volley of off-color jokes, most of them aimed at girlfriends and spouses. "You married?" I asked my neighbor, a man about my own age.

"Uh huh. Two kids." I asked how his family felt about his hobby. "If it wasn't this, it'd be golf or something," he said. He propped on one elbow and lit a cigar butt from an archaic box labeled Friction Matches. "At least there's no room for jealousy with this hobby. You come home stinking of gunpowder and sweat and bad tobacco, so your wife knows you've just been out with the guys."

From a few mummies down, Joel joined in the conversation. "I

just broke up with my girlfriend," he said. "It was a constant struggle between her and the Civil War. She got tired of competing with
something that happened a hundred thirty years ago."

Joel worried he might never find another girlfriend. Now, when
he met a woman he liked, he coyly let on that he was "into history."
That way, he explained, "I don't scare her off by letting the whole cat
out of the bag."

"What happens if you do tell her straight?" I asked him.

"She freaks." The issue wasn't just weekends spent away; it was
also the money. Joel reckoned that a quarter of his income went to
reenacting. "I try to put a positive spin on it," he said. "I tell women,
'I don't do drugs, I do the Civil War.'" He laughed. "Problem is, the
Civil War's more addictive than crack, and almost as expensive."

The chat gradually died down. Someone got up to pee and walked
into a tree branch, cursing. One man kept waking with a hacking
cough. And I realized I should have taken off my wet boots before
lying down; now, they'd become blocks of ice. My arm was caught
awkwardly beneath my side, but liberating it was impossible. I'd dis-
turb the whole spoon, and also risk shifting the precarious arrangement of blanket and coat that was my only protection from frostbite.

My neighbor, Paul Carter, was still half-awake and I asked him
what he did when he wasn't freezing to death in the Virginia hills.
"Finishing my Ph.D. thesis," he muttered, "on Soviet history."

I finally lulled myself to sleep with drowsy images of Stalingrad
and awoke to find my body molded tightly around Paul's, all awkwardness gone in the desperate search for warmth. He was doing the
same to the man beside him. There must have been a "spoon right" in
the night.

A moment later, someone banged on a pot and shouted reveille:
"Wake the fuck up! It's late!" The sky was still gray. It was not yet
six o'clock.

The pot, at least, was an encouraging prop. I hadn't eaten since
lunch the day before, and then only lightly in anticipation of a hearty
camp dinner. But no one gathered sticks or showed any signs of fixing breakfast. I saw one man furtively gnaw on a crust of bread, but
that was all. Recalling the hunk of cheese I'd packed the day before—
the only item of mine that had escaped confiscation—I frantically

searched my jacket pocket. The cheese was still there, hairy with lint and nicely chilled.

The Guardsmen rolled up their bedrolls and formed tidy ranks, muskets perched on shoulders. As a first-timer I was told to watch rather than take part. One of the men, acting as drill sergeant, began barking orders. "Company right, wheel, march! Ranks thirteen inches apart!" The men wheeled and marched across the orchard, their cups and canteens clanking like cowbells. In the early morning light, their muskets and bayonets cast long, spirelike shadows across the frost-tinged grass. "Right oblique, march! Forward, march!"

The mood was sober and martial, nothing like the night before. Except for a hungover soldier who fell out of line and clutched a tree, vomiting.

"Super hardcore!" his comrades yelled.

I spent an hour watching the men march and wheel as the drill sergeant called out his monotonous orders. "Shoulder arms. Support arms. Carry arms." The field was skirted by a split-rail fence. Just beyond stood the plantation house, a handsome brick edifice ringed by stately oaks; I'd been told the night before that the Confederate guerrilla John Mosby had once climbed out a window of the house and down a tree to escape capture by Federal cavalry. To the west loomed the Blue Ridge, gentle and azure in the morning sun. There wasn't a single modern intrusion. Looking at the scene, I thought about Mathew Brady's black-and-white photographs, and the false impression they conveyed. The War's actual landscape was lush with color and beauty. The sky, always a featureless white in Brady's photographs, was a brilliant, cloud-tufted blue.

The sergeant broke my reverie, handing me his musket and suggesting I practice the drill steps behind the other men. At first, the maneuvers reminded me of learning to square-dance, with the sergeant acting as caller and soldiers taking turns as the lead dancer. The main difference was that a misstep here could result in a rifle butt to the chin instead of a step on the toe. The moves were also crisp and angular, lacking the fluid motion of a reel or do-si-do. "On the right by files, into line, march!"

Finally, after several hours of nonstop drilling, the Guardsmen stacked their weapons and sprawled under a tree. Reaching into their haversacks, they began wolfing down cornbread, unshelled peanuts, slabs of cooked bacon. One of the Guardsmen, a new recruit named Chris Daley, offered me what looked like a year-old piece of beef jerky. I asked him why he'd joined up.

"I work as a paralegal on Long Island," he said. "This is escapism. For forty-eight hours you eat and sleep and march when someone else tells you to. There's no responsibility."

Chris chomped into the jerky, adding, "I think there's a lot of people like me who want to get back to a simpler time. Sandlot baseball, cowboys and Indians, the Civil War."

Rob Hodge agreed. "When you get into the grim details of the War, you realize you've lived a soft life. I think we all have some guilt about that. Doing this is a way of making things a little hard for a change."

This prompted debate about just how hard a hardcore's life should be. Rob favored total immersion in soldierly misery: camping in the mud, marching barefoot on blisters, staying up all night on picket duty. If he caught ticks and lice, so be it. "If that happened, I'd feel like we'd elevated things to another level," he said. "It would suck, but at least I'd know what it was like to scratch my head all day long."

A Guardsman named Fred Rickard went Rob one better. "There's something in me that wishes we could really go the whole way," he said. "I'd take the chance of being killed just to see what it was really like to be under fire in the War." He paused, munching on salt pork and biscuits. "At least then we'd know for sure if we're doing it right."

Fred leaned over to spit out a bit of gristle and noticed something in the grass. "Rob's bloating," he announced. Rob lay splayed on his back, cheeks puffed and belly distended, eyes staring glassily at the sky. Joel walked over and poked a boot in his ribs. "Suck in your gut a bit," he said. "It looks like you sat on a bike pump." Fred rearranged Rob's hands. "They don't look rigor mortal enough," he said. Then the two men returned to their meal.

Rob sat up and wiggled his fingers. "Hands are a problem," he said. "It's hard to make them look bloated unless you've really been dead for a while."

○ ○ ○

I stuck out the drill until late afternoon. The temperature was dropping fast and another night of spooning loomed ahead. Better to farb
out, I decided, than to freeze or perish from hunger. Rob urged me to
come out with the Guard again when the battle season got under
way, and I said I would. But there was something else I wanted to do
in the meantime. Lying awake in the night, pondering Civil War obsession, I'd plotted a hardcore campaign of my own. Super hardcore.

2

North Carolina

CATS OF THE
CONFEDERACY

The South is a place. East, west, and north are nothing but directions.
—Letter to the editor, *Richmond Times-Dispatch*, 1995

Historians are fond of saying that the Civil War occurred in 10,000 places. Poke a pin in a map of the South and you're likely to prod loose some battle or skirmish or other tuft of Civil War history. The first pin I pushed turned up the town of Salisbury, North Carolina.

The scheme I'd plotted while spooning in the night was to spend a year at war, searching out the places and people who kept memory of the conflict alive in the present day. As my territory I'd take the actual ground over which the Civil War raged. This dictated a Southern strategy; apart from Gettysburg and stray Confederate raids on towns like Corydon, Indiana, the War occurred below the Mason and Dixon line. Given my mission, a Southern tour made sense. "We have tried to forget the Civil War," Edmund Wilson observed. "But we have had the defeated enemy on the premises, and he will not allow us to forget it."

It also seemed fitting to start in Charleston, where the War began with the shelling of Fort Sumter. But speeding south from Virginia, I tired of the interstate and pulled off at Salisbury to pick up a small road to South Carolina. Searching for a nonfranchise snack, I noticed a sign marked "Historical Salisbury" and followed it to an old train depot. An elderly woman sat reading a paperback with lovers in antebellum dress embracing on the cover. I asked her if historical Salisbury included anything to do with the Civil War.

"Oh yes," she said, riffling through a desk drawer. "The national cemetery." She handed me a yellowed pamphlet and a self-guided driving tour. "The graveyard's right next to the textile plant," she said, returning to her romance.

Strolling down Salisbury's main street, I passed a pawn shop, a Textile Products Outlet Store, the modestly named OK Wig, and an historical plaque stating that George Washington slept here in 1791. Reaching Spanky's Cafe, I settled in for a cup of coffee and a scan of the tourist literature. At first glance it looked unpromising, like Salisbury itself: a drab textile town with a doomed tourist trade built around a few old homes, a smattering of graves, and a cavalry raid three days after Appomattox.

A young black man sat at the next table gazing into space. He wore a blue bandanna around his neck, beneath a carefully trimmed beard and mustache. From time to time he scribbled in a leather-bound notebook. I leaned over and asked what he was writing.

"I'm trying to figure out what I'm doing here." He eyed the pen and pad I'd laid on my table. "How about you?"

"Same thing, I guess."

He smiled, exposing a gold-capped front tooth. James Connor was thirty-two and had just separated from his wife of ten years. "We married too young. Never had a chance to explore on our own." So after their split, Connor quit his hairdresser's job in Atlanta and hopped a bus for Salisbury, where his uncle lived in a trailer outside town. "I wanted to see some of the world for myself. I was tired of relying on what people told me about it."

He'd arrived in Salisbury at night. There were no blacks in sight. "I freaked," he said. "I was wondering, 'Where's mine? What did they do to 'em?'" He laughed. That was three days ago. "White people here treat me like any human being. That's the first thing I learned. I thought out here in the sticks it would be *Deliverance* and shit."

He lifted his pen. "My turn," he said.

"Fire away."

"How would you define prejudice?"

"Hmm. Big question. Can I think on that?"

"Okay. Question two. If I was to ask you, what are you looking for and how do you fit into the big picture, what would you say?"

I glanced around the coffee shop. A half-dozen customers stared back. "Got any easy questions?" I asked.

"Yeah." He pointed at the visitors' map and audiotape. "What's all that?"

"Driving tour of Salisbury. Want to come?"

We found the Civil War dead beside a denim plant with a billboard that said, "Bringing Fabric to Life!" On the other side of the cemetery stood a Frito-Lay warehouse. The din from the two buildings drowned out our audiotape, so we parked the car and walked among the headstones.

The first said "Unknown." Then "Two Unknowns." Then a monument that read: "Neither hunger, thirst, nor offered bribes affected their loyalty." The memorial had been erected by the state of Maine.

"Where's the dead rebs?" Connor asked.

I looked again at the tourist literature. The blandly named "national cemetery" was actually the burial ground for Northerners who died at a Confederate prisoner-of-war camp. We walked a bit farther and saw eighteen headstones in a line labeled "Unknown U.S. Soldier." Each marked the foot of a burial trench almost the length of a football field.

We found the cemetery's director in a small caretaker's building adorned with an incongruously sunny painting of inmates playing baseball in the prison yard. Abe Stice kept a computer log of the men buried outside. The log for Union soldiers wasn't long. "Most of the corpses were stripped of their clothes, tossed on dead-wagons and dumped in those trenches," Stice said, "so we don't know a whole lot of names." Salisbury's tiny graveyard held more unknown dead than any other national cemetery in America.

Most prisoners died from malnutrition and disease: smallpox, dysentery, scurvy and dengue or "breakbone" fever, so-called because it caused aches so intense that sufferers thought their bones were snapping. "The official figure's eleven thousand seven hundred dead, but we're really just guessing," Stice said. If the guess was correct, over a third of the inmates perished, making Salisbury among the deadliest of all Civil War prison camps, including Andersonville.

Stice showed us a few books and diaries about the camp. One Iowan weighed 181 pounds when he arrived at the prison and 87 when he left six months later. Another prisoner wrote: "It is not hunger or cold, sickness or death, which makes prison life so hard to bear. It is the utter idleness, emptiness, aimlessness of such a life, with nothing to fill the vacant mind, which always becomes morbid and turns inward to prey on itself."

Oddly, not all the prisoners were Yankees. There were also Southern deserters, Carolina Quakers jailed for being conscientious objectors, and convicts imprisoned for petty theft, drunkenness, or "trading with Yankees and inducing Negroes to go to Washington D.C." The roster also listed the teenaged son of David Livingstone, the famous missionary and doctor in Africa. Robert Livingstone dropped out of school in Scotland and caught a ship to America, apparently in search of adventure. Fearing his family would disapprove, he enlisted under an alias. "To bear your name here would lead to further dishonoring it," Robert wrote his father from Virginia, adding, "I have never hurt anyone knowingly in battle, having always fired high."

Confederate guards at Salisbury weren't so kind; they shot Livingstone dead during a mass break-out attempt. Hundreds of other inmates also died while trying to escape. "Our men will Shoot them now On every Occasion," one rebel guard wrote his wife. "I saw one shot Down yesterday like a Beef."

Like most Civil War buffs, I'd always focused on the grim but glorious history of battle. Salisbury was just grim: men eating mouse soup, "skirmishing" with lice, and "tiered up like sticks of wood" on dead-wagons. But none of this surprised Abe Stice. "You know what Sherman said: 'War is cruelty and you cannot refine it.'" Stice turned around; the back of his jacket said Vietnam Remembered. "I dished out my share of cruelty in 'Nam and got some back." A twice-wounded helicopter pilot, Stice spent fourteen months in hospital before coming home. "I can't forget Vietnam. But I hope the next generation won't be hung up on it the way mine is," he said.

The same sentiment didn't extend to the Civil War. Stice had worked in Salisbury a year, long enough to recognize that memories endured here much longer than in his native Oklahoma. "In school I remember learning that the Civil War ended a long time ago," he said. "Folks here don't always see it that way. They think it's still half-time."

Stice scribbled down the phone number for Sue Curtis, who headed the local chapter of the United Daughters of the Confederacy. "Go talk to this lady and you'll see what I mean," he said, closing up for the night.

Connor and I sat in the car with the heater running as smoke belched from the denim plant and clouded the graveyard. The place depressed me, but Connor didn't see it that way. Gazing out at the graves, he said, "Their dying was my freedom, straight up."

Connor had a job tryout at a hair salon. I had a date with Fort Sumter, or so I'd planned. But Stice's last comment intrigued me. "Want to meet a Daughter of the Confederacy?" I asked.

Connor laughed. "You heard what the man said. Some folks here think it's still Scarlett and Mammy days."

I remembered something. "You asked how I'd define prejudice. That's it. Making assumptions about people you've never met."

Connor shook his head. "You call it prejudice. I call it sense." So I dropped him off at the hairdresser's. He told me to stop by the salon next time I came through Salisbury. "Maybe by then you can answer my other question," he said.

I found a phone booth and dialed Sue Curtis. She seemed oddly unsurprised when I explained that Abe Stice recommended I come speak to her about the Civil War.

"I'm so sorry, I'd ask you over but I'm getting ready for our meeting tonight," she said. "It's our annual Lee-Jackson birthday party."

Robert E. Lee's and Stonewall Jackson's birthdays fell two days apart and were once major holidays across the South. I hadn't realized anyone still commemorated the dates.

"Is the meeting open to the public?" I asked.

"Usually not, but it might be." There was a pause on the line. "The Sons of Confederate Veterans are meeting across the hall from us. If you'd like, I can tell them to expect you."

At the Rowan County library, I was greeted by three men who introduced themselves in order of rank. "Jim White, commander," said a man with a pastor's dog-collar and a long, coiffed beard.

"Ed Curtis," announced a second. This was Sue Curtis's husband, a tall, lean man with aviator glasses. "First lieutenant commander."

"I'm Mike Hawkins," said the third man, standing erect, like a marine cadet. "Color sergeant, Rowan Rifles, Army of Northern Virginia."

None of the men wore uniforms. The army they served had disbanded in 1865, or so I'd last heard. The best I could do was stammer out my name and town, which at least lay in northern Virginia.

"And where were you raised, Tony?" the commander asked. I took this as a diplomatic allusion to my lack of a Southern accent. "Maryland," I said. Actually, I was born and schooled in Washington, D.C., but my family lived a few blocks outside the one-time Yankee capital.

The commander clapped me on the back and sang out a line from Maryland's state song: "Huzzah, she spurns the Northern scum!" Maryland stayed neutral in the War, but harbored many Southern sympathizers. Apparently, as a Marylander, I might still qualify as one—or at least not as Northern scum.

"We can't boast Virginia's claims to aristocracy," the commander went on, "or South Carolina's fame as the cradle of secession."

"You know what they call North Carolina," Ed Curtis added. "'A vale of humility between two mountains of conceit.'" He smiled. "Of course that's a conceited thing to say about yourself. But at least we're humble about how much better we are than anyplace else."

As the meeting got under way, the twenty or so men in the room pledged allegiance to the Stars and Stripes. Then the color sergeant unfurled the rebel battle flag. "I salute the Confederate flag with affection, reverence and undying devotion to the Cause for which it stands," the men said, effectively contradicting the pledge they'd just made to "one nation, under God, indivisible, with liberty and justice for all."

Then came a banner with N*C on one side. "I salute the North Carolina flag and pledge to the Old North State love, loyalty and faith," the men intoned, with heightened fervor. Yet another flag appeared, this one showing the familiar rebel cross, but arranged on a field of white with a red stripe along the border. "As I'm informed," the commander said, "the third national flag is still the official flag of the Confederacy."

I looked quizzically at the color sergeant, who took his seat beside me. "That's the last political flag of the South," he whispered. "It can't change until the Confederate Congress convenes again."

The birthday party that followed was even stranger. First, the commander pointed to a table spread with food: lemon snaps to honor Stonewall Jackson, who allegedly sucked the sour fruit during combat, and a snack called "Chicken-in-a-Biskit" to honor Lee, who toted a pet hen in his wagon during the campaigns of 1863. Then one of the Sons stood up and recapped Lee's military career—though only his successes up to July 1863. "Gettysburg—there were some mistakes made there, it's a sad thing and I'm not going to go into that," he concluded. "Then came the rest, to Appomattox. Lee died on October 12, 1870." He sat down to polite applause.

The next speaker, Dr. Norman Sloop, spoke about Stonewall. "I'll focus on the medical aspects of Jackson's career," he said, before discussing the general's dyspepsia, myopia and famed hypochondria (Stonewall believed, among other things, that one arm and leg weighed more than the other). Sloop ended with Jackson's mortal wounding by his own troops while leading the rebels to victory at Chancellorsville.

"Like the boxer Rocky Marciano, who died in a plane crash without ever losing a fight, Stonewall went out when he was still on top," Sloop concluded. "And when he reached heaven, the Lord used the words, 'Well done, thou good and faithful servant.'" The source for this last anecdote wasn't entirely clear. But the audience loved it and applauded uproariously.

Then the men in the room split into two teams—the lemons and the chickens—for the evening's main event: a Lee-Jackson trivia quiz. Ed Curtis, the lieutenant commander, stood at the front of the room and read from a pile of index cards.

"How did Jackson graduate in his West Point class?"

"Seventeenth!" Dr. Sloop called out.

"Correct. What wound did Jackson receive at First Manassas?"

"Shot in the left hand. Broke his middle finger," the doctor said.

"Correct. What did Robert E. Lee weigh at the start of the War?"

"I'm wanting to say one eighty but maybe it's one seventy-three," called out the commander, who led my team, the lemons.

"No. One hundred seventy," Sloop corrected.

"Right. Who played the part of Johnny Yuma in the TV series *The Rebel*?"

It quickly became obvious the chickens would triumph, thanks to Dr. Sloop. So midway through the quiz, the lemons resorted to satire.

"In the Mexican War, what hazardous action off the battlefield did Braxton Bragg encounter?"

"Gonorrhea," the pastor-cum-commander shouted.

"No, I'm sorry. He was almost assassinated twice. General Lee's most famous mount was Traveller. Name one other."

"Mary Custis Lee!" the commander yelled again.

"Ajax," Dr. Sloop corrected.

"Right. How many Confederate regiments went into Pickett's Charge?"

"Too many," the color sergeant said.

"Forty-six to be exact. What were the odds of surviving a head wound in the War?"

"Not too good," I volunteered, getting into the spirit of things. The correct answer was one in six. Dr. Sloop again.

"Oh gee, fellahs, this one's a giveaway," Ed Curtis said, reaching the last question. "How many horses did Nathan Bedford Forrest have shot out from under him?"

"Twenty-nine!" the audience shouted in unison. Of sixty-five questions, only Jeff Davis's middle name—Finis—had stumped everyone. I quietly resolved to hit the books. The store of Civil War trivia I'd carried around since childhood clearly wouldn't suffice if I hoped to hold my own among latter-day rebels.

After the quiz, we were joined by the women of the United Daughters of the Confederacy, who had met across the hall. Sue Curtis was a stout woman with large-framed trifocals and a suit the color of strawberry daiquiri. Draped over her ample chest was a ribbon pinned with shiny medals, in the style of a Latin dictator.

"I've got seventeen Confederate ancestors I can prove," she said, "and one who I think went Union." She laughed. "I'm not doing any more research on him."

I told her about the journey I'd just begun, and asked why she thought Southerners still cared about the Civil War.

"War Between the States," she gently corrected me. "The answer is family. We grow up knowing who's once removed and six times down. Northerners say, 'Forget the War, it's over.' But they don't have the family Bibles we do, filled with all these kinfolk who went off to war and died. We've lost so much."

Strictly speaking, she was right. Roughly half of modern-day white Southerners descended from Confederates, and one in four Southern men of military age died in the War. For Yankee men, the death rate was about one in ten, and waves of post-War immigration left a far lower ratio of Northerners with blood ties to the conflict. Still, I was struck by Sue Curtis's tone. She spoke as though her kinsmen died yesterday, not 130 years ago.

"Caleb Senter, my great-great-grandfather, was captured at Cold Harbor," she said, fingering an "ancestor pin" that bore his name. "He was on his way to Elmira Prison, but a drunk telegraph man directed his train right into a coal freighter in Pennsylvania. Poor Caleb was squashed to death and buried by the tracks." Her eyes misted over. "I made a magnolia wreath for his grave."

We were interrupted by her husband, Ed. "Sue boring you with her War stories?" he asked.

"Not at all. Actually, I'm kind of jealous. I don't even know the names of my great-great-grandfathers."

Ed winked. "Don't get her started on her great-great-uncles."

The others began drifting out of the library. It was almost nine o'clock. "We're going across the street to Miss Lucy's for some iced tea and French silk pie," Sue said. "Would you care to come along?"

I suddenly didn't feel in any rush to reach Charleston.

Awakening the next morning in a $27 room at Salisbury's Econo Lodge ("Spend a Night, Not a Fortune!"), I recognized the appeal of dwelling on the South's past rather than its present. Stepping from my room into the motel parking lot, I gazed out at a low-slung horseshoe of ferroconcrete called Towne Mall, a metal-and-cement forest of humming electricity pylons, a Kmart, a garish yellow Waffle House, a pink-striped Dunkin' Donuts, plus Taco Bell, Bojangles, Burger King, the Golden Arches of McDonald's and the equally gaudy signs for Exxon, BP and Shell hoisted like battle flags above the melee of competing brands. A few exhaust-choked bushes poked from the greasy asphalt.

I'd gone to bed reading about the Confederate general Albert Sidney Johnston, who urged his men into battle at Shiloh by declaring, "Remember the fair, broad, abounding land, the happy homes and ties that would be desolated by your defeat!" I wondered sleepily what Johnston would make of the view from the Econo Lodge.

Over coffee at the Waffle House, I also began wondering about the crowd I'd met the night before. It had included not only the doctor and pastor, but also a textile worker, a rose grower, a gun-shop owner, a state bureaucrat and several farmers in overalls. Apart from sports, I couldn't think of many interests that comfortably bridged such a wide range of people. I was curious to know more of what drew them together.

"Blood," Sue Curtis said. "That's all you really need to join this club."

I'd tracked her down at the Rowan County library, where she spent several mornings a week verifying applications for membership in the United Daughters of the Confederacy, or UDC for short. This meant hours of scrolling through microfilm copies of military records from the 1860s. I squinted into the machine at a muster roll.

In terse language and careful script, the records listed each soldier's home, occupation, age, and eventual fate. "Died in hands of enemy," read a typical entry. "Effects none."

From scraps like this, Sue reclaimed whole lives. Muster rolls led to pension records, wills, marriage certificates, gravestones. Diaries and letters fleshed the story out. She showed me a notebook filled with documents on Caleb Senter, her great-great-grandfather. "I have seen the cannon-balls strike men and the pieces of clothing would fly as high as the trees," he wrote his wife. In another letter he told of his constant hunger and pleaded, "If there is anybody coming to this company, send me a small ham of meat and some chickens and a few pies and a couple of onions and so forth." Soon after, Caleb was captured and killed in the Pennsylvania train wreck Sue had told me about the night before.

"When you've researched these people, it gets very personal," she said. "You know what color hair they had, if their eyes were brown or green, how tall they were, their dreams for when they came home. After a while the War doesn't seem that far away. It becomes part of your life." She paused. "Or it takes over your life."

When I asked what she meant, Sue laughed. "Come over to our place tonight and you'll see," she said, returning to her microfilm.

LATE THAT AFTERNOON, I went to see Mike Hawkins, the color sergeant I'd sat beside at the Lee-Jackson meeting. His fourteen-foot-wide trailer perched next to a narrow road through the red-clay farmland that surrounded Salisbury's sprawl of tract homes and malls. Inside, cluttering the main living space, was a guinea-pig cage, a large TV and an elegant table Hawkins's great-grandparents received as a wedding gift in the 1890s.

Hawkins was a spare man with pocked skin and a wispy mustache. He wore the same outfit I'd seen him in the night before: black denims, cowboy boots, red flannel shirt. He sat squeezed beside his wife, Kaye, a big woman who took up most of the couch.

"Mike told me he met a paper man last night," Kaye said, with a nervous high-pitched laugh. "Never met a paper man."

"Actually, I'm doing research for a book."

"Oh, books," Kaye said, laughing again. "Mike loves his books. Loves 'em more than me, I think."

Kaye was Hawkins's second wife. His first marriage had ended in an ugly legal fight that left him with limited visitation rights for his three kids. He pointed to their pictures on the wall. "It's in the Lord's hands," he said. "I tell Him, 'Do for me what you can.'"

It was soon after his divorce that Hawkins became obsessed with the Civil War. To meet child support payments, he'd moved in with his parents and worked seven days a week at a textile factory. At night, he went to the genealogy room at the library. "I was trying to get my life back together," he said. "I had this want to find out about my kin."

One night, combing muster rolls, he found his great-great-grand-father listed as a private in a North Carolina regiment. Fields Hawkins was a twenty-year-old farmer when he volunteered. Shot twice in the spring of 1862, he married while recovering from his wounds, then returned to the War—though only for two months. "He got his leg shot off at Sharpsburg," Hawkins said.

Hawkins showed me Fields's application for an artificial leg, and census records from the early twentieth century that listed Fields and his wife, then in their sixties, as cotton mill workers. "Just like me," Hawkins said. But one crucial detail still eluded him: the site of his great-great-grandfather's grave. "It's been seven years, but when I find it I'll finally feel like I've accomplished something. A connection with my past that I can reach out and grab hold to."

Hawkins had taken his documents to the Sons of Confederate Veterans and paid $33 in annual fees to join up. He'd made every meeting since. "It brings people together, like the War did," he said. "I sit in a room with a doctor and pastor and such, and I don't see them otherwise. We're all together for the same reason." The only other club to which he belonged was his factory's softball team, which competed in North Carolina's Industrial League.

Hawkins took particular pride in his status as the Rowan Rifles' color sergeant. "If we were going into battle, I'd be in front of everybody," he said. "It's an honor, though it would have been a short honor." Flags had another appeal; Hawkins could buy them cheaply at flea markets and souvenir shops.

He took me into the trailer's cramped bedroom, lined with secondhand volumes on the War. Hawkins read everything he could find on Sharpsburg (known in the North as Antietam) and dreamed of visiting the Maryland battlefield, particularly the sunken road known as Bloody Lane where Fields Hawkins lost his leg. "I go there a lot in my head," he said, flipping open a book with photographs of the Antietam dead. "I look at these pictures and it's like the music from *Twilight Zone* kicks on, like I was there way back when."

Kaye turned on the television and started fixing dinner. Hawkins lowered his voice. Late at night, he said, when Kaye fell asleep, he often slipped out of bed and continued reading, by oven light. "It's an escape," he said. "When I'm reading, I feel like I'm there, not here. And when I finish I feel content, like I've been away for a while." He smiled. "Sometimes I get brain fry from all the reading."

I asked him if he thought "there" was better than "here."

"Not better," he said. "I mean, my great-great-grandpap got his leg shot off. But I feel like it was bigger somehow." Hawkins flipped through pages of Civil War pictures. "At work, I mix dyes and put them in a machine. I'm thirty-six and I've spent almost half my life in Dye House No. 1. I make eight dollars sixty-one cents an hour, which is okay, 'cept everyone says the plant will close and go to China." He put the book back on the shelf. "I just feel like the South has been given a bum deal ever since that War."

Hawkins unstuck a rebel banner from a small flag stand by the bed. He waved it and said, "Here's a trivia question they didn't ask last night. What state sent more troops to the Confederacy than any other, and took more casualties, too?"

"North Carolina?"

Hawkins smiled. "Not too many people know that. We gave a hundred twenty-seven thousand and lost forty thousand. Do you know one reason North Carolinians are called Tar Heels?"

"No. Why?"

"Because Lee said we stuck in battle. At Chickamauga, for instance—"

Kaye poked her head in the bedroom. "Suppertime," she said. Hawkins looked startled, like he'd been away for a while. Kaye invited me to stay, but I said I had to be going. For a few moments we stood awkwardly by the trailer door, as a chill wind rattled the storm window.

"We were honored, really," Kaye said.

I blushed and said, "I was honored, too."

"I liked you right away last night," Hawkins said. "There were all those doctors and such at the meeting. And you wanted to talk to me."

Navigating my way to Ed and Sue Curtis's home, I discovered that Salisbury was a far more pleasant and prosperous town than I'd at first supposed. Its residential streets were lined with parks and gardens and gracious homes (funded, I later learned, with the millions that locals earned from investing years ago in a Salisbury-based supermarket chain called Food Lion). From the outside, the Curtis home appeared ordinary enough: a modest brick ranch house fronted by an American flag. But stepping inside, I found myself in a museum of Confederate kitsch. Portraits of Jeff Davis and Robert E. Lee adorned one wall. A bell-jar model of Ashley Wilkes perched on a side table. Statuettes of Lee, Davis, Jackson and Jeb Stuart sat atop the mantel. "I always wanted something just the right color for that spot," Sue said of the gray figurines. She nonchalantly pulled off Stonewall's head. The figurines were actually flasks with necks made of cork.

There were also Lee and Jackson paperweights, a music box that played "Dixie," and a seashell filled with spent minié balls. "Goes with the painting," Sue explained, pointing to a watercolor just above the shell showing General Beauregard on the beach at Charleston.

That was just the living room. In the dining room there were plates and cups decorated with rebel generals and paintings of battles in which the Curtis forebears fought. Sue pushed open the door to the kitchen. I glimpsed rebel-themed fridge magnets and mugs decorated with Rhett Butler. "It sort of flows from here all the way to the garage," Sue said. "But the War does not come to the bedroom. That's where we draw the line."

Somewhere in this ancestral lava was the Bible a rebel forebear had carried into battle. One of Ed's ancestors, a Confederate scout, had also preserved a piece of shin bone he lost after being shot from a tree. "He kept it in a bottle by his bed," Ed said. But most of the Curtises' relics and trinkets were gifts Sue and Ed had given each other on birthdays and anniversaries. They'd even courted on Civil War battlefields. "Instead of bells ringing I heard cannons boom," Ed joked.

It wasn't until after their marriage, though, that the Curtises' interest in the War turned from a casual hobby to an obsession. The spark was Sue's curiosity about her rebel ancestry. "A lot of people like me first got deep into Confederate history in the late seventies, when genealogy really took off," she explained.

Ironically, Alex Haley's novel *Roots* helped trigger this trend, inspiring blacks and then other Americans to dig through archives and ship records. Tracing pedigree wasn't new to the South, but it had traditionally been most popular among blue bloods such as the FFVs, or First Families of Virginia. In the past twenty years, Sue said, there'd been a dramatic upsurge of interest in common forebears, including rebel foot soldiers.

Sue's duties as registrar often took her to the state archives in Raleigh. As a special treat, Ed sometimes drove her to the National Archives in Washington. I asked when they'd last taken a trip unrelated to the Civil War.

Ed looked at Sue. "Have we ever?"

She shrugged and shook her head. "Not that I can think of."

Rarely a week passed without some meeting, or a ceremony marking one of the anniversaries scattered like saints' days through the year: Lee's and Jackson's birthdays, Confederate Flag Day, Confederate Memorial Day, Jefferson Davis's birthday. Sue also corresponded with Northern women whose ancestors lay in Salisbury's cemetery, and had even held a memorial service for a Michigan soldier with a wreath laying and the singing of the "Battle Hymn of the Republic." "My great-great-grandfather died on his way to prison up North," she reminded me. "I like to think some Northern lady might have done the same for him."

The Curtises had no offspring of their own to enroll in the Sons or Daughters of the Confederacy. At least no blood kin. "I started the first chapter of the Cats of the Confederacy," Sue said, stroking a diabetic feline named Flurry Belle. "We wear gray ribbons with cat pins and get together and tell stories about cats in the War." For instance, a Confederate mascot named Tom Cat who became the only casualty during a Federal bombardment of Savannah in 1863.

Given all this, it seemed remarkable that the Curtises managed to hold down day jobs; Ed helped veterans find employment, Sue filled volunteer posts at schools, libraries and hospitals. But their passion for the War had crowded out everything else, including church.

"We were raised Methodists," Sue said. "But we converted to the Confederacy. There wasn't time for both."

"War is hell," Ed deadpanned. "And it just might send us there."

But Sue didn't worry about the afterlife. In fact, she looked forward to it. "The neatest thing about living is that I can die and finally track down all those people I couldn't find in the records." She pointed at the ceiling and then at the floor. "Either way, it'll be heaven just to get that information."

At the Lee-Jackson birthday party, a shopkeeper named Michael Sherman had given me a business card labeled Firearms Etc. When I'd asked what etcetera included, he replied, "C'mon out and see for yourself." So the next morning, I followed a country road winding out of town until I found a cement-block building with a sign in the shape of a revolver.

Sherman stood behind the counter, demonstrating an assault rifle with a retractable bayonet. A man and a boy of about ten looked on. "The beauty of this one," Sherman said, thrusting the gun at the wall, "is that if you're down to just a few rounds, you can poke the guy through instead."

Across the shop sat two other men I recognized from the meeting: a bloated fellow in overalls and a camouflage jacket, named Doug Tarlton, and an even doughier figure, Walt Fowler, who sat drinking a diet soda and wolfing down Bugles.

"Had to cut down on the sugar," Fowler said. "Gout's got me again. 'Course it could be the acid in those tomatoes I ate this morning, or the cheeseburger they came on."

"Walt's a restaurant inspector," Tarlton explained, "so he's got to sample everything to make sure it's safe for humanity. If you can call Walt human."

Fowler acknowledged this friendly jibe by rummaging in a plastic bag beside his chair and pulling out a crude, photocopied cartoon showing several men aiming pistols into a toilet bowl. "Polacks shooting crap," Walt said, convulsing with laughter.

Tarlton smiled. "Walt's not prejudiced. He hates all minorities the same." Tarlton pointed to a chair and offered me a chocolate-colored wafer that I took at first for a Mars bar. "Want some 'backer?" he asked. I tore a small piece from the dense plug of chewing tobacco and stuffed it in my cheek. For a few minutes, I concentrated on my cud and took in the rest of the shop. There were cases filled with Lugers, scopes, holsters, pepper spray, banana clips, Bowie knives, and felt bags labeled "soft cases for your dreaded ASSAULT RIFLE!" A sign by the door declared, "Shoplifters will be shot. Survivors will be shot again!"

The only nonlethal item in the shop was a picture called "The Last Meeting," a popular reprint of the most hallowed of Confederate images: Lee and Jackson parting at Chancellorsville on the day Stonewall was shot while flanking the Federal army. I pointed at the picture and asked Tarlton why he thought memory of the Confederacy was so enduring.

"You're looking at it, or at least one reason for it," he said, gesturing around the crowded shop. "Southerners are a military people. We were back then, still are today. Every man in here has carried a gun for his country and probably a few of the women, too."

Tarlton had served in Vietnam and taken so much shrapnel in his leg that he'd had seven operations and now wore a prosthetic knee. "Up close, war's kind of a stomach-turner," he said, tapping the leg of his overalls. "I like it better in books."

After Vietnam, Tarlton worked as a police detective before turning to farming. He was also licensed as a lay minister.

"What do you do now?" I asked.

"Die for a living." He lifted his hunting cap to reveal an entirely bald scalp. "Advanced leukemia."

I realized now that the puffiness around his eyes was watery and unnatural, due to chemotherapy or cortisone rather than Southern cooking. "I'm sorry," I said.

"Don't be. Doctor told me I'd be dead by Christmas. I'm enjoying the borrowed time."

Tarlton spent much of it studying the Civil War. "The present—I live it, it holds no mystery," he said. "The past does." He paused. "Plus the present to me is not all that attractive right now. When you're puking in the commode, the past looks a whole lot better."

The Civil War also kept his detective skills sharp. Tarlton helped friends track down proof of rebel ancestry. As a detective, he'd spent much of his time busting drug dealers and blowing up backwoods liquor stills. "Basically I was a narc," he said. "So I had a close-up view of all the sickness out there. Junkies. Thugs. Guys who'd pimp their daughters for dope. You deal with that all day and you feel kind of soiled." He pointed at the picture of Lee and Jackson. "When I read about them, I feel like man's a noble creature, like maybe humanity's just going through a bad patch."

He chuckled and pointed at Fowler, who was finishing off his box of Bugles. "Take Walt," he said loudly. "You'd never guess it from looking at him, but when his great-great-uncle, Henry Fowler, got killed in battle, his commanding officer sent a note saying he 'behaved with great coolness and courage.'"

I asked Tarlton what he knew about his own Civil War forebears. "Bunch of poor dirt farmers, like most folks were around here, and like a lot still are," he said. "Didn't own any slaves."

"Why do you think they fought?"

"The way I see it," Tarlton said, "they were fighting for their honor as men. They came from stock that was oppressed and they felt oppressed again by the government telling them how to live."

"Same as today," another man chimed in. "Government's letting the niggers run wild."

"Amen," said a third, looking up from a case of bayonets. "What they need to do is put all those crackheads on work crews and let them chop the right-of-way for a few years. You can bet your sweet bippy that'll adjust their attitude."

I plugged my mouth with a fresh wad of tobacco. Walt Fowler

broke the awkward silence by reaching into his plastic bag again. He extracted a piece of parchment that looked like one of those homilies people put on their living room walls. Fowler solemnly intoned: "Lord, give me the serenity to accept the things I cannot change, to change the things I can, and the wisdom to hide the bodies of those people I had to kill because they pissed me off." He hooted and slapped his thigh.

I got up to go and told Tarlton I might stop by to see him again. "Don't count on it," he said. "I told those doctors to quit everything. No more chemo." He tipped his cap. "Life's a bitch and then you die. If God wants me, he can take me. I'm ready."

Then, as if on cue, he and Fowler pulled revolvers from their coat pockets and held them stiffly across their chests, mimicking young Confederates posing for studio portraits at the start of the War. "Still armed and ready for action!" the two men shouted in unison.

IN THE CATALOGUE of Confederate organizations to which Sue and Ed Curtis belonged, one in particular had piqued my curiosity: the Children of the Confederacy, or C. of C. for short. An auxiliary of the United Daughters of the Confederacy, the C. of C. was designed to prep youngsters for Confederate citizenship in rather the way that Future Farmers of America readied teenagers for agricultural life. "You age out of the C. of C. at eighteen," Sue explained, "and hopefully then you move right into the UDC or SCV."

Sue had "reactivated" a dormant C. of C. chapter in Salisbury and she invited me to attend a state meeting at the Plantation Inn Resort in Raleigh. This turned out to be a faux-plantation motel on a busy suburban road, right across from Kmart. About a hundred kids and their parents crowded inside a climate-controlled annex to recall and honor the suffering of their forebears.

At the front of the room sat girls in flouncy white dresses and red sashes labeled "page," beside boys in clip-on ties marked "aide." Parents popped up from the audience with video cameras, like proud and indulgent parents anywhere—watching a school play, say, or a junior-high debate. This illusion of normality evaporated as soon as the program got under way, first with the salutes to various flags, then with the singing of "Dixie" and the pronouncement of the C. of C.'s "Creed."

"We pledge ourselves to preserve pure ideals; to honor the memory of our beloved Veterans; to study and teach the truths of history (one of the most important of which is, that the War Between the States was not a REBELLION nor was its underlying cause to sustain slavery); and always to act in a manner that will reflect honor upon our noble and patriotic ancestors."

One of the aides handed out copies of the "Catechism," a sixteen-page pamphlet that served as the Children's guiding text. It was published in 1954 (the same year that *Brown* v. *Board of Education* declared school segregation unconstitutional), and arranged in a question-and-answer format.

Q. What causes led to the War Between the States, from 1861 to 1865?
A. The disregard of those in power for the rights of the Southern states.
Q. Where was the first slave ship built and launched?
A. In Marble Head, Mass., in 1636.
Q. What was the feeling of the slaves towards their masters?
A. They were faithful and devoted and were always ready and willing to serve them.

The treatment of battlefield history also hewed to traditional notions about Southern valor.

Q. What is considered by historians as the decisive battle of the war?
A. Gettysburg.
Q. Why?
A. Because it was conclusive evidence to an unbiased mind that the Federal supplies and forces greatly outweighed and outnumbered the Confederate forces.

Actually, Gettysburg was the rare clash in which the Confederates weren't badly outmanned. If the battle proved anything, it was that Lee could blunder and that Northerners could fight as doggedly as Southerners. Reading through the rest of the Catechism, I began to hear echoes of defeated peoples I'd encountered overseas: Kurds, Armenians, Palestinians, Catholics in Northern Ireland. Like them, Southerners had kept fighting their war by other means.

After a break for milk and Animal Crackers, the children took their seats for what was known as the Catechism Quiz. A teenager posed questions from the text, and a group of twelve-and-unders competed to be the first to answer correctly, often with verbatim recitations of the Catechism. If no one could answer within fifteen seconds, the moderator called out "Books!" and the children riffled through their Catechisms until they located the correct response. The kids were stumped only a few times. It was an impressive display of rote learning and reminded me of my own childhood passion for Civil War trivia, though this was a level of fine print I'd never reached.

After the quiz, I went with the Curtises and a couple named the Crowders to a Southern-style restaurant chain called Morrison's. We loaded our trays with un-Confederate heaps of cornbread, fried chicken, mashed potatoes and collard greens. I was about to shovel in the first bite when Violet Crowder loudly cleared her throat. Then she turned to her four-year-old son, Warren. "Lord," he intoned, "we thank thee for this meal and especially for the great and wonderful Confederacy."

Violet smiled proudly. "You have to set them on the straight and narrow at an early age. Then, even if they stray, they'll come back to the faith."

I wasn't sure which faith she meant: the Confederacy or Christianity.

"We all stray, I know I did," Violet went on, hoeing into black-eyed peas. "I was a liberal once."

"No!" Sue Curtis exclaimed.

"Vi's even got a jail record," her husband said. "For a protest in Washington in 1969."

Violet blushed. "I grew up in a tiny town where everybody knew my grandmother and her grandmother. You never got wild. So when I went to college I did." She sipped her iced tea. "I've straightened out since."

Her son sat quietly completing a connect-the-dot picture of the rebel flag and filling in a coloring-book map of America: gray for the Confederacy, blue for Union, green for border states. "Warren," his mother said, "tell this nice man from Virginia, is there anything you hate more than Yankees?"

"No sir! Nothing!" he shouted. Then he dove under the table, yelling, "Someone told me there's Yankees around here! They hate little children!"

In the afternoon, the C. of C. convened again for a memorial service at Raleigh's Confederate cemetery. The children read short profiles they'd composed about the dead, then recited sentimental poems about "sleeping Confederates" and laid wreaths at a mausoleum called House of Memory. Sue Curtis explained that the C. of C. spent many weekends this way: raking and fertilizing Confederate plots, decorating graves with flowers, visiting monuments and shrines.

One girl lingered long after the others, gazing back at the ranks of stones. "You know what I hate?" she said. "When people say that history repeats itself. That's the scariest thing I can think of."

Beth was a tall, intense girl of twelve with braces and a black barrette stuck crookedly in her hair. I told her I wasn't sure I understood the appeal of all this devotion to crypts and alabaster, which was beginning to strike me as a bit morbid for a children's group.

"To tell you the truth, I was kind of embarrassed to come today," she said. "When I told a friend at school about it, she said, 'What's that, some kind of redneck thing?'" Beth frowned. "I'm not prejudiced and I don't agree with all this 'South is great' stuff. I'm sure there were some good things about the North." She looked around. "I hope nobody hears me say that."

Even so, Beth served as president of her C. of C. chapter and reckoned she'd join the UDC when she aged out. But her passion for the Confederacy didn't spring from the C. of C. Catechism. In school she'd just learned about the Holocaust and become obsessed with Anne Frank and other Jews killed by the Nazis.

"What gets me is the heart of the Jews. They were underdogs, they knew they were going to die but didn't give up the faith," she said. "Just like the Confederates."

Beth saw another connection between the Civil War and the Holocaust. "I like the gruesome stuff, like about the prisons," Beth said. "I like Auschwitz—I mean, I don't like it, but I like to learn about it. That's my favorite concentration camp. It makes me wonder how human beings can possibly do that sort of thing to each other, and how you keep your spirit in that situation. Then I got to thinking about Salisbury's prison." Her voice lowered, the way a twelve-year-old's does when she's about to say something awful. "You know how some prisoners killed themselves at Salisbury? They drank potty water." She grimaced. "I guess if you were really sick already, that would do it. But you'd really have to want to die."

We caught up with the others at a punch-and-cookies reception at an antebellum mansion, followed by a banquet of fried chicken, potatoes with cheese, green beans, biscuits and peach cobbler. Digging into my third sclerotic meal of the day, I recalled a conversation I'd once had with the Tennessee writer John Egerton over a heart-stopping lunch in Nashville. "This meal's got all six of the major food groups in the South," he observed. "Sugar, salt, butter, eggs, cream and bacon grease."

The dinner was followed by speeches and awards: for the Catechism quiz winner, for the chapter "sending in the greatest number of accurate membership papers" (won by Sue Curtis's group, of course) and for "the youngest child registered in the division," a five-month-old who would become the C. of C.'s state "mascot" for the following year. This post was so coveted, Sue said, that some parents registered their children at birth, even asking the labor-room doctor to sign the application form.

It was ten-thirty when the meeting finally adjourned. I promised Beth I'd send her some material from the Holocaust Museum and told her about another museum, in Tel Aviv, where I'd dug up details on my forebears in Eastern Europe. Beth's eyes lit up. She'd recently become interested in genealogy, too, and was now tracing her rebel ancestry.

"My father's mother's maiden name is Frank, and they came from somewhere in central Europe originally," she said. "Maybe, oh maybe, I'm praying that I'm kin to Anne Frank. That would be the greatest thing in the world."

I STAYED A WEEK in Salisbury, attending several more meetings with the Curtises. By the end, I knew the words to every stanza of "Dixie" and had learned to distinguish the rebel battle flag from the first, second and third national flags of the wartime South. I'd also begun to realize that the Curtises logged more miles for the Confederacy each year than the Army of Northern Virginia.

But my last day in Salisbury, I decided to attend a remembrance of a different sort. The third week of January marked not only the birthdays of Lee and Jackson, but also of Martin Luther King Jr. In the reconstituted world of the 1990s South, the Confederates' birthdays were now discreet affairs, celebrated in library back rooms, while King's was a national holiday. Virginia, I later learned, had attempted a bizarre fusion of the Civil War and civil rights, creating "Lee-Jackson-King Day" (all three men were "defenders of causes," the state legislature proclaimed). But the hybrid didn't take and most Virginians continued to celebrate their heroes separately.

The same was true in Salisbury. Blacks observed King's birthday with a parade and a service at a small church a few blocks from the town's Confederate monument. Ushers handed out paper fans decorated with King's picture on one side and a funeral home advertisement on the other. A dozen or so whites sat near the front, including the mayor, sheriff and county judge.

The service began, like the other meetings I'd attended, with the pledge of allegiance and with tunes that echoed Southern history, albeit from the opposite shore of racial strife and liberation.

> *Heaven help the black man if he struggles one more day.*
> *Heaven help the white man if he turns his back away.*
> *Heaven help the man who kicks the man who's had a fall.*
> *Heaven help us all.*

The "birthday message" by a visiting minister also spoke to the legacy of the Civil War. "Frederick Douglass said over a century ago that America cannot remain half slave and half free," he began. "He said the sky for blacks was dark but not rayless. I would say the same today. Do you hear me?"

"Yessir!"

"Some of us are still ashamed to be known as African-American. We have tried to assimilate harder than any other. We try to talk like other folk, we are afraid to laugh. When I was coming up, you could hear us laugh a block away. Talk to me, somebody!"

"Tell it, Rev!"

"We're not cannibals. We don't stew folks in pots or wear bones through our noses. When I was a child I read about L'il Black Sambo putting tiger butter on pancakes. At school I learned about Robert E. Lee. But nobody told me about the peanut man, Booker T. Washington. I didn't hear about *our* heroes. We can't all be superstars. Most of us are just hardworking average folk. But you are somebody special because God didn't make any junk. I'm going to pick at this bone just a little bit and then leave it alone."

"Nossir! Go on now!"

"Dr. King said you must be willing to stand for something or you will fall for anything. Jesse Jackson said it doesn't matter what boat brought you to this country. We're all in the same boat here. So let's come together. Let's hold hands now and smile at each other."

The choir broke into song and everyone joined in, belting out "The Battle Hymn of the Republic." I'd heard Julia Ward Howe's anthem to abolition a hundred times before. But listening to it now, through the prism of the Civil War, I was struck by its explicitly martial tone and its vivid imagery of 1860s army life.

"He hath loosed the fateful lightning of His terrible, swift sword . . . I have seen Him in the watch-fires of a hundred circling camps . . . He has sounded forth the trumpet that shall never call retreat . . . As He died to make men holy, let us die to make men free, while God is marching on!"

If "Dixie" was elegiac, a nostalgic evocation of cotton fields, buckwheat cakes and gay deceivers, the "Battle Hymn of the Republic" was its antithesis: apocalyptic, ironfisted, and almost industrial in its summoning of God's legions to march forth and crush iniquity. It would be a stretch to suggest that the two songs offered a tuneful synopsis of what had separated North from South—and what had fueled the North's triumph. But hearing the songs sung in such close succession, I couldn't help feeling the emotional distance between the two causes.

When the singing ended, I chatted with others in my pew, including a tall, aristocrat-looking man with pomaded gray hair. I told him about the Lee-Jackson gatherings I'd attended and asked how he felt about people still celebrating the Confederacy.

"I'm happy they have the freedom to celebrate those men, the same way we celebrate King here," he said. "But you didn't see nobody black at those meetings, did you? We had white folks here, at least a few. Anything you got to do with your own kind in secret, something's wrong with it. You feel bad about it inside." A wry smile creased his lips. "I got one word for those folks—Appomattox. The game's up, you lost. Get over it."

The other blacks in our pew didn't seem to care about whites honoring Lee and Jackson. "Whites have their day, now we've got our own," one woman said. But one man didn't share this indifference. Michael King was a young preacher with horn-rimmed glasses and a close-cropped beard and mustache. "The Bible says, if eating meat offends your brother, eat meat no more," he said. "Worship of the Confederacy offends me."

When I asked why, he walked me to the Confederate monument, which occupied a median strip on Salisbury's busiest street. The 1909 memorial depicted a bronze angel cradling a dying rebel soldier and holding forth a laurel crown. Chiseled on the granite base was the Confederate motto, *Deo Vindice*. With God As Our Defender.

"What's the message here?" King said. "God dispatched an angel to ferry this brave rebel to heaven. As a Christian pastor, I got a problem with that. The whole notion that God was involved with one race putting down another, that's going against the grain of a Christian nation. God ain't with racism or anything to do with subdividing people."

The monument bothered King for another, subtler reason. "It's idol worship. I feel sorry for folks who feel like they have to put up idols to feel good about themselves."

King had lived in Salisbury his whole life. He knew his was a minority view. Most blacks were apathetic, he said, or didn't want to ruffle Salisbury's racial calm by talking about old monuments. He had done so publicly once, questioning at a public meeting why the monument—owned by Sue Curtis's UDC chapter—should stand in the middle of a busy street where "I got to worship it every time I'm stuck at a red light," King said.

In reply, King had received hate mail. His protest also prompted an avalanche of letters to the local paper stating that the monument wasn't racial, it was just a symbol of great-grandfathers who fought and died for their beliefs. "The way I see it," King said, "your great-grandfather fought and died because he believed my great-grand-father should stay a slave. I'm supposed to feel all warm inside about that?"

I asked King if there was any way for white Southerners to honor their forebears without insulting his. He pondered this for a moment. "Remember your ancestors," he said, "but remember what they fought for too, and recognize it was wrong. Then maybe you can invite me to your Lee and Jackson birthday party. That's the deal."

3

South Carolina

IN THE BETTER
HALF OF THE WORLD

South Carolina is too small for a republic
and too large for an insane asylum.
—JAMES L. PETIGRU, describing his native state in 1860

The *General Beauregard* eased out from the pier and steamed slowly into Charleston harbor. Trapped mid-deck in a coffle of schoolkids, camera straps and windblown maps, I could barely see the fort or hear the ferry's crackly soundtrack. *"With the first shot on Fort Sumter, America's greatest moment of conflict, the War Between the States, had begun."*

Wriggling free, I joined a few stoic passengers gazing into the wintery breeze from the *Beauregard's* bow. Sumter lay three miles offshore. Other Civil War ramparts occupied fingers of land poking into the water. "The Forts, faintly blue on the twinkling sea, looked like vague marine flowers," Henry James wrote of his visit to Charleston in 1905. From the bow of the *Beauregard*, Sumter looked more like a manhole cover bobbing atop Charleston harbor.

A man to my left stared at his tour book. "They fired three thousand rounds at that thing," he said. His wife nodded with the trance-like glaze of a teenager in first-period history class. To my right stood a heavyset man about my own age. He had a shaved head, sunglasses and a camouflage jacket with safety pins where the buttons should have been.

"It's heart-breaking, huh?" he said, staring out to sea. I wasn't sure if he meant the Civil War or the scene on the *Beauregard*.

"Tony Horwitz," I said, extending my hand.

"Joel Dorfman." He paused. *"Shalom."*

Dorfman was an unemployed truck driver from Long Island. I asked what brought him to Fort Sumter.

"This is the end," he said.

"The end?"

"Yes, the end, my friend. I just got into town about an hour ago."

"Me, too."

"Took a look around to see which way the wind blows."

I don't know what I'd expected to find on the ferry to Fort Sumter, but it certainly wasn't this: a shaved-headed Jewish truck-driver from Long Island, talking in Doors' lyrics.

"I've been a rider on the storm for four months," Dorfman went on. The journey began when he lost his trucking job. Ever since, Dorfman had traveled through the Civil War, as I now planned to do. Only Dorfman was doing it backwards: from Lee's surrender at Appomattox, to Petersburg, to Gettysburg, Antietam, Manassas and now Fort Sumter. Later today, he'd begin the long retreat to New York.

"Why'd you do it in reverse?" I asked him.

Dorfman looked at me quizzically. "If we could travel back in time, wouldn't we hit the end of the War first?"

THE *Beauregard* docked at Sumter. Up close, the "consecrated object," as Henry James called it, looked even less impressive than it had from sea. The fort, a low pentagon of brick, squatted atop a bleak man-made atoll. Its walls were covered with an ugly, lavalike spill of black pitch. Seagulls screamed and shat around us as we clambered ashore for the hour until the boat returned.

A Park Service ranger stood atop a cannon barrel inside the fort's walls. He explained that Fort Sumter wasn't yet finished when the Confederate commander in Charleston, Pierre Gustave Toutant

Beauregard, received orders to "proceed to reduce it." Beauregard carried out this dietlike instruction at dawn on April 12, 1861, when the rebels unleashed an artillery barrage from batteries ringing the harbor.

The Union garrison inside Sumter fired back until the fort's wood barracks caught fire, forcing the men to surrender. Incredibly, the only fatality during the thirty-four-hour artillery duel was a Confederate horse. But when Beauregard permitted his foes to fire a 100-gun salute before lowering the Stars and Stripes, one of the shots misfired and killed two Northern soldiers—the first of 620,000 men who would die in the four-year struggle that followed.

"No climbing, no crossing barriers and please don't take Fort Sumter home with you," the ranger said, as his audience dispersed across the rubbled fort. The ranger, a young black man named Joe McGill, said his warning against carting off chunks of the fort was only partly in jest. Many Southerners regarded Sumter as a Confederate shrine; marines often came here to reenlist and couples to exchange marriage vows. "Every once in a while someone gets carried away and tries to pry loose a sacred brick," McGill said.

Mostly, though, the fort attracted ordinary tourists, many of whom possessed a muddled grasp of American history. Visitors often asked McGill why he didn't mention the "Star-Spangled Banner." He had to explain that the national anthem was composed during the shelling of a different fort in a different conflict: Baltimore's Fort McHenry in the War of 1812. Others asked whether it was true that John Brown fired the first shot at the fort. They were thinking of the abolitionist's raid on Harpers Ferry, eighteen months before the attack on Sumter. "One guy even asked me why so many Civil War battles were fought on national parks," McGill said.

I was curious if McGill felt any awkwardness guiding tourists through a shrine to the slaveholding Confederacy. "I would if that was the whole story here," he said. He pointed to a spit of land a short way across the water. It was near there, he said, that black Union troops launched a suicidal attack on a Confederate redoubt called Battery Wagner. The assault, which formed the climax of the movie *Glory*, changed white attitudes both North and South about the fighting ability of black soldiers.

McGill also told me about Robert Smalls, a Charleston slave and harbor pilot who hijacked a Confederate ship called the *Planter*, slipped past the guns at Sumter, and turned the ship over to the Union navy. Smalls later became the ship's commander, as well as a five-term U.S. congressman from South Carolina. McGill smiled. "I see my role here a little the same way," he said. "Maybe I can slip in a few things that will change how folks think about the War."

McGill excused himself and went over to tell a school group about the fort's crumbled bulwarks. The mortar was made from oyster shells and lime, and the ugly black coating I'd noticed from sea was the legacy of the fort's renovation following the Spanish-American War. The army converted Sumter into a gun battery and sealed it with reinforced concrete, painted black to deaden glare.

I wandered outside and found Joel Dorfman lurking in the mud-flats by Sumter's original gate. A few artillery shells were still embedded in the wall. "These are the original stones and the original cannonballs," Dorfman said. He pressed his palms against the sun-warmed bricks and closed his eyes. "Break on through to the other side," he intoned.

A ship's horn tootled, recalling us to the *General Beauregard*. Steaming back to Charleston, we gazed at the palmetto-lined seawall where women and children gathered in 1861 to watch the bombardment of Sumter. "All the death," Dorfman said. "It starts to get to you. Shiloh. I was there. Bloody Pond. It was horrible. The Wilderness. I was there. During the battle the woods caught fire and burned hundreds of wounded men." He paused. "I've been to a lot of cemeteries. Did you know three thousand Jews fought for the South? There's some buried here in Charleston."

Suddenly a cry went up and the other passengers started pointing at the sea. "Fin!" someone shouted. A pair of dolphins had broken water. "Quick, get the camcorder!"

Dorfman shook his head. "I've been to a lot of these places," he said. "I couldn't get much higher. But ninety percent of these people don't know why they're here. They'll be standing on top of ten thousand graves and it might as well be Disneyland."

We docked in Charleston at sunset. I walked Dorfman to his car. The backseat of the battered Dodge was piled with crumpled clothes, a stained pillow, Civil War books, crushed boxes of Ritz crackers, and a Styrofoam tray holding a gravy-stained biscuit. "The end, my friend," Dorfman said, climbing inside. He rolled down the window and shouted *"Shalom"* as he puttered off in a cloud of exhaust. I waved and smiled, wondering if I would reach the end of my own journey in similar shape: death-obsessed, bloated on biscuits and gravy, sleeping in a car littered with dirty laundry and Ritz crackers.

As a CIVIL WAR bore, I'd arrived in Charleston naively expecting to confront the 1860s at every turn. But climbing off the *Beauregard,* I quickly saw that the Confederacy represented only a four-year blip in Charleston's long history. The first clue to the city's other lineage was the regal procession of street names—King, Queen, John, Mary—so reminiscent of colonial Williamsburg. In fact, Charleston predated Virginia's first capital and was named for a monarch who ruled England two thrones before William of Orange.

Charleston even had its own creation story, a Southern version of the *Mayflower.* Hardy colonists sailed from England in 1669 aboard three ships; hurricanes wrecked two, forcing settlers to crowd onto the *Carolina* before alighting in Charleston the next year. When modern-day Charlestonians intimated that their ancestry went back to the "three ships," they were letting you know, in genteel code, that their blood was of the bluest Charleston pedigree.

In the eighteenth century, Charleston was the largest city south of Philadelphia and boasted the colonies' best theaters, finest homes and first public library. Each summer, while slaves toiled in the rice and indigo fields, the gentry escaped the malarial torpor of their coastal plantations and took up residence in urban pleasure-domes that rivaled the Robber Baron "cottages" in Newport, Rhode Island. "The gentleman planters are absolutely above every occupation but eating, drinking, lolling, smoking and sleeping, which five modes of action constitute the essence of their life and existence," a colonial doctor in Charleston observed.

This sybaritic splendor had helped ignite the Civil War and was, in turn, destroyed by the conflict. On the eve of the Civil War, white

Charlestonians had the highest per capita income in America. In much of the Lowcountry, as the swampy coastal lands around Charleston were known, slaves outnumbered whites by nine to one. It was mostly wealthy planters who gathered at a Charleston hall one December night in 1860 to unanimously pass the South's first ordinance of secession.

By War's end, Charleston had been ravaged by fire and by an eighteenth-month blitz by Union naval guns. While post-War Atlanta and other cities remade themselves in the image of the North, Charleston abided in a sultry drowse: a poor, proud ghost of the defeated South. But destitution proved a blessing of sorts, sparing Charleston the wrecking ball. By the time prosperity crept back during War II—fueled, ironically by the same federal navy that pummeled the city eighty years before—Charleston's grand homes had been recognized as historic and architectural gems worth preserving, and the city was reborn as a playground for tourists. Having vanquished the Old South, Northerners could now partake of its luxuries by staying at planters' city homes, touring their plantations, riding carriages along cobbled streets, and dining elegantly on the Lowcountry's colorfully named dishes: hoppin' John, frogmore stew, wild-cat shrimp and she-crab soup.

I opted for the low-rent tour, staying at a B and B and lolling about the peninsula tip on which the heart of historic Charleston rested. This square mile or so was the most agreeable piece of urban real estate I'd yet visited in America. The low skyline, hurricane-swept flora and well-spaced buildings gave Charleston's streets the sun-flooded brilliance of a Van Gogh landscape, with architectural coloring to match. I gazed at the lollipop-colored facades lining "Rainbow Row" and peered through wrought-iron gates at secret gardens and grand side porches called piazzas, a Caribbean import designed to catch sea breezes and offer shade against the summer sun. Even in winter, it was easy to conjure a pair of Charleston aristocrats perched in wicker settees on one of these piazzas, idling away the day over rum, tobacco and whist.

I finally found the Civil War again at the Market, a former fish and produce mart that was now a tourist bazaar, including a stall devoted to Confederate paraphernalia: rebel flags, Dixie shot glasses, bumper stickers proclaiming, "If at First You Don't Secede, Try Try Again." Just beside the stall, a black woman sat weaving coiled baskets from palmetto fronds, pine needles and sweetgrass. She perched in a fold-out chair with a blanket over her legs and cardboard scraps as shields against the breeze. "Can't bear the cold," Emily Haynes said of the sixty-degree day. Tucking a windblown wisp of gray hair under a bright green headwrap, she had the worn look of a woman who could be anywhere between forty-five and ninety.

Haynes was a sharecropper's daughter and had spent much of her childhood in the fields, using the baskets she now wove for tourists. "You tossed the rice up and down and let the wind blow the chaff away," she said. "Fan-'em baskets, what we called 'em." She laughed, exposing a solitary molar. "Now white folks use 'em for fruit and flowers and such."

It was in the rice fields that Haynes learned what little she knew about the Civil War. "I forgot the tune but the words went like this." She cleared her throat and recited:

> *Abraham Lincoln, King of the Jews,*
> *Pinchbeck britches and cowbelly shoes.*

She resumed her weaving. "Pinchbeck meant funny pants, blown up like a balloon," she said. "Don't know about cowbelly shoes. Sounds poor. Abe was a hick, I guess." I asked why he was known as King of the Jews. "Cause he led slaves to freedom, same as Moses," she said. "That's why the gang got him, same's they got Martin Luther King. The gang didn't want him to have their chair."

The "gang" had also kept poor people down. Blacks once owned much of the farmland around Charleston but they'd been "fooled out of it," Haynes said. "My daddy always said, 'White people will out-figure you and take your money.'" This reminded her of another ditty, popular during the Depression:

> *A nickel's worth of sugar, a dime's worth of lard,*
> *I would buy more, but times too hard.*

Times were better now. Haynes sold her baskets for $30 each—more, she reckoned, than her father cleared in a year. I let her fool me out of $30 for one. As I got up to go, I asked how she felt about her neighbor selling rebel trinkets in an adjoining stall.

Haynes shrugged, gathering fronds in her lap for a fresh basket. "They can remember that war all they want," she said. "So long's they remember they lost."

Charleston—tourist industry Charleston—preferred to forget the War altogether. The city's main museum displayed a few Confederate relics but made no mention of secession or Sumter. Across the street, at Charleston's huge visitors' center, the introductory slide show opted for a passive construction of events: "Shots were fired on Fort Sumter and Charleston was plunged into the dark days of the Civil War." Then the show moved quickly to other calamities in the city's history: fires, earthquakes, the hurricane Hugo. I asked a woman at the desk about Civil War sites I might visit. Apart from Sumter, she couldn't name any. "There's used to be an old museum in the Market, I think," she said, loading me instead with brochures for carriage rides, garden shows, plantation visits.

Returning to the Market, I found an antebellum building modeled on the Temple of Nike in Greece. A sign above the portico said "Confederate Museum" but there were boards over the windows; the building had been closed since Hugo damaged it in 1989. It was only by chance, at a shop down the street, that I noticed a handwritten flyer saying that the museum had set up temporary digs on a back street and was open for a few hours each weekend.

The location turned out to be a kindergarten, and the museum's curator a Daughter of the Confederacy who taught there during the week. "The kindergarten said it was okay if we put a few of our things here for the time being," June Wells said, gesturing at a small, dimly lit room cluttered with dusty cases.

The "things" included the first rebel flag to fly over Fort Sumter and wooden wheels from the first Confederate-made cannon—crammed, for lack of space, in one of the kindergarten's toddler-sized toilet stalls. "We're not politically correct, you see," Wells said of the museum's circumstances. "The city says it can't fix our building downtown because of money. But they've built a new park, a new school, a new aquarium and have fixed all the other buildings damaged by the storm."

Wells told me this without rancor. She was about seventy, with delicate features and an hourglass figure. I found myself wondering what she had looked like as a young woman. It wasn't just her appearance. It was also her gentle laughter and direct, almost coquettish gaze. "You're from Virginia? Oh, we're deeply flattered," she said as I signed the guest book. Mine was the first name on a blank page labeled January.

I told her about my travels so far, and the impressions I'd begun forming about Civil War remembrance. "What a wonderful project," she said. "May I offer you a few of my own thoughts?"

"Of course, m'am. I'd be grateful to hear them." The best thing about Southern manners was that they seemed to improve my own, at least temporarily.

"We're a different sort of people in Charleston, then and now, and I'm sure that's why we started it all," she said of the War. "We were a well-educated city that cared about issues and had never been through the poverty stage of colonization."

Wells's own family arrived on the "first ship" and had stayed in the city ever since. She knew dozens of families with similar pedigrees. "We're not a migrating people," she said. "We live in our old houses and eat on our old dishes and use the old silverware every day. We're close to the past and comfortable with it. We've surrounded our lives with the pictures of all these relatives hanging on the walls, and we grow up hearing stories about them. It gives these things a personality beyond just the material they're made of."

She stood up and smoothed her paisley dress. "May I show you what I mean?" She gently grasped my wrist and led me to a glass case with a punch bowl inside. The woman who donated it, she said, was the daughter of the chief Confederate engineer at Fort Sumter. At a Confederate reunion in the 1890s, the woman served punch from the bowl to hundreds of distinguished veterans.

"Although she was a young woman, she had false teeth," Wells said. "As she leaned over to pour the punch, her teeth fell in the bowl. She looked at the line of people waiting to be served, and she looked at the punch. The dentures had sunk to the bottom. So she decided to go ahead serving until she could discreetly remove her teeth." Wells laughed. "She told me that forty years ago, but I still can't look at that punch bowl without thinking of those teeth."

She moved on to another glass case and another strange story. "A woman I'd never heard of in my life calls the museum one day and says, 'I'm going to die before tomorrow. I have a uniform. If you want it you have to come and get it.'" When Wells arrived, the woman served her sherry in a silver goblet and talked for two hours. "Then she said, 'I'm dying now, so if you want my granddaddy's uniform it's upstairs in a closet.'"

Wells pointed at the uniform and said, "It's very valuable because it has pants. Few pants survived because the soldiers just wore them till they gave out." I asked what became of the old lady. "Oh, she still calls me from time to time, to check on grandpa." Wells smiled. "She's just as fine as she could be. But she doesn't like her relatives. I think she gave me the uniform to spite them."

Every item in the museum seemed to carry a similarly Gothic tale, told with the same blend of decorum and dirt that left me guessing whether Wells meant to praise or skewer her subjects. "Pierre Gustave Toutant Beauregard was a charming ladies' man," she said of the euphoniously named Creole. "This is one of his silver matchboxes, which shows his exquisite taste." She paused, reaching for her pearl-handled stilletto again. "Did you know he brought a servant with him from Louisiana to wax his mustache every day? He also brought his own cow, by train from New Orleans. He had stomach troubles and claimed he couldn't drink the milk of any other animal. Can you imagine?"

Wells's own family wasn't spared. Both her grandfather and great-grandfather had fought for the Confederacy. "Very esteemed men in Charleston," she said. At least outside the house. The two men lived together and both survived to ninety-five. "So my grandmother had to take care of these two ancient men, her husband and father, arguing about the War until the end of time. You know that lady had her hands full."

Wells had joined the Daughters of the Confederacy as a young woman. At that time, the group still included many true daughters of rebel soldiers and even a few widows. Wells often ferried them to meetings. "These were real Charleston ladies, in gloves, hats and heels. I'd do up their corsets. Eighty-five years old, sucking in their breath to show off their slender waists."

It was these women who had presided over the UDC during its heyday at the turn of the century, when the organization boasted 100,000 members and erected monuments of rebel soldiers on court-house lawns across the South. It seemed strange to me that women had been so much more active than veterans in hallowing battlefield glory. But Wells, who once served as the UDC's president, felt the women were honoring themselves as much as their menfolk.

"Before the War, Southern women—white Southern women of means—were basically protected people, they didn't do much," she said. "But then the men went off to war and the women were left to take care of the homes, the businesses, the farms. They suddenly had to be self-reliant, and they found that they could be." By 1865, one of every three Confederate soldiers had died from battle wounds or dis-ease. Those who straggled home, from Northern prisons or the killing fields of Virginia, were defeated, dispirited, often maimed. "But the women had found in a strange way that they were stronger than before," Wells said. "They took care of the widows and orphans and wounded men. And they felt a solidarity and sentimentality about the South."

They also cherished the War's physical remains; it was the Daugh-ters who had started the Confederate Museum in 1896. Many of the items still bore yellowed, handwritten labels scribbled by veterans themselves. A typical one read: "Button from the coat of C.P. Poppen-heim, with stain of wound received at battle of Sharpsburg." One vet-eran presented a glass box filled with pressed flowers from Manassas. Another hauled home the trunk of a bullet-riddled tree. Some even toted home rocks. "When they weren't shooting Yanks they were hunting souvenirs," Wells said.

Nor did relic hunting end with the War. Wells showed me a letter with a lock of gray hair sewn to it. "This is our most popular item," she said. The letter was from Robert E. Lee's barber and read: "The lock of hair I send you was cut by me from the head of the great Hero after his death." Another case contained a lock of Jeff Davis's hair and splinters of wood from the tree under which he was arrested by Union troops in 1865.

Hair. Bits of wood. Blood-stained clothing. The kindergarten was beginning to feel less like a museum than a saints' reliquary. "Why do you work here?" I asked Wells.

"Volunteer," she corrected me. Then, in answer to my question, she showed me a pair of drumsticks with a caption that said, "Found in the hands of a lad killed in battle." There was also a little trunk in which the drummer boy had carried his childhood belongings off to war.

"I always show these to young people because I'm very anti-military," Wells said. "That's why I do this museum. Everything here is real. It isn't television. I hope that people seeing these things will make them never want to fight again."

To Wells, defeat and devastation were the true legacy of the War; they set the South apart from a nation accustomed to triumph. She liked to think this made Southerners a little wiser and perhaps a little more considerate of one other. "I always felt sorry for Northern people," she said. "I have a Yankee relative in New York and when I go to visit her I'm uncomfortable, people are so suspicious and cold." She shrugged. "I guess I still feel the South is the better half of the world somehow."

There was a knock on the door and a weary-looking woman came in with a boy of about ten. Catching sight of the museum, the boy's face brightened. "I'm so glad we finally found you," his mother said. "He's mad on the Civil War."

The boy pressed his face to a glass case displaying a pile of Confederate money. "When we were girls," Wells told him, "we'd play house with this money and use it to start fires with." Wide-eyed, the boy began wandering toward the weapons and uniforms, dragging his mother along.

"We have some drumsticks used by a boy about your age," Wells said. "Make sure I show them to you before you go."

BY DAY, CHARLESTON in January seemed quiet and genteel. By night it went wild. One evening, I was almost run down by a brigade of drunk college students charging through the streets shrieking, "Can't lick those Cocks!" The "Gamecocks" of the University of South Carolina had recently triumphed in a football bowl game, prompting a week-long bender in the bars lining the Market. Not that Charlestonians needed much of an excuse. South Carolina had just elected a Christian Right governor. During the same election, Charlestonians passed a referendum allowing Sunday drinking.

A few days after my arrival, I phoned a local woman whom a friend had recommended as a guide. She offered to take me on "the walk."

"The walking tour of the Battery? I did that. It was lovely."

She laughed and said she'd meet me at dark. "The Walk," it turned out, was Charleston slang for a pub crawl that ended when its participants were too stupefied to stagger any farther.

It seemed only fitting, then, that a saloon called Moultrie's Tavern became my base for Civil War operations in Charleston. Moultrie's looked at first glance like a tourist trap. Billed as a tavern "set in 1862," it offered period music, Civil War decor and glass cases filled with minié balls and buttons unearthed by the bar's relic-hunting proprietor. But while tourists hoed into cutely named dishes like Blockade Salad and Ham and Shrimp Sumter, a curious mix of well-dressed professionals and roughneck laborers clung to the bar, endlessly debating the Civil War.

As I ate lunch one afternoon, I overheard a man bellowing to several other drinkers, "The whole Southern cause was manipulated by a bunch of Charleston fat cats and that's what got us into the mess at Sumter. Don't get me wrong. I'm real proud of states' rights. Hell, I believe in city rights."

He paused to drain his beer, leaving me to wonder what depredation of the state government he was about to decry.

"Columbia has no business running us," he said of the state capital. "It's in the goddamned Bible Belt. I grew up being told that Baptists don't fuck standing up because people might think they were dancing. That's how staunch they are."

I moved my lunch to the bar and offered to buy the man a drink. He ordered four beers, shoving one to me. "I drink beer so I can drink liquor," he said. "You've got to lay down a foundation in your stomach before you start in on the hard stuff."

Idiosyncrasy was a point of pride in Charleston. Several people had already boasted to me about the city's police chief, a Berkeley-educated black Jew and former rodeo cowboy named Reuben Greenberg who roller-bladed his beat and decorated his office with miniature rebel flags. But even by Charleston standards, Jamie Westendorff ranked as a bonafide eccentric. Broad-shouldered, with watery blue eyes and a coronel of brown curls, Westendorff was, among other things, an alligator wrestler, fifth-generation Charlestonian, and descendant of a Confederate blockade runner.

"Those captains did it for the Cause, and that cause was money," he said. "Running the blockade back then wasn't much different from running dope today. Except they were smarter than dope runners because they didn't get into their own junk."

Westendorff worked as a seaman, too, gathering shellfish for his catering business. He specialized in Lowcountry feasts—fried shrimp, softshell crabs, hogs cooked in vinegar and pepper—and he always cooked on a Rabelaisian scale. "I'm like those blockade runners. Whatever you can do, do it for the most. So if I can cook for a hundred, why not a thousand?"

Westendorff also worked as a plumber, which had led to his principal hobby: privy digging. Using nineteenth-century insurance maps of Charleston, he looked for small squares marked W.C. and tried to find their remains in present-day backyards. "Fortunes were thrown down those holes," he said. Medicine bottles. Crockery. Kitchen utensils. And liquor jugs. "Guys who didn't want anyone to know they drank used to do it in the outhouse. That's where we get the phrase 'shithouse drinker.'"

Westendorff drained the last of his beers. "Got a hog to cook," he said.

"Mind if I tag along?" I asked.

He shrugged. "If you don't mind riding in the stankiest truck in the South."

Two reeking mutts, Rut and Rut-Lite, perched in the cab of his battered pickup. Plumbing snakes, peanut shells and Civil War shrapnel littered the dashboard and floor. Starting the engine with what looked like a paper clip, Westendorff asked what I'd seen of Charleston. I told him I'd visited Sumter, various museums, gone on a walking tour, poked my head in a few gardens and interiors.

"In other words, you seen nothing yet," he said, offering to show me a few of his favorite sites in "peninsula city," as he called downtown. We stopped first at a street of grand homes by the harbor. "I've worked inside—or at least under—most houses in the Battery," he said. "What they don't tell you on those tours is what these houses really are—the world's biggest money pits." Termites, humidity and sea air corroded facades and porches. Simply painting the larger houses, in some cases an annual job, cost $40,000.

Westendorff pointed at a sprawling mansion with a peeling front and rotted shutters. "That's typical of old Charleston money," he said. "Too poor to paint, too proud to whitewash." He edged the truck forward and pointed to several homes in much better repair. "That's new Charleston dough. Outside money. Nouveau riche." One of the houses belonged to a Wall Street trader, another to the founder of Wendy's, a third to a McDonald's executive. Westendorff whistled. "Must be big bucks in burgers."

Where others saw grandeur, though, Westendorff saw dung. Pointing through an iron gate at an elegant garden, he said, "I reckon the privy would have been just over there. Could be a real gold mine a few feet down." But Westendorff suspected he'd never plumb its depths. As new owners bought up Charleston, privy treasure was becoming endangered feces. "Used to be, I'd finish a job in someone's house and they'd let me poke around the yard. But the new money people aren't so prone to have you dig up their camellias."

A horse-drawn carriage clip-clopped past, piloted by a coachman in nineteenth-century livery. A leather diaper dangled beneath the horse's hindquarters to keep the animal from soiling Charleston's streets. This daintiness extended to the tour guides' vocabulary:

slave quarters were called "dependencies" or "carriage houses," and privies were airbrushed into "houses of necessity." Westendorff watched a gaggle of tourists poke cameras out the carriage window. "I call them 'people of necessity,'" he said. "Got to have 'em, just like you got to have craphouses. But they're turning this town into a fake."

Westendorff preferred the real thing, most of it tucked on back streets or torn down long ago. He turned down an alley and stopped at a slatternly wood building. "Last of the great hoe-hooses," he said.

"Great what?"

"Hoe-hoose," he repeated. "What are you, a goddamned Baptist?"

Hoe-hoose. Whorehouse. Westendorff was the first white person I'd met with a true Charleston accent. The dialect had high and low forms, with the latter known as Geech or Geechee. "It's a lazy way of talking," he said. "Slurs words, cuts corners." He began counting: one, two, shree, fo. The area between Shultz Lane and Michelle Court became simply "Shellcourt." Then there was Charleston slang. Near the hoe-hooses had once stood dozens of "peanut shops," hole-in-the-wall joints that sold pint bottles of booze after hours—with peanuts, cigars and other wares serving as fig leaf for their illicit trade. Charleston also once harbored countless speakeasies, known as "blind tigers." It was at one such dive that black jazz musicians were believed to have created the dance known ever since as "the Charleston."

"As long as there's been people in this town, there's been parties," Westendorff said. He did his best to uphold this tradition. Pulling over to the curb, he took me inside an unmarked brick building. Paintings of wigged colonials gazed down from the walls at a room filled with card and dice tables. This was the Fellowship Society, founded in 1762, one among scores of private clubs in Charleston. Westendorff had gambled there the night before. "I figured, why stay up all night? So I cut a card with a guy for five hundred bucks. He got a queen. I got a shree." He shrugged. "Whatever you do, do it for the most."

Church bells chimed outside. Westendorff fingered an ancient pair of black and white orbs, once used to vote on potential new members and "black-ball" those who didn't pass muster. "Growing up here, you can't help being obsessed with the past," he said. "Nothing ever dies in this town. It's like a bottle of wine, just gets older and better."

Westendorff had to pick up a few things at his house, so we drove over the Ashley River to what looked like an ordinary suburban ranch home. Except that a huge missile perched where a boxwood should have been. "Union shell, two-hundred-pounder, dug it out of a privy," he said.

Outhouse treasure also filled the interior. Westendorff picked up a nineteenth-century bottle and showed me the words "to be returned" on the base. "People think recycling's new, but back then people recycled everything. People didn't throw shit away." Except down privy holes, of course.

Westendorff unearthed a yellowed notebook filled with invoices and letters of lading. This was the log of a company that managed blockade runners. "No romance here—all of this is strictly business," he said. He opened the log to early 1863 and read aloud: "'News has just arrived of another terrible defeat to the Yankees. We have offered our client the goods or any portion he may select at 300% on cost.'" Westendorff whistled. "These guys sure as shit didn't give anything away."

He read on: "'We think by the spring the Yankees will be tired of fighting. We have no more doubt of our ultimate success than we have in our own existence.'" Standard Confederate boosterism. Then business again: "'We hope therefore to sell as many goods as possible before 1863 expires.'"

Westendorff chortled. "The romance is that a blockade runner was so rich he could throw stuff around, like Robin Hood. But look at this journal—the guy's so tight he fills every inch of paper rather than waste any." Sure enough, tiny scribbles filled the margins and back of every page. "You can bet that for every pistol they ran in, there was twice that amount of perfume and ale. Even if you did fifty dollars for the Cause, you'd get rich."

Westendorff's own blockade-running forebear hadn't done so well. Captain of a ship named the *Bermuda*, he sailed to Liverpool soon after the War started and loaded up with cannons. But the cargo made his ship too heavy to run the blockade. So he docked at a Caribbean island to refit and was seized by the Union navy. After his release from prison he was caught again. He never succeeded in running the blockade and died soon after the War, a destitute man whose four children ended up in an orphanage.

"That's where the Cause got most people," Westendorff said. "Prison. Downward mobility. An early grave." Even so, Westendorff had named his own boat *Bermuda* in honor of his seafaring ancestor.

We climbed back into Westendorff's truck and returned to town. I thanked him for the tour and asked directions to an old Jewish cemetery that Joel Dorfman had mentioned on the Sumter ferry. This gave Westendorff an excuse to tell me about his own tombstone. "I did a cook-out for a memorial company. The owner was broke so he cut me a stone instead." The inscription read: "He loved life and tried everything. Take it back—two things he never tried. Sucking dick and suicide." Westendorff laughed. "My mother about died when she saw that."

I left him cooking his pigs and walked a half-mile to the iron fence enclosing the Jewish cemetery. Charleston was the cradle not only of secession but also of Reform Judaism in America. Jews began arriving in Charleston in 1695; until the early nineteenth century, the city had the largest Jewish population in the country, with a quarter of all American Jews living in South Carolina. The nation's first Reform congregation was founded in a converted cotton gin in Charleston in 1824. Jewish names still dotted businesses and law offices across the city. They also filled the headstones before me, mingling Hebrew lettering and Jewish stars with insignias of the Confederacy.

One monument honored a twenty-two-year-old named Isaac and a seventeen-year-old named Mikell: "Victims in Their Early Youth to the Horrors of War, They Freely Gave Their Lives to Their Country's Needs." Other stones bore the names Moses, Hilzeim, Poznanski, and also told of early deaths on battlefields or in prison camps. One among the dead was the son of Charleston's chief rabbi.

I knew that several thousand Jews had fought for the Confederacy and a number had become prominent in the government. David Yulee, an ardent Florida secessionist, was the first Jew elected to the

U.S. Senate. David De Leon served as the Confederacy's surgeon general. And Judah Benjamin, a close confidant of Jeff Davis, became the Confederacy's attorney general, secretary of state, and secretary of war.

Still, the image of Southern Jewish foot soldiers discomfited me. I thought of my draft-dodging great-grandfather and of the Passover service, with its leitmotif of liberation from slavery in Egypt. Yet here were young Jews—a rabbi's son, even, who had perhaps recited the four questions at his family's seder—going off to fight and die in defense of the South and its Pharaonic institution. I was much more comfortable with the image Emily Haynes sang about while weaving her sweetgrass baskets. Abraham Lincoln, King of the Jews, killed by "the gang" because he brought blacks out of bondage.

Blacks, of course, had struggled hard to liberate themselves. A third of all Africans brought to this country as slaves first touched American soil in Charleston, and it was here that a free black named Denmark Vesey plotted one of the South's most ambitious slave revolts. A carpenter and preacher who bought his freedom with winnings from a city lottery, Vesey planned to seize Charleston's arsenal and arm slaves across the Lowcountry. Betrayed by one of his men, Vesey went to the gallows in 1822 with thirty-four co-conspirators.

A famous shrine to Denmark Vesey still stood, though few people recognized it as such. After the failed revolt, Charleston erected a well-fortified arsenal to guard against future insurrections. This bastion became the Southern military college known as the Citadel (or "the house that Denmark built," as some blacks called it). The Citadel was now best known for guarding against women, who were struggling to gain admission to the school at the time of my visit.

The Citadel's modern campus centered on a parade ground ringed by mock-Moorish fortresses that reminded me of sand castles I'd made from plastic molds as a child. At the school's small museum, I found a room devoted to the Civil War.

"first shots," announced a sign at the start of the exhibit. I'd had my fill of Fort Sumter and was about to move to the next display when a line of text jerked me back: "On Jan. 9, 1861, cadets under command of Major P. F. Stevens opened fire."

January 9? Open any history book and you'll learn that the War's first shots were fired on April 12, 1861, when Beauregard attacked Sumter. But according to the Citadel, four of its cadets beat Beauregard to the punch—by three months.

"Cadet George E. Haynsworth," I read on, "pulled the lanyard firing the first shot across the bow."

Bow? Of a fort?

Outside, I found a small monument by the parade ground with a bronze bas-relief of four cadets firing a small cannon out to sea. "In the early dawn of Jan. 9, 1861, the first shot of the War between the States was fired from Morris Island by Citadel cadets," the plaque read, "and the defense of the South became real."

Had there been some sort of cover-up?

I headed for the library and was greeted by a massive mural, depicting the same scene. I asked the librarian for material on the incident. She handed me a folder labeled "Star of the West," bulging with yellowed clips and faded monographs that told the hidden history of the War's beginnings. After South Carolina seceded, federal troops in Charleston moved from a land fort to the safer redoubt at Fort Sumter. Charleston officials responded by posting militiamen to the beaches and islands ringing the harbor. Among them was a detachment of Citadel cadets.

A few weeks later, a Northern steamer called *Star of the West* left Brooklyn with supplies for the Sumter garrison. A Southern sympathizer in New York telegraphed Charleston. When the *Star of the West* tried to enter Charleston harbor at dawn on January 9, 1861, it was a Citadel cadet who sounded the alarm. He and three classmates then fired across the ship's bow. Several other guns also opened fire. Three balls struck the ship's side and the captain prudently steamed back to New York. That was it.

Curious to know more, I went to see Colonel Bill Gordon, the Citadel's resident expert on the *Star of the West*. Colonel Gordon was a ramrod-straight marine with close-cropped hair and black shoes polished to a blinding sheen. He said he took students on field trips to Morris Island, though the site of the famed cadet battery had eroded into the sea years ago.

"I look at it this way," he said. "It was Christmas, 1860, just before exam period. And someone says to these cadets, 'Would you rather take your exams in calculus and English composition or go out to Morris Island and shoot at Yanks?' It's a no-brainer. You go."

The adventure quickly became a wretched camping trip. The cadets were housed in an abandoned hospital filled with coffins. It was buggy, cold, and most of all, dull. So one morning, when a Yankee ship appeared, the adolescent cadets fired their guns. "I don't think these kids had a cotton-picking clue what they were getting into, unless they were lunatics," Gordon said.

The War that followed hadn't been kind to the cadets. Two died in battle and a third fought four long years until the South's surrender. Nor did he or the other gun-battery survivor enjoy any fame for their actions. "The romance set in later, when their families took an interest," Gordon said. "The guys themselves probably didn't give a rat's ass about the War."

Gordon's irreverence surprised me, and I told him so. He explained that he'd seen plenty of combat in Vietnam. "Nothing romantic, let me tell you," he said. Also, like June Wells's at the Confederate Museum, his study of the Civil War seemed to have bred a certain pacifism. "I guess it's fair for the Citadel to claim the first shot of the War," he said, "but given the slaughter that followed, I'm not sure that's much to be proud of."

Others at the Citadel evidently disagreed. The school even had a prize called the Star of the West Medal, awarded each year to the best-drilled cadet. The prize consisted of a gold medal bearing a wooden star carved from what Gordon called "the sacred wood"—an actual sliver from the hull of the ship. The *Star of the West* also formed part of "knob knowledge," the rote that first-year cadets—called "knobs" because of their shaved heads—were required to memorize and "pop off" whenever upperclassmen demanded it.

Gordon walked me to the door. It was Friday, when cadets drilled in dress uniform across the parade ground. Clad in gray, they toted rifles and the same Palmetto flag displayed with such pride by South Carolinians during the War. With their close-cropped hair and crisp uniforms, the cadets didn't much resemble the raffish, bearded rebels of old. But the drill ended with an appropriate flourish. A crew of artillerymen wheeled a cannon in front of the *Star of the West* monument. One of the cadets yanked the lanyard, a blank fired loudly, and a cloud of acrid smoke billowed out across the parade ground. The cadets in the gun crew smiled.

After visiting the Citadel, I made a point of perusing the indexes of Civil War histories, searching for scraps on the *Star of the West*. I rarely found more than a footnote. In the view of historians who bothered mentioning the incident at all, the cadets' action proved inconsequential, resulting in nothing more than the ship's return to New York. So the *Star of the West* remained a lost shard of Civil War history, hermetically sealed inside the Citadel, as if in a pharaoh's tomb. In a sense this seemed fitting. What better vault than the Citadel, arguably the most mummified institution in America?

Nonetheless, I felt a furtive pleasure at being in on the secret. I doubted even the trivia whizzes back in Salisbury, North Carolina, knew this one. So I stored it away, looking forward to the day when I could slap a dollar on the bar while drinking with a Civil War buff and unleash my hidden weapon from the Citadel's silo. "Buck says you don't know who fired the first shots of the Civil War."

T HE WAGER WOULD HAVE TO WAIT for some bar other than Moultrie's Tavern, the one place I'd be sure to lose. Idling away another lunch hour there one afternoon, I noticed a vivid portrait behind the bar. Titled *The Relic Hunter*, it showed the bar's proprietor scanning the beach with a metal detector. I was struck by how well the portrait captured its subject and asked the bartender about its creator.

"Manning Williams?" The bartender laughed. "Where to begin? As you can see, he's a first-class artist. Also a college professor. A reenactor. Charleston's leading secessionist. Among other things."

In other words, another Charleston eccentric. I phoned Williams from the bar and was immediately invited to his house. Following his directions to a neighborhood north of town, I wondered if I'd become lost. The area was predominantly black. This shouldn't have surprised me; statistically, Southern cities were far better integrated than Northern ones. The second surprise was the figure who greeted me at the door of his bland modern home. Williams was a wiry, muscular man of about fifty, with piercing blue eyes, paint-stained fingers and a pointed beard that reached almost to his breastbone. He looked like a roguish rebel officer—a resemblance that was entirely intentional.

"It seems peaceful out there," he said, shutting the door behind me, "but don't be fooled. The War is emotionally still on. I call it the thousand-year war. It'll go on for a thousand years, or until we get back into the Union on equal terms."

Williams led me into a studio littered with half-empty coffee mugs, half-finished beers, half-smoked cigars. Civil War tomes and copies of a super-hero comic book called "Captain Confederacy" lay propped atop chairs and easels. "This is the work I'm finishing now, though the subject's something I'll never be finished with," he said, pausing beside a large canvas. "It's called *Lincoln in Hell.*"

The oil painting brought to mind Hieronymus Bosch's inferno in *Garden of Earthly Delights*. The sky was a florid orange and streaked with exploding shells. In the foreground, a gaunt figure in a black frock coat and stovepipe hat strode across a mound of skulls, cannonballs, and bits of blue and gray uniform. Behind him loomed other stacks of bones, with blurry figures perched atop each.

"That's Napoleon," Williams said, "and over there's Genghis Khan." Like Lincoln, these leaders were warmongering tyrants who had therefore earned a place in Williams's underworld.

"I've done some studies for a painting called *Southerners in Hell,* too," he added. "It shows a bunch of rebels sitting with their hands over their ears as Lincoln recites the Gettysburg Address for the rest of eternity." Williams broke into a wide, tobacco-stained grin. "I poke holes in icons. I'm suspicious of all agendas, most of all my own."

For the rest of the afternoon, Williams prowled restlessly around the studio, delivering a monologue that skipped from the Lost Cause to lost souls to Christian evangelists to calculating how long a pair of wool army socks would have lasted in 1863 ("until the stink became too much," he hypothesized). Often, he spanned two or three topics in a single sentence. And every fifteen minutes or so, he'd lasso a runaway thought and rope it back toward his central theme: the ineradicable divide between North and South.

"Take driving habits," he said, detouring from a discourse on regional voting patterns. "Down here, you stop in a line of traffic to wave someone in and a single car pulls in front of you. Up north, you pause five seconds and ten cars butt ahead."

Williams hated cars, particularly car tires, and railed against Goodyear and Firestone ads. Again, it took me a moment to see where this was leading. "Car tires are the footprint of Northern industrial society," Williams said. As a subtle protest, he stuck tires into his paintings—a stray radial, say, perched anachronistically in the foreground of an unflattering portrait of William Tecumseh Sherman.

We were back to the Civil War, though Williams didn't call it that. "A civil war is an internal revolt. But this was a war between two independent nations, one of which was exercising its constitutional right to secede." Like many Southerners, Williams preferred the phrase War Between the States, or the War of Southern Independence. "Of course, the War to Suppress Yankee Arrogance is also acceptable," he said.

In a convoluted way, Williams was introducing me to a subject dear to the hearts of latter-day rebels: neo-Confederate thought. This loosely defined ideology drew together strains of Thomas Jefferson, John Calhoun, the Nashville Agrarians (who took the title of their manifesto "I'll Take My Stand" from a verse of "Dixie"), and other thinkers who idealized Southern planters and yeoman farmers while demonizing the bankers and industrialists of the North. In the neo-Confederate view, North and South went to war because they represented two distinct and irreconcilable cultures, right down to their bloodlines. White Southerners descended from freedom-loving Celts in Scotland, Ireland and Wales. Northerners—New England abolitionists in particular—came from mercantile and expansionist English stock.

This ethnography even explained how the War was fought. Like their brave and heedless forebears, Southerners hurled themselves in frontal assaults on the enemy. The North, meanwhile, deployed

its industrial might and numerical superiority to grind down the
South with Cromwellian efficiency. A military historian and neo-
Confederate guru named Grady McWhiney put it best: "Southerners lost the War because they were too Celtic and their opponents
were too English."

Viewed through this prism, the War of Northern Aggression had
little to do with slavery. Rather, it was a culture war in which Yankees
imposed their imperialist and capitalistic will on the agrarian South,
just as the English had done to the Irish and Scots—and as America
did to the Indians and the Mexicans in the name of Manifest Destiny.
The North's triumph, in turn, condemned the nation to centralized
industrial society and all the ills that came with it. Including car tires.

"If you like the way America is today, it's the fruit of Northern
victory," Williams said. Abandoning a lit cigar for a wad of chewing
tobacco, he sent a stream of brown juice into his coffee mug. "The
South is a good place to look at what America used to be, and might
have become if the South had won. If something's fucked up, the
North did it, not us."

But the fight was far from over; as Williams had said, this was a
thousand-year war. As an artist, Williams chose to take his stand on
cultural grounds. "If the South had won the War, we never would
have had a movie like *Pulp Fiction*," he said. I'd recently seen the
Quentin Tarantino film and been put off by its gratuitous bloodshed.
But what irked Williams was a detail I'd missed.

"Tarantino goes out of his way to turn every stereotype upside
down—except one." The boxer, played by Bruce Willis, was white.
The drug dealers were yuppies. The hitman, John Travolta, made
jokes in French and read novels on the toilet. "But when two good ol'
boys appear in the film, what do they do?" Williams asked. "They
rape a black guy in front of the Confederate flag." He paused, disgusted. "Rednecks are about the only group it's still okay to kick
around. Not counting Nazis, of course."

It was sunset. We'd been talking for hours; or rather, Williams had
been talking and I'd been trying to sift what sense I could from his
torrent of art criticism, car criticism, profanity, political philosophy.
Much of what Williams said seemed little more than a clever glide
around race and slavery, rather like the slick-tongued defense of the

Southern "way of life" made by antebellum orators, South Carolinians in particular.

But parts of his diatribe unsettled me. It was certainly true that Northern zeal for righting Southern wrongs had a way of evaporating when similar wrongs surfaced close to home. To a degree I'd succumbed to the same hypocrisy. Born and schooled in Washington, D.C., a city sharply divided along race and class lines, I'd gone to work after college as a union organizer in rural Mississippi, urging impoverished loggers, most of whom were black, to go on strike and confront their white bosses. I'd burned out after eighteen months, but clung nostalgically ever since to this one bright flare of youthful idealism. Williams, I felt sure, would put a different spin on my Mississippi sojourn. He'd say I behaved like sanctimonious abolitionists and 1960s Freedom Riders who swooped down on the South while neglecting injustice in their own backyards.

"Listen closely while you're down here and take a hard look at your own prejudices," Williams said, slapping me on the back as he saw me out. "We may just make an honorary cracker out of you yet."

4

South Carolina

SHADES OF GRAY

Oh I'm a good old rebel, that's what I am. . . .
I won't be reconstructed, and I don't give a damn.
—INNES RANDOLPH, "A Good Old Rebel," 1870

Since my arrival in the Carolinas, hardly a day had passed without some snippet about the Civil War appearing in the newspaper: a school debate on whether to play "Dixie" at ball games; an upcoming Civil War reenactment; a readers' forum on the rebel flag. But one morning a short feature jumped off the page like a tabloid item about Elvis on Mars.

YANKEE STATUE FOUND IN KINGSTREE

Kingstree, S.C.—Another Civil War soldier—AWOL for nearly a century—has been found deep behind enemy lines. While a Rebel statue stands watch over the cold New England coast, a granite Yankee keeps close watch over this small Southern town.

Switched at birth?

Neither community knows for sure.

The story reported that townsfolk in York, Maine, had discovered that their decades-old Civil War memorial bore "a striking resemblance to Colonel Sanders." Meanwhile, citizens of Kingstree, South

Carolina, had long harbored doubts about *their* Civil War statue, which looked suspiciously like Billy Yank. "The mixed-up monument mystery," the story concluded, "may never be unraveled, and it is growing weirder by the day."

Things sounded weird enough already to merit a look. So I drove into the Carolina hinterland to see this AWOL Yankee for myself. Forty-five minutes from Charleston, sluggish streams and piney woods gave way to desolate farmland and derelict crossroads. Weatherboard shacks careened at gravity-defying angles beside fields choked with weeds. I crossed Flea Bite Creek and stopped to pump gas at a hamlet of four buildings, three of them vacant. The gas station attendant lay sprawled inside on a pool table, sound asleep. Back on the road, I passed an occasional brick home, trailers with satellite dishes perched in the yard, and a few weak pulses of economic life: stands selling boiled peanuts, fields of soggy "storm cotton" left unpicked from the year before, and a huge hand-painted sign that read, "Catfish for sale. CHEAP!"

Kingstree announced itself with a sign identifying the town as the birthplace of Joseph Goldstein, winner of the 1985 Nobel Prize for Medicine. Then came a ragged commercial strip: pool hall, wig shop, car wash, Piggly Wiggly supermarket, pawn and gun shop. Kingstree looked as though it had peaked in about 1930 and gone quietly to seed ever since.

Stopping for lunch, I asked a waitress with a name tag reading "Phyllis!" about the monument mix-up reported in the paper. "Oh sure, everyone here grows up knowing that," she said. "My dad always called it our 'Confederate Yankee' statue."

Phyllis! poured me sweet tea. "The way I look at it," she went on, "he's just one more prisoner of war who never got home. We're taking good care of him. I hope they're doing the same with ours. Anyway, there's lots of people here from somewhere else. I was born in North Carolina."

A man down the counter piped in, "We got plenty bigger issues to get us bent out of shape. Like the worst unemployment in the state."

"And the worst corruption," Phyllis added.

The cashier and cook materialized atop stools on either side of me. The cashier thought the Yankee statue was a Northern trick by post-War carpetbaggers. The cook suspected some Northern town had stiffed its stonemason, who then sold the statue to Kingstree instead. Phyllis wondered if the man on the monument was a Confederate after all. "Lots of rebs had to wear Yankee stuff they picked up on the battlefield," she said.

Clearly, Kingstree's cross-dressing Confederate was not just an open secret, but also a welcome distraction in a town known for little but its poverty, its graft, its forgotten Nobel laureate. "You know, Goldfarb, the Jewish guy," Phyllis said. "He won a big prize—don't ask me what for—something about blood, I think."

The luncheonette crowd suggested I go see Frances Ward, who worked at the farm bureau and also ran the local historical society. I found her at her desk, sifting insurance claims. She, too, seemed delighted by a chance to chat about the statue instead. "Off to see the Yank," she gaily announced to her co-workers.

We stopped first at a pawn shop to borrow a pair of hocked binoculars. When we reached the monument, I saw why we needed them. The soldier stood atop a thirty-two-foot column. Maybe this was why the Yank had evaded detection for so long. "I don't know what it is," Ward said, handing me the binoculars. "He just don't look right."

The soldier had short hair and a trim mustache. He held his cap by his side. "Most other monuments, there's a slouch hat," Ward said. "And he looks too clean, not ragged enough." The soldier also had a knapsack on his back, as Yankees generally wore them, rather than a haversack slung over one shoulder, in traditional rebel fashion. Ward showed me a photograph of the monument in Maine. Slouch hat, long beard, haversack dangling against his waist. Textbook Confederate. "Odd, isn't it," she said.

One thing about the Kingstree monument was right. The soldier faced vigilantly north toward the oncoming enemy, like a stone rebel should, gazing above Kingstree's abandoned storefronts, its wig shop and pool hall and Hardee's restaurant, all the way to York, Maine, where his long-lost twin gazed back at him. Ward said she'd learned of the turncoat memorial as a teenager in the 1960s. The news came as a shock. "This is a very Southern town," she said. "I grew up with this picture of my great-grandfather with a long beard and a sleeve pinned up because he lost an arm in Virginia somewhere. Discovering that the guy on top of our monument was a Yank was like being told there's no Santa Claus."

Over time, though, Ward had warmed to the stranger. "He's been there a long time. We might as well keep him." Also, like the folks at the diner, she felt the mystery was a "big joke" that offered relief from the reality of life in Williamsburg County, of which Kingstree was seat. "It's good to have some positive—or at least not too negative—news about this county. Mostly it's been about our sheriff being arrested, our chief deputy in jail for selling drugs, or about the county losing its credit rating and the rubber-glove factory closing."

Neighboring Lee County boasted a new maximum-security prison and a cotton museum. But Kingstree was a long way from the interstate and offered little to visitors. Ward smiled. "'Cept maybe this monument." She conceded, though, that I was the first person who had to come to Kingstree expressly to see it.

There was another, touchier reason for leaving the monument alone. Williamsburg County was two-thirds black. "If we made a big deal about that Yank and took him down, it would maybe offend people," Ward said. The year before, two new memorials had gone up beside the statue: plaques to Thurgood Marshall and Martin Luther King Jr. "Some whites about died when that happened, right here by the War memorial." After all, neither man had ever visited the county, much less gone to war for it. "Then again," Ward observed, "neither did our Yank."

She walked me to the historical society, a former bank now cluttered with bits of porcelain, an old Polaroid camera, a picture of a local football coach, and an enormous canoe of dubious Indian origin. "Basically junk out of people's attics," Ward said. She led me to a creaking microfilm machine and dug out dusty reels of the county newspaper. As I cranked through them, the monument story grew weirder still. The statue had been commissioned by the United Daughters of the Confederacy in 1910 at a cost of $2,500, a huge sum for a small, impoverished community. Two thousand people turned out for the statue's dedication. A Confederate colonel delivered a stem-winder, which was received with "enthusiastic sympathy by the staunch old vets in the audience, no one of whom respect the molly coddles who feel regret for acting the part of men in obeying their country's call."

But this fulsome news dispatch was oddly muted about the statue itself. The reason lay buried in the final paragraph: "It is a matter of regret that the statue to be placed on top of the granite column failed to reach here in time for the unveiling." The statue's arrival was held up by "unforeseen delays," the paper said, assuring its readers: "When it is done it will be the pride of future generations." A month later, the statue arrived and was hoisted atop its shaft without ceremony.

The story raised several intriguing possibilities. Had the mason realized his error and delayed shipment in hopes of avoiding discovery? Had he genuinely faced "unforeseen delays" and mixed up his clients in his haste to ship late orders? Or had some wise Daughter of the Confederacy, upon receiving the statue, prudently chosen to keep it under wraps rather than risk a riot by unveiling it before all those "staunch old vets"?

Surely, Ward said, someone must have noticed a problem when they unpacked the crate. "It was probably done the Southern way," she hypothesized. "Whispered about in homes but kept quiet so that no one would be embarrassed."

More recent news clips yielded another crop of odd details. When folks in York, Maine, learned of their Confederate and Kingstree's Yank, a resident wrote a letter proposing a "friendly exchange of our last two prisoners of war." But a Daughter of the Confederacy in Kingstree politely demurred, writing back, "We are contented with our handsome Yankee friend." In fact, there was no evidence the two monuments had ever been switched. Kingstree's was cut in 1910 by a South Carolina company; York's went up four years earlier and was sculpted by an Englishman living in Massachusetts. "As a former native of England, his knowledge of the Civil War may have been foggy," a news clip on Maine's statue speculated. Or, "the figure may have been sculpted for a Southern town that reneged."

Nonetheless, the myth of a Kingstree-York connection endured, a sort of proto-urban legend that popped up from time to time, as it had in the newspaper feature I'd read. Whatever the exact truth of the matter, Ward felt the tale carried a redeeming message. "What were they putting up monuments to in the first place? A lot of Southerners dying for nothing. And look at us now, still arguing about the rebel flag. To me that says we're still a lost cause in a lot of ways." She dumped an armful of old documents in the canoe and turned off the lights. "Maybe the message of the whole mix-up is that we shouldn't make such a fuss about these old symbols. Forget it. There's real things to worry about."

WARD'S PARTING COMMENT came back to me a few days later, when I opened the morning paper to find a rebel battle flag splashed across the front page. South Carolina's legislature was about to debate whether the Confederate banner should keep flying above the capitol dome, as it had since 1962. Demonstrations were anticipated for later in the week. So I reluctantly departed the seductive Lowcountry for the state's rolling midriff, two hours' drive west.

After Charleston, Columbia seemed a colorless burg with few historic buildings and a drab downtown that died after dark. This wasn't entirely Columbia's fault. Sherman brought urban renewal to the city in 1865 during his return march from the sea. Fire finished off what Union shells missed. Even a Northern reporter, touring the South six months after the War, was stunned by the "ruins and silent desolation" he found in Columbia. "In no other city that I have visited," wrote John Dennett, a correspondent for *The Nation*, "has hostility seemed to me so bitter."

Rather than rebuild and forget, in the manner of Atlanta, Columbia had turned its capitol grounds into a memorial to Yankee depredations. "Burned by Sherman's troops," said a gravestone marking the site of the bygone wooden statehouse. Brass stars marked where each of Sherman's shells had scarred the walls of the current capitol, which was under construction in 1865. A nearby bronze of George Washington bore a plaque recording that Sherman's troops "brickbatted this statue and broke off the lower part of the walking cane." The damage had been left unrepaired.

Just beside the capitol stood the Confederate Relic Room, a museum whose keepsakes included a torch used by Sherman's men, a ruglike suitcase of the sort toted by Northern carpetbaggers, and the Confederate Roll of Dead, a handwritten list of South Carolinians killed in the War. The Roll, recently published in book form by the state archives, had become an overnight bestseller in local bookshops.

"We resent playing second fiddle to Charleston when it comes to the Confederacy," said Dotsy Boineau, the Relic Room's curator. In fact, secessionists had originally gathered in Columbia to vote themselves out of the nation; they only moved to Charleston because of a smallpox scare in the capital. "I think we're not yet sure we want to be part of the Union," Boineau went on. "We still think this little state of ours has the right to decide a lot of the questions that big government is taking over."

As I spoke with Boineau, her neo-Confederate views were enjoying a degree of vindication at the nearby capitol. A conservative, states-rights governor was taking the oath of office, having pledged to keep the battle flag flying (a promise on which he would later attempt to renege). South Carolina had also elected a Republican majority to its legislature for the first time since Reconstruction. The party of Lincoln, anathema to earlier generations of Southerners, now spoke to antigovernment tendencies across the region. There was even a striking consonance between the GOP's "Contract With America" and the Confederate constitution; both called for term limits, budget balancing, curbs on taxation and other restraints on the state.

"Our ancestors were a little off with their timing, but their rebellion against federal government is finally seeing fruition," a Republican legislator told me as we chatted in his office beneath paintings of Lee and Jackson.

The legislator's rebel forebears, though, might have been surprised to see the Confederate battle flag flying above the statehouse. It had never done so in the 1860s. The banner most Americans now called the rebel flag—a diagonal blue cross studded with white stars and laid across a field of red—served only as a combat standard during the War. The political flag of the South, as I'd learned in Salisbury, took a different design and changed several times in the course of the War.

But in South Carolina and several other states, the better-known battle flag had been hoisted over capitol domes a century after the War, in the midst of civil rights strife. Flag defenders now maintained that the flag was raised to honor soldiers' valor and sacrifice on the occasion of the War's centennial. But for many white Southerners, the flag had also symbolized defiance and segregation at a time when they felt under siege again by the federal government and by Northerners who wanted to change the South's "way of life."

On the morning of the legislature's opening session, I met a pro-flag group called the Council of Conservative Citizens, or CCC for short, over breakfast at the Capitol Restaurant a few yards from the statehouse steps. The group was easy to spot; a small rebel flag waved from an orange-juice glass at the center of their table. But the dozen or so men eating grits and fried eggs looked more like members of the local Rotary Club than a rabid band of battle-flag defenders.

"You found the wild-eyed rednecks, eh?" joked a man in a pin-striped suit. He spoke with a Northern accent and handed me a business card embossed with the name of an export/import firm in Philadelphia. Sitting beside him was a middle manager from New Jersey. There was also an engineer from New Hampshire who wore a Mickey Mouse watch and boasted that his hometown of Peterborough was the setting for Thornton Wilder's *Our Town*. "Southern heritage is as much a part of American history as Plymouth Rock," he said with a jarring New England accent. "But for me, the flag's mainly a symbol of resistance against government control, not a symbol of the South."

Sitting across from me was a man with long curly hair, a black beret and a plaid shirt. He looked like a Beat poet. "I'm Walt," he said, amiably thrusting his hand across the clutter of breakfast dishes. "I'm here to defend my race against the government and the Jewish-controlled media."

Before I could respond, the group's leader arrived: William Carter, a thirty-eight-year-old chiropractor who wore a charcoal gray suit with a rebel-flag pin. I asked about his plans for the group's protest at the capitol. "We'll make a mock presentation of a petition, hold up some banners, shout a few slogans," he said. "Propaganda, essentially."

I asked if he had any Civil War ancestors. Carter shrugged. "Yeah, but I don't know the details. Anyway, that's not why we're here. This fight's about today, about the ethnic cleansing of Southern whites—same thing that's happening in Bosnia. There's black history month, there's a black Miss America pageant, there's even a black yellow pages in South Carolina. Can you imagine a yellow pages for whites? No way. Anything for whites is PIC—politically incorrect."

The New Hampshire engineer gestured at his Mickey Mouse watch. Carter leapt up to lead his troops into battle. "Let me slick up," he said, jerking a comb through his thin, Brylcreemed hair. By now, about forty or so people had gathered, including two men in camouflage pants and plumed slouch hats, several members of a motorcycle gang, and a man in a gray tuxedo carrying a portable phone and a briefcase with a sticker that read "I HAVE A DREAM, TOO"—beneath a picture of the U.S. Capitol with a rebel flag flying from the dome.

Television cameramen waited on the statehouse steps. Though Carter and his lieutenants had reviled the media over breakfast, they now rushed forward to pose for the cameras, waving rebel flags and chanting, "Never take it down!" Carter brandished a pro-flag petition with 40,000 signatures and lambasted companies whose executives in South Carolina had spoken out against the banner. AT&T came in for extra vitriol. "We won't spend any of our rebel money on a phone company that likes queers!" Carter yelled. What exactly this had to do with the rebel flag wasn't clear.

The marchers moved inside the capitol, posting themselves by doors and elevators so arriving legislators had to run a gauntlet of protesters waving placards and shouting. The representatives exhibited their best Southern manners; even black legislators smiled and nodded, as if greeting supporters.

I wandered outside and found one of the CCC demonstrators studying a memorial to the Confederate dead, who, the inscription said, "glorified a fallen cause by the simple manhood of their lives." Bud Sharpe was a fifty-five-year-old construction foreman. "Once the flag's gone, they'll want to go after this," he said, gesturing at the statue. "We may have lost the War, but at least we should have this to look back on." It seemed a wistful logic; the Cause was lost but the Lost Cause shouldn't be.

"I feel like the flag's the only thing working people like me have left," he went on. "All my life it's been one thing after another. First they integrated the schools. Then they integrated everything. Then they say 'colored' ain't right anymore, it's got to be 'black,' then 'African-American.' But nothing changes for us. We're still 'crackers' and 'peckerwoods' and 'rednecks.' I feel like I've swallowed enough for one lifetime."

I asked Sharpe if things would be better if the South were still segregated. "Damn right, they would," he replied. "In my town, there were no blacks until recently—they knew they wasn't supposed to live with white people. Now, they're all around. They even have interracial dating."

Sharpe paused, trying to contain himself. "Look, I'm a labor foreman. I've got blacks working for me. We eat lunch together. But at the end of the day I go to my home and they don't come along. This isn't hate, it's just not wanting to mix your seed with another race."

Sharpe picked up his placard—"KEEP IT FLYING!"—and headed off to rejoin the other protestors. "I'm here today to stand up for heritage," he concluded. "That's what the flag's all about."

I sat at the monument for a while. For the past several weeks people had been talking to me about "heritage." But, like the flag, this obviously meant very different things to different people. For the Sons of Confederate Veterans I'd met in North Carolina, it meant the heritage of their ancestors' valor and sacrifice. For Bud Sharpe, it was the heritage of segregation and its dismantling over the past forty years. Was it possible to honor one heritage without upholding the other?

I went back to the Capitol Restaurant for a cup of coffee and a look at several copies of the CCC newspaper. The flag debate was right there on the front page, beside a story headlined: MALCOLM X FOLLOWERS RAPE, MURDER WHITE WOMAN.

The waitress came over to refill my coffee. She'd served the CCC at breakfast and formed her own views about the flag dispute. "You know what the state should'a done? Send someone to the capitol in the dead of night to take the flag down without telling anyone. I'd bet a week's worth of tips that not a single person in South Carolina would'a noticed it was gone." She sighed. "It's too late now. As soon as you make an issue of something, everyone feels they got to pick sides, same as they done back in eighteen-whatever."

This was the most concise analysis of the flag controversy—or of events in eighteen-whatever—I'd yet heard in South Carolina.

I returned to my CCC paper and read about a secret plan to create a black-controlled "Republic of New Afrika" in six Southern states. It was tempting to dismiss the CCC as a dinosaur remnant, an evolutionary dead end of Southern bigotry. But maybe such an offhand dismissal was an exercise in prejudice, too. Right-wing extremism was thriving across America; it behooved me to hear it out. So that evening, I drove to a trailer park outside Columbia to visit Walt, the beret-clad man who'd sat across from me at breakfast and scribbled his address on the CCC paper.

A rebel flag covered one window of Walt's mobile home. A cardboard sign filled another with the words "Walt's Nest." It was an appropriate nickname; the chaotic interior was feathered from floor to ceiling with piles of *Time* magazine, *Playboy* and *The Wall Street Journal;* wall photos of Robert E. Lee and Mr. Spock; ceiling posters of Michael Jackson and swimsuit-clad models.

Walt pointed me to a ratty couch and returned to chopping vegetables in the trailer's cramped kitchen. "I'm a vegetarian," he said, slicing a red pepper, "because I don't trust federally inspected meat."

There wasn't much that Walt did trust about the State—or "the Snake," as he called it. That was why he'd taken a day off work, without pay, to demonstrate for the rebel flag. "I'm not an American, I'm a citizen of the Confederate States of America, which has been under military occupation for the past hundred thirty years."

Putting down his paring knife, Walt rummaged through a stack of newspapers and handed me a photo of an anti-Communist rally in East Germany, held just before the Berlin Wall came down. Amid the sea of protesters stood a man waving a rebel flag. Walt had circled the grainy AP photo with yellow Magic Marker. "I doubt that German knew a thing about the Confederacy," he said. "But he knew what that flag stood for. Being a rebel, raising hell."

This was the anarchic, James Dean–ish side of the South that had once appealed to my own adolescent soul, particularly in rock 'n' roll.

As a teenager in the 1970s, I'd swilled Rebel Yell and thrilled to the music of The Band ("The Night They Drove Old Dixie Down"), the Allman Brothers ("Ramblin' Man"), Little Feat ("Dixie Chicken"), and other groups that either came from the South or romanticized its folk culture. To me, these tunes evoked a freethinking defiance that dovetailed nicely with my pubescent alienation from "the System"—a loose-knit cabal linking Richard Nixon, Henry Kissinger, my parents and most of my teachers.

Walt, who was forty-nine, had once demonstrated against the Vietnam War. He opened a drawer where he kept the beads and McCarthy button he'd worn back then. His fondness for berets, long hair, organic vegetables and *Star Trek* also were vestiges of a sixties self that he'd otherwise left behind. Somewhere in the intervening quarter century, Walt's instinctive rebelliousness had turned reactionary. Since graduating from a technical college, he'd bounced from job to job and now found himself living in a beat-up trailer, driving a Toyota with 200,000 miles on it, and working for $5.45 an hour at a small factory that repaired cable-TV converters.

"I became an angry man," Walt said. "I knew something was wrong but I didn't know what. I blamed myself." He reached into the fridge for broccoli. "Now I'm not angry anymore. I understand why the world is the way it is."

Walt walked across the trailer and threw back a madras spread covering a tall bank of pigeonholes. The slots were stuffed with literature and divided into sections, each carefully marked with typed labels: "Hittites," "Semites," "Asiatics," "Freemasons," "Homosexuals." There were pamphlets from the National Alliance, a neo-Nazi group, and copies of a rabidly xenophobic newspaper, *The Truth at Last: News Suppressed by the Daily Press*, which claimed the nation was being overrun by immigrants who ate insects and dogs. Other publications targeted gun-control advocates, blacks, feminists, Catholics.

"Blacks are a primitive race, not as intelligent as we are," Walt said, pulling a mimeograph from a pigeonhole labeled "Bushmen." "They look human so you give them the benefit of the doubt, but really they're savages. They have bigger teeth than we do, for chewing things, but their brains are small. They need supervision to survive."

Blacks' natural overseers were whites—descended from Hittites.

But Hittites also were a subject race. The world's true masters were Semites and their descendants among modern-day Jews. "They're a predatory race with higher intelligence than us," Walt explained. The superiority of Semites flowed from a single source: racial purity. Jews bred only with their own, while encouraging other races to mix. This ensured that Jews' own genetic fiber stayed intact while others' weakened. "That way, Jews stay in control," Walt explained.

Through this anti-Semitic window, Walt had come to see everything anew. The Christianity of his youth was a Semitic plot to undermine whites; Jesus told his followers to turn the other cheek rather than fight back. Walt had also disavowed *Star Trek* and his beloved Mr. Spock, who was half-human and half-Vulcan—a coded message encouraging miscegenation. Then there was Uhura, the sexy black officer who broke taboos by engaging in TV's first interracial kiss with Captain Kirk.

"Our government is run by a foreign power—Israel," Walt concluded. "The only way to escape that is a political dissolution of the United States. And the only hope for that I see is a revival of the Confederacy."

Walt returned to his vegetables while I pondered how to respond. "Have you ever met a Jew?" I asked him.

"I knew one in high school. He seemed normal. But that was before I knew anything."

"Well, you've just met your second."

Walt looked up from a pile of oyster mushrooms. "You're a Jew? You don't look Jewish." He studied me, searching for some telltale Semitic clue. "What's your last name again?"

"Horwitz."

"I should'a guessed." He cut another mushroom. "Well, you know exactly what I'm talking about, then. Anyway, it's the big people I'm against, the ones pulling strings." He reached for tofu. "Just because a race is bad doesn't mean everyone who belongs to it is. There's one black I respect a lot." Walt riffled through his library again. "This guy," he said, handing me a picture of Louis Farrakhan speaking at a Nation of Islam rally. "He thinks mixing the races is wrong, that blacks and whites should go their separate ways. And he's down on Jews, too."

Walt also made an exception for Michael Jackson—"he's an android, he's not really black"—and for the rap group known as 2 Live Crew. A South Carolina official wanted to ban the group's latest album because of its raunchy lyrics. Walt had immediately gone out to buy their music. "Anything the state's against, I'm for," he explained. This segued, once again, into his defense of the rebel flag. "Until they started criticizing that flag, I'd never given it a thought. But once you attack something, that's exactly when I'm going to support it."

Walt took down a wok and slicked it with sesame oil. "Want some dinner?" he asked.

"Some other time."

Walt shrugged and walked me to the door. Then he reached into a pigeonhole and planted a sticker on the cover of my notebook. "Earth's Most Endangered Species: THE WHITE RACE!" He thrust out his hand, as genial as he'd been that morning at breakfast. "It's been real nice talking to you," he said. "Come again, will ya?"

"I just might." His words seemed genuine and so were mine. There was a feisty iconoclasm about Walt that I couldn't help admiring, even if he was on the mailing list of every hate group in America.

THE NEXT MORNING, on my way out of Columbia, I stopped at the airport industrial park where Walt said he worked. Partly, I was curious to test his grasp on reality. He'd told me he worked beside a militant NAACP member and that his employer was "brain-poisoned" because he promoted blacks over whites and made Walt clean the bathrooms.

The plant was a windowless hanger where forty or so workers crouched beneath fluorescent lights, tinkering with cable converters. Walt, wearing his beret, sat across from a young black man with wire-rim glasses, a turtleneck and a gold earring. "Hey guys!" Walt shouted, as soon as he spotted me. "Here's the Jew I was telling y'all about!"

The young black man rolled his eyes. "Don't pay him no mind," he said. "Walt's a crackpot."

Walt smiled, as though he'd been paid a compliment. "I've given Sam some of the stuff I showed you last night. He disagrees with me."

"Disagree? Shit," Sam muttered. "I think that stuff should be burned." He turned to me again. "Walt thinks black people are being recognized too much. But white folks have been recognized since the day they were born. We're just getting into this world."

The plant's supervisor appeared. "Can I help you?" he asked. This was James Padgett, whom Walt had described as "brain-poisoned." I told him I'd met Walt at a flag rally the day before and was curious to see where he worked. Padgett took me to his office and shut the door. "You can't fire someone for their politics," he said. "Anyway, Walt breaks the monotony here."

Padgett confirmed the broad outline of what Walt had told me. Sam was indeed an outspoken NAACP member; some blacks earned more than whites; and yes, Walt cleaned the bathrooms. "He's not a top producer, so if he wants to make more money he has to clean the toilet."

I asked what he thought of Walt's views. "Paranoid," Padgett said. "And silly." He paused. "Listen, I'm thirty-eight, I grew up in the New South. We've all got to get along, black and white. If we do, we can really go somewhere. If we don't, we'll keep getting dumped on."

"Dumped on?"

"Let me show you something." Padgett walked me to the plant's shipping dock and pointed at a mountain of crates. "We're part of a national company that converts cable boxes so folks can watch pay TV. Look at the return addresses on these orders. Massachusetts. New York. Oregon. They send all the toughest jobs South because we're the best."

Padgett's face reddened. "I used to go to company meetings in New York and everyone was looking down on me because of my hick accent," he said. "But then it turned out we're not so dumb down here. In fact, we're the toughest unit in the company and we make a ton of money. So now, when I go to the meetings in New York, I'm not some savage anymore—I'm the hero." Padgett shook his head. "I'm the same person I always was. All that's changed is their image of me."

Padgett walked me to the door. He seemed a bit embarrassed by his unprompted outburst. "Enjoy the rest of your trip," he said. "And keep your eyes and mind open. The South may surprise you."

The South had surprised me plenty already, as had Padgett's words. They echoed the same sense of Southern grievance I'd picked up across the Carolinas: from the gunshop crowd in Salisbury, from Manning Williams at his Charleston art studio, from the rebel-flag protestors at the state capitol. In their view, it was the North—or Northern stereotypes—that still shadowed the South and kept the region down.

But something was wrong with this picture. An Arkansan occupied the White House. The vice president came from Tennessee. A Georgian served as Speaker of the House. States' rights, or "devolution," was the political fad of the day. And the South had become the nation's most economically vibrant region.

"The South is a good place to look at what America used to be," Manning Williams had told me. It was a thought that appealed to my romantic image of the South as a rural backwater, rich with history and character so absent in most of the nation. But viewed from Columbia's capitol grounds and the industrial park by the airport— as well as from the strip malls and housing tracts and new factories I'd passed all across the Carolinas—the South was exactly the opposite: a good place to see what America was becoming. Suburban and exurban, politically conservative, anti-union, evangelical, a booming part of the global economy.

I later put this to A. V. Huff, a historian of the South at Furman University in upland South Carolina. He responded by reminding me just how recent and profound the South's transformation had been. Huff told of picking cotton as a child in the 1940s, when the rhythm of the school year still moved to the cotton crop. Children attended class in midsummer, during lay-by season, and returned to the fields for the autumn harvest.

Yet in Huff's own lifetime, this most fundamental of Southern rites had all but vanished from the experience of most Southerners. Many of Huff's students—mostly middle-class kids from the suburbs of Atlanta and other cities—had never even seen a cotton crop. Huff illustrated his point by inviting me to sit in on one of his classes. Lecturing on Eli Whitney's invention of the cotton gin, he produced a boll from his family's farm as a teaching prop. The students passed the boll around, gazing at it with wonderment, as if at a mastodon's tooth.

Fewer than 5 percent of present-day Southerners now worked the land, and Dixie was fast becoming the nation's new industrial heartland, with car plants sprouting across the former cotton belt. Per capita income in the South—half the national average when Huff was born in 1937—now ranked close to the rest of America. The eleven states of the Old Confederacy comprised the fifth-largest economy in the world.

To Huff, this transformation helped explain the resurgent nostalgia for the Confederacy he sensed across the South, even among his mostly affluent students. "The South—the white South—has always had this powerful sense of loss," he said, as we chatted in his office between classes. First, it was the loss of the War and antebellum wealth. Later, as millions of Southerners migrated to cities, it was the loss of a close-knit agrarian society. Now, with the region's new prosperity and clout, Southerners wondered if they were losing the dignity and distinctiveness they'd clung to through generations of poverty and isolation.

"All those things Southerners say they hold dear they're selling out now for a mess of pottage," Huff said. "So there's this feeling, 'If I wrap myself in the flag, maybe Grandma will forgive me for selling the farm and dealing with the Yankees.'"

Huff pulled a book from his shelf and read me a poem called "The Conquered Banner," composed by a Confederate chaplain after the Civil War.

> *Furl that Banner, for 'tis weary;*
> *Round its staff 'tis drooping dreary;*
> *Furl it, fold it, it is best;*
> *For there's not a man to wave it,*
> *And there's not a sword to save it,*

And there's not one left to lave it
In the blood which heroes gave it;
And its foes now scorn and brave it;
Furl it, hide it—let it rest.

Huff closed the book and headed off to teach another class on the Cotton Kingdom. "It's too bad nobody reads that poem much any-more," he said

5

Kentucky
DYING FOR DIXIE

When I was younger I could remember anything,
whether it happened or not, but I am getting old,
and soon I shall remember only the latter.
—MARK TWAIN

The cinder-block building by the Tennessee line looked more like a bunker than a bar. Wire mesh concealed windows the size of medieval arrow slits. Man-high razor wire ringed an adjoining yard. A military jeep painted in desert camouflage sat parked out front, beside pickup trucks and Harley choppers. Scarlet letters splashed across the building's facade: REDBONE'S SALOON.

Inside, "Confederate Railroad" wailed on the jukebox. Behind the bar stood a man in a polka-dot cap and a T-shirt adorned with a swastika. This was the proprietor, Redbone. He served me a beer and huddled with a man whose shirtfront proclaimed: I've Got a Nigger in My Family Tree. The back of the shirt showed a lynching—a cartoonish black man, dangling from a branch.

A week earlier, Redbone's Saloon had celebrated Martin Luther King Jr.'s birthday with a "Thank God for James Earl Ray Party."

Flyers posted in the nearby town of Guthrie, Kentucky, proclaimed "Fuck Martin Luther King's B.Day" and invited folks to play pool and eat "Chicken-Ribs-Fixins" for three bucks a plate.

That same weekend, a nineteen-year-old named Michael Westerman drove through Guthrie with a rebel flag flying from his pickup. Several carloads of black teenagers gave chase; one of the youths shot Michael Westerman dead. Then crosses started burning in Guthrie. The FBI, the KKK, the NAACP, and reporters from Kentucky and Tennessee all hustled to the stateline town. So did I, startled by a newspaper squib—"Rebel Flag Is Catalyst to Killing"— that appeared in Carolina newspapers. Until then, I hadn't realized the nineteenth-century conflict I'd set out to explore was still a shooting war.

But arriving late on a Saturday night, I knew little about the place, except what a gas-station attendant told me. The Kentucky side of Guthrie was dry, she said. If I wanted a beer, there were two bars in Tennessee, just across the state line at the southern edge of town. "There's Billy's, which is kinda country-and-western," she said, "and Redbone's. That's a biker bar. Real bad news."

The music at Redbone's blared too loudly for conversation. So I sipped my Budweiser and studied the walls. Amidst the usual biker-bar decor—pictures of half-naked women splayed across motorcycles, a pistol mounted beside the words "We Don't Bother Calling 911"—I noticed a curious anthology of hand-scrawled verse. The poems mingled biker and Confederate themes, evoking nihilistic scenes of the ruined South as viewed from the back of a Harley.

> It was 1865, homes burnt to the ground,
> Everything lost, I took my stand.
> Riding through the fog,
> Rebel flag in hand,
> Fighting for my freedom,
> Fighting for my land.

Beneath the poetry appeared a cryptic insignia: "F.T.W." Between songs on the jukebox, I turned to a man on the next stool and asked what F.T.W. stood for.

"Who's asking?" he replied. "F–B–I?"

This provoked howls from the bar. "I'm a writer, not a cop," I said, inanely flashing a spiral pad with "Reporter's Notebook" stenciled on the cover.

The man looked at me dubiously, but muttered, "F.T.W. Fuck the World."

Another man, bulging from a Lynyrd Skynyrd T-shirt, lurched over and bellowed, "Write this in your damned notebook. We got a few people standing up for white rights. The rest are pussies who let niggers trample all over them. Like those boys who shot Westerman did t'other day." He reeled for a moment. "You've got your KKK and your BBB—that's Badass Black Brothers. Two sides of the same coin. If they want war, come on. Let's get it on."

He sat down with a thud and gazed blankly at a TV behind the bar. Male ice skaters in tights glided across the screen. As I scribbled down his words, I sensed someone looming behind me. Then a hot, beery breath whispered in my ear: "That shorthand or chicken scratches?"

I looked up to face a leather-clad giant with bloodshot eyes and long, straggly hair. "Shorthand," I lied, hoping he couldn't decipher my notes about swastikas and lynchings. He bent down, tore a few pages from my notebook, and stuck the wadded paper in his mouth. "You know," he said, chewing loudly, "I shit out a turd this morning that was bigger than you."

Unsure as to the appropriate response, I glanced around the bar for support. The other drinkers had vanished into a cloud of cigarette smoke by the pool table. Only Redbone remained, eyeing us warily from behind the bar. "The question is," my inquisitor resumed, "should I beat the shit out of you right here and now, or let it slide this time?"

The veins in his neck began throbbing. One of his hands curled into a fist. I weighed whether to take off my glasses, so shards wouldn't lodge in the back of my head, or keep them on in the faint hope that spectacles might cause the giant to let it slide this time. A snatch of poetry swam on the wall behind his head.

Like the Rebels of Old,
Still Bursting With Pride,

Don't Take no Shit,
On Harleys We Ride.

I eased slowly off my stool, nodded toward the door and said, "Maybe I should just—"

The man grabbed my coat and ripped it cleanly from armpit to wrist. Redbone lunged across the bar and seized the man's arm, shouting "Cool it!" I ducked under the giant and dove through the door, sprawling on the gravel outside. Then I sprinted toward the lights of town. Slowing to a jog, I reached the Kentucky line and a sign that read:

WELCOME TO GUTHRIE
BIRTHPLACE OF ROBERT PENN WARREN
FIRST POET LAUREATE OF THE UNITED STATES.

DURING ROBERT PENN WARREN's childhood at the start of the century, Guthrie was a raw railroad town ringed by fields of dark-leaf tobacco known as "the Black Patch." Warren, who lived in Guthrie until he was fifteen, later described his hometown as "very un-Southern," a new community that lacked "a sense of belonging in any particular place or having any particular history." Eighty years later, Guthrie exhaled the depleted air of a thousand other towns across the back-country South, bypassed by the interstate and drained of vitality by decades of migration to the city. Guthrie's main street wound past a Piggly Wiggly, a pool hall, The American Cafe ("country cookin' makes you good lookin'"), a hog-feed elevator, a garment factory, and convenience stores crowded with people scratching lottery tickets (locals drank on the Tennessee side of town but could gamble only in Kentucky).

At the end of the strip, next to the Tinytown Baptist Church, I found a rundown place called the Holiday Motel. The motel's neon sign flickered WE ARE REASONABLE, which sounded comforting after the conversation I'd just had at Redbone's Saloon. A large woman in a baggy housedress sat smoking behind the reception desk.

"I'd like a single room for the night," I said.

"Why is that?" She had a German accent and stroked a schnauzer in her lap. A German flag and pictures of the Bavarian Alps adorned the wall behind her.

"Why do you ask?"

She shrugged. "Your car plates are out of state. Your coat is torn. You look pale. There is a Holiday Inn over in Clarksville, much nicer than this."

I told her I wanted to stay in Guthrie to learn about Michael Westerman's shooting. Then I mentioned my visit to Redbone's.

"You crazy?" she exclaimed. "When that bar closes, that's when I turn on my No Vacancy sign. They stupid to begin with, but once they start drinking and doing drugs, they have no brains left."

As I filled out a registration form, a police scanner crackled behind the desk. "I'm nosey," the woman said, twiddling the dial and looking through the motel's picture window. "Not much ever happens here, until they shoot that Westerman boy." She chuckled. "You know, I think there's some pride. Guthrie had its first drive-by."

I sat up most of the night with Maria Eskridge, sipping peppermint schnapps and sifting the trove of newspaper articles and gossip she'd collected on the Westerman killing—and on everything else in Guthrie. The daughter of a Munich brewmaster, Eskridge had married an American soldier and moved to his native Kentucky. While he worked a small farm, she ran the motel, which she freely conceded was a fleapit. "Holiday Motel—it is a sort of joke," she said. "Who takes a holiday in Guthrie?" But she loved to gossip, and the motel gave her ample chance for that. She herself had become part of local lore, a strange blend of Bavaria and Kentucky who spouted things like "kiss my grits" with a guttural accent. "People here call me the crazy Kraut of Tinytown," she said.

But after thirty years in Guthrie, Eskridge still felt like a stranger, never more so than in the days since Michael Westerman's death. She told me about the crude, scrap-lumber crosses that burned in the night, and about Michael Westerman's funeral procession; rebel flags draped his coffin and flew from the 120-car caravan trailing the hearse to Guthrie's all-white graveyard. Now, well-dressed strangers had begun appearing in town, distributing literature that proclaimed Michael Westerman a Confederate martyr, the first man to die for the rebel flag in 130 years.

Aryan Nation and other white supremacist groups had also turned up in Guthrie. "I know from Aryans," Eskridge said, fingering one of the group's flyers. She reached inside her desk and pulled out a German newspaper clip from the 1950s. It showed a shirtless man with a shaved head, harnessed to a road grader. Eskridge translated the headline: "The Galley Slaves of Our Times." The man in the picture was her father, imprisoned at Dachau during World War II for speaking against the Nazis. "That's what an Aryan nation looks like," she said, studying the photograph.

Eskridge had one other thing to show me. She led me across the motel's forecourt to a fence enclosing picnic tables, beach umbrellas and a rectangle of patchy grass. "That used to be our swimming pool," she said. Guthrie had no public parks or pools, so locals paid two dollars to swim at the motel. Then, two summers ago, several black kids paid their money and jumped in. "It was like we sent an electrical charge through the water," she said. "As soon as the blacks got in, all the whites got out." Whites demanded that Eskridge tell the blacks to leave. Her response: kiss my grits.

When whites kept complaining, Eskridge and her husband filled the pool with pond dirt rather than let it become the scene of racial strife. A dogwood and weeping willow now sprouted in the deep end.

"Enjoy your stay in Guthrie," she said, handing me a room key and retreating inside with her schnauzer.

I STAYED TWO WEEKS at the Holiday Motel, enduring its lumpy beds and stained carpet and threadbare covers, which forced me to deploy my ripped jacket as an extra blanket. Each morning, I breakfasted on a Styrofoam cup of watery coffee and a scratch-off lotto ticket from the convenience store across the road. I visited Robert Penn Warren's childhood home, a Victorian bungalow at the corner of Third and Cherry, now a well-kept but forgotten shrine open only a few hours each week. I went to church on Wednesday night and heard a two-hour sermon titled: "If you were arrested and charged with being a Christian, would there be enough evidence to convict you?" Most other nights, I drank at Billy's, where the same two songs—"If Hell Had a Jukebox" and "I Like My Women a Little on the Trashy Side"—played over and over again as the barmaid wailed along. I decided that if hell had a backwater, it would look a little like Guthrie, Kentucky.

But what Guthrie lacked in atmosphere it made up for in intrigue. The mystery began with the circumstances surrounding Michael Westerman's death. Westerman and his wife, Hannah, had been high school sweethearts, about to enjoy their first night out since the birth of their twins five weeks before. They planned to buy Hannah a denim dress before going to dinner in Nashville, an hour south of Guthrie. En route, at about four o'clock, Michael stopped for gas at a convenience store called Janie's Market, on Guthrie's main street.

Westerman's truck caught the eye of four black teenagers who were parked in a car nearby. The pickup was hard to miss: a big red Chevy 4 × 4 with a jacked-up chassis, a rebel-flag license plate, and a large rebel flag flapping from a pole in the truck's bed. The car's driver, Damien Darden, thought he'd seen the flag-waving truck before, cruising through Guthrie's black neighborhood.

"Let's go whip that dude," he told his friends, speeding off to recruit others for the brawl. Because the Westermans' truck had dark tinted windows, Darden and his friends couldn't see that the pair inside were former neighbors and classmates.

Michael Westerman pumped gas and bought watermelon bubble gum, then sat chatting in the cab with Hannah. The two weren't in any hurry. They'd left the twins with Michael's parents and had the whole evening to themselves. Hannah told police that Michael had teased her and joked about "getting some" later that night.

Damien Darden returned to Janie's Market trailed by two other cars, and pulled alongside the pickup. Several of the black teenagers later testified that a white hand reached out the truck's sliding back window and shook the rebel flag. One of them said he heard someone in the truck shout "Niggers!" Hannah denied that she or Michael had said or done anything.

Michael pulled out of Janie's and drove south into Tennessee. Hannah glanced back and saw the three cars from Janie's trailing

behind. "Kick it!" she said, and Michael floored the accelerator, hurtling down the two-lane highway.

At about the same moment, in the backseat of Darden's car, a
seventeen-year-old named Freddie Morrow told his friends he had a
gun. "No you don't," the others taunted. Freddie reached inside his
belt and brandished a cheap .32 pistol. Damien Darden sped up,
gaining ground on the flag-bearing truck.

A few miles south of Guthrie, near a forlorn railroad siding, Freddie fired wildly out the window. Then the gun jammed. Damien ac-
celerated and pulled into the oncoming lane. He and Michael now
raced side by side, going eighty-five. Michael shoved Hannah to the
floor. Freddie unjammed his gun, stuck his hand out the window and
fired again.

Hannah didn't hear the blast but she saw her husband clutch his
side and moan, "Oh my God, they shot me." As the truck slowed, she
somehow scrambled over Michael into the driver's seat. Damien's car
had stopped in the road just ahead; another car from Janie's pulled up
behind the pickup. Hannah thought the cars were trying to box her
in. So she swerved off the road, did a U-turn, and sped back toward
Kentucky as Freddie fired again.

By the time Hannah reached a hospital emergency room, Michael
was in shock. A bullet had passed through his heart. Surgeons closed
the wound and rushed him by ambulance to Nashville, where he died
the next day. When police searched the Westermans' truck, they
found a single bullet hole in the door, Michael's loaded .380 auto-
matic on the floor, and his black cowboy hat with a big wad of watermelon bubble gum stuck to the brim.

The episode bristled with question marks. Who was Michael Westerman and what did he mean by flying the flag in a largely black
town on Martin Luther King's birthday weekend? Why had this so
provoked Damien and his friends that they chased down and killed a
white man in broad daylight? And why had violent rage over the
rebel flag erupted here of all places, in Warren's "un-Southern"
hometown, in a state that never joined the Confederacy?

On a Sunday morning, I went looking for clues in the Todd
County seat of Elkton. Located at the county's main crossroads, ten

minutes north of Guthrie, Elkton was home to the high school that both the Westermans and their assailants attended. It was also here that Michael had sometimes cruised with his rebel flag, circling the courthouse square and crawling past an adjoining stretch of fast-food joints. In a dry county with no mall or movie theater (or even a stoplight), looping between the Dairy Mart and the Dairy Queen provided what little action was available. Teenagers called this 1950s-style ritual "flipping the dip."

When I arrived, the dip was flipping with rebel-flag-toting trucks. There were also two cars with holes crudely drilled in their rooftops and flagpoles poking out, like mutant hair follicles. One member of this ersatz color guard wore a rebel kepi and carried a loaded .22 pistol in his lap. He told me he'd only begun flying the flag since Michael's death. "One goes down, two fill his space," he said. Then, flag hoisted high, he shouted "These colors don't run!" and sped off toward the Dairy Queen.

Nearby, a dozen people in jungle fatigues and combat boots stood at strategic points around the square, handing out flyers to the after-church traffic. I approached the troop's leader, a bearded man with a walkie-talkie, and asked what was up. "Literature roadblock," he said, handing me several flyers. The first was headlined: "The only Reason You are White! Today is Because Your Ancestors Practiced & Believed in Segregation YESTERDAY!" The second commanded: "I WANT YOU FOR THE ALMIGHTY KU KLUX KLAN!"

The literature was signed "Yours for White Victory, Ron Edwards, Grand Dragon for Christ, Race & Nation." This was the same bearded man who stood before me, barking un-dragonlike orders into his walkie-talkie. "Cross the street only on the crosswalks, and stay on the goddam sidewalks!" he commanded his underlings. Then to me: "I don't want us breaking any laws."

Ron Edwards was a water-blaster by trade and ruler over "the Realm of Kentucky." Two subalterns shared the corner with him: an Exalted Cyclops named Jim, and a Klaliff named Velma. Velma wore furry earmuffs, snug booties and green mittens with her military fatigues. "Jelly doughnut?" she asked, proffering a cardboard box.

Passing cars honked and gave the thumbs up. Several motorists swapped church pamphlets—"What Must I Do To Be Saved?"—for

the Klan's exclamatory literature: "Justice For Our People NOW!"
Then a burly pedestrian in a farm cap stopped to grouse, "I've had
enough of niggers telling us what to do."

Jim and Velma quickly escorted the man to a rusted Buick, which
served as the Klan's recruiting office. I tagged along and climbed
into the backseat with Velma while Jim sat up front, delivering the
Klan's sales pitch. "You move up quickly," Jim said. "Any day now I'm
going to be promoted to Great Giant."

"My son just joined," Velma added, "and he's a Grand Titan
already!"

The burly man seemed impressed. Jim went on: "You can get
started today for just twenty-five dollars and two photos, and if your
wife wants to join, too, the price is the same." He paused. "That's
sort of a special we've got going this month."

While Jim kept pitching God, Race and Nation, Velma showed
me snapshots of her grandchildren. She talked about her crafts shop,
the macramé she'd made for Christmas, and an upcoming cross-
burning she hoped to attend. Before going, Velma had to pass an
exam that would qualify her for full citizenship in the Realm. "It's
like a driver's test where they try and foul you up," she said. "I need
to know the whole book of knowledge. Like if someone asks, 'Why
do we hate Jews?' I didn't know before, but I found out. It was Jews
that put Christ on the cross."

If she passed the exam—and avoided Klan infractions, such as
committing a felony or sleeping with a black man—Velma would
don a satin hood and robe for the cross-burning, which marked her
full "naturalization" into the Klan. I asked why she and the others
weren't wearing their hoods and robes today.

"It's a good look," she said. "But we've had a lot of events lately.
The cleaning bills will kill you."

THE KLAN HANDED OUT 750 flyers and signed up ten new
acolytes before melting back into the Kentucky hills, leaving Elkton
Sunday-quiet. The only place open on the square was a luncheonette
called the Town Grill. A petition lay on the counter: "We the under-
signed believe the rebel mascot should stay at Todd County schools.

We are the South, let us wave our pride." The waitress explained that Todd County Central High School called its sports teams "the Rebels" and took as its logo two flag-waving Confederates. But just before Michael Westerman's shooting, a committee of prominent citizens had quietly recommended that the school drop the rebel motif to ease racial tension.

To the waitress and many other whites, this assault on the rebel mascot by local elites, meeting behind closed doors, mirrored the assault on Westerman and his flag by angry young blacks. "They're fixin' to strip white people—whites that ain't rich—of what little they got," the waitress said.

The petition drive was led by a retired nurse named Frances Chapman. I called her from the grill to ask to come chat. En route, I stopped at Todd Central, a low-slung brick school with bright hallways and new computer labs. It looked like any other public high school, except for a vast mural in the foyer of the notorious mascot: two cartoonish Confederates clutching battle flags and blowing bugles emitting the words "Go, Rebels, Go."

I was surprised that these flabby caricatures had provoked such a storm. They seemed to mock rather than exalt the Confederacy. But Frances Chapman didn't see it that way. "The fat men, oooh, I think they're wonderful!" she exclaimed. "They make me feel so proud."

Chapman was a tiny woman with oversized glasses and an electric-green pants suit. Her words were equally arresting. As soon as I sat down, she showed me a newspaper story quoting her recent comments on a local radio show. "Slavery was not all that bad," she'd declared. "A lot of people were quite happy to be living on large plantations."

Chapman smiled sweetly. "Blacks just need to get over slavery," she said, as though talking of the flu. "You can't live in the past."

I gently observed that she herself might be accused of living in the past by defending the rebel flag. "Oh no, that's about now," she said. "Blacks don't really have anything against the flag. They just don't want us to have it. They want the best jobs, the biggest money. Now they want this. If we lose the mascot, it'll just be a matter of time before we lose everything." Her voice quivered with rage. "Don't put *us* where *they* used to be."

It was the same bitterness I'd heard from Bud Sharpe, the pro-flag demonstrator in Columbia. For both Sharpe and Chapman, the rebel banner represented a finger in the dike, the last brake against a noisome tide of minority rights that was fast eroding the status of whites. "The pity of it is," Chapman went on, "blacks have a great legacy. They had Ray Charles, Duke Ellington, George Washington Carver. They first learned dancing and singing—we learned that from them."

Chapman had learned something else from blacks: the idiom and tactics of civil rights. She and her supporters had launched a school boycott, with scores of white families pulling their kids out of Todd Central and threatening to withhold county taxes unless the rebel mascot was retained. They also planned a sit-in at the next school board meeting. Chapman had printed a special T-shirt for the protest, adorned with the Confederate flag and the words: SHOW RESPECT—You're in Rebel Country.

Seeing me to the door, Chapman raised her small fist above her head. "We shall overcome," she said.

THE NEXT DAY at Elkton's library, I learned a strange thing. Todd County wasn't rebel country, at least not historically. According to the volumes of local history I perused, most Todd Countians supported the Union in the Civil War. Like much of the upper South, the county split along geographic lines. Whites from the county's fertile plantations bordering Tennessee tended to side with the South. But the more numerous yeoman farmers in Todd County's hilly north (where slaves were few) supported the Union. Kentucky also stayed in the Union, though the first Confederate Congress optimistically allotted a star for Kentucky on the Confederacy's flag in hopes the state might secede.

Despite this history, almost all whites I spoke to echoed Frances Chapman, proclaiming their county rebel territory and believing it had always been so. As proof, they pointed to a 351-foot concrete spike soaring at the county's western edge. The obelisk marked the birthsite of Confederate president Jefferson Davis, who was born there in 1808 (only a hundred miles and eight months apart from his future antagonist, Abraham Lincoln).

The obelisk was identical in shape to the Washington Monument and two-thirds as tall. Rebel veterans, who first planned the memorial in the early 1900s, believed the father of the Confederacy deserved a memorial almost as lofty as the one honoring the father of the nation. But the shaft's Ozymandian dimensions belied the slightness of Todd County's claims on Jeff Davis. At the time of his birth, Todd County didn't yet exist (it was carved out of neighboring Christian County a decade later). Nor could anyone say for certain whether the Davis's log homestead had stood on the Todd side of today's county line. Also, Davis's parents were peripatetic folk; they moved to Louisiana when "little Jeff" was two. It seemed doubtful the Confederate leader had any memories of his old Kentucky home.

No matter. Each year on Davis's birthday, Todd Countians crowded around the spike for a bizarre rite: the crowning of a local teenager as "Miss Confederacy." Contestants were judged on their poise, hair, hooped skirt, and answers to questions such as, "What will you do while holding the title to promote and defend Southern heritage?" At the end of the pageant, a young man in Confederate uniform escorted the tiara-clad winner down the monument steps as a local band played "Dixie."

Robert Penn Warren, who watched the monument's construction as a child, later recalled the bemusement he felt as this "immobile thrust of concrete" soared above his native soil. Remembrance of the Confederacy, he wrote, "had never been of burning importance in Guthrie, where to a certain number of contemporary citizens the Civil War seemed to have been fought for the right to lynch without legal interference."

But in the intervening decades, something curious had happened, an act of what psychologists today might term "recovered memory." Locals had reclaimed a past of their own creation, in which Todd County was staunch rebel territory, a pastoral land of Southern belles and brave Confederates. "History, like nature, knows no jumps," Robert Penn Warren once wrote. "Except the jump backward."

◗ ◗ ◗

As FRANCES CHAPMAN had promised, hundreds of people packed the bleachers of a middle-school gym for the next meeting of the Todd County school board. Some wore kepis and rebel-flag bandannas, others the "SHOW RESPECT—You're in Rebel Country" T-shirts Chapman had printed for the meeting.

A few black families sat by the exit, as did all four members of the Sheriff's Department. The school board perched around a table on the gym floor, awkwardly conducting routine business. Finally, as the crowd grew restive, a board member set up a microphone and invited the public to comment.

The first to speak was a military widow. "My husband was a Yankee and I converted him to a rebel and I'm damn proud of it!" she shouted. "I will not compromise my values and equal rights to satisfy a minority. God bless America, God bless our rebel flag!" She threw open her cardigan to reveal the "SHOW RESPECT" T-shirt she wore underneath. The crowd behind her roared.

Next, a lean, bleached-blonde woman strode to the microphone and jabbed her finger at the school board. "Listen to us—we put you there!" Flushed with rage, she said her son at Todd Central was forced to take off a rebel-flag T-shirt the week after Westerman's murder. Metal detectors had also been installed at the school to prevent further violence.

"They even took away my boy's pepper spray!" someone shouted from the bleachers.

"Sure ain't right!" the woman at the microphone yelled.

The crowd began stamping its feet and chanting, "Discrimination! Discrimination!" As the woman returned to her seat, she pumped her fists in the air like a prizefighter leaving the ring.

The meeting went on like this for two hours. As the twentieth or so woman spat venom at the school board, it struck me that recent media attention lavished on "angry white males" neglected the considerable depths of female rage on display here, and everywhere else I'd been in Todd County. Nor did their wrath have much to do with the rebel flag's historic symbolism. The banner seemed instead to have floated free from its moorings in time and place and become a generalized "Fuck You," a middle finger raised with ulceric fury in the face of blacks, school officials, authority in general—anyone or anything that could shoulder some blame for these women's difficult lives. Tonight, at least, these trailer-bound, factory-trapped women could vent their rage and affirm the race consciousness that blacks had exhibited for decades, even flashing their "RESPECT" shirts with Aretha-like pride.

Frances Chapman claimed the last word. Waving her petition, which now bore 3,000 names, a quarter of the county's population, she shouted, "Don't ever count us out!" Then she and the other whites stormed from the gym and into the flurrying snow. They lingered outside, waving flags and shouting, as though vaguely dissatisfied. Neither the school board nor the few blacks at the meeting had responded.

Inside the gym, a half-dozen black women stood waiting for the parking lot to clear. "I work in Todd County," one woman said softly. "I pay my taxes and my children go to school, too. I feel like, why shouldn't we have a say about the school mascot? Kids are killing kids over this. Don't you think it's time we at least start talking about it?"

I asked why she hadn't made this sensible comment during the meeting. She looked at me as though I was crazy. "Who's listening?" she asked.

Another woman had the blank, haunted look of a shell-shocked soldier. Before Michael Westerman's death, she said, white rancor toward blacks was contained. "We were living with it. I felt like they respected us." But now she wondered if she'd been fooling herself her whole life. "That flag opens up a racial door we've been keeping closed for so many years. It's a way of saying what white people have kept bottled up."

She paused as the sound of chanting—"equal rights for whites!"—drifted through the open gym door. The woman shook her head. "They've gone loco on us," she said.

IN THE WEEK FOLLOWING the school meeting, I made the rounds of local officials, ministers and long-time residents, searching for clues about what was happening to Todd County. From both blacks and whites came the same, bewildered refrain. Though Jim Crow hadn't been as rigid in Kentucky as it was farther South, the past three decades had witnessed extraordinary change. Blacks and whites mingled freely at schools, workplaces, restaurants and other public places. Yet for reasons no one fully understood, this intimacy had spawned a subterranean rage, which had boiled over with the shooting of Michael Westerman and the tumult following his death.

"We're a little ol' Southern Mayberry," Guthrie's mayor told me. "Or I thought we were." A portly man of thirty-six, he'd campaigned for mayor of the town of 1,600 with the slogan "I'm a good guy and will work hard for you." I found him fastidiously sweeping Guthrie's diminutive town hall. "When I was a boy, no one cared about that flag," he went on. "Heck, I never even thought of myself as Southern. But today there's this intolerance, white and black. People feel they have to wave their beliefs in each other's faces."

A few blocks away, a middle-aged black storekeeper echoed the mayor's words. "Kids today, they're weaker and wiser," she said, sifting turnip greens and smoking Kools. "A lot of things we didn't pay attention to, they do. If we were called nigger, we shook it off. Just went about our business. Not now. It's strange, my kids have white friends, which I never did. But they got white enemies, too."

Michael Westerman's brief life seemed to typify this paradox. He grew up on the same street of modest brick ranch homes as two of the black youths who would later be charged with his murder. They went to the same schools and shot hoops in the Westermans' driveway. Michael's father, a tenant farmer, served on the volunteer fire department with relatives of the black teenagers. Michael's mother ran a sewing machine at Guthrie Garment, a plant whose workforce was evenly divided between black and white. At Todd Central, interracial dating had become common. A few months before Michael's death, a black student was voted Homecoming Queen over several white competitors.

But amid this apparent racial amity, a low-grade guerrilla war brewed between some blacks and whites. Earlier generations of blacks in Todd County had quietly endured exaltation of Jeff Davis,

the rebel flag, and the defunct nation for which it stood. Black athletes at Todd Central dribbled basketballs across a gym floor painted
with the school's rebel mascot; they wore class rings decorated with
rebel emblems; they bought the "Rebel" yearbook, which for many
years included a photo of two students annually anointed "The General and His Southern Lady" and pictured in hoop skirt and Confederate uniform.

   "Back then, parents told you to sit your butt down, work hard and
keep your mouth shut around white people," said Kim Gardner, a
Todd Central student in the late 1970s. I was visiting Gardner at her
trailer outside Elkton. Her daughter Shanekia, a junior at Todd Central, sat beside her mother in tight jeans and Timberland boots, beneath a poster of Malcolm X. As I spoke with Kim, Shanekia shook
her head. "We aren't going to just take it like our parents did," she
said. "I keep telling Momma times has changed."

Times had changed across the South, and in some ways Todd
County was just catching up. Though black hostility to Confederate
totems lay relatively dormant for two decades after the civil rights
struggles of the early 1960s, it resurfaced in the mid-1980s and
had escalated ever since. In 1987, the NAACP launched a campaign
to lower Confederate flags from Southern capitols and eventually
helped bring Alabama's down. Black cheerleaders refused to carry
the rebel flag at college ball games. Schools started banning "Old
South" weekends and the playing of "Dixie." In some cities, blacks
called for the removal of Confederate monuments and rebel street
names. And in 1993, black senator Carol Moseley-Braun successfully
challenged renewal of the patent for the United Daughters of the
Confederacy insignia, which incorporated the Confederacy's political banner.

   But this growing militancy provoked a backlash among Southern whites, many of whom already felt aggrieved over the Martin
Luther King Jr. holiday, affirmative action, and other race-tinged
issues. Self-styled "Southern heritage" or "Southern nationalist"
groups spread like kudzu across the region, preaching the gospel of
states' rights, regional pride and reverence for the Confederacy.

These groups also cleverly tapped into the culture of self-esteem and identity politics common across the land. When Spike Lee's movie on Malcolm X launched a wave of "X" clothing, a counter-symbol quickly sprouted on T-shirts and bumper stickers across the white South. It showed the diagonal cross of the rebel flag beside the words "You Wear Your X, I'll Wear Mine."

By the time Marcus Flippin became a teacher and sports coach at Todd Central in 1992, students were brandishing their separate Xs like duelling pistols. A white kid would show up in a rebel-flag bandanna, a black kid in an X cap. A fight would break out, and the next day still more students would show up wearing Xs and start the cycle over again.

Flippin, one of only three black teachers at the school, became a sounding board for black students. "They'd see on the news about the flag coming down in Alabama, or 'Dixie' being banned," he said, "and they'd come to me and ask, 'How come whites still get away with that stuff here?'"

Flippin also realized that coaches of visiting sports teams were using Todd Central's rebel logo to whip up their own black players, saying, "You know that flag represents slavery and the Klan. We have to go over and show those racists." Flippin convinced school officials to repaint the gym floor with an innocuous outline of Todd County. This only enraged white students still more. Graffiti started appearing in school bathrooms: "KKK," "Go Back to Africa," "How to have a good time—kill Niggers!" One afternoon, as black students waited for a bus in front of the school, a white student drove by in his truck; hitched to the bumper was a chain with a black Barbie doll dragging from the end. Both black and white students started packing knives and guns in their cars and pickups.

Flippin tried to calm both blacks and whites, but felt he simply couldn't break through. "I don't know if it's the movies, the music, the music videos," he said, "but there's no respect for adults, or for human life. You just had the feeling all the time that something bad was about to happen."

Marcus Flippin's first year at Todd Central was the last for Michael Westerman, who graduated in 1993. A tall, slim teenager with long dark hair and an engaging smile, Michael was named the Future Homemakers of America "sweetheart" his senior year. A mediocre student, he struggled through with the help of his long-time girlfriend, Hannah Laster. They married soon after graduation and went to work at a sawmill owned by Hannah's father. Michael cut timber, Hannah drove the forklift.

The sawmill lay on a gravel road in the hilly northern half of Todd County. Hannah's parents, Billy and Nancy Laster, lived in a home they'd built themselves beside the mill. "None of this would'a happened if everyone had just stuck to their own," Billy said. He was built like the oak trees that churned through his mill, and prescribed hard work as the remedy for all ills.

His wife hewed to a biblical injunction against cutting hair; hers was pinned in a gray helmet that rose a full six inches above her head. "Michael picked and plucked at people and laughed about everything," she said. He raced his four-wheeler, played pranks, made animal noises, licked his sister's face, told jokes about fat people. When he wasn't cutting logs, Michael wore what amounted to a personal uniform: black Levis, black cowboy hat, cowboy boots and a huge silver-plated belt buckle.

"He loved Jeff Foxworthy jokes more than anything," said Hannah's sister, Sarah. She quoted a few of Michael's favorites. "You might be a redneck if your family tree doesn't fork." Or: "You might be a redneck if you refer to fifth grade as 'my senior year.'" Just before he died, Michael bought a decal for his truck windshield that said "Redneck Ride."

The family said Michael first met Hannah on a bus to night vocational classes, where he'd studied welding and she nursing. Michael later used his welding skills to attach a flag pole to the diamondback toolbox in the bed of his pickup. Then, a few months before he died, he got a tattoo on his arm of the cartoon character Tasmanian Devil clutching a Confederate battle flag.

"It was a school symbol, that's all," Billy Laster said. "I don't think he knowed the history of it."

Sarah thought there was more to it than that. "The flag was a symbol of him," she said. "He was a rebel, a daredevil, outspoken. He'd do anything."

Michael's aunt, Brenda Arms, gave Michael's devotion to the flag a very different spin. A retired nurse and the self-appointed historian of the Westerman family, Brenda had given Michael his first rebel flag as a child. "Michael was raised with that flag, just like my own son," she said. "It's just part of our life."

We sat in her kitchen drinking coffee from mugs decorated with the rebel flag. Brenda said Michael displayed the banner on his bedroom wall as a boy, then moved it from his bicycle to a three-wheeler he raced through the fields, then to his car, and finally to his truck. "It was his first flag," she said, weeping softly. "He treasured it just the way I do the doll I've been carrying around since I was a little girl."

Since her nephew's death, Brenda had become the point-person for a parade of Southern groups seeking to contact the Westermans. First came members of a nearby chapter of the Sons of Confederate Veterans. They volunteered to set up a bank fund for Michael's widow and children, and deposited several thousand dollars to kick off the effort. They also helped Michael's parents catch up on bills. Soon, solicitations for the "Westerman Twins Fund" began appearing in the Sons' national magazine. "His death causes us to reflect upon the continued sacrifices made in the name of heritage and honor," read a message accompanying the ad.

Southern heritage groups now planned a major memorial in Todd County for Confederate Flag Day in early March. Organizers had asked Brenda to read a short biography of her nephew. She handed me a flyer for the Flag Day event. It was headed: "In Honor of a Fallen Confederate Patriot."

After two weeks in Guthrie, I took the motelkeeper Maria Eskridge's advice and decamped to the Holiday Inn in nearby Clarksville, Tennessee, where I could relax at night watching a basketball game on the bar's cable TV. One evening, the bartender asked what brought me to the area. When I told him, he said, "Oh yeah, Westerman. He used to wash dishes here. Tight jeans. Shitkickers. The hundred-pound belt buckle. Your basic total redneck."

He called over two waitresses, who offered an even less flattering picture of the Fallen Confederate Patriot. "How would I describe Mike? Goofy and obnoxious, kind of ignorant," said a twenty-two-year-old named Lydia. "He'd do a few dishes, then sit reading comic books and annoying anybody who walked by. He took things to extremes."

One night Michael had argued with a waitress, then picked her up and carried her around the kitchen. The waitress screamed "Put me down!" and struggled to get free, but Michael wouldn't let her go. When a black cook intervened, Michael shouted "nigger" and other slurs. "Mike had a racial hang-up," Lydia said. "He thought the races shouldn't mix." Soon after the incident—the third for which he'd been reprimanded—Michael was fired.

The waitress Westerman harassed that night had since taken another job. She wasn't surprised by the news that Westerman had been killed while flying his rebel flag. "I hate to walk on a dead man's grave, but the best word to describe him is bully," she said. "Everyone around him needed to know he was bigger than them." She paused. "I'm prejudiced too, I guess. But I know when to keep my mouth shut. He was the kind who never did."

A few weeks later, I finally saw Michael's truck, which Hannah drove in one of the half-dozen memorials held in her husband's honor in the weeks following his death. This particular wake was organized by motorcycle clubs in Kentucky and called, with conscious irony, "Freedom Ride '95."

Arriving at the procession's gathering point beside a Cracker Barrel restaurant, I found a sea of Harleys, bomber jackets, and T-shirts as loud as the bikes: "Drunk and Ready to Fuck," "Shit Happens," "Helmet Laws Suck." Someone shouted "Pulling out!" and the iron horses charged down through the hills of southern Kentucky, rebel flags flapping in the wind. As I trailed the mile-long cavalcade, it struck me that I might be witnessing the largest assemblage of rebel flags since Appomattox.

The bikers growled down Guthrie's main street to a vacant lot beside a grain elevator. Several bikers erected a makeshift stage and auctioned leather jackets and other items, with the proceeds donated to the Westerman family. Parked beside the stage was Westerman's truck, with the rebel flag flying from a pole in back. Well-wishers filed solemnly by, poking their pinkies in the small bullet hole in the door and peering at Michael's cowboy hat, perched on the dashboard with the watermelon bubble-gum still stuck to the brim.

Hannah, a tall, hefty woman with permed strawberry-blond hair, stood impassively beside the cab. I asked her why she thought Michael had displayed the flag. Was it Southern pride?

"He wasn't into all the Confederate history and that," she said, echoing her father. "He didn't, like, dig into it."

"School spirit?"

She smiled. "Michael was glad just to graduate from the place." She said a few of Michael's friends had started flying the flag from their pickups about the time he bought his truck. He decided to do the same.

"Why?"

Hannah shrugged. "He'd do anything to make his truck look sharp. The truck's red. The flag's red. They match."

By the time of the Confederate Flag Day rally, six weeks after the shooting, Michael Westerman's biography had undergone a rewrite. Now, according to official lore, Michael and Hannah first met during a school outing to Fort Donelson, a Confederate redoubt where one of Michael's forebears served. The Sons of Confederate

Veterans also claimed that Michael was an avid student of his family's rebel genealogy and had planned to join their group. A Kentucky camp inducted him posthumously and helped refurbish his grave. Chiseled on the new granite headstone was Michael's pickup and flag. Planted beside it was an iron cross identical to those marking the graves of actual rebel veterans, with C.S.A. on one side and 1861–1865 on the other, beside the Confederate motto, *Deo Vindice.* With God As Our Defender.

Michael's new Confederate profile appeared to comfort his relatives, giving a larger meaning to what had seemed a senseless death, and drawing the family into a world beyond the provincial confines of Todd County. Michael's parents, who had previously kept their grieving private, now began granting newspaper and TV interviews defending their son's display of the flag. An SCV member connected to the Nashville music scene arranged tickets and backstage passes for the family to see Lynyrd Skynyrd, Confederate Railroad and other shows. Contributions to the Westerman Twins Fund poured in from sympathizers across the South, as did letters and poems. The Klan also sent its condolences, even offering the family help in writing thank-you notes.

But no one wanted the Klan to distract attention from the Flag Day memorial. The KKK more or less obliged, staging another "literature roadblock"—in robes and hoods this time—but donning street clothes before joining others at the cemetery. Aryan Nation also politely called Michael's aunt Brenda ahead of time and agreed to leave its literature at home. The few skinheads who showed up kept a respectful distance from a 200-car convoy that wound down Guthrie's main street, across the railroad tracks and past a corrugated-cardboard plant that adjoined the cemetery.

At the grave site, Confederate reenactors unfurled a rebel flag embroidered with the words "Michael Westerman Martyr" and fired their muskets in salute. Women dressed as Confederate mourners wept. The service concluded with the playing of "Dixie" and a eulogy by an SCV "commander" from Mississippi. Michael Westerman, he declared, had joined "the Confederate dead under the same honorable circumstances" as rebels who fell in battle. "He was simply one more casualty in a long line of Confederate dead of over one hundred thirty years of continuous hostility towards us and our people."

The convoy wound across Todd County to the Jefferson Davis memorial, where members of the Westerman family briefly shared details about Michael's life. Brenda Arms said, "Michael's personal reason for flying the Confederate flag was to show the pride he felt in his ancestors who fought and died for the flag, as well as to show his Southern heritage." His father, David, a ruggedly handsome man, said Michael died because of his "beliefs and his constitutional rights."

Then a succession of speakers from across the South turned the memorial into an overtly political rally. An official with the Atlanta-based Heritage Preservation Association ripped into "the goose-stepping stormtroopers of the political correctness movement," announcing that "the NAACP, Queer Nation and others have been fomenting hatred against the honorable culture of the South." Jared Taylor, editor of a right-wing newsletter, cited statistics about black-on-white crime. "Any given black person," he shouted, "is about seventeen times more likely to kill a white person than the other way around." He listed brutal black-on-white murders, rhetorically asking the crowd each time, "Are we to remain silent?"

"No!" the crowd replied, with a few shouting, "It's time for revenge!"

Michael Hill, an Alabama history professor, cast Michael's death against a much broader canvas. Head of the newly formed Southern League, Hill called for secession from "a corrupt Yankee nation" and proclaimed: "The South represents the only remaining stumbling block to the imposition of an American police state." This state, he added, would plunge America into a "New World Order" marked by a "Godless" and "mongrelized" multiculturalism.

Hill also linked Michael's murder to FBI action against David Koresh's band of Branch Davidians in Waco, Texas, and white separatist Randy Weaver at Ruby Ridge, Idaho. The message of all these incidents: "It is open season on anyone who has the audacity to question the dictates of an all-powerful federal government or the illicit rights bestowed on a compliant and deadly underclass that now fulfills a role similar to that of Hitler's brown-shirted street thugs in the 1930s."

Jefferson Davis, for one, might have been startled by these remarks. A plaque on the monument, a few feet behind the speakers, quoted from Davis's last public speech, to a group of young Southerners shortly before his death: "The past is dead; let it bury its dead, its hopes and its aspirations; before you lies the future. Let me beseech you to lay aside all rancor, all bitter sectional feeling, and to take your places in the ranks of those who will bring about a consummation devoutly to be wished—a reunited country."

But the Flag Day speeches weren't really about the South, and Michael Westerman had metamorphosed once again, from a fallen Confederate patriot to a front-line soldier in a contemporary war, one that pitted decent God-fearing folk against what Michael Hill called "an out-of-control government and its lawless underclass."

This apocalyptic spin on a small-town tragedy appeared to confuse and alarm many Todd Countians, including Michael's aunt Brenda. When I visited her a few days after the rally, she opened a trunk stuffed with literature that had begun turning up in her mail. "Some of this stuff is a little wild," she said, handing me neo-Nazi newspapers, white supremacist screeds, and paranoid militia-style tracts. "South-Hating Liberals Are to Blame for This!" read the headline of one story on Michael's death. Another, in a newspaper called *Confederate Underground*, described Michael's assailants as "menacing black gangsters" and alleged that the cross-burnings following his death were a ploy by civil rights agitators to attract sympathy. A publication called "WAR: White Aryan Resistance" warned of a coming racial Armageddon.

Brenda closed the trunk and slipped a video of the Flag Day rally into her VCR. Midway through the tape, as the fiery speeches played again, Brenda began weeping. "I feel like my grandchildren will see another civil war," she said. "Between black and white, not North and South. People just can't seem to get along."

WHILE DEMONSTRATIONS CONTINUED in southern Kentucky, the prosecution of Michael Westerman's assailants wound through the Tennessee courts. Though the defendants were minors—one just fifteen—prosecutors won a motion to try them as adults on a stiff list of charges: first-degree murder, civil-rights intimidation (a reference to Michael's right to display the flag) and aggravated attempted kidnapping (stemming from Hannah's allegation that the teenagers tried to box her in with their cars). All except the trigger-man, Freddie Morrow, were released on bail.

By law, juveniles couldn't be housed with adults in Tennessee prisons. But Robertson County, at whose border the shooting occurred, lacked a juvenile facility. So Morrow found himself in solitary confinement at the county jail, an overcrowded pen under court order to improve its wretched facilities. The jail was a squat box the color of slightly-off salmon, with a rooftop exercise yard wrapped in chain link and razor wire. As I walked across the parking lot, inmates began rattling their rooftop cage and shouting.

"Yo, snow! What's your name?"

"Hey sugar, come up and get some sweet stuff."

"You coming to see Freddie?"

"They gonna fry that little dude?"

"Shut the fuck up!" a guard shouted, escorting me inside to a converted cell that served as the prison's library. Then he brought in Freddie Morrow. Wearing orange prison pants and a white T-shirt, he stood a lanky five feet ten and flashed me a chip-toothed grin. His head was shaved but he had a wispy teenager's goatee, which he fingered self-consciously. He looked even younger than his actual age of seventeen.

We sat knee to knee in the cramped cell and made desultory small talk about basketball. I'd heard from Freddie's family that he'd become a passionate reader in prison and I asked him what books he'd most enjoyed. Morrow perked up. He'd just finished *Native Son* and said he identified with Richard Wright's protagonist, Bigger Thomas.

When I asked why, he launched into the long, tangled tale of his own troubled upbringing in Chicago. The story unspooled in a rush of urban images: a struggling single-parent home (his father died in a car crash soon after Freddie's birth), rough schools, drugged-out parties, gang skirmishes, pregnant girlfriends, curfew violations and juvenile court hearings. Eventually, Freddie's mother sent him to live with in-laws in Guthrie, hoping the small-town atmosphere might calm him down.

At first it did. He began dating a girl and attended church with his relatives. The Kentucky quiet agreed with him. "I thought I was in heaven," he said. But things started to unravel soon after he entered Todd Central. Freddie's baggy pants and earring and inner-city slang aroused suspicion and fear among white students and teachers. Black classmates caused problems for Freddie, too.

"Being in gangs, that's the main thing they want, they want to be bad," he said. "They came and asked me about gang colors, stealing cars, crazy stuff."

Before long, Freddie fell into his old ways, playing the part of street-savvy tough that both blacks and whites seemed to expect of him. He showed off the star-shaped tattoo marking him as a member of the Gangster Disciples, a notorious Chicago gang. He talked back to teachers and brawled with classmates. The way Freddie told it, these fights always followed the same pattern. Someone would provoke him, he'd walk away, then a taunt or internal prompt would lead to a fight. He kept repeating an odd, fatalistic phrase: "Go on ahead." As in, "He picked up a bottle and broke it and was talking about putting it in my back, and I was like, 'Go on ahead, just go on ahead.'"

At the start of his second year at Todd Central, Freddie fell in with a rough crowd in Clarksville, a mid-sized city ten minutes from Guthrie. He bought a Czech semiautomatic for $50 at an abandoned baseball diamond in Guthrie, and purchased bullets at Wal-Mart. Then one night he fired off a few rounds in the chill Kentucky air. "It felt good," he said, "like all my worries was through." He stuffed the gun under his mattress and didn't take it out again until the Martin Luther King birthday weekend.

Just before Christmas, Freddie got into a fight after being taunted during a school assembly. Freddie was suspended, then told by school officials that he'd missed so much class time that he'd flunk for the second year running. It was during this suspension that he shot Michael Westerman. Freddie's lawyer had barred us from discussing details of the killing. So I asked Freddie the question that had gnawed at me ever since I'd arrived in Guthrie. He was a new-comer in Todd County and didn't know Michael Westerman. Yet the sight of Michael's flag had apparently sparked so much rage that one teenager now lay in a Guthrie grave and Freddie sat here in solitary confinement, facing the possibility of life imprisonment (as a juve-nile, he could not receive the death penalty). What exactly did the rebel flag mean to him?

Freddie shrugged and looked at me impassively. "I thought it was just the *Dukes of Hazzard* sign," he said. *The Dukes of Hazzard* was a popular TV show that featured a car decorated with a rebel flag. Growing up in Chicago, that's all Freddie had known about the Con-federate banner.

After moving to Guthrie, he gradually began to sense whites' at-tachment to the flag and blacks' hostility toward what they consid-ered a symbol of slavery. "They was telling me about how they had a war for it back in the days and all this," Freddie said. That was all he knew of the Civil War. To him, the banner was simply something whites knew that blacks hated. He suspected whites brandished the flag as a sort of schoolyard taunt, "just doing it out of spite, to see what we would do."

Now they knew. Freddie's words fit the picture of events I'd begun to form during my weeks in Todd County. What happened on that lonely road outside Guthrie wasn't the portentous clash that outsiders—from the Southern League to the NAACP to journalists like me—imagined it to be. It seemed instead a tragic collision of insecure teenaged egos: one prone to taunts and loutishness, the other to violence and showing off. In a way, Michael Westerman and Freddie Morrow had a lot in common.

Freddie had grown morose during our three-hour chat. He talked of his frequent nightmares about the shooting, and began to cry. "No matter what I do—ever since I turned myself in I've been saying 'sorry,' but that just ain't gonna do." One night, he'd torn up a bed sheet and decided to hang himself. But a prison guard and former preacher pulled him back from the brink. The guard had since per-suaded Freddie to study the Bible and think about the future. Freddie said he now planned to take up drawing again, a hobby he'd enjoyed as a child. He also fantasized about his release from jail, which he spoke of as though it was imminent.

"My main plan for when I get out is to be back in touch with my family, go to church every Sunday," he said. He wanted to stay in Guthrie—nothing fancy, just settle down with his girl and get a job at an appliance factory where several of his relatives worked. "I was thinking when I turn eighteen I can get on at State Stove with my cousin Jeff," he said.

INSTEAD, FREDDIE CELEBRATED his eighteenth birthday by moving out of solitary and becoming "rock man," prison slang for toilet cleaner. His mother could no longer pay the private lawyer she'd hired, so a public defender took over the case. Meanwhile, back in Todd County, the atmosphere had calmed since the Flag Day rally. The county's school board quietly shelved plans to change Todd Central's rebel mascot, allowing Frances Chapman and her followers to declare victory and abandon their school boycott. Guthrie hired its first black cop. And when town officials learned that a new tattoo parlor in Guthrie acted as a front for the Klan, they quickly used building-code violations to shut the place down.

I went one peaceful afternoon to see the crowning of a new Miss Confederacy at the Jeff Davis monument. A succession of young belles sashayed past the crowd: twirling parasols, flicking fans, and smiling as best they could in their oxygen-depriving corsets. The winner, a tenth-grader named Rebecca, cinched the contest with her crowd-pleasing answer to the question, "What was the proper role of a Southern lady as a wife and mother?"

"As a wife, she supported and respected her husband and believed in the Cause," Rebecca said. "As a mother, she looked after her children and spent a lot of time with them."

Heritage groups kept a low profile at the Miss Confederacy contest, sensing perhaps that locals were weary of rallies and anxious to restore some normality to their lives. But outside the county, the mythical status of Kentucky's teenaged martyr continued to grow, culminating in Michael's induction into the pantheon of Confederate

heroes at Franklin, Tennessee, one of the foremost shrines to Southern sacrifice. It was at Franklin one afternoon in the autumn of 1864
that the South suffered over 6,000 casualties in a frontal assault even
braver and bloodier than Pickett's Charge.

A Sons of Confederate Veterans' museum at Franklin now featured
a Westerman exhibit, including the rebel banner that had draped
Michael's coffin, a photograph of the teenager, and a retelling of his
death that carried overtones of a nineteenth-century regimental history: The "Confederate Martyr" had "succumbed to his wound" after
being "accosted by a carload of black youths who made racist remarks concerning the flag."

The exhibit occupied pride of place in the museum's foyer, right
beside a portrait of Pat Cleburne, the most renowned of six Southern generals killed at Franklin. Cleburne had two horses shot from
under him before leading his men forward on foot, waving his cap
and shouting, "If we are to die, let us die like men!" He was found the
next day, shot through the heart and stripped of his boots, saber and
watch. Cleburne's death site lay only a hundred yards from the museum, beneath the parking lot of a Pizza Hut.

THE TRIAL OF Michael Westerman's assailants was held in
Springfield, Tennessee, forty-five minutes south of Guthrie, in a
brick Victorian courthouse with glass globes dispensing gum for a
penny and clouds of cigarette smoke hanging in the air. The Westerman family sat behind the prosecution bench, wearing pictures of
Michael pinned to their breasts. Friends and neighbors clustered behind, as did several SCV members and a publisher of Southern books
who spent each break peddling copies of "Facts the Historians Leave
Out," a Confederate apologia from the 1920s. Two local Klansmen
also sat in, sans robes and literature.

Across the gallery gathered a smaller group of blacks, mostly
the defendants' families. Conspicuous among them was Freddie's
mother, Cynthia Batie, who had come from Chicago by Greyhound.
Afflicted with a crippling nerve ailment, she rode into the courtroom
in a motorized cart.

There was no jury. The pool of potential jurors had proved overwhelmingly white and pro-prosecution, so the defense lawyers chose to try the case in front of a judge instead. In opening arguments, the defense likened the car chase and shooting to a schoolyard brawl that spilled tragically out of control. Freddie had fired wildly, intending only to scare the truck's passengers. In the defense view, this amounted to manslaughter rather than felony murder, which carried a mandatory life sentence.

The lawyers also attempted what Freddie's attorney called "the cockroach defense." If you lack strong evidence that might exonerate your client, he told me, "you shit all over what the other side's got." As a result, much of the trial focused on holes in the police investigation. No ballistics tests were ever performed on Michael's gun to see if it had been fired. Police failed to do gunshot-residue tests on the black teenagers' car and didn't inspect the damage to Michael's truck until 116 days after the crime (better tests might have shed light on whether Freddie fired wildly or intended to hit the truck).

Questions also arose about Michael's medical care. Emergency-room doctors had accidentally severed one of his phrenic nerves, which control the diaphragm. And in a bizarre twist, the coroner who signed Michael's autopsy report was unavailable for questioning. He'd fled Tennessee amid allegations of incompetence and necrophilia; colleagues said he fondled corpses' breasts and conducted anogenital exams that were "inappropriate and degrading to the deceased."

These and other questions, as well as the recently concluded O.J. Simpson trial, raised hopes among the defendants' families that the prosecution case would collapse due to flawed or tainted evidence. But the defense team—a public defender, two court-appointed lawyers, and a black attorney working on the case pro bono—didn't have the sort of resources available to the O.J. "Dream Team." And the defendants had made incriminating statements to police, before any of them had lawyers and before they knew that Michael's wound was fatal.

The state also had two potent witnesses in Hannah Westerman and Tony Andrews, a passenger in the black teenagers' car who had agreed to testify against his friends in exchange for two years' probation. Hannah took the stand clutching a picture of Michael and told about the premature birth of her twins (named Michael and Michaela), the couple's first night out, and Michael's fateful stop for gas in Guthrie. She said neither Michael nor she did anything to provoke the black teenagers at Janie's Market. Asked why Michael displayed the flag, Hannah repeated what she'd told me: "It matched his truck and made it look sharp."

Tony Andrews corroborated Hannah's story, calmly fingering Damien Darden as the driver and instigator of the car chase, and Freddie Morrow as the willing triggerman. But he testified that he'd seen someone in Michael's truck reach out and shake the flag at Janie's, just as Damien was having second thoughts about a brawl. Tony said this action, combined with one of the passengers hearing someone shout "Nigger," reignited the teenagers' desire to fight.

When Tony was done, the judge called a break and the families drifted out of the gallery, silent and stunned. Tony had fragged his friends, but he'd also blown a hole in Hannah's story—and Michael's reputation—by suggesting that racist gestures and remarks were made at Janie's. As Freddie's mother steered her motorized cart out of the chamber, she ran into Michael's family standing just on the other side of the door. Hannah, arms crossed, fixed Cynthia Batie with a flinty-eyed scowl.

"What's your problem?" Batie snapped.

"Bitch," Hannah said.

"What did you say?"

"You heard me, bitch."

Hannah's family pulled her away as Batie yelled, "The truth is going to come out! Then we'll see who the bitch is!" The two camps huddled at opposite ends of the hall, chain-smoking and venting their rage. Batie groused that Hannah and her family were bigoted rednecks. To Michael's mother, Freddie's crippled mother was a "motormouth with a motor," an uppity city black just like her son. Watching the scene, it was hard not to see a depressing adult mirror of the anger and racial stereotyping that had afflicted their sons.

On the trial's third day, Freddie took the stand. He showed none of the emotion or remorse he'd displayed during our prison chat. Instead he seemed numb with anxiety and dully mumbled "Yessir" or

"I don't know" as the prosecution asked one incriminating question after another. In the gallery, the county's chief deputy leaned over and whispered to the man beside him, "He started in a ditch about six inches deep with a shovel. Now he's in with a backhoe digging himself as deep a grave as he can."

Ironically, it was left to the prosecution to point out the provocative role played by the rebel flag. The defense feared that dwelling on the flag, or on racial strife in Todd County, might bolster the state's claim that the crime was premeditated, and also incriminate the defendants on the charge of violating Michael's civil rights.

But in closing arguments, a defense attorney quoted Hannah's testimony about the flag making the truck look sharp, rather than expressing any political belief. In his view, this undermined the charge of civil rights intimidation. "Aesthetics are not protected by the Constitution," he dryly observed.

This prompted an emotional reply from one of the prosecutors, an owlish man who rushed to the podium carrying several tomes. The key issue, he said, wasn't the intent of the person displaying the flag, but "stereotypical assumptions" made by those who saw it.

"If a person feels it is symbolic of keeping African-Americans back, then it's easy to believe that the people displaying it are bigots." Whites in the audience began to shift uncomfortably. "They'd get mad," the prosecutor went on, "they might want to drag them out and beat them up. A stereotypical assumption was made in this case, and that's why it happened."

Then he opened William L. Shirer's *The Rise and Fall of the Third Reich* and quoted Nazi laws proscribing Jews, which he said offered further illustration of how "stereotypical assumptions" led to violence. He opened another book, Carl Sandburg's biography of Abraham Lincoln. "I'll probably offend some people," he said. Then he read part of the Gettysburg Address, lingering on the phrase, "All men are created equal."

The prosecutor cited Lincoln to buttress his central point: whites had the same right to fly the rebel flag as blacks had to wear X caps. Still, it was strange to hear the Confederate Antichrist invoked in a Tennessee courtroom filled with family and friends of a man killed because of his rebel flag.

As the judge deliberated, the families stood at opposite ends of the courthouse, holding hands and praying. When the judge returned after a ninety-minute recess, the chamber filled with undercover police. There had been anonymous death threats against the judge, and police also feared a post-verdict brawl between the families.

Fingering a Styrofoam coffee cup, the judge spent several minutes staring at a legal pad. Then he read the charges against Freddie, finding him guilty of felony murder, attempted aggravated kidnapping, and civil-rights intimidation. "The court imposes sentence of imprisonment for life," he said. Damien Darden received the same. The third defendant, a fifteen-year-old who had apparently just been along for the ride, was found not guilty on all counts.

Freddie's head slumped on his chest. Damien stared blankly ahead. Behind them, relatives burst into tears, as did the women in the Westerman family. Except for Hannah. Striding out of the courtroom, she paused before a TV camera and declared, "They got what they deserved—well, they deserved to die." But she seemed satisfied by her day in court. "It's about time," she said, "someone who's white got to stand up and say, 'Our civil rights were violated.'"

A FEW HOURS LATER, at Billy's Bar in Guthrie, I watched Hannah again on the six o'clock news. The barmaid raised a beer bottle in salute and everyone at the bar cheered—before turning on the jukebox again. Down the street, at Janie's Market, trucks pulled into the gas pumps with rebel flags flying from their beds. Banners also appeared in windows along the main street. But after a few days, this white triumphalism stopped. Most locals recognized the severity of the verdict: justice had been served, tribal blood money paid.

At the cemetery, I found two teenaged girls smoking beside Michael's grave. They said Todd Central High School was calm now, but a chilly distance separated blacks and whites. "No one wants to talk—we go our separate ways," one girl said. She flicked ash on the ground. "It's probably for the best."

The black teenagers I spoke to felt much the same. A growing number had decided to escape Todd County by joining the army at the earliest chance. Many of their parents now felt awkward and un-wanted around local merchants and shopped in nearby Clarksville instead. Some blacks avoided going out after dark.

On the Sunday after the trial, I went to a service at Guthrie's black Baptist church attended by members of the defendants' fami-lies. Several relatives got up to thank the community for their sup-port. "God will deliver his verdict, but in his own good time," Freddie's aunt said. "We look at the little pictures, He takes the big view." Another woman wailed, "I don't want to go to hell, Lord. It's hell here." Then the pastor set the trial in the broad context of black suffering. "We have been o-pressed and de-pressed for over two hun-dred years," he said. "Ain't nothing change but the years."

After the service, Freddie's mother invited me to her in-laws' house, a small bungalow across from the church. Showing me a pic-ture of Freddie at age two, hugging a Teddy bear, she pondered how her youngest child could have ended up in prison for murder. Per-haps, she said, it was her fault, for losing her job when Freddie was a young teenager; after that, she'd had to move to a rough area of Chicago she described as New Jack City. It was there that her son first got into trouble.

Or maybe adolescent hormones were to blame. "Boys got this thing, showing your manhood, that you're bad," she said. "It's a man thing." But she was also angry that racism and the rebel flag hadn't really been aired at the trial. "The flag and 'nigger'-calling—you can deny that it hurts you, but it builds up," she said. "You keeping putting it on people, it's going to blow up."

She reached in her purse for a card from prison. The front showed a calm winter landscape with farms and horses. Inside, Freddie had scribbled a poem.

> *I'm hitchhiking to heaven. I'll get there someday.*
> *Others have made it now. I'm on my way.*
> *I'm here on life's highway. My thumb up high!*
> *I can see the sinners laugh as they go by.*
> *And there comes an Angel. Riding on a cloud.*
> *That's my ride to Glory. I'm Homeward Bound.*

The card was signed, "Peace and much love Mama. I love you." Freddie also asked her to pass on a message to his siblings and their kids. "Much love from little bro and uncle on lock down."

Cynthia Batie began weeping and put the card back in her purse. "My baby," she cried.

Ten minutes up the road, at the Westermans' house in flat farmland north of Guthrie, fourteen rebel flags were on display. One flew at half-mast, the others draped across porch furniture. Inside, Hannah sat with her in-laws watching *Oprah* as her twin children frolicked on the floor. One toddler wore a rebel-flag shirt: "American by Birth, Rebel by the Grace of God." The den was also cluttered with Confederate paraphernalia, most of it gifts from well-wishers across the South.

Michael's mother, JoAnn, joined us. A wiry woman of forty, she said she now took tranquilizers and had entered counseling with her husband to deal with their son's death. Returning to work at the garment factory had also been tough. "Blacks I consider myself close to, deep down inside there's something in between us now," she said. "We leave that void there and don't discuss it."

Michael's father, David, offered to show me a home video. Images of Michael rolled across the TV screen: as a baby, as a seventh-grader on the football team, at home making a science-fair telegraph with his father, at the senior prom with Hannah, and finally, cradling his newborn twins. David Westerman began to cry. A modest, soft-spoken man, he was, like Freddie's mother, still trying to make sense of what had happened to his son.

"Look at this," he said, opening an album of family history he'd been given by his sister, Brenda Arms. David ran his finger along a list of rebel ancestors: one captured, another shot dead at Gettysburg, and a private "killed in action, 24th May, 1862." His age was listed as nineteen.

"Just like Michael," David said. He wiped his eyes. "They say that war ended a long time ago. But around here it's like it's still going on."

6

Virginia

A FARB OF THE HEART

Who knows but again the old flags, ragged and torn, snapping in the wind,
may face each other and flutter, pursuing and pursued, while the cries of
victory fill a summer day? And after the battle, then the slain and wounded
will arise, and all will meet together under the two flags, all sound and well,
and there will be talking and laughter and cheers, and all will say:
Did it not seem real? Was it not as in the old days?
—BERRY BENSON, Confederate veteran

I returned home to Virginia badly in need of a furlough. My Southern journey had taken a long and dispiriting detour in Todd County. Apart from brief visits to Fort Sumter and a few other sites, I'd hardly set foot on the historic landscape of the Civil War I'd originally planned to explore.

Salvation arrived soon after my return in a telephone call from Robert Lee Hodge, the hardcore reenactor I'd met bloating on the road months before. He said the first major event of the campaign season was coming up: the Battle of the Wilderness. Eight thousand reenactors were expected to attend, plus twice that number of spectators. "It'll be a total Farbfest," Rob predicted.

Hardcores were ambivalent about battle reenactments. After all, it was hard to be truly "authentic" when the most authentic moment of any battle couldn't be reproduced, though Rob did the best he could with his bloating. Hardcores also felt that crowds of spectators interfered with an authentic experience of combat. But Rob and several other Guardsmen planned to go anyway, to scout fresh talent and see what changes the long winter layoff had brought to the hobby.

I was curious to go, too. Since spooning with the Southern Guard, I'd been doing some research. Before, I'd assumed that reenacting was a marginal part of Civil War memory, a weekend hobby for gun-toting good ol' boys—with the emphasis on boys. My reading suggested something altogether different. Reenacting had become the most popular vehicle of Civil War remembrance. There were now over 40,000 reenactors nationwide; one survey named reenacting the fastest-growing hobby in America.

Also, while battles remained the core event, reenacting now encompassed all the nonmilitary aspects of the Civil War, mirroring a similar trend in scholarship on the conflict. Soldiers were joined by growing ranks of "civilian" reenactors who played the part of nurses, surgeons, laundresses, preachers, journalists—even embalmers. A generation ago, a young person with a keen interest in the War would likely have joined a Civil War "roundtable," one of the hundreds of scholarly clubs nationwide. In the 1990s, the same person was more likely to join a reenacting unit, perhaps with his wife and kids.

Not that women needed men to get involved. On the Internet, I found multiple chat groups for reenactors; on one, the topic of the day was "Top Ten Civil War Studs," a discussion among women about "gents who would most belong on the cover of a romance novel." The designated "Dishes" included P. G. T. Beauregard ("Continental charm in Creole packaging") and Robert E. Lee ("a gerontophile's dream with sugar daddy possibilities"). The "Dud" list featured Braxton Bragg ("less style than a Nehru jacket") and William Tecumseh Sherman ("sinister expression").

Reenacting had also bred a vast cottage industry of tailors, weavers, and other "sutlers," a Civil War term for merchants who provisioned the armies. For advice, reenactors could turn to a dozen publications, ranging from the oxymoronic *Civil War News* to the

Camp Chase Gazette, a monthly crammed with how-to articles titled "Bundling Paper Cartridges for Field Use" and personal ads such as, "DWF ISO S/DWM between 45–55. Must be in good shape and ready for some hard campaigning. No TBGs need apply." Translation: divorced white female in search of single or divorced white male in trim condition—not one of those tubby bearded guys (TBGs), or what Rob would call a "fat flaming farb." There was even a *Consumer Reports*–style quarterly called *The Watchdog*, which rated the historic accuracy and quality of the various products on offer to the Civil War shopper.

Standards hadn't always been so high. When reenacting first became popular during the Civil War centennial in the 1960s, many soldiers wore work shirts from Sears and fired BB guns. But in the three decades since, the hobby had matured and so had the quality of soldiers' "impressions." Even so, reenactors differed on just how far they should go in seeking "authenticity." Hardcores were a small minority within the reenacting community and regarded by many as elitists. Mainstream reenactors also feared that the hardcore faith, taken to its fundamentalist extreme, would turn the hobby into a performance art that no one would want to watch—much less participate in.

"They're pushing the envelope in terms of authenticity," the *Camp Chase Gazette* editor, Bill Holschuh, told me when I phoned for his opinion. "About the only thing left is live ammunition and Civil War diseases. I hope it doesn't come to that."

THE DAY BEFORE THE Wilderness battle, Rob dropped by to lend me some gear: foul-smelling socks that might once have been white but were now splotched amber, a butternut "trans-Mississippi officer's shell jacket," gray "JT Moore" trousers, a "smooth-side 1858 model" canteen, and a "tarred Federal haversack." None of this meant anything to me, but I was given to understand that I'd resemble a walking museum piece. "With this kit," Rob said, "people will think you're hardcore even if you act like a total farb." Rob wasn't sure about the Southern Guard's plans, so we arranged a vague rendezvous at the reenactment, held on a private farm near the historic battle site.

The real battle of the Wilderness, as its name suggested, was a confused struggle fought in jungly Virginia woods in May 1864. Lee slammed into Grant's advancing army, hoping that surprise and the tangled terrain would disorient his much more numerous foe. For two days whole units became lost in the scrub oak and slash pine. The woods caught fire, cremating hundreds of wounded. Grant lost 17,000 men, twice as many as Lee. But the North could bear such losses better than the South, and Grant pressed on, waging the grisly war of attrition leading to Lee's surrender the next spring at Appomattox.

Today's Civil War "battles" were scheduled months in advance and conveniently signposted. I drove across the Rappahannock and the Rapidan and turned at a roadside placard marked Battle of Wilderness. A bit farther on, another sign pointed to the C.S.A. Parking Area. A woman sat behind a bridge table, chatting on a cellular phone. "Are you preregistered?" she asked me. I mumbled something about the Southern Guard. "Well, just fall in," she said, glancing at her watch. "Afternoon battle's about to begin."

Just beyond the parking lot and a long line of Porta-Johns, several thousand Confederates mustered as drums rolled and flags unfurled. I scanned the long lines of gray but couldn't find any of the Southern Guard. A ragtag troop marched past, led by a lean, strikingly handsome figure. He wore wire-rimmed spectacles and a battered slouch hat, brown and curled, like a withered autumn leaf. Long blond locks brushed the shoulders of his butternut jacket. He looked like a cross between Jeb Stuart and Jim Morrison.

I saluted him and said, "Sir, I've lost my unit. May I fall in with yours?"

He peered through his spectacles at my uniform. "Certainly, private," he drawled. "I regret to say that one of our men fell in this morning's fight. You may take his place."

He pointed me to the rear rank, between two middle-aged men. The one to my left, named Bishop, had graying hair and what looked like red finger paint smeared on his cheek. I asked about the soldier whose place I was taking. "His wife wanted him back for their kid's birthday party tonight," Bishop said. "So he took a hit early and drove home."

Bishop had been wounded in the same clash. He pointed to his stained cheek. "Yankee bullet just bounced off me," he said. Then he reached into his pocket and pulled out a tube labeled Fright Stuff: Fake Blood. "Got it at a gag shop," he said. "It's mostly corn syrup, with some dye and chemicals mixed in."

The soldier to my right, a huge man with long stringy hair named O'Neill, said he'd fought as a marine in Vietnam. The experience had evidently left him embittered. When the rebel army halted, confused over where it was headed, O'Neill groused, "Just like the real military—a continual fucking screw-up."

I'd joined Company H of the 32nd Virginia, from the Tidewater area in the state's southeast. The handsome man in command was Captain Tommy Mullen, a carpenter by trade. O'Neill worked at a museum. Bishop was a cop. Many of the others worked in the shipyards around Newport News. "We're a bunch of average Joes, pretty much like the Confederates of old," Bishop said.

"Bullshit," O'Neill interjected. "We're a bunch of fat slobs who couldn't hack it in the real Civil War for an hour."

The 32nd wasn't hacking the unreal war particularly well, either. Our line kept wavering, and every time the captain gave an order someone got it wrong. "Git back up in the ranks!" the captain shouted. "I said right face! Do you know right from left?"

We reached a line of trees. "Watch the poison ivy!" one of the lead men called out. Then, marching through a pasture littered with cowpies, someone yelled, "Watch the landmines!" A few yards farther on, he yelled again, "Watch the cable!" I looked down and saw an electrical cord snaking through the scrub. O'Neill explained that a film crew was recording the battle. "My brother's on the other side, in the Sixty-ninth New York," he said. "He lives in New Jersey. I'm hoping to get filmed capturing him."

We stumbled through brambly woods until Captain Mullen ordered us to halt. Then he gave us a few stage directions for the upcoming fray. "The Yanks get hit big-time, forty-five percent casualties," he said. "But those rebs to the right of us are going to get overrun so we've got to counterattack and chase the Yanks back." He glanced at his watch. "Ten minutes to battle so take a piss and eat something if you need to."

The men pulled out pieces of store-bought beef jerky, minus the plastic, and Marlboros repackaged in old cigar cases. As we ate and smoked and urinated, I asked my fellow soldiers what they thought of hardcore reenactors.

"We try to be authentic," O'Neill said. "But no one wants to eat rancid bacon and lie in the mud all night. This is a hobby, not a religion."

Bishop gestured at his motley garb: work boots he'd bought at a yard sale, a homemade canteen, a haversack he'd crafted from an army surplus bag. "The way I see it, soldiers back then threw together whatever they could lay their hands on, like me. Was it perfection? No way." He also resented the snobbishness of hardcore units. "Back then, the army took all available men. So why turn away someone who wants to fight just because he's fat or doesn't look the part?"

He had a point. I also realized I felt far more at ease here, among fellow bumblers, than I had at the Southern Guard drill surrounded by perfectionists.

Artillery began pounding in the field just beyond the woods. Each time the cannons boomed, the ground shook and pine needles showered down around us. A foul gray smog seeped in among the trees. "Suck it in, boys," Captain Mullen said, resuming his Civil War persona. Troops to the right of us hoisted their guns and flags and rushed from the woods, vanishing into the smoke and noise. There was a keening rebel yell and the crackle of small-arms fire. I started to feel butterflies. Crouching in the woods, peering into the smoke and listening to the percussion of guns and artillery, I sensed a little of what a soldier must have felt, with no clue who was winning the battle he was about to join, or what his part in it would be.

Then I realized I had no role myself. "Prime muskets!" the captain barked. All around me the men of the 32nd bit open paper cartridges and poured black powder down their rifle barrels. Since I'd failed to hook up with Rob, I was the only man without a gun. I asked the captain what part I might play in the upcoming combat.

"If one of our men should fall, pick up his musket and fight on," he said. Then he added, sotto voce: "If no one goes down, run around awhile and then take a hit. We can always use casualties."

Back in line, I shared my orders with Bishop. "Casualties are a problem," he said. "Nobody wants to drive three hours to get here, then go down in the first five minutes and spend the day lying on cowpies." Sometimes, he said, officers began the battle by asking everyone for their birth dates. "Then they'll say, 'all Januarys and Februarys die. March and April, serious injuries.'" Another trick was to hand out different-colored cartridges with a particular hue designated as "death rounds."

"Usually, though, it's an honor system–type situation," Bishop said. "If someone takes a bead on you and fires, go down. Otherwise you wait until you're tired or you've run out of ammo."

O'Neill cut in with a safety tip about dying. "Check your ground before you go down," he said. "I've gotten bruises from falling on my canteen. Also, don't die on your back, unless you want sunburn."

Shoulder to shoulder, we marched out of the woods and into the clouded field. We marched forward, then sideways, completely blinded by the smoke. Somewhere in the fog a fife tootled "Dixie." Then we seemed to be marching away from the noise. There were no other Confederates in sight.

"Halt!" the captain shouted. He took out binoculars and peered through the gloom. Just ahead, we heard the murmur of voices and what sounded like triggers cocking.

"Form battle lines!" Mullen shouted. Ten men knelt, rifles at the ready, with the other ten standing right behind. Then the smoke cleared, revealing a crowd of spectators in lawn chairs, aiming cameras and videos back at us. "There they are!" one of the spectators shouted, and a hundred shutters clicked at once.

"Company, left!" Mullen yelled, wheeling us sharply around, back into the smoke. Suddenly, fifty or so Yankees appeared just in front of us, as startled and disorganized as we were. "Fire at will!" the captain shouted. Flames licked from the muskets and bits of white cartridge paper fluttered all around us. The blanks made a deafening roar. Like street mimes, the Yankees aped our motions precisely. Then both sides frantically loaded and fired again. "Pour it in, boys!" the captain shouted.

I put my fingers in my ears and crouched beside O'Neill. The Yankees were no more than twenty yards in front of us, firing round after round. But I waited in vain for one of our men to go down.

"Damn Yanks can't shoot straight," O'Neill said, lips black with powder. Apparently, the rebels couldn't aim either. Despite the withering fire, only one Federal had gone down. "Yanks never take hits," O'Neill griped. "Fuckin' Kevlar army."

Then, obeying the battle's script, the Yankees suddenly turned and ran. "Look boys, they're turning tail!" Mullen shouted, drawing his saber. "Drive em, boys! Drive 'em!"

"No-account Yankees!"

"Candy asses!"

"Take no prisoners! Kill 'em all!"

We reached a field littered with blue figures. Several of the dead lay propped on their elbows, pointing Instamatics at the oncoming rebs. Fifty yards farther on, we ran into a storm of Yankee fire and repeated our previous drill: battle lines, fire at will, reload, fire again. "Okay boys," the captain said, after we'd poured imaginary lead at each other for fifteen minutes. "Time to take some hits."

Bishop reached into his pocket for the Fright Stuff. Smearing the bright red goop on his temples, he asked me, "Want a squirt?" I shook my head, imagining what Rob Hodge would say if I returned his uniform with fake bloodstains. "Watch for landmines when you go down," Bishop reminded me.

The Yankees unleashed another volley. I clutched my belly, groaned loudly and stumbled to the ground. O'Neill flopped on his side like a sick cow, bellowing, "I'm a goner, oh God, I'm a goner." Then he spotted his brother from New Jersey, lying in the grass nearby. "Hey Steve, they got you, too! Just like the Civil War, brother against brother!"

Bishop sprawled with his eyes wide open, Fright Stuff dribbling down his chin. Another man lay on his stomach, convulsed with laughter. He was wearing foam earplugs, the type they give you on airplanes. I wondered how I'd report the scene to Rob Hodge. Died and gone to farb heaven.

As the battle raged on, I chatted with a young Virginian named Butch McLaren who had fallen beside me. I asked about his wound.

"It was mortal," he said. "A lot of internal bleeding. But I died for an honorable cause."

McLaren rolled on his side and lit a posthumous cigarette. During the week, he said, he worked as a rigger at a Norfolk shipyard. He passed the long days dreaming about these weekends and thinking about his great-great-grandfather, Private R. J. Dew. "He was wounded three times at Chickamauga and once marched four days with no food," McLaren said.

We sprawled flat again as rebel reserves rushed past us and poured another volley into the Union line. "You know," McLaren said, face pressed to the grass, "if I could trade places with my great-great-grandpappy, I'd do it in a second. Life was harder then but in a way it was simpler. He didn't have to pay phone bills, put gas in the car, worry about crime. And he knew what he was living for."

We lay in the grass until a bugle sounded Taps, signaling the end of hostilities. Captain Mullen rose to his knees and gave a final order to his men: "Resurrect!" We stood up and shook hands with enemy corpses as the spectators gave a lusty round of applause.

Combat wasn't scheduled to resume until the next day, so the soldiers and spectators scattered: to the parking lots, to the Porta-Johns, to a huge tent encampment called the sutlers' row, or "the Mall." Here, brought to life, was the strange world of civilian reenacting I'd read about. North and South mingled peaceably along dirt streets lined with shops. The atmosphere was tongue-in-cheek quaint, with stores labeled The Carpetbagger or War Profiteer Serving Both North and South. A commissary sign said, "No Likker Sold to Soljers." Shoppers could have their picture—or rather, ambrotype—taken in period dress by a man with a hooded camera, or buy "period" love poetry penned on handmade stationery.

I watched couples promenade in uniforms and hoop skirts, quaffing Doc McGillicuddy's Sarsaparilla, then wandered over to explore the "civilian camps." At a Confederate tent, I found a "Soldiers Aid Society" where women clad as Southern belles sat knitting socks. They sipped Confederate coffee (parched corn sweetened with dark molasses) and gossiped about their Northern counterparts. "Yankee women, of course, may not be of the highest moral order," one woman drawled.

On the Union side, a tall man in a black frock coat and stovepipe hat held forth before a crowd of wide-eyed children. "As a nation, we are a great deal more similar than we are different," he proclaimed. "Woe be it to any foreign power that incurs the wrath of the United States."

In real life, the orator worked as a nurse practitioner in Virginia. He played a Confederate soldier during combat, but preferred Abe Lincoln for his civilian impression. "I look the part," he said. Problem was, there were two other Lincolns at the Wilderness (and no less than three Robert E. Lees). "But I think I'm the only Lincoln with a Southern accent," he said. Then, resuming character, he slapped me on the shoulder and asked, "Can I count on your vote in November?"

The scene deepened the impression I'd begun to form from my reading. Contrary to its martial stereotype, reenacting seemed a clean-cut family hobby, combining elements of a camping trip, a county fair and a weekend-long costume party. Between battles, the schedule included a square dance, a trivia quiz for kids, a women's tea, a period fashion show, and an outdoor Sunday church service at which two reenactors would be married. "It's an era lost that we're trying to recapture," a woman named Judy Harris told me as she washed clothes in a tub at the Union camp. "Men were men and women were women. It was less complicated." A soldier walked past, tipped his hat at Harris and said "'Evening, m'am." She smiled back, then said to me, "See what I mean? No one's that polite in real life anymore."

In real life, Harris worked as a data processor. "But here, no one asks what you do for a living. You could be a dentist or a ditchdigger. See that general over there? He's probably pumping gas at Exxon during the week."

Women weren't quite as welcome on the battlefield. A female re-enactor dressed as a male soldier had successfully sued the National Park Service following her expulsion from a 1989 battle (she was caught while coming out of the women's bathroom). Ever since, a small number of women had dressed and fought as soldiers, despite

frequent grumbling from male reenactors who regarded this as
farbish.

However, a different sort of cross-dressing—Southerners clad
as Northerners, and vice versa—was common, even encouraged.
The reason became obvious as I toured the Union camp. Though
blue outnumbered gray almost two to one at the real battle of the
Wilderness, the opposite was true here. In fact, a shortage of Yankees was endemic to reenactments, particularly those staged below
the Mason and Dixon line. So it helped to carry two outfits, in case
the other side needed your services. Reenactors called this "galvaniz-
ing," the Civil War term for soldiers who switched sides during the
conflict.

"The rebs have to take turns shooting us because there's always
more of them," a Union reenactor, John Daniel, told me. Though a
schoolteacher from Virginia, Daniel preferred to wear blue. He disliked what he called the "Redneckus Americanus" element on the
Southern side. "There's a biker mentality. Long hair, squirrel gun,
South will rise again." Some unreconstructed Confederates even
tried to rewrite history by turning reenactments of Southern losses
into latter-day rebel victories.

Daniel also preferred Northern style. Historically, the Union
tended toward spit-and-polish ranks of blue, while Southern uniforms were often homespun and differed from state to state. "If you
want to portray a generic Yank, you can pretty much dress off the
rack," he said. "If I were dressing Confederate, I wouldn't know
where to begin. Do I wear gray today, or butternut? Slouch hat or
kepi? Boots or barefoot?"

But it was precisely this stylistic latitude that appealed to many
Confederate reenactors. As I'd learned from Rob Hodge, rebel fashion gave new meaning to the grunge look; it was acceptable—even
commendable—for Confederates to wear patched, threadbare duds
covered in mud, pan grease, coffee grounds and tobacco spittle. Bad
hair days were obligatory ("Try to use the dullest scissors you can
find," a *Camp Chase Gazette* article on haircuts advised, "and comb
your beard with your fingers"). The South's raffish look also made
Confederate garb, on average, a bit cheaper than Union.

Other, subtler differences underlay the preponderance of rebels.

There was, first of all, Americans' instinctive allegiance to underdogs, the same sentiment that had fueled my own preference for
Confederates as a child. "When I play Northern, I feel like the Russians in Afghanistan," one reb from New Jersey explained. "I'm the
invader, the bully." The South also won hands-down when it came to
romance. Conformist ranks of blue couldn't compete with Jeb Stuart,
Ashley Wilkes and the doomed cavaliers of the Confederacy. This
also helped explain why foreign reenactors, bred on *Gone With the
Wind*, almost always donned gray, even though their forebears in
1860s Europe and Canada had typically supported the other side.

But then, ideology rarely intruded on the hobby. If reenactors had
a mission beyond having fun, or raising money for battlefield preservation, it was educational and nonpartisan. "We're not here to debate
slavery or states' rights. We're here to preserve the experience of the
common soldier, North and South," said Ray Gill, a gray-clad Connecticut accountant. "I hate to call it a hobby, because it's so much
more than that. We're here to find the real answers, to read between
the lines in the history books, and then share our experience with
spectators."

Gill and other reenactors were indeed knowledgeable about the
men they portrayed. Touring the camps, I was regaled with minutiae
about the units represented: what they ate, where they served, their
exact casualties at each battle. But this bookish devotion to the War
rarely extended to the passions underlying the conflict. "Why did
they fight? I guess it was like the Persian Gulf, you just signed up
and went because it was the thing to do," Ray Gill speculated. "I
don't think there was that much difference between North and
South."

There was historical precedence for this studied neutrality. Reenacting evolved from the reunions, called "encampments," held by
Civil War veterans themselves. Veterans bivouacked at actual battlegrounds, donned their old uniforms, and occasionally performed
mock versions of the heroic deeds of their youth. In 1913, hundreds
of geriatric rebels rushed as best they could across the field they'd
crossed during Pickett's Charge, toting canes instead of muskets and
greeting their erstwhile foes with handshakes rather than bayonets.
By then, bitterness over the War had mellowed and the two sides

met in an atmosphere of reconciliation, to celebrate their common valor rather than their sectional differences.

Now, reenactors were doing much the same. Those who professed deep ties to North or South typically did so only because it was the side their forebears fought for. "I have eighteen Confederate ancestors—it just doesn't feel right to wear blue," one Virginian said. "My grandmother always talked about the 'War of Northern Aggression' and she had a Currier and Ives print of Lee hanging in the front parlor. When she heard I'd played a Union soldier at Gettysburg, she shook her head and said, 'Your grandfather would have been disappointed in you.'"

Others gave their Southern leanings a 1990s spin. In the rebel camp I heard a Long Island twang and traced it to a railroad conductor who marched at the head of other Long Islanders: farmers, factory workers, even a few whalers. "We play Confederate because we don't like one group of people trying to rule over another," the conductor said. "It's not the U.S. we're rebelling against, it's the black-hearted businessmen who want to lord it over the working man." He gestured at his comrades, adding, "We've been squeezed, laid-off, down-sized, put down. We're fighting for our freedom, on and off this battlefield."

The freedom of slaves didn't figure much in this picture. Although *Glory* inspired several units modeled on the black regiment depicted in the film, the Wilderness reenactment and a half-dozen other battles I later attended were blindingly white affairs. This, too, was an issue both blue and gray preferred to sidestep. When I asked a Southern Guardsmen about his unit's views on race, he replied: "Damn right we're prejudiced. Against farbs."

I'd finally found several Southern Guardsmen at the rear of a sutler's tent. The unit had chosen to skip combat at the Wilderness because of the "farb quotient" and were busy planning their next event, a skirmish restricted to hardcore units. "Let's talk about how we're going to bring out the dead," one Guardsman said, drawing in the dirt. Evidently, the order to "resurrect" would never be heard at a hardcore event.

Abandoning this austere crew (Rob Hodge was mysteriously

absent), I wandered back to the rebel camp and found my erstwhile comrades from the 32nd Virginia seated around a bonfire, draining a case of Busch beer. One man poked at a can of tuna with his Swiss Army knife. Another scooped his fork into a plastic sack that I recognized from my Gulf War reporting as an MRE, or meal-ready-to-eat. "Have some hardtack?" one man asked, proffering a paper plate piled with Ritz crackers.

As they ate and drank, the men digested the day's battle. "If that were a real firestorm of lead like we saw today," one man opined, "we would'a all been dead now."

"No shit, Sherlock. I wouldn't go back and fight in that war unless I could do it in an F-15."

"And with a pocket full of penicillin. The only Scarlett they knew back then was fever, not O'Hara. We're pussies compared to them."

The conversation drifted from syphilis to semantics, and a cataloguing of words with alleged Civil War origins: hooker from Joe Hooker, the Union commander famed for his tolerance of female camp followers; sideburn from Ambrose Burnside, the Union general with bushy muttonchops; tampon from tompion, a wooden plug used to protect rifle barrels from dirt and rain; heavy metal from mid-nineteenth-century slang for large artillery pieces. Then, as the beer disappeared, the chat became increasingly right-wing and profane, wandering from gun control to Hillary Clinton to a recent news report about the health risks of movie popcorn. This was greeted as yet another example of left-wing bureaucrats trying to dictate behavior. "If I want to go in a movie theater and grease my popcorn with eighty million grams of cholesterol, that's my right and kiss my ass," one man drunkenly shouted.

Bishop, the Fright Stuff soldier I'd marched beside, invited me to join him at a civilian tent where several families were preparing dinner. Here, the scene was markedly more genteel. Hoop-skirted women cooked ham, cornbread and black-eyed peas over an open fire while their kids frolicked around the camp.

Peeling vegetables with a woman named Debbie, I asked what she did while her husband went off to battle. "Wash dishes, make the camp bed, wait for him to come back," she said. Debbie sewed her own dresses from calico cloth and pinned her hair in a "snood," or hairnet. For meals, she consulted period "receipts," as nineteenth-century recipes were known. "I'm not a purist, though," she said, opening a can of apple pie filler.

During the week, Debbie worked as the manager of a shipping department in Newport News. "It's high pressure, every minute of the day is scheduled. Then you get out here without TV or appliances and for two days you sit around a campfire talking to strangers and helping each other. We've lost the art of conversation, of just being neighbors." The only thing she disliked was the letdown she felt at the end of the weekend. "You climb in your car and head back home, and the twentieth century starts flooding in again. It's depressing."

After dinner, rain began pelting down and I headed back to the 32nd's camp in hopes of finding a dry spot for the night. One soldier had retreated to his car, leaving his tent vacant. Crawling inside, I quickly saw why. The canvas was so leaky and crookedly pitched that it resembled one of the wretched lean-tos in photographs of Andersonville. I found a bit of straw to put down on the wet ground, but in minutes the hay was soaked through. Then a river of rainwater drained into the tent and over my legs.

Rob Hodge, at least, would approve. But as I lay there on the wet hay, in my wet uniform, with rain beating against wet canvas a few inches from my face, I couldn't help wondering what actual Confederates would do if they could rise from the dead, as we had that afternoon. Offered the chance, wouldn't any soldier worth his salt be sleeping in a car with the heater on instead of lying out here in the mud?

I AWOKE AT DAWN to a hissing sound deeply resonant of my suburban childhood. Pulling aside the tent flap, I saw one of the Virginians squirting lighter fluid on a pile of briquettes. Using his cigarette lighter as torch, he ignited the charcoals and perched a modern coffeepot on top. All around the camp, Confederates performed their morning ablutions. A man cleaned his teeth with a horsehair toothbrush and swigs from a Diet Pepsi bottle. Men wandered off to pee in the woods while women in hoop skirts lined up beside a row of Porta-Johns marked "Ladies Only."

I headed off in search of Rob Hodge again and found the Guardsmen bedded down in a sutler's tent. One of the men said Rob had left
at midnight to camp in a nearby field. I found him there, wringing
out his socks over a sodden fire. Rob said he'd lain awake in the
sutler's tent, listening to the torrential rain, and become disgusted
with the softness of his quarters. "I wanted to see what it's like to
be soaked and cold on the night of battle," he said. "Now I know. It
sucks the big one."

I sat with Rob while he cooked slab bacon in a half-canteen that
served as his fry pan, poking the victuals with his bayonet. A stream
of young Confederates stopped by to swap stories and also, I sensed,
to pay their respects. Some had met Rob the day before, or at previous events; others had heard of him through the reenactors'
grapevine. Robert Lee Hodge, baddest reb in the whole damned
camp, sleeping out in monsoon rain and cooking blackened pork
with a bayonet.

"Rob," one young disciple asked. "I got this shirt at one of the sutlers' tents. What do you think?"

Rob eyed the garment. "Hmmm. It's almost there. What you want
to do is cut those farby wood buttons off. Then go to an antique
store and get some mother-of-pearl."

The youth sloped off and another approached, caked with mud.
Rob rubbed grease from his fry pan into the man's trousers. "Want
some for your beard?" he asked.

The man dabbed a bit on his chin and said, "I hear you're doing a
fifteen-mile march next week."

"That's right. Wanna come?"

"Hell yeah. Let's do the first ten miles barefoot!"

Rob smiled approvingly. "Super hardcore," he said.

This was a side of Rob I hadn't appreciated before. His reputation
and odd magnetism made him a missionary or guru, drawing acolytes to the hardcore faith. "If you can turn just one guy, he can
bring his whole unit around," Rob explained.

Rob planned to spend the day searching for fresh talent to recruit.
He slipped on a red armband marked "ambulance corps" and issued
a spare one to me. As nineteenth-century medics, we could wander
the battlefield without taking part in combat. Rob even had a flask of

gin in case we needed to administer anesthesia to the wounded. "Gives you the best seat in the house," Rob said, perching atop an embankment.

The second day's script called for a reenactment of the Mule Shoe at Spotsylvania, a bloodbath soon after the Wilderness during which Union and Confederate troops fought hand-to-hand. As the Army of Northern Virginia took up positions in the trenchworks, Rob cast a discerning eye at each unit's impression. He wasn't impressed.

"Look at that guy with the derby hat. Ridiculous. It's 1880s Butch Cassidy stuff."

"See the big officer over there? Great uniform, but the weight's way out of line. And who's the guy behind him with the red pants? He looks like a circus clown."

"Ouch, way too much red trim on those artillery uniforms. They look like Shriners."

I spotted the 32nd Virginia and pointed the unit out to Rob. "Those were my guys yesterday. What do you think?"

Rob frowned. "Poor cut. Wrong trouser color. And way too much blubber. The whole unit needs liposuction."

I pointed hopefully at Captain Mullen, the dashing officer who had struck me the day before as possessing that Confederate *je ne sais quoi*. Rob *savait exactement quoi*. "*Très* farb," he said. "A real Confederate would eventually have cut that hair to keep the lice under control. And what's with the hat? It's all wrong—the Boer War maybe, not this one."

Rob scouted for another hour, gradually sinking into despair. But as the battle got under way, he finally spotted a prospect. Pointing at a mud-caked rebel, he said, "Garment's hung fine and the bedroll's just right." Then the youth took a hit and sprawled backwards, thrashing wildly and ripping his shirt open to get at the imaginary wound.

"Wow, you see him get popped? He's a natural. C'mon." We rushed over to the wounded youth. I checked his pulse while Rob cradled his head. "Great hit," Rob said, sloshing gin down his throat. "I liked the bouncing around. Looked like a nerve wound. You ever heard of the Southern Guard?"

As Rob evangelized, there was a pause in the fighting. A Union officer sprinted into the rebel trench "Stop shooting," he shouted. "This is unscripted! We're supposed to do hand-to-hand." He conferred with a rebel officer and retreated to his position. Then the Confederate officer climbed atop the breastwork and waved his saber. On cue, the Yankees poured across twenty yards of open ground and into the trench. The blue and gray tangled in a melee of swinging rifle butts and mock bayonet thrusts. Several men abandoned their weapons and began groping on the ground. I was reminded of fake wrestling matches I'd watched on TV as a child.

After half an hour, Taps played. The battle was over and so was the weekend's reenactment. But as the dead resurrected and shook hands, I noticed a dozen men still sprawled on the ground. One clutched his arm, another writhed and moaned. Their impressions looked remarkably good and I searched for Rob to see if we should recruit them. Instead, an officer ran up and asked of my armband, "Are you doing nineteenth-century medical or twentieth?"

"Nineteenth."

"Damn. Some guys got really carried away."

A moment later, modern medics appeared in an ambulance. They bandaged a broken nose, toted off a man with broken ribs, and stuck an oxygen mask on an older man struggling for breath. I later learned that fifty-seven people were hurt in the weekend's reenactment, and two required hospitalization. At some events, casualties were mortal: several men had expired from heart attacks and one froze to death during an unseasonably cold night in Tennessee.

Rob had vanished with his new recruit, so I wandered off the field alone as reenactors and spectators streamed toward the parking lots. One woman lingered on the grass long after the others had left. Slim and delicate-featured, she wore a black hooped skirt, a tight black bodice and held a black parasol over her lace-covered head. I bowed slightly and asked what had brought her to the Wilderness.

"A reb shot my husband at Gettysburg," she said. "I came here to remember him."

Playing along, I offered the view that the rebel who killed her husband was simply following orders. "But I'm very sorry just the same, m'am."

"That's very kind of you, soldier," she said, wiping away what looked to be a real tear. I asked what she did on the home front now that her gallant husband was gone.

"Empty bedpans and take blood," she said. "I'm a registered nurse in Tonawanda, New York."

She smiled, signaling that we were now "out of character," and reached out a black lace glove so I could pull her from the grass. "This getup weighs ten pounds," she complained. "I can't wear it two days in a row because it starts to smell."

As we strolled toward the parking lot, Karen Meinhold told me how she'd become a Union widow. Six years before, while visiting the chocolate factory in Hershey, Pennsylvania, she'd stopped off at Gettysburg and been stunned by all the graves. Knowing little about the War, she began reading and gradually became obsessed. Now, she often drove twelve hours after work on Fridays to reach Virginia in time for the opening shots of reenactments.

But she didn't want to play any of the usual female roles, least of all nurse. "After all, that's what I do in real life," she said. Thirty-four and single, she'd settled on widowhood, hand-sewing her seven-layer outfit: pantalets, chemise, corset, corset cover, hoop, petticoat and dress. "At Gettysburg last year it was 108 degrees. I almost fainted."

Her distress must have been fetching; she'd fielded eleven proposals of marriage during the battle and suspected not all were in jest. But Karen brushed off the overtures, intent on remaining a widow. "It may sound silly," she said, "but I really do mourn the Union dead."

We'd reached the hot dog stand that divided our two nations; one sign pointed to a parking area marked "Union," another to a pasture labeled "C.S.A." A traffic jam had already formed, heading back to the twentieth century.

"After these battles, all the soldiers just get up and walk away," Karen said, as though she wished the drama ended otherwise. "But in real life, it didn't happen that way. Glory had a cost. I'm here so people will remember that."

Footsore and dirt-encrusted, I climbed in my car and crawled toward the highway behind hundreds of other Confederates. I turned

on the radio, then quickly turned it off. There was something to
what the others had said. Despite the weekend's discomforts and
phony moments, it had provided a pleasant taste of the enforced
leisure and sociability of nineteenth-century life: chatting with the
women as we peeled carrots, lazing beside Rob as he slow-cooked his
breakfast, ambling down the mile-long country lane between the
Union and Confederate camps, a distance that a car would have covered in a minute. Modern life rarely allowed for these simple, unhur-
ried pleasures.

Reaching the highway, I stopped for coffee at a 7-Eleven. The
store was crowded with black shoppers. Several of them stared
quizzically—and, I sensed, with some hostility—at my Confederate
uniform. Clunking self-consciously to the counter in my hobnailed
boots and gray trousers, I felt like blurting out, "I'm just play-
acting," or "It's only a game."

Instead, I returned to my car feeling confused and ashamed. This,
too, was an aspect of the twentieth century that reenactors were
fleeing: a heterogeneous society still raw with historic wounds and
racial sensitivities. In principle, remembrance of the War could be a
way to probe these scars, many of which trailed back to the 1860s.
But reenactments did precisely the opposite, blandly reconciling
North and South in a grand spectacle that glorified battlefield valor
and the stoicism of civilians.

Driving back north across the Rappahannock and the Rapidan, I
felt like a farb of the heart. Flags and muskets and uniforms weren't
just toys for adult boys to play with, nor could their symbolism be
shed like so much dirty clothing. When I arrived home, a grungy
Confederate foot soldier, even the dog didn't recognize me. Peeling
off my socks and boots and gray wool trousers, I resolved that next
time I'd be true to my views and wear blue.

7

Tennessee

AT THE FOOTE
OF THE MASTER

The Southerner talks music.
—MARK TWAIN

Soon after the Wilderness battle, I headed south again to keep an engagement of a different sort. From the start of my journey, I'd thought about contacting Shelby Foote. This proved surprisingly easy to do. His number was listed in the phonebook. But after picking up the phone a few times, I decided to type a long letter instead, requesting an interview. He responded with a succinct message, handwritten on delicate white notepaper. "I'll be glad to talk with you if we can find the time."

I took this as a summons to Memphis. Foote lived in a 1930s Tudor ringed by blossoming plum, dogwood and magnolia trees. A maid showed me into a handsomely appointed den with a pitched timber ceiling, dark wood flooring and liquor bottles set on a trolley. The setting wasn't quite what I'd expected: suburban baronial, more Henry the Eighth than William Faulkner.

The figure who strode briskly into the room a moment later also surprised me. Wearing trim gray trousers and a polo shirt, the silver-haired sage of Ken Burns's Civil War documentary looked as though he might have played a few sets of tennis before breakfast.

He also seemed more aloof than the grandfatherly figure on television. Without so much as a handshake or hello, Foote led me into a study with a throw rug at the door that said, "Go Away."

A bed occupied most of the study and Foote pointed me to a chair on one side of it. He took a seat across the bed, as far away as he could get. Angled with his back half-turned to me, he reached for one of a dozen pipes scattered across the desk behind him, tamped tobacco into the bowl, and said by way of small talk, "What can I do for you?"

I wasn't exactly sure. Foote's mellifluous drawl and folksy stories on television had captivated me, as had his three-volume narrative history of the Civil War, still a hot-selling classic twenty years after its publication. The seventy-eight-year-old writer had become a curious phenomenon—a Civil War celebrity—and I'd somehow imagined that my cathode-tube acquaintance with him would make it easy to just chat about my travels, and to get his views on some of the impressions I'd formed.

Instead, I found myself groping for one of a dozen Big Theme questions I'd rehearsed just in case on the taxi ride over. When I finally lobbed one across the bed—why was memory of the War so enduring?—Foote smashed it straight back. "Because it's the big one. It measures what we are, good and bad. If you look at American history as the life span of a man, the Civil War represents the great trauma of our adolescence. It's the sort of experience we never forget."

Foote lit his pipe. I lobbed another one: Why did the South in particular cling to remembrance of the War? "It was fought in our own backyard," he immediately replied, "or front yard if you will, and you're not apt to forget something that happened on your own property. I was raised up in a rough-and-tumble society. I was in a lot of fistfights, maybe fifty in my life. The ones I remember with startling clarity are the ones I lost."

How did the experience of defeat define the post-War South?

"It gave us a sense of tragedy, which the rest of the nation lacks. In the movie *Patton* the general talks about how 'We Americans have never lost a war.' Well, Patton's own grandfather was in Lee's Army of Northern Virginia. He damn well lost a war."

We went on like this for half an hour, each question prompting a perfect sound bite of the sort Foote had mouthed for interviewers a hundred times before. I felt as though we were working our way through a responsive liturgy. I also felt like a jerk for wasting his time. It was a relief when the telephone rang.

"You're speaking to him," Foote gruffly told the caller, who, like me, must have been surprised to reach the Great Man so easily. As Foote answered a question about rebels in Missouri, I looked around his study. The room appeared as though it hadn't changed much in the thirty years since Foote began writing there. The phone had a rotary dial. There was no computer, printer or modem. I'd read that Foote wrote longhand, using an antiquated pen dipped in ink. He regarded even the fountain pen as a "mechanical intrusion" and a concession to a modern era of which he didn't wholly approve.

Foote hung up the phone. "It's a nightmare, ever since that Burns thing," he grumbled. "I'm trying to write a novel but mostly I work at answering that phone."

I asked him why he bothered answering it. "Stupid stubbornness," he said. "I've worked my whole life without a secretary or research assistant. I will not let all this hoorah make me hire one, or take my name out of the book. I don't want to live in a different way."

Then, leaning back in his chair, Foote began to speak a bit more personally, as I'd hoped he would. "It's been a helluva century," he went on. "I was born during the First World War, spent my adolescence in the Depression and came of age in the Second World War. This is the bloodiest century there ever was." He paused, smiling into his pipe. "Now I'm living to see another terrible thing—the South joining the party of Lincoln."

Republicans had recently won a number of congressional seats across the South, in some cases for the first time since Reconstruction. I asked Foote how the party of Lincoln had been viewed in his youth. He put down his pipe, cleared his throat and recited a tuneless ditty:

> *Abraham Lincoln was a son of a bitch,*
> *His ass ran over with a seven-year itch,*
> *His fist beat his dick like a blacksmith's hammer,*
> *While his asshole whistled the Star-Spangled Banner.*

Foote chuckled. "When I was thirteen or so, I knew reams of obscene doggerel about Lincoln, but that's the only bit I remember."

I threw away the rest of my canned questions and listened to
Foote reminisce about his childhood in Greenville, Mississippi. In
the 1920s and 30s, he said, the sting of Civil War defeat was still so
vivid that Mississippians refused to observe July 4th, the day Vicksburg fell. Only the post office—a federal facility—closed for the day.

"I remember in the 1930s there was a family from Ohio in town,
God knows why," Foote recalled, "and on July Fourth they drove
their car up on the levee and spread a blanket and had a picnic. They
didn't set the brakes on the car and it ran down into the Mississippi
River and everyone said, 'It served them right for celebrating the
Fourth of July.'" Foote chuckled again, adding, "We despised Yankees, just on the face of it."

Greenville was more tolerant of other outsiders. The Delta town
attracted large numbers of foreign immigrants. Foote's maternal
grandfather, Morris Rosenstock, was a Viennese Jew who emigrated
to America in the 1880s, found work as a plantation bookkeeper and
married his employer's daughter. Until the age of eleven, Foote attended synagogue each Saturday with his mother. He didn't recall
any anti-Semitism in Greenville; there were more Jews than Baptists
in the local country club. But Foote never took to Judaism, and as
he got older he realized the broader society wasn't so accepting as
Greenville. This became painfully obvious at college in North Carolina, when the fraternity his friends had joined turned Foote down
because of his background.

"I knew all the trouble I'd have down the line," he said of his Jewish heritage. "I was always not wanting to take on that kind of trouble. It just added one more problem, an added awkwardness to life."
So in his twenties he was baptised and confirmed as an Episcopalian.
But he didn't take to Christianity, either. "I never had much use for
turning the other cheek," he said. "I always buck back, particularly
when any authority leans on me."

This combativeness cost him dearly. Eager to fight the Germans,
Foote joined the National Guard in 1939 and rose to the rank of artillery captain. While stationed in Northern Ireland, preparing for

the Allied invasion of the Continent, he tangled with a colonel who he felt had insulted one of his men. Soon after, Foote fudged a mileage report so he could visit Belfast, two miles beyond the fifty-mile limit for weekend trips in army vehicles. The colonel and another superior had him court-martialed for falsifying documents.

Returning to America, Foote enlisted as a private in the marines and went through boot camp. But the war ended just as he was bound for combat again, this time in the Pacific. To paraphrase what he'd said of the Civil War, Foote had missed the great trauma of his own generation's adolescence.

"I felt cheated, as though I was dealt out of the big adventure," he said. Foote also wondered if the experience of war might have enriched his later writing. "I often wonder how much I could have learned from being shot at and having others fall all around me—assuming I wasn't one of the ones who fell."

What Foote had done instead was marry the Belfast woman he'd gone to visit on the fateful trip that led to his court-martial. This struck me as more romantic than going off to fight, but Foote didn't see it that way. "I felt as though I'd made a fool of myself," he said. Foote also felt he'd fallen short of what was expected of him as a Southerner and a descendant of Confederates. "Growing up in Mississippi, they were the embodiment of gallantry and chivalry," he said. "You were expected to measure up to those standards, most of all with regard to physical and moral courage."

Foote gestured toward a framed certificate on the wall from the United Confederate Veterans. It was dated 1892 and honored his great-grandfather, Colonel Hezekiah William Foote. Before the War, Hezekiah owned five plantations and over one hundred slaves. "I was given clearly to understand as a child that I was a Southern aristocrat," Foote said.

His great-grandfather had opposed secession but fought without hesitation for the South. "Just as I would have," Foote said. "I'd be with my people, right or wrong. If I was against slavery, I'd still be with the South. I'm a man, my society needs me, here I am. The difference between North and the South in the War is that there was no stigma attached to the Northern man who paid two hundred dollars to not go to war, or who hired a German replacement. In the South you could have done that, but no one would. You'd have been scorned."

Foote's retroactive allegiance to the Confederacy surprised me. It was the honor-bound code of the Old South. One's people before one's principles. The straitjacket of scorn and stigma. "It's a bunch of shit really," Foote conceded. "But all Southerners subscribe to this code to some degree, at least male Southerners of my generation." In Foote's view, this same stubborn pride had sustained Southerners during the Civil War. "It's what kept them going through Appomattox, that attitude of 'I won't give up, I will not be insulted.'"

It took almost a century after Appomattox for Confederate blood to cool. Southerners' "abiding love" for Franklin Delano Roosevelt tempered their prideful regionalism, Foote said; so, too, did the patriotic fervor surrounding World War II. It was in 1945 that Mississippians finally dropped their eighty-year ban on celebrating Independence Day. This was also when many Southerners stopped referring to the Civil War as the War Between the States. "It was a big admission, if you think about it," Foote said. "A civil war is a struggle between two parts of one nation, which implies that the South was never really separate or independent."

Nonetheless, Southern identity—Foote's included—remained fierce. His National Guard unit was known as "the Dixie Division" and its members stood at attention each time the anthem of the Old South was played. As he trained for war against the Germans, Foote devoured books on Stonewall Jackson. He saw a Union monument for the first time in 1946 when he traveled to Santa Fe with his boyhood friend and fellow writer, Walker Percy. "We immediately made plans to dynamite it," Foote said.

They didn't, though the idea obviously stuck with Percy, who later used it in his writing to mock the South's obsession with the Civil War. In his 1967 novel *The Last Gentleman*, Percy's young Southern protagonist confides to a doctor: "When I was at Princeton, I blew up a Union monument. It was only a plaque hidden in the weeds behind the chemistry building, presented by the class of 1885 in memory of those who made the supreme sacrifice to suppress the infamous rebellion, or something like that. It offended me. I synthesized a liter of trinitrotoluene in the chemistry lab and blew it up one Saturday afternoon. But no one ever knew what had been blown up. It seemed I was the only one who knew the monument was there. It was thought to be a Harvard prank."

Like Percy, Foote valued fiction above all else. He never finished college, nor did he ever receive any formal training as an historian. It was only as a break between novels that Foote accepted a commission to write a "short history" of the Civil War—a project that grew to three volumes and consumed twenty years of his career. "It took me five times as long to write a history of that War as it took the country to fight it," he said.

When he finished in 1974, Foote told Dick Cavett in a TV interview that he was busily "forgetting everything I know about the Civil War" so he could return to fiction. Despite having spent so long on the history, Foote regarded himself as a novelist, not a scholar (many professional historians agreed, sniping privately about his success and his anecdotal style). But the Ken Burns series catapulted Foote back to his historical work, and forward into the strange world of Civil War renown. Five years after the Burns series aired in 1990, Foote still couldn't go anywhere without having copies of his books thrust at him to sign—something he refused to do.

"When you sign a book for a friend, it means something, but it means nothing if you sign everyone's," he explained. "Also, I find autograph-seekers obnoxious, very unmannerly. I rebuff them for that reason, too."

I was glad I'd forgotten to bring several of his books to sign. I also sensed that Foote's initial aloofness, which I'd taken for a distinctly un-Southern frostiness on his part, was more akin to gentlemanly reserve: an old-fashioned, rather English sense of friendship and respect for personal space. There are people one knows and people one doesn't. One shouldn't cheapen the former by feigning intimacy with the latter. Like so much else about Foote, there was irony here. A private, almost reclusive man who wrote with a dip-pen and distrusted modernity, Foote had gained his greatest fame appearing before millions of television viewers in the guise of a warm and folksy raconteur.

Many Southerners I'd spoken to felt betrayed by Foote's appear-

ance in the Burns series, which diehards regarded as wicked Northern propaganda. Foote disagreed, though he did feel "there is some
justice to the claim that slavery was overemphasized." To Foote, the
Confederacy's avowed commitment to states' rights wasn't simply a
fig leaf for a defense of slavery. "It's ridiculous now to talk about the
right to secede; it was not ridiculous in 1861," he said. "Not one of
those thirteen colonies would have joined the Union if they hadn't
believed they could get out of it."

Foote's views on race were also complex. He'd been raised during
a period of frequent lynchings and unthinking bigotry. "Brazil nuts
were called 'nigger toes' and a sling shot was a 'nigger shooter,'" he
said. But Foote had bucked the Southern trend and supported integration early on. He also quit his Sons of Confederate Veterans' chapter when it chose to honor George Wallace on a visit to Memphis,
and later abandoned plans to build a home on the Alabama coast because of a strong Klan presence there.

Nor did Foote subscribe to romantic Southern views of the Lost
Cause. Militarily, he believed, the Cause was always lost. Ideologi-
cally, the Cause was easy to mythologize precisely because it was
lost. "The Civil War monument in my hometown calls the Confederacy the 'only nation that lived and died without sin,'" he said. "Well,
it's easy to stay pure if you're never put to the test."

The victorious North *had* been put to the test, and in Foote's view
it had flunked. "Slavery was the first great sin of this nation," Foote
said. "The second great sin was emancipation, or rather the way it
was done. The government told four million people, 'You are free. Hit
the road.' Three-quarters of them couldn't read or write. The tiniest
fraction of them had any profession that they could enter."

Foote felt the consequences of Reconstruction were still with us.
But the fault wasn't all with the government or with white Americans. "What has dismayed me so much is the behavior of blacks.
They are fulfilling every dire prophecy the Ku Klux Klan made. It's
no longer safe to be on the streets in black neighborhoods. They are
acting as if the utter lie about blacks being somewhere between ape
and man were true."

Like the obscene ditty about Abraham Lincoln, this was a side of
Shelby Foote that hadn't come through in Burns's documentary.

Foote also displayed an intricate sympathy for the early KKK, which ex-Confederates formed immediately after the War to combat what they regarded as the cruel excesses of Reconstruction. "The Klan takes some careful talking about, it's easy to misinterpret what I'm fixing to say," Foote cautioned. "But in some ways the Klan was very akin to the Free French Resistance to Nazi occupation. To expect people who fought as valiantly as these people did to roll over and play dead because there was an occupying army is kind of crazy."

Foote also admired Nathan Bedford Forrest, the Klan's first Imperial Wizard, a slave trader before the War, and a rebel commander who allegedly permitted the slaughter of surrendering black troops at a battle called Fort Pillow. Foote regarded Forrest as one of the "two authentic geniuses" of the War (Lincoln being the other). A daring cavalry commander, Forrest was the only soldier on either side to rise from private to lieutenant general in the course of the War, and his lightning tactics later inspired Rommel's use of blitzkrieg in World War II.

In Foote's view, Forrest was also "a fine man. My black friends abhor him. They want to take his statue down, dig up his and his wife's bones, and throw them to the wind. But it is not known generally that he dissolved the Klan when it turned ugly."

Disbanded around 1870 (owing not only to Forrest, but also to a government crackdown), the Klan revived in 1915 following the success of the movie *Birth of a Nation* and quickly became a potent force nationwide. "The Klan that people remember today is the Klan of the 1920s," Foote said. "Anti-Catholic, anti-Jewish, anti-black. Forrest's Klan was anti-black but not opposed to all black people. It was trying to keep illiterate blacks from occupying positions like sheriff and judge."

Foote's views on the Confederate battle flag were equally nuanced. In his view, those who saw the banner as synonymous with slavery had their history wrong. The battle flag was a combat standard, not a political symbol. "It stood for law, honor, love of country," Foote said, and the banner was revered as such by the veterans who had fought under it.

At the same time, Foote recognized that the flag had become "a banner of shame and disgrace and hate." But he pinned the blame for this on educated Southerners who allowed white supremacists to misuse the flag during the civil rights struggle. "Freedom Riders were a pretty weird-looking group to Southerners," Foote said. "The men had odd haircuts and strange baggy clothes and seemed to associate with people with an intimacy that we didn't allow. So the so-called right-thinking people of the South said, 'They're sending their riffraff down here. Let our riffraff take care of them.' Then they sat back while the good ol' boys in the pickup trucks took care of it, under the Confederate banner. That's when right-thinking people should have stepped in and said, 'Don't use that banner, that's not what it stands for.' But they didn't. So now it's a symbol of evil to a great many people, and I understand that."

Foote paused to answer the phone, as he'd done several times. There had been a request to give a speech (denied), a query about Methodism in the War (answered), a question about slavery in Kentucky (deferred). And always the same curmudgeonly tone, as Foote glared at the phone, then picked it up, wearily telling each caller, "You're speaking to him."

Reminded that I was yet another consumer of his scarce time, I moved to the topic I'd most wanted to ask Foote about. I'd enjoyed his novel *Shiloh*, and also read about his frequent visits to the battlefield, a place he evidently regarded with mystic awe. Shiloh lay several hours' drive east of Memphis. I wanted to know what Foote found so special about Shiloh, and what I might look for during my own visit there.

"For me, something emanates from that ground," he said, "the way memory sometimes leaps up at you unexpectedly." His great-grandfather fought at Shiloh. And it was a landscape Foote had traveled over many times in his literary imagination. "If you've drawn a picture or written about a particular historical incident in a particular place, the place belongs to you in a sense. I feel that way about Shiloh, a sense of proprietorship."

Foote had visited Shiloh over twenty times, and once escorted Faulkner there (stopping en route to find a bootlegger so the bibulous writer could down a Sunday morning whiskey). Foote always tried to visit on the anniversary of battle, if possible at dawn when the battle started, and then follow the fighting through the day. This allowed him to reconstruct the battle and appreciate how everything from the foliage to the angle of sunlight influenced the outcome. "If the light and the leaves and the weather are right," he said, "I swear I can see and hear soldiers coming through the trees."

The phone rang again. Hanging up, Foote glanced at his watch. I'd been there all morning and sensed my audience was through. We stepped out of his study and back into the present. For all its faults, the late twentieth century had its rewards, including the Mercedes sports car in which Foote offered me a lift to a hotel downtown.

As we tooled into Memphis, past a hideous strip of franchise outlets, Foote retreated again to the 1860s. He'd recently read several soldiers' memoirs and been struck, as so often before, by the essential difference between their mindset and ours. "It is the simplicity of the people that fascinates me," he said. "Their minds don't seem to have been cluttered like ours, they didn't have all the hesitations about things being right or wrong. They knew, and they acted."

Foote pulled over at a small park, almost lost amid the mess of modern Memphis. Disheveled men with brown bags lay splayed across benches. At the center of the park rose a massive equestrian statue of Nathan Bedford Forrest. "They ruined it when they cleaned it," Foote said. "It used to be a dark green bronze. Now it looks like it's made out of Hershey bars." The statue had also been vandalized on several occasions.

Staring at the monument, I tried to understand a little of what drew Foote to Forrest. The cavalryman's deep-set eyes, narrow face and long, pointed beard certainly matched the sobriquet Sherman had once given him: "the very Devil." Here was a man who had little hesitation about right and wrong. He knew and he acted. "War means fightin' and fightin' means killin'," Forrest famously declared.

To Foote, Forrest also epitomized certain "antique virtues," such as cunning and initiative, which had been lost in our own century's warfare. "A soldier is no longer a thinking bayonet. He's a blip on a radar screen. You can abolish him by pushing a button." Forrest, by contrast, almost single-handedly changed the outcome of several battles. He also had twenty-nine mounts shot from under him, while managing to personally kill thirty Yankees—a feat that led Forrest to boast that he came out "a horse ahead at the end."

There was something else Foote admired about Forrest. The crude and contentious cavalryman offered an obvious contrast to the gentlemanly perfection of Robert E. Lee. "In my day, and I think still to a considerable degree, Lee was a Christ figure, without sin," Foote said. "Nothing pleases me more than to find some shortcoming in Lee, because it humanizes him."

We returned to the car and pulled back into traffic. "I abhor the idea of a perfect world," Foote said. "It would bore me to tears."

8

Tennessee
THE GHOST MARKS
OF SHILOH

History, n. *An account mostly false,*
of events mostly unimportant, which are brought about
by rulers, mostly knaves, and soldiers, mostly fools.
—AMBROSE BIERCE, *The Devil's Dictionary*

I'm late for Western Civ. A blue exam notebook lies on my desk. Everyone else is already taking the test. I open the blue book. A question
about Greece swims before my eyes. "What's wrong?" the student next
to me asks. "Didn't you study?"

The motel alarm jolted me awake. I lay staring at the digital red
4:00 winking from beside the bed, wondering where I was. Corinth.
Corinth, Mississippi. Corinthian columns. Western Civ.

An all-night omelet shop cast a sallow glow across the motel
parking lot. It looked like a place Edward Hopper might have gone
to sketch a solitary diner. Except that the restaurant was packed. I
wedged onto a stool beside a man with "Jerry" stitched on his work
shirt. He drank black coffee and blew perfect smoke rings. I asked
him why the place was so busy at 4 A.M.

"Busy? Shit. You should'a been here an hour ago, when the bar
crowd was here."

Bar crowd? Arriving in Corinth late the night before, I'd had trouble finding a hamburger, much less a beer. "Hard to believe, but this used to be a rowdy-ass town," Jerry said. That was before the Baptist majority voted to go dry and close the town's beer joints. Later, they repented and voted to permit hard liquor (which for some reason citizens judged easier to control). After several decades of losing beer revenue to nearby Tennessee, Corinthians had changed their mind again. "At the last election," Jerry said, "we voted liquor out and beer in." So the bars were hopping again.

Jerry, though, didn't look like the late-night drinking type. "What brings you here?" I asked him.

"Force of habit. Ate here for ten years before punching in at the garment factory at six." These days, Jerry raised laboratory mice instead. "Rat cage don't open till eight," he said. But he couldn't break the predawn ritual. The other customers were mostly loggers, farmers and truckers. Jerry dropped his cigarette in a pile of grits. "How's about you, stranger?"

"Just passing through." I paused. "It's the anniversary of the battle of Shiloh. I'm headed up there to check things out."

"At four in the fucking a.m.?" Jerry said it so loud that everyone at the counter turned their heads.

I looked into my coffee. "The battle started at five. I'd sort of planned to be out there by then."

Jerry shook his head. The others shrugged and returned to their eggs. "Guess you got to go the whole nine yards," he said.

The road north from Corinth climbed through gentle hills and crossed into Tennessee. My headlights picked up the occasional logging truck and the usual snapshots of rural Southern life: a railroad crossing called Cotton Plant, a G-Whiz convenience store, a trailer labeled Worms for Sale, a small wooden church with a huge sign that blared, PRAYER IS A TRUCK HEADED FOR GOD'S WAREHOUSE.

In half an hour I sped across terrain that the rebel army spent three days slogging through in the muddy spring of 1862. Ulysses S. Grant and 40,000 Federals lay camped by the Tennessee River, near a log church called Shiloh. Grant awaited reinforcements so he could move south and attack the crucial rail junction at Corinth. But the

Confederate commander, Albert Sidney Johnston, decided to strike first and dispatched his men north from Mississippi to surprise the encamped Federals. "Tonight we will water our horses in the Tennessee River!" he told his officers at dawn on the day of battle.

Instead, at midafternoon, Johnston lay dead near Shiloh's Peach Orchard after leading a charge on his horse Fire-eater. The rebels fought on, almost pushing Grant's men into the river. But during the night, steamboats ferried Federal reinforcements across the river; the Union army counterattacked at dawn, recapturing the ground it had lost the previous day. The Confederates straggled back through the mud to Corinth, which they abandoned seven weeks later. At Shiloh, the South lost its last best chance to halt Grant's conquest of the western Confederacy.

In April 1862, the Shiloh church had ministered to a backwoods settlement of 150 souls who eked out a living from fruit orchards, beeswax and small plots of cotton and corn. Today, Shiloh wasn't much more: an unincorporated crossroads with a gas station, a convenience store, and a run-down building labeled "Shiloh Souvenirs" with a window display of minié balls, rusted pocketknives, and slivers labeled "Petrified Wood. Very old."

Spotting a sign for the battlefield, I became suddenly giddy. Like Shelby Foote, I'd always felt drawn to Shiloh, though for me the tug came from childhood fantasy rather than family ties or firsthand visits. When I'd first read about and painted the battle as a boy, Shiloh—"place of peace" in the Bible—sounded haunting and beautiful, nothing like the bluntly named Bull Run or the Germanic towns of Gettysburg and Fredericksburg. Only Antietam rolled off the tongue in as lovely a way. But Antietam lay within the same fifty-mile orbit of my boyhood home as the Virginia and Pennsylvania battlefields.

Shiloh lay a world away, in a wilderness of lazy rivers, log cabins and tersely named creeks: Dill, Owl, Snake, Lick. Deepening Shiloh's mystique was the dearth of documentary images from the battle. Wartime photographers rarely ventured west of the Appalachians. The photographic history of the War I'd studied with my father included only one unstaged picture from Shiloh: a tantalizing shot of Union paddle wheelers docking at Pittsburg Landing, beside the battlefield. The wide, slow Tennessee snaked behind. I could almost see a log raft floating past with a boy in a straw hat and britches tossing a catfish line over the side.

Now, the real battlefield lay before me in the predawn gloom. I turned in at the park gate, switching off my headlights lest a ranger apprehend me for entering outside of official hours. Inching along in the dark, I parked near the spot on my tourist map labeled Fraley Field. It was here in J. C. Fraley's cottonfield, at dawn on April 6th, that Northern sentries first encountered the oncoming rebel army.

Crumpled Bud Lite cans lay on the ground beside a parked car. A match flared inside. Another Civil War addict waiting for dawn? I rapped lightly on the window. The glass came down just enough for me to glimpse two startled teenagers smoking in the front seat. "Do you know how I get out to Fraley Field from here?" I asked. The driver shook his head, started the engine and sped off. Shiloh, like many other battlefields, doubled as a lovers' lane after dark.

I stood in the gloom, shivering and feeling suddenly silly. My breakfast companion was right; what *was* I doing here at four-what-ever in the fucking a.m.? If tramping through the woods before dawn was so damned transcendent, why hadn't Shelby Foote accepted my invitation to come along?

Twigs crunched and a voice called out from the dark. "Fraley Field's over here, I think." A figure approached and flicked on a cigarette lighter. He was heavyset, prematurely bald and about my own age, clad in a windbreaker and ski cap. "My great-great-grandfather was doing picket duty out here right about now, a hundred thirty-three years ago. Weird to think, isn't it?"

The lighter flicked off. It was 4:55—the precise moment when the battle began—and stars still winked in the pitch-black sky. "In the books they talk about 'gray streaks of dawn' when the fighting started," the man said. "But I don't see any gray or any dawn." I was confused, too. Then it occurred to me. "They didn't have daylight savings back then." So 4:55 in April 1862 would be equivalent to 5:55 today. In Shelby Foote's terms, we were an hour too early.

We found a log and sat talking by intermittent Bic-light. Bryson Powers was a thirty-eight-year-old bus driver from Minneapolis. Laid off a year before, he'd moved in with his mother. To escape the house during the day, he visited the genealogy section at the local library and learned that his great-great-grandfather had served in the Civil War. Powers followed the paper trail from birth records to enlistment papers to muster rolls and finally to the files of the Cincinnati Sanitary Commission.

"He joins the Sixteenth Wisconsin in the late fall of '61, travels by train from Wisconsin to St. Louis, then by boat to Pittsburg Landing just in time to march out here," Powers said. "Then he gets shot in the knee and sent to a hospital in Cincinnati. He dies there a few weeks later. That's his war."

Powers's war remained incomplete. "I want to know the whole story," he said. Rehired to his bus-driving job, he'd saved enough money to take a week off and come down here. He flew to Memphis and rented a car because he didn't want to tour the South with Minnesota plates. "In case I broke down on some back road," he said. Even so, he'd been stricken with panic when the car rental agent told him the quickest route to Shiloh cut through the northern rim of Mississippi. Powers had taken the long way instead, through Tennessee. "This is the first time I've been South, just like my great-great-grandfather." He laughed nervously. "Hope my trip ends better than his."

The sky had edged from black to dark gray, allowing us to make out a path through the woods. As we emerged at the fringe of Fraley Field, Powers grasped my arm and pointed at something in a clump of trees about fifty yards off. "A deer?" he whispered. The form shifted and split into two. There was a murmur of voices and I thought I could see the silhouette of a rifle. It was just as Foote had described; you could almost see soldiers coming through the trees.

As we crept forward I heard a man say, "Breckinridge and Polk must have come up right through there." It was the familiar banter of Civil War bores. I relaxed. But Powers still held back. I guessed he'd never met reenactors on his bus route in Minneapolis.

"Looky there," one of the men called out in an exaggerated drawl. "Some goddamn Yankee sentries." He lowered the gun from his shoulder. "Twenty-fourth Tennessee," he called out. "Who goes?

"Sixteenth Wisconsin," Powers called back.

"We gave you blue-bellies a helluva time here, didn't we?"

"Shot me in the knee," Powers replied. He checked his watch.

"Right about now, my guys are breaking up campfires and saying 'oh shit' as you guys start charging through the woods."

The four of us stood silently in the ankle-high dew, listening to the hum of truck traffic out beyond the shield of trees. Then, as the sky shifted from gray to pink, the scene around us began to unfold: a gently swelling field, a stream bed, dogwoods blooming white along the edge of the dark woods.

We could also see each other's faces and awkwardly introduced our modern selves. The man with the musket—and a Diet Dr. Pepper in his other hand—was Steve Oxford, a big, bushy-bearded man in a leather jacket and jogging pants. His friend, a lean, clean-cut man in jeans, was Mike Brantley. They both worked for phone companies in Nashville and timed their vacations to coincide with the anniversaries of Civil War battles.

"This was my great-grandfather's gun, so I thought I'd bring it back," Oxford said. "Actually, he was shot here, dropped his gun and picked this one up from a Yankee." He showed us where the gun's original Northern owner had carved his name in the butt. "You didn't have an ancestor named Melton, did you?" he asked hopefully.

Powers shook his head. "My great-great-grandfather was in Peabody's regiment, on picket." He pointed back the way we'd come. "He would have been somewhere back there, I guess, standing behind a tree. The way I understood it, he stuck his leg out for a moment and got shot."

Oxford's rebel forebear had charged out from the other side of the field. "His unit got waxed somewhere over there," he said, pointing at the stream bed. "He took one in the hip." Brantley's great-grandfather traveled the same route. He survived the battle, but not the War.

The three men turned to me. I explained that I had no ancestors here and told them about my visit with Shelby Foote. Then I asked why they were out here at dawn.

"Time travel, like Foote talked about," Brantley said. "I always think of Patton in the movie. You know the scene when he looks out at that ancient battlefield and hears a trumpet, like he's been there before, way back when?"

Oxford nodded. "I'm half hoping this gun will start glowing and shaking and getting real heavy. You know, telling me exactly where my great-grandfather picked it up." He laughed. "He's probably looking down from heaven at me now and thinking, 'You damned fool, let it go. If I'd had any brains, I'd have hung back from the charge shouting "I'll be right there!" like I had the Tennessee two-step.'" That was Civil War slang for the runs.

Powers felt the same ancestral tug. "I guess I want to know more about him," he said. "I mean, I've got the paperwork. He was born in 1834, had three kids, enlisted in Oconomowoc, Wisconsin. So did his father. It was fall, they probably wanted a paycheck. They were probably thinking, 'It's going to be winter in Wisconsin, not going to get anything done, so let's go South.' They put Xs next to their names. Couldn't write a thing."

He paused. "I drive a city bus in Minneapolis. I've had lots of blacks on the bus call me names. There's some kind of irony to that. My great-great-grandfather wore blue and got killed so blacks could come up North and call his great-great-grandson a motherfucker."

The others laughed. "What do you think of the South?" Brantley asked.

"Well, your friend here has a gun so I don't know what I should say. I've heard Southerners are more likely to knock your block off."

"We'll let it slide this time, Yank," Oxford drawled. "Have you tried some of our fine Southern food?"

"Not yet. I've been hitting McDonald's and Taco Bell so far. Food groups I'm used to."

"You got to try some scratch biscuits and red-eye gravy," Brantley said.

"What's red-eye gravy?"

"Basically water and grease."

A woodpecker banged madly in the woods nearby. "Machine gun!" Oxford joked, ducking to the ground.

It was full dawn now. My feet were soaked with dew and I suddenly felt cold. The magic had slipped away, and so had the easy intimacy of standing in the dark telling personal history to strangers. "Well, this is going to be a regular thing for us," Oxford said, extending a hand. "Maybe we'll see you Yanks out here next year."

We strolled back through the woods. I noticed now that my sedan lay a few yards from a Nissan Sentra and a Chevy Bronco. Unlike the armies of North and South, we could take a break from battle, sit inside our vehicles and turn on the heat for a few minutes before marching on.

When the Tennesseans drove off, Powers got out of his car and came over to mine. "I didn't want to say it in front of the others," he said, "but when that guy asked how I felt about the South, I wanted to say, 'I've been to Canada and everyone talks and seems pretty much like me. But down here, it's like a foreign country.'"

"What do you mean?"

"Maybe it's the Civil War thing, my being shot here—Henry Powers I mean. But I still feel like they look at me and say to themselves, 'Damn Yank.' I know it sounds silly but I almost feel like it's dangerous down here. That guy with the gun—I saw him at first and thought, 'He's pointing it at me.'"

Powers laughed at himself, not so nervous now. "But you know, those guys were okay, and I found myself thinking, if they were up in Minnesota or I was down in Tennessee, maybe we'd be friends. Then I started thinking, maybe it was the same for my great-great-grandfather. That reb who shot him in the leg was probably a farmer like him, and about the same age. If they'd ever had a chance to talk instead of shoot at each other, maybe that whole bloody mess would have turned out different."

Powers had one more mission before leaving Fraley Field. Shiloh, like other battlefield parks, was dotted with historic markers recording the movements and deeds of individual units. Powers pulled out a map of Shiloh he'd bought at the park headquarters the day before. It looked like an oil prospector's chart, with tiny, numbered dots and an index that you needed a magnifying glass to decipher.

"I think I'm just over there," Powers said, pointing to the edge of Fraley Field. We hiked over and found a post with a plaque that said: "21st Missouri and Pickets of Peabody's (Ist) Brig., Prentiss's (6th) Div., Army of the Tennessee. The 21st Mo., 3 companies of 25th Mo., 2 companies of 12th Mich. and 4 companies of 16th Wisconsin were engaged here April 6, 1862."

Somewhere in this forest of numerals was an illiterate twenty-seven-year-old from Wisconsin named Henry Powers. I left his great-great-grandson there, silently studying the plaque and the field surrounding it.

THE DAY DAWNED just as it had on April 6th in 1862—"clear, beautiful and still," in the words of Sam Watkins, a Confederate private who wrote a famous memoir about the War called *Co. Aytch*. It was at Shiloh that Watkins experienced his first true taste of battle—"seeing the elephant," as Civil War soldiers called it. Fully 85 percent of rebels at Shiloh and 60 percent of Federals had never seen the elephant before. Advancing toward what Watkins called the "bang, boom, whirr-siz-siz-siz" of battle, he saw many of his comrades stricken with loose bowels, and glimpsed one man shooting off a finger to avoid the fight. Watkins's own bravado faltered at a field littered with dead and wounded. "I must confess that I never realized the 'pomp and circumstance' of the thing called glorious war until I saw this," he wrote.

A staggering number of soldiers at Shiloh would never see the elephant again. One in four became casualties of the two-day battle, and the toll on both sides—24,000 in all—surpassed the *combined* American casualties in the Revolutionary War, the War of 1812, and the Mexican War. This "grim arithmetic," as Shelby Foote called it, sobered those both North and South who thought the War would end quickly and with little bloodshed.

I left my car parked by Fraley Field and pushed north on foot, as the Confederates had done after crushing the thin blue line of Yankee scouts. My plan was to take Foote's advice and follow the battle as it progressed through the first day. This would take me across a broad plateau that ended abruptly at a hundred-foot-high bluff by the Tennessee River. Apart from the cliff and several streams and ravines, there were few landmarks. Nor had the battle much altered the terrain. In 1862 generals still hewed to Napoleonic tactics; they thought trench-digging would demoralize troops and discourage them from going on the offensive.

So early on the first day of battle, Confederates easily overran the surprised and unfortified Union camps. Some rebels paused to loot greenbacks, rations and clothes from their better-supplied foes. But the Federals quickly regrouped, and by midmorning Shiloh became a hot, pitched battle. Near Fraley Field, I found a marker quoting a rebel's first sight of stiff Union resistance. "I at last saw a row of little globes of smoke streaked with crimson, breaking out with spurtive quickness from a long line of bluey figures in front; and, simultaneously, there broke upon our ears an appalling crash of sound." The author of this stilted prose was a young journalist-to-be from Arkansas who would later become famous for uttering another improbable phrase: "Dr. Livingstone, I presume?"

Henry Stanley was but one among a cast of future celebrities at Shiloh. The Union generals included Grant (then still an up-and-comer shadowed by rumors of alcoholism), his deputy William Tecumseh Sherman (who had recently returned to the army after a nervous breakdown) and Lew Wallace, later to become author of *Ben Hur*. Also on hand were John Wesley Powell (who lost an arm here, but still navigated the Colorado River and Grand Canyon after the War), William Le Baron Jenney (a future Chicago architect and "father of the skyscraper"), and a young soldier named Ambrose Bierce, whose morbid short story, "An Occurrence at Owl Creek Bridge," would become a staple of junior high reading lists.

Bierce also wrote a nonfiction essay called "What I Saw at Shiloh." What he saw, through his Midwest farmboy's eyes, was a forest so primeval that "I should not have been surprised to see sleek leopards." Leaving the paved road and plunging into the woods, I sensed a bit of what Bierce described. Treetops blotted out the sun. Each path dwindled to a rutted trace before dead-ending in a tangled thicket or brambly streambed. Advancing through these woods, rebel units became so lost and confused that they began slaughtering each other. Friendly fire, or "fratricide incidents" as they were known then, were so endemic at Shiloh that a Louisiana colonel later recalled, "We feared friend more than foe."

Bushwhacking over moss-slick stones and fallen trees, I finally found my way back to a road. It was still an hour before the park's opening time. But I spotted a man in what looked like a rebel uniform, marching alone with a walking stick and a flag I didn't recognize. Catching up with him, I called out hello. He turned, nodded solemnly, and said, "It's a good day to die."

The man's long black hair, droopy mustache and unkempt beard looked appropriately nineteenth century. But his uniform was a mishmash: gray Confederate kepi, blue jeans, work boots, and camouflage jacket. It was the sort of motley getup of which Rob Hodge would disapprove. But Scott Sams wasn't a reenactor, at least not in the usual sense. "This is a religious thing for me," he said. "Christians have Easter Sunday and midnight mass. I've got Shiloh on the anniversary of battle."

Sams was thirty-five and worked at what he called "a pretty dull job," putting phones in boxes at a factory in Chattanooga. Eight years ago, while driving home from Graceland, he'd stopped at Shiloh on what happened to be the battle's anniversary. "The whole Elvis thing seemed so phony to me, but sunrise here was different. I felt this incredible rush I couldn't explain." So he'd returned every April 6th since, driving all night after work and sleeping in his car for the few hours until dawn.

Each year, Sams explored a different aspect of the battle: the role of artillery, for instance, or a theme, such as fear. His costume was a way of getting deeper into the experience, a sort of pilgrim's scallop. The army jacket was the one he'd worn during his own army service in Germany. The flag was a replica of the banner carried by a Tennessee unit at Shiloh.

Sams also carried the same map of the park Bryson Powers had shown me, covered with topographical lines and tiny circles and squares labeling monuments and markers. "I'm a concrete person, not an abstract one," Sams said. "I try to look out over the field and see what they saw. It doesn't fall into place until I look hard at the ground, but then it's click, click, click."

Running his finger across the chart, he explained that the hundreds of red circles denoted "the good guys," while blue represented Union positions. Pointing at a rash of blue and red dots in an otherwise blank section of map labeled Lost Field, he plunged straight into the woods. "My theme for this year is chaos," he called over his shoulder.

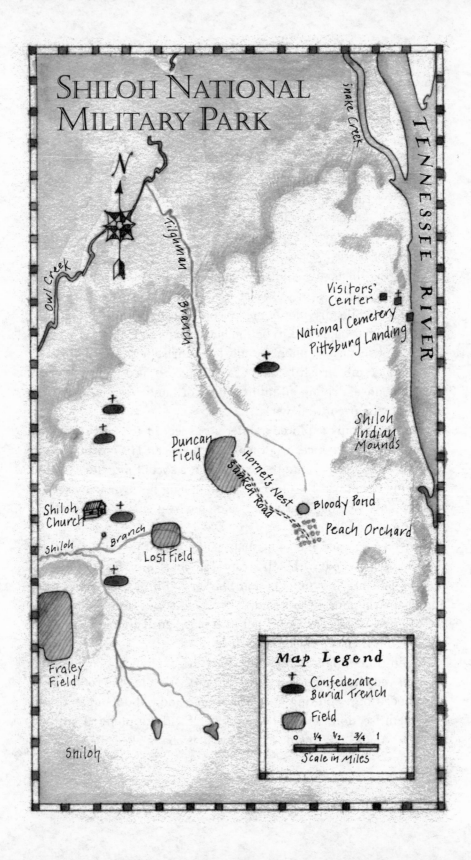

I scrambled after him. Ten minutes later, scratched and sweaty, we emerged in a small clearing. This was the aptly named Lost Field. Several markers to Mississippi units skirted one edge. A marker labeled Burial Place: 49th Illinois Infantry perched at the field's center. Judging from the close-packed graves, this lonely glade had witnessed one of the short, sharp clashes that together comprised what Foote called the "disorganized, murderous fistfight" that was Shiloh.

Sams turned to me with a contented grin. "You always read about the confusion," he said, "with all these panicked units wandering through the woods and bumping into each other." He gazed across the cramped, grave-strewn field. "Click, click, click," he said.

As we straggled back to the road, Sams showed me another grave: a stone in the shape of an oak stump, etched with the name "J. D. Putnam." A short text on the stump said: "His comrades buried him where he fell and cut his name in an oak tree which stood here. In 1901, Thomas Steele recognized the burial place, the name he helped to cut in 1862 still being legible on the stump." The Wisconsin veterans replaced the stump with this granite replica as a permanent marker of their position at the battle.

"I like to think of these old guys coming back and remembering what they went through as young men," Sams said. "No other war in America could both sides come back and say, 'This is where it happened, this is what I did.'"

Glancing at Sams's map, I realized we stood near the scene of the battle's climax, at the so-called Hornet's Nest. I asked Sams if he wanted to have a look. He shook his head. The park opened soon and he wanted to finish his mission before Shiloh filled with visitors. "I've got some chaos to check out over by Bloody Pond," he said, vanishing into the trees.

The Hornet's Nest was a tangled copse of small trees and brush. A split-rail fence ran along its front, just beside a wagon trail known as the Sunken Road. On the other side of the road lay a bucolic pasture called Duncan Field. On the first day at Shiloh, 6,000 Federals crouched in the Hornet's Nest and Sunken Road, fighting back eleven rebel charges across Duncan Field. The twelfth charge—aided by what was then the largest artillery barrage in U.S. history—finally forced the Union defenders to surrender. But the Yankees' staunch defense of the Nest turned the whole battle, stalling the rebels long enough for Grant to regroup and take on reinforcements. Or so I'd always read.

I walked into the middle of Duncan Field and turned slowly in a circle. Here was a 360-degree panorama that corresponded to the Platonic ideal of a Civil War battleground I'd carried in my head since childhood. A broad meadow bounded by wilderness, with a mud-chinked log cabin lying in amongst the trees. The crooked, hand-hewn simplicity of a split-rail fence. The Sunken Road, worn down by pioneer wagons toting apples and timber and corn. Bronze-snouted cannons poking out from between tall oak trees.

Succumbing to a boyish impulse, I rushed the Union line, trying to conjure the buzz of bullets that gave the Hornet's Nest its name. Then, reaching the Nest, I turned and became a Yankee, crouched in the Sunken Road with an imaginary musket resting on the split-rail fence. When I was a boy, the field would have instantly filled with smoke and flame and shrieking rebels. But now, as a fantasy-impaired adult, I found myself glancing around self-consciously to make sure no one was watching.

I sat on a log and gazed at the pastoral scene through grown-up eyes. The Nest was lovely, covered in pine needles and moss and speckled by sunlight glinting through the trees. From this vantage, the whole notion of a "battlefield park" seemed a contradiction in terms. Preserved here for eternity was peace, beauty and quiet—the precise opposite of the events memorialized.

When Ambrose Bierce arrived at Shiloh on the battle's second day, he found a "smoking jungle" quivering with cannon fire and "the sickening spat of lead against flesh." The woods had been reduced to blasted stumps. "All the wretched debris of the battle still littered the spongy earth as far as one could see," Bierce wrote. "Knapsacks, canteens, haversacks distended with soaken and swollen biscuits, blankets beaten into the soil by the rain, rifles with bent barrels or splintered stocks." Mutilated horses lay everywhere, as did men, "all dead apparently, except one."

Bierce studied the wounded man. "He lay face upward, taking in his breath in convulsive, rattling snorts," Bierce wrote. "A bullet had clipped a groove in his skull, above the temple; from this the brain

protruded in bosses, dropping off in flakes and strings. I had not previously known one could get on, even in this unsatisfactory fashion,
with so little brain." Bierce debated whether to bayonet the dying
man, but decided otherwise and marched on.

Now, where 100,000 men had clashed that April day in 1862, I sat
alone on a moss-covered log, listening to a solitary bird warble
somewhere in the trees above.

IF THE RAW FEEL of battle eluded me, another piece of Shiloh's
history was easier to grasp. As Scott Sams pointed out, Shiloh had
two pasts: the actual battle, and its remembrance by those who
fought there. "In our youth our hearts were touched with fire," wrote
Oliver Wendell Holmes, twice wounded in battle. "We have felt,
we still feel, the passion of life at its top." In later life, these same
men helped lay out Shiloh and other battlefield parks, recalling in
Wordsworthian tranquillity the brave deeds of their youth and
memorializing themselves for posterity.

When Shiloh became a park in the 1890s, each state was allowed to
build one monument cut from enduring materials, such as granite,
marble or bronze. Iowa's memorial stood seventy-five feet high,
weighed over half a million pounds, and had to be hauled to Shiloh by
barge and ox. It showed a woman symbolizing "Fame," inscribing the
names of dead Iowans into the monument's stone. A nurturing breast
slipped from her loose robe. Park rangers later confided to me that
Fame nurtured Boy Scouts these days, who snapped pictures of each
other sucking on the monument's marble nipple.

The post-War South couldn't afford monuments on this scale.
Nor were all Southerners enamored of battlefield parks, which diehards regarded as a perfidious scheme to glorify Yankee victory. In
the end, most Southern states did erect monuments at Shiloh, but
not the hundreds of additional memorials to individual units constructed by the North. So, as in war, blue massively outnumbered
gray at Shiloh and most other battlefields.

Also, while Northern monuments tended toward the grandiose
and triumphalist, Southern memorials possessed an elegiac quality
that was somehow more powerful, at least for me. The most striking

by far was a monument honoring soldiers from all Southern states, "Whether sleeping in distant places, or graveless here in traceless dust." Erected by the Daughters of the Confederacy near the high-water mark of the rebel advance at Shiloh, the memorial showed a downcast angel surrendering a laurel wreath to a Grim Reaper–like figure. The sculptor titled his work *Victory Defeated by Death and Night.* The death was that of General Johnston; night referred to the darkness that denied the rebels a chance to complete their near-triumph on the battle's first day.

This was a microcosm in marble of the Lost Cause romance that took hold in the South after Appomattox. The Civil War became an epic might-have-been, a "defeated victory" in which the valorous South succumbed to flukish misfortune—Johnston's untimely death, for instance, or Stonewall Jackson's mortal wounding by his own men at Chancellorsville—and to the North's superior manpower and materiel. I later found a program from the monument's unveiling in 1917, which revealed another side to the unreconciled South. It noted the various objects placed in the monument's cornerstone for eternity: flags, coins, a lock of General Johnston's hair, and a photograph of two local dignitaries "in Ku-Klux regalia."

Just beyond *Victory Defeated,* I reached a simple hunk of stone chiseled with the names of Alabamans who fought at Shiloh. A mini-van drove up with a bumper sticker that read "World's Greatest Grandpa." Leaping from the van, an elderly woman in a floppy hat ran her finger along the monument. "He's still here!" she shouted toward the van. Then to me: "That's my great-grandfather, Captain Thomas Jenkins."

His great-granddaughter was a retired Alabama teacher named Edwina. She'd first visited Shiloh with her children in the 1960s and had now returned with her teenaged grandson. "We're here so he can learn about his Southernness," she said. Her grandson sat in the van's backseat, listening to a Walkman. The world's greatest grandpa perched impatiently behind the van's wheel with the engine running.

I asked Edwina what she meant by "Southernness."

"My husband's a Northerner—from Boston, the worst kind—and

he'll always be one," she said. "We're like night and day and we've been married forty-three years. He's English and I'm Scottish, in ancestry and temperament. I'm very careful about how I come across to others. Not him. The other day we're at the movies and people in front of us are talking. I was bothered but I didn't say anything. He shouted at them, 'You know there are others here!' I could have melted through the floor."

I wasn't sure what to make of this civil war. But Edwina reminded me. "He wants to tell people how to do things, the same way the North tells the South how to live, and did back then."

Her husband honked the horn. From what Edwina had said, it seemed remarkable that she and the world's greatest grandpa had stayed together forty-three years. "My South is my South," Edwina shouted as the minivan sped off, leaving me alone with Captain Thomas Jenkins and his brave Alabamans. I reckoned they'd be pleased to know their efforts hadn't been entirely in vain.

I pressed on, to Bloody Pond. It was here, at the height of the first day's fighting, that men from both armies crawled to drink water and soak their wounds. Like other stops on the battlefield, the pond's bank had a stand with a small audio speaker. I pushed a button and heard the testimony of a local man who visited soon after the battle. "There were dead men and horses, broken artillery carriages and dismounted guns in the pond. Soldiers taking dead men out of the water and laying them in rows on the bank. The water looked like blood." Now, a father and daughter stood on the bank, skipping stones across the clear, cool water.

Parked nearby was a convertible Mercedes with a vanity license plate: MAYS. A paunchy man in an Izod shirt stood riffling through a briefcase balanced on the roof. Bill Mays was a lawyer from Missouri. He'd arranged his caseload so he could slip away from his office and drive six hours to be here on Shiloh's anniversary. Like the bus driver I'd met at Fraley Field, Mays had come to track the path of his forebear, a rebel private named Elijah.

Mays dug through his briefcase for one of the elaborate park maps I'd seen several times already. "I'm a lawyer, so I always look for what the preponderance of the evidence suggests," he said. He knew that Elijah fought with the 52nd Tennessee, in a place called Cloud Field. A red dot on the map, near where we now stood, denoted a marker to the Tennessee men. But Mays was having trouble finding the corresponding spot on the ground.

I followed him as he plunged, briefcase in hand, in what he guessed was the direction of the monument. Within minutes, we were lost in thigh-high undergrowth. "I've been to battlefields in Virginia—they're like golf courses compared to this," he said, Izod shirt stained with sweat. As we rested on a log, swatting gnats, I asked Mays why it was so important to track his great-grandfather's precise movements 133 years ago.

"I'm here because the issues are still here," he said. "People still want to be independent of central authority. The evidence suggests that rebels like Elijah believed strongly in their individual right to determine what their government should be." He started to open his briefcase, then paused, as though realizing he wasn't in court. "I'm a Republican," he went on. "Tracking down Elijah gives me some perspective on what it is I believe in, and what commitment to your beliefs is all about."

It went deeper than that. The South's failure to stop the North at Shiloh ultimately led Elijah's unit to another great battle at Chickamauga. Captured there, Elijah was sent to a prison camp in Indiana where he died a few weeks before the War's end. Soon after, Elijah's widow died of cholera, so their kids were raised by a brother who moved to Missouri, near where Bill now lived. "Ultimately, I guess, I'm trying to figure out what my place in the big picture is," Mays said. "I am who I am, geographically and politically, because of what happened here."

Mays picked up his briefcase and headed deeper into the woods. I stayed on the log and rested awhile. Until now, I'd regarded others' retracing of their ancestral footsteps as a bit odd and obsessive. Like birdwatchers who tramped around the globe, fanatically compiling "life lists," these combat genealogists seemed to be missing the forest for the trees.

But Mays's story forced me to recall a lonely trip of my own, ten years before, to a remote region of what was then still the Soviet Union. Armed with old maps and a family memoir, I'd trudged through ankle-high mud until I found the wagon road my father's father traveled on the day his family fled Czarist Russia. The road ultimately led to a Baltic seaport, to Ellis Island, to me. As Mays had put it, I was who I was because of what happened on that muddy trace in 1906. Thinking back on the trip, I felt envious of Mays and the others I'd met at Shiloh. They had a blood tie to a patch of American soil that I never would.

AT MIDDAY I REACHED the visitors' center, a modern building near the Tennessee River. A park ranger named Paul Hawke collected my two-dollar entrance fee. I confessed that I'd already gotten my money's worth wandering Shiloh since dawn.

Hawke smiled. "One of the pilgrims. We get them every year. Every day, really." Hawke's last posting was Pea Ridge, an Arkansas battlefield just off the interstate. "You could tell that half the people stopping there had just seen a sign for a national park on the highway and thought, 'Clean bathrooms—let's stop!'" He'd also worked at Gettysburg, which drew thousands of tourists who knew little about the battle, except that it was one of those sites to which all parents should drag their kids. But accidental tourists rarely turned up at Shiloh. "It's not on the way to anyplace," Hawke said, "so you tend to get a very devoted breed."

Shiloh's isolation, though, hadn't spared it a growing problem at battlefields across America. The boom market in Civil War relics had unleashed scores of treasure hunters who scavenged after dark with metal detectors. Rangers now patrolled the park with night-vision goggles and had once nabbed two men toting over 130 artifacts. Relics also turned up accidentally; just a month before my visit, a gardener found a live cannonball while planting grass near the visitors' center. "The dud ratio for Civil War ordnance was fifty percent or more," Hawke said, "so there's still a lot of unexploded stuff lying under the ground."

Hawke, it turned out, specialized in such half-hidden remnants of the Civil War. As part of his park duties, he tramped through the woods around Corinth, searching for earthen defenses thrown up by the Confederates. Hawke had even founded the "Civil War Fortification Study Group," which met annually to discuss new research on earthworks. The prosaic nature of the subject appealed to Hawke's modest nature. "We tend always to focus on the biggest and bloodiest events in war," he said. "But if you think about it, earthworks are the one tangible survival from the Civil War put there by soldiers themselves for the express purpose of fighting."

Hawke conceded, though, that earthworks weren't always that tangible. Most had so eroded that they remained invisible to the naked eye at ground level. But their imprints could be spotted in infrared photographs taken from the air.

"Wars leave what's called 'ghost marks' on the landscape," Hawke said. This struck me as an apt metaphor for the traces of Civil War memory I myself had been searching for in the course of my journey.

As I chatted with Hawke we were joined by an imposing figure with a handle-bar mustache, tight jeans, cowboy boots, a Stetson and tortoise-shell glasses. He looked like a bookish gunslinger. He turned out to be the park's historian, Stacy Allen, who agreed to take a few minutes to answer some questions I had about Shiloh.

As it happened, we spoke for three hours and toured the whole battlefield. By the time we were done, this somber, bespectacled Kansan had made me wonder if everything I thought I knew about Shiloh—and about many other battles—was closer to fiction than to fact.

Allen's revisionism sprang from his academic training as a physical anthropologist. "Traditional historians tend to ignore the best primary source out there—the ground," he began. "If you read it right, you realize a lot of the written history is simply wrong."

Most history books, for instance, described the 1862 terrain at Shiloh as covered in impenetrable spring woods. But after watching spring unfold for six years at Shiloh, Allen began to wonder if this was really so. Studying old weather charts and nineteenth-century farm records, he discovered that spring came to Shiloh very late in 1862. Most trees remained bare. Allen also learned that Shiloh's farmers cleared their land for crops and fenced livestock out of the fields. So cattle and hogs roamed the woods, chewing the undergrowth and trampling it down. "Overall, the landscape was still pretty wintry at the time of the battle," he said. The confusion at the battle, he added, was probably due more to smoke, dust and poor maps than to dense foliage.

Allen also studied what lay under the ground. After the two-day fight in 1862, Grant ordered the dead of both armies buried in mass graves "along the line of battle"—in other words, where they fell. It was therefore logical to conclude that the burial trenches indicated where the heaviest fighting occurred. Yet no burial trenches had ever been found near the Hornet's Nest, where Union defenders supposedly turned the battle by beating back repeated rebel assaults across Duncan Field.

"Strange, isn't it," he said, driving me back to the Sunken Road and gazing out at Duncan Field. "There were supposedly eleven or twelve charges here, yet we can't find many bodies to speak of." Allen had also studied the rosters of the units that fought in and around the Hornet's Nest. He found that their casualty rates were much lighter than for others at Shiloh.

Again, the landscape offered a clue, at least in Allen's view. The historic tablets scattered across Shiloh had been carefully placed by a battlefield commission in the 1890s, with the help of returning veterans. Each tablet was intended to mark the exact spot where individual units fought. Yet there were no such markers in Duncan Field. Instead, markers for Southern units that fought here clustered in the woods on either side of the pasture.

"Grandpa was brave but he wasn't stupid," Allen said. "He avoided that field. Wouldn't you?" In the end, he'd documented only one attempted charge across Duncan Field and concluded that the other assaults—seven in all, not eleven—worked their way along the thicket bordering the pasture.

Allen also believed that heedless assaults across open ground were much rarer throughout the War than was commonly supposed. The most notable exceptions, such as Franklin and Pickett's Charge, proved the rule: frontal attacks had become suicidal because of newly improved rifles that could kill at seven hundred yards. Rifled guns, which replaced the much faultier smoothbore muskets used in earlier wars, also cut down another romantic staple of Civil War lore: bayonet combat. Allen had found almost no hard evidence of hand-to-hand fighting at Shiloh, and suspected the same was true at other battles. In fact, bayonets and sabers accounted for only one half of 1 percent of wounds in the Civil War. I later learned that there wasn't one confirmed bayonet wound in all of Pickett's Charge.

Allen's sleuthing revealed another twist to the story of the Hornet's Nest. He'd done time-and-motion studies of units that later claimed to have fought in and around the Nest. It turned out many of them couldn't possibly have done so. Allen smiled. He'd come to the kicker of his story. "When you look at the whole battle," he said, "what actually happened here was almost incidental to the outcome."

In Allen's version, the crucial combat at Shiloh occurred on either side of the Nest, where the South concentrated its first-day attack. Some rebel units from these flank assaults made piecemeal contact with the Nest during the day. But it was only after the rebels had pushed the Union back on both flanks that they converged on the Nest, which had by then become a lonely Union salient. So the main reason the Federals in the Nest hung on so long was because the Confederates were busy hammering other positions for most of the day.

The obvious question, then, was why the Hornet's Nest assumed such prominence in history books. Here, Allen turned from physical anthropology to psychology. "Let's put ourselves in the heads of those Yankees in the Hornet's Nest," he said, pacing up and down the Sunken Road. "We're in this thicket where we can't see the rest of the battlefield. There's rebels coming at us, in bits and pieces, all day long. Then suddenly we're still here and everyone else has retreated. It seems like we fought the whole battle on our own."

As prisoners, Allen went on, the 2,200 men captured at the Nest had months to talk over the battle and also to bond with each other. After the War, they formed a vocal veterans' group called the Hornet's Nest Brigade, led by their commanding officer, Benjamin Prentiss, an influential politician who outlived most of his contemporaries. "He was eager to foster the impression that the Hornet's Nest and his role there were crucial to the battle," Allen said. "He played it up big, particularly later in his life."

So gradually the myth grew, until the Hornet's Nest became the battle's turning point. The Sunken Road, in fact, wasn't even called that in initial reports of the battle. But as time passed, the shallow wagon trace became deeper and deeper in veterans' memories, eventually leading to its nickname. "Grant once said that Shiloh was the most misunderstood battle of the Civil War," Allen concluded. "It's taken me awhile to grasp how true that was."

From the Hornet's Nest, Allen led me to the woods and narrow fields near the Shiloh church, where he believed the battle had in fact turned. It was here that the oncoming rebels almost crushed the Federal right flank. But Sherman's men held, fell back, counterattacked and stalled the Southern advance. Again, the landscape told the story. All around us rose monuments to Midwestern units that sustained losses of 30 percent or more. Scattered among these slabs were Confederate burial trenches, well-manicured rectangles of grass bordered by cannonballs. They looked rather like putting greens. One burial pit held over 700 rebels, stacked seven deep. Four of the five known burial trenches at Shiloh lay near here.

Allen said that rangers on morning patrol sometimes found Ouija boards, divining rods, notes to the dead—even a funeral card with a picture of a man whose cremated ashes had been spread here in the night. "One woman came into the visitors' center saying she'd been meditating by one of the pits and had communicated with a soldier named Billy Joe, who told her 'he wanted out of there,'" Allen said. "I'm sure he did."

Allen believed the actual body count at Shiloh was double the official figure of 3,500 dead. At this early stage of the War, neither army had any real system for handling casualties. On the first night at Shiloh, hundreds of soldiers lay ungathered on the battlefield. Allen had found accounts of hogs enjoying a "carnival feast" of the dead. Some parts of the battlefield also caught fire, roasting both dead and wounded men. Ambrose Bierce, of course, made a clinical examination of one such assembly: "Their clothing was half burnt away—their hair and beard entirely; the rain had come too late to save their nails." In the end, many bodies may simply have vanished without ever being counted.

Wounded men who survived long enough to receive medical care also fared poorly. Allen guessed that fully 2,500 of those listed as wounded at Shiloh later perished from their wounds, often super-ficial injuries that became infected. Prisoners also died at a stagger-ing rate, usually from dysentery.

A few weeks before visiting Shiloh, I'd gone to the National Archives in Washington and perused reports from wartime field hos-pitals. Doctors listed the treatment given each soldier, typically am-putation, splinting, or a "water dressing," a wet bandage that did little but spread infection (doctors didn't learn about sepsis until after the War). Doctors also wrote brief follow-ups on their patients. Among the most common notations: "probably mortal," "died of tetanus," and the oddly redundant "mortally, died."

But what had struck me most were the doctors' notes on what they called the "seat of injury" for each soldier. An astonishing number of wounds were seated in the "testicle" or "thigh and privates" or "leg and scrotum." Allen explained the grisly logic of this. Officers con-stantly implored their men to "aim low" to avoid firing over the heads of the oncoming enemy. "Also, human beings have a tendency to shoot towards the center mass," he added. "So you see a lot of hits to the abdomen and groin."

To Allen, the full details of these and other horrors of Civil War battle were only beginning to emerge from the mythic haze envelop-ing the conflict. "Each generation sees the War differently, and that's why interest in it will never die," he said. The first generation—the veterans themselves—tended to couch tales of battle in high-blown Victorian prose about courage and sacrifice. "It wasn't their style to dwell on the graphic details of injury and death," Allen said. (An ob-vious exception was Ambrose Bierce, shot in the head at Kennesaw Mountain and deeply embittered by his wartime experience.)

Later historians, relying heavily on veterans' accounts, also glossed over the War's grisly side, highlighting instead the battle tactics and personalities of generals. But Allen, born in the mid-1950s, belonged to a generation that had grown up watching the Vietnam War on the nightly news.

"I think the next phase of Civil War scholarship—my generation's phase—will be to hit the American public with the reality of how horrible the War really was," he said. "You read surgeons' reports and learn that a big problem wasn't just missiles, but also bits of clothing and leather and grime and flesh that got blown into wounds. The teeth and bone from others ahead of you could be deadly projectiles, too." He paused, pointing at a line of cannon on the battlefield. "We look at these nice beautiful weapons and tend to forget what they did to the human body."

Driving back toward the visitors' center, Allen pulled in at the most popular stop on the Shiloh auto tour: the site of Albert Sidney Johnston's death. I'd recorded the scene in the crude cyclorama painted on the walls of my childhood attic, with a bullet arcing cometlike across the woods and striking Johnston in the chest. In reality, Johnston bled to death from a wound in the back of his knee and might have been saved by a simple tourniquet.

Allen walked me to a tree stump marking the site. The stump listed so precariously that it had to be supported, like a ship's mast, by halyards running between the tree and an iron fence surrounding it. A plaque said the stump was all that remained of the tall oak tree under which one of Johnston's aides, Isham Harris, found his wounded commander reeling in the saddle. Harris dragged Johnston into a ravine, where the general soon expired. In 1896, Harris returned to identify the spot for posterity.

Allen let me study the stump for a moment, then said, "We haven't done dendrochronology to determine the stump's age, but we have studied old photos of the tree it belonged to." He paused. "It probably wasn't here in 1862, and if it was it couldn't have been more than a sapling."

Before permanent monuments went up across the park, key sites were marked with signs nailed to trees. So after Isham Harris located the spot, a sign went up on the nearest tree, saying "Johnston death site"—though the ravine where he actually died lay some distance away. Early visitors apparently became confused and assumed the tree marked the exact spot and the exact tree under which Johnston died. Allen also thought it likely that the septugenarian Harris, searching Shiloh's woods thirty-four years after the battle, got the site wrong altogether.

"Either way," Allen said, "we're worshiping a rotten piece of wood that probably wasn't here at the time of battle." But the storm-damaged tree had been revered for so long that efforts by Allen and other rangers to uproot the stump had provoked protests—even anonymous letters threatening, "If you remove that tree you'll be sorry." So the stump survived, a relic of misremembered history. "Legends die hard," Allen said. "But Mother Nature is doing a good job on that tree for us. It'll be gone before long."

Allen left me there, beside the oak impostor, feeling exhilarated but also unsettled by his decoding of the battlefield. Before setting off on my journey, I'd known that heated debate still raged around the War's causes and legacy. But I'd naively assumed that scholars had closed the book on battlefield matters. After all, Shelby Foote and others relied on the authoritative-sounding *Official Records of the Union and Confederate Armies*, known as the O.R. to Civil War buffs. The O.R., 128 volumes in all, were compiled by the government soon after the War, mostly from firsthand reports. Historians could also turn to the vast, Talmudic body of interpretive literature published on the War since.

But if Allen was right, this received wisdom was riddled with inaccuracies, false memory and self-serving distortions. Nor was he a lonely revisionist. I later learned that Civil War scholars were rethinking numerous battles and questioning the reliability of long-revered sources. After Gettysburg, for instance, Robert E. Lee—presaging the doctored body counts in Vietnam—fudged his report on the debacle and the appalling casualties he sustained. Lee also ordered George Pickett to destroy his scathing report on the disastrous charge that bore his name.

Even pictures could lie. New research revealed that the captions on many well-known photographs were wrong. And some of the War's most famous pictures were staged, with corpses dragged across battlefields and posed for dramatic effect. Historians had also found previously untapped sources—wartime diaries, unpublished letters, obscure court records—that led to wholly new assessments of familiar subjects.

Trying to make sense of all this, I later called back Shelby Foote. He calmly acknowledged that Stacy Allen's view of Shiloh might well be valid, and that all of his own generation's work was open to challenge. "I could redo my entire three volumes on the Civil War without using one bit of source material I used the first time," he said, "and probably come to very different conclusions."

But this didn't bother Foote. Like Stacy Allen, he felt each generation had to reinterpret the Civil War by its own lights. "I don't think that I could have written what I wrote in less than a hundred years after the War," he said. "It took that long for North and South to see each other honestly through the dust and flame."

Now, it seemed, a new generation had to cut through some of the dust and flame kicked up by Shelby Foote and his peers.

LEAVING JOHNSTON'S DEATH SITE, I trudged back to the Sunken Road. It was now ten hours since my arrival on the battle-field. I was famished, footsore and burnt by the Tennessee sun. Resting for a moment, I caught sight of a lanky figure in sky-blue trousers, a trim blue jacket and a Federal kepi. The only Northerner I'd met at Shiloh was the bus driver from Minneapolis. So I decided to ambush one more Yankee before calling it a day and retreating, like the rebels, to Corinth.

Up close, the man's "impression" appeared carefully crafted: hand-made brogans, period spectacles, a bayonet scabbard and a canteen slung just so across his chest. He stood before a tall monument with a book open in his hands.

"Excuse me," I said, "could I ask you something?"

The man looked up from his reading. "Yes?"

"I'm researching a book about memory of the Civil War—"

"That's odd," he interrupted. "So am I." He spoke formally, with a slight accent I couldn't place. Then he said, "Are you by any chance Tony Horwitz?"

I studied him again. "Do I know you from somewhere?"

He smiled and thrust out a hand. "I am Wolfgang Hochbruck of the University of Stuttgart in Germany. I sent you an e-mail months ago. You never responded."

Before setting out on my journey, I'd posted an Internet query with a Civil War chat group, searching for ideas and contacts. The first flood of responses proved so soporific—mostly lists of unpublished monographs on obscure regiments—that I'd quickly stopped tuning in. Then I'd hit the road and forgotten all about my cyberspace foray. Wolfgang must have tried to contact me some time after that.

"Sorry," I said. "What did you message me?"

"That we should compare notes," Wolfgang said. "What were you about to ask me a moment ago?"

"Why you're standing out here in the sun in a blue uniform, looking at that monument."

He handed me the book he'd been studying: Shelby Foote's *Shiloh*. Wolfgang said he'd first read the novel at age nine in German translation and identified with one of the characters, an immigrant artilleryman named Otto Flickner. Foote based Otto's story on the history of an actual unit from Minnesota, Munch's Battery, which saw action near the Hornet's Nest.

Thirty years later, Wolfgang was now making the same sort of pilgrimage as the lawyer from Missouri and the bus driver from Minnesota. Lacking a real forebear at Shiloh, he'd found a surrogate in the fictional Otto Flickner and was retracing his steps across the battleground. The monument he now stood before showed a Minnesota artilleryman holding what looked like a giant cotton swab. "I am wearing the uniform," Wolfgang said, "because I thought it would add to the experience of being Otto."

Otto Flickner was an odd choice of characters to inhabit. In the novel, Otto abandoned his position and fled all the way to the Union rear. This, too, was based on fact; during the first day's fighting, many Union soldiers broke and ran.

Wolfgang knew all about Otto's flight; it's what drew him to the character. "He watched the Confederates come charging, again and again, shooting and screaming. Then he ran." Wolfgang paused. "Wouldn't you?"

He opened *Shiloh* again and consulted a map to locate the next stop on Otto's retreat route. This German professor and I obviously had a lot to talk about. So I bummed a few swigs from his canteen and hobbled along as he hiked briskly through the woods.

En route, I learned about Wolfgang's boyhood in the 1960s, which eerily mirrored my own. His father often traveled to the United States on business and returned with Civil War gifts for his son. Wolfgang played with the same plastic soldiers I had. He'd built cabins out of Lincoln Logs. He'd even pored over the same, wonderfully illustrated Time-Life book on Civil War battles that I'd studied.

As he recounted these memories, Wolfgang pointed out an obvious circumstance I'd somehow missed. The early 1960s coincided with the Civil War centennial. Battle reenactments began in earnest; hundreds of Civil War books were published; war-related games, toy cannons and other mass merchandise abounded as never before. This helped explain why Wolfgang's father returned home with Civil War trinkets. It also shed light on my own childhood fixation, which I'd tended to view, in a self-congratulatory way, as the eccentric passion of a boy born in the wrong century. Perhaps I'd been the opposite, a creature of twentieth-century commercial culture who had simply latched onto a product line current at the time. Other boys thrilled to John Glenn and spaceship models; I preferred Honest Abe and Lincoln Logs.

We reached a riverside bluff topped by flat-topped mounds. A marker explained that the mounds were believed to have been platforms for ancient Indian temples. Scrambling on top of one of the mounds, as Confederate scouts had done during the battle, we gazed down on the Tennessee. It was just as I'd imagined: a wide, lazy river coiling through the countryside, with sandy bluffs and deep woods lining the opposite shore.

Wolfgang was also matching the vista against his childhood imagining. Just below us lay the steep cliffs beneath which Otto Flickner and several thousand real-life skulkers had sought refuge from the battle. Some even waded out in their frenzy to flee the fighting. "So this is it," Wolfgang murmured. "I have always wondered what became of Otto on the second day of battle."

When I asked why he identified so strongly with Otto, Wolfgang told me about his own military service. Drafted into the German navy at eighteen, he'd served as a torpedo man on a destroyer and found himself, like Otto, cramming projectiles into guns, in this case antisubmarine weapons. Wolfgang proved a capable seaman and the navy wanted to promote him. But he'd seen one of his fellow crewmen commit suicide and several others "turn into monsters around all these weapons." So he chose to become a conscientious objector and argued his case before a military panel. Citing Gandhi and Martin Luther King, he won release from the navy and later convinced three other torpedomen to follow his lead.

"I said to myself after that, 'I'll never wear a uniform again.'" He fingered his Yankee costume. "Now, here I am."

Like me, Wolfgang had retrieved his childhood passion only recently. Accompanying his wife to America while she researched a Ph.D. thesis, Wolfgang discovered all the contemporary publications devoted to the Civil War. Then, on a weekend outing, he stumbled on a reenactment. "I realized there was this whole culture, or cult really, surrounding memory of the Civil War," he said. Returning to Germany, Wolfgang began teaching American Studies classes that took as their syllabus *The Red Badge of Courage, Gettysburg, Gone With the Wind,* and other Civil War novels and films.

Wolfgang had also formed a reenacting troop in Stuttgart, modeled on a German-American unit, the 3rd Missouri. The original 3rd Missouri included many left-wing political exiles who carried a red flag emblazoned with a hammer smashing chains. The new 3rd Missouri was almost as odd, including several women, four conscientious objectors and a U.S. Army chaplain. All portrayed privates. "Our democratic traditions must be remembered," Wolfgang explained. The proceeds his troop solicited at reenactments were donated to a refugee camp in Bosnia.

We sat there quietly for a while, watching barges float past on the river. I felt as though I'd stumbled on a body-double, a doppelgänger, here in the woods of Shiloh. Like Wolfgang, I'd drifted from a childhood fascination with the Civil War to adolescent embarrassment about it, and then to a deep distrust of all things military. Yet both of us had found outlets for our childhood obsession. Wolfgang studied war, I wrote about it. During my time overseas, I'd kept gravitating toward combat zones: in Iraq, Lebanon, the Sudan, Bosnia, Northern Ireland. For someone who professed a hatred of guns, I'd spent an awful lot of time watching people shoot at each other. "Nothing in life is so exhilarating as to be shot at without result," Winston Churchill memorably observed of his own time as a war correspondent.

For Wolfgang, as for many Germans of his generation, fascination with war was freighted with a much more complex self-doubt. "It is not easy to grow up with the knowledge of belonging to one of the most destructive people in world history," he said. "I think some of the Confederate reenactors in Germany are acting out Nazi fantasies of racial superiority. They are obsessed with your war because they cannot celebrate their own vanquished racists. Most of these people are Bavarians, of course."

Wolfgang, on the other hand, always played Union soldiers. He also hoped that both his academic work and his reenacting would ultimately buttress a pacifist message. "My thesis so far is that Civil War remembrance reflects a movement towards more civility and peace," he said. "In reenactments, North and South get along, they work together. And look at all the people who dress as civilians. Maybe if we played at war more instead of really using weapons, our world would be a better place." He laughed. "Of course, it is possible my thesis is nonsense."

We walked toward the last stop on Wolfgang's tour, the National Cemetery, where Union dead were moved after the War from their original burial trenches. It was now late afternoon and the monuments cast long, cool shadows across the freshly mowed grass. Most of the graves were marked only with stone stumps labeled "Unknown." Some recorded a few initials or other fragments of soldiers' identities: J. Pe——Ia, Mosely, H.O.K. I'd learned from the park historian Stacy Allen that neither army at Shiloh had dog tags to identify corpses. Comrades of the dead sometimes pinned bits of paper to their friends' uniforms, or put names in bottles or Bibles, which were then placed in dead men's pockets. Even so, the names of all the Confederates buried at Shiloh and most of the Federals remained unknown.

As we left the graveyard, a man in a Confederate kepi spotted Wolfgang and shook a fist, shouting in mock fury, "We'll git you next time, Yank!"

"Oh yes?" Wolfgang replied, playing along. "At Gettysburg?"

The man smiled. "What unit you in?"

"The Third Missouri. Stuttgart, Germany."

"No shit!" The man fumbled in his haversack and took out a camera. "Mind if I snap a picture? This'll blow my buddies' minds."

Wolfgang posed politely. Then the man thanked him and shook his hand. "Yankees in Germany. Man, that's something."

As the man wandered off, Wolfgang smiled wearily. He often got odd responses when he told people he was German. Occasionally, reenactors would confide that they liked to do World War II re-enactments—dressed in SS uniforms—when they weren't doing the Civil War. Mostly, though, people just thought Wolfgang was strange. Tired of explaining himself, he'd concocted a phony German-American ancestor in the 3rd Missouri. "That way, when people ask why I'm here, I can just mention him. Otherwise, they think I've gone off the rails."

Wolfgang's wife, Sabine, stood waiting at the visitors' center with the indulgent smile of a mother watching her muddy son trudge home from a football game.

"How did you spend your day?" Wolfgang asked her.

"Like an adult. Reading a book at the motel."

When Wolfgang introduced us, Sabine asked me if I liked to collect Civil War relics. I shook my head. "Your wife is lucky, then," she said. "We only have two rooms in Stuttgart. Last time in America Wolfgang started gathering—what do you call it, grape nuts?"

"Grape shot," I said.

"Actually," Wolfgang said, "they were minié balls."

"He also wanted to buy a rusty thing," Sabine said.

"A bayonet," Wolfgang said.

"It was big, like a sword. It would have taken up the whole shelf."

Even so, Sabine now participated in her husband's obsession. At first, she said, reenactments made her uncomfortable. "We still have real civil wars going on in Europe. It does not seem like play to me." But Wolfgang had persuaded her to join in, dressed as a nineteenth-century nurse or as a teacher of freed slaves. "It is like Carnival in Brazil," she said. "You get in costume and be who you want to be for a few days. It is a second chance." It was also a refreshing break from her own academic field: American political rhetoric in the 1960s. "In the 1860s, I think, people spoke more plainly than in the 1960s," she said.

I went with Wolfgang and Sabine to dinner at a nearby catfish restaurant, then back to their motel, where we drank sourmash bourbon and sifted through the clutter they'd accumulated in their travels: battle flags, reenactors' mess kits, a windup toy in the shape of a cotton boll that played a tinny rendition of "Dixie." "Research material," Wolfgang said. Sabine rolled her eyes. At midnight we stood in the motel parking lot, exchanging addresses and phone numbers and promises to stay in touch.

"I'll answer your e-mail next time," I said.

"I am glad you didn't before," Wolfgang said. "It was much better that we met on the field of battle."

9

Mississippi
THE MINIÉ BALL
PREGNANCY

The old South was plowed under.
But the ashes are still warm.
—HENRY MILLER, *The Air-Conditioned Nightmare*, 1945

Backwoods Mississippi, a myth-encrusted badlands for so many Americans, was for me the most familiar ground in the South. As a union organizer in the early 1980s, I'd trolled thousands of miles of Mississippi byways in search of new members. Fifteen years later, I could still recite the litany of absurdly named crossroads I'd chanted to myself during long, lonely drives: Hot Coffee, Its, Soso, Chunky, Whynot, Scooba, Shivers, Jumpertown, Prismatic, Basic City.

But rereading the diary of my time in Mississippi, I was struck by how rarely I'd noted anything to do with the Civil War. Here and there I'd recorded a monument's inscription ("The Men Who Wore the Gray Were Right and Right Can Never Die"), or pondered a clump of rebel graves poking from the weeds between a Jiffy-Mart and a shoe factory. But at twenty-two my Civil War virus still lay in remission; blues bars and Ole Miss coeds stirred me more deeply than cannons and cemeteries. Also, compared to other Southern states east of the Mississippi, the homeland of Faulkner and Foote compassed relatively few sites of Civil War renown.

Except, of course, Vicksburg, where I headed now after winding through the state along the Natchez Trace, an antebellum trade route that had become a scenic highway. Perched on steep bluffs overlooking a meander loop of the Mississippi, Vicksburg once commanded the river's narrowest and wildest point south of Memphis. Boats bobbed and twisted in Vicksburg's eddies, often running aground; before the War, the life span of a Mississippi steamboat averaged only two years. In wartime, Union gunboats faced the added challenge of firing accurately from yawing decks. The Confederates, firing back from Vicksburg's swamp-skirted bluffs, were able to choke traffic down the river and cling to the city long after other ports fell. It was only by attacking from land as well as from water, and then laying siege, that Grant finally brought down "the Gibraltar of the West."

Ten years after the War, the Mississippi River changed course, leaving Vicksburg high and dry and accomplishing in an instant what Grant fought for months to achieve: a way past the town. Engineers later cut a channel, redirecting a nearby waterway beneath the city's bluffs. Now, instead of the mighty Mississippi, it was the uneuphonious "Yazoo Diversion Canal" that lapped at the shore of what Mark Twain, in a rare lapse from cynicism, dubbed the "lofty hill-city."

Vicksburg's waterfront underwent another transformation with Mississippi's embrace of legalized gambling in the early 1990s. During my last visit, in 1981, the town had seemed picturesquely seedy, a sort of downmarket Natchez with cannons and kudzu. Now it was just seedy. Washington Street, once the town's elegant main thoroughfare, had become a hideous gash catering to the gambling trade: cheap motels, pawn shops, check-cashing shops, J. M. Fly Rent-All, Dr. Junk's buy-sell-trade!, Mrs. Harris Spiritual Advisor, and RV parks with streets named Double Diamond Drive and Avenue of Aces.

The occasional cannon or bronze Confederate bust were now lost amidst neon billboards flashing REEL WINNERS! and LOOSEST SLOTS

IN TOWN! During the wartime siege, Confederates set cotton bales alight on the riverbank so gunners could see Union ships slipping by in the night. Now, it was Harrah's and other casinos that cast an eerie, twenty-four-hour glow across the water.

Stopping at the grandly named Vicksburg Convention and Visitors' Bureau, I chatted with the office manager, a woman named Lenore. She'd first started working in tourism twenty years before. "Back then, we were just a double-wide trailer off the interstate," she said. "When people stopped in, I'd take out a city map and circle all six tourist sites—basically the battlefield and a few old houses." Now Vicksburg boasted "27 bonafide attractions," though bonafide seemed a strange word to describe faux-riverboat casinos ringed by theme parks, putt-putt golf courses and Bayou Bash Bumper Boats.

Few gamblers, though, bothered to see Vicksburg's historic sites. So Lenore lay awake nights, trying to dream up a visitors' slogan that might encourage more crossover. At the door, she tried one on for size. "Gamble in the Lap of History." She paused. "What do you think? Too tacky?"

It was hard to think of anything too tacky to describe a town with a Casino Faulkner's Gift Shop, a street named Cool Millions Lane, and flyers that proclaimed: VIVA LAS VICKSBURG. One casino, the Ameristar, replicated a nineteenth-century steamboat, with a paddle wheel, smokestacks and layer-cake decks. The historical resemblance was ruined somewhat by the casino's size—seven times that of an actual steamboat—and by the boat's immobility. Fixed to a permanently moored barge, the boat squatted like an oversized bathtub toy in a small, shielded lagoon (Mississippi gaming laws required that all casinos occupy bodies of water, however contrived).

I checked into Harrah's, which mercifully limited its old-timey touches to blackjack dealers in dark cravats and murals of nineteenth-century river scenes. After a brief, losing visit to the slots, I left the cucumber-cool casino and started up the steep bluff leading to Vicksburg's old town. The sky was the color of unpolished pewter, the air so leaden that I seemed to be pushing through a force field. Halfway up, my shirt and hair were soaked with sweat and my customary trot had slowed to a plod. It was May, the same month when the siege of Vicksburg began in 1863. I tried to imagine Union soldiers, mostly

Midwestern farm boys, sweating through their wool uniforms and praying that the rebels would capitulate before they themselves succumbed to the Deep South summer.

Crowning the hilltop was the Vicksburg I dimly recalled from my earlier visit: brick Victorian storefronts and antebellum mansions, some still harboring Union cannonballs in their walls. I shuffled along the one level street in sight, toward a comforting-sounding dot on my map marked Coca-Cola Museum (the beverage was first bottled in Vicksburg in 1894). On the way, I paused at a quaint, false-fronted shop marked "Corner Drug Store." Cannonballs flanked the door and a curious mix of items—dueling pistols, dice, old medicine bottles—filled the window.

Inside, one aisle displayed shampoo, laxatives and D-Con rat poison, the next a row of patent medicines and quack potions labeled "Dr. Otto's India Smash Compound" or "Wa-Hoo Blood and Nerve Tonic." Another aisle featured medical instruments from the Civil War. The owner, a small, silver-haired man named Joe Gerache, filled out prescriptions behind the counter. "In this life I'm a pharmacist," he said, when I asked about the store's schizophrenic display. "In my other life I'm a Civil War surgeon." He waited until a few customers departed, then locked the front door and gave me a tour.

"These are some of my favorite things," he said, beginning with the medical instruments. He picked up what looked like a carpentry-shop hacksaw. "This was the most popular tool in the Civil War. They sawed a lot of bones in that war." Beside the saw lay a trepanning tool, a corkscrew-like instrument used to bore holes in skulls. "By the time you finished with this, the guy went home in a box or with a drool bucket. That was the beginning of neurosurgery."

Gerache reached for an anesthesia mask. "Luckily, we had painkillers, ether and chloroform mostly," he said. "But if we administered them wrong, it was a one-way trip." When drugs weren't available, soldiers bit bullets during surgery. Gerache showed me a minié ball scarred with teeth marks. "Soldiers bit so hard that they'd throw their jaws out. So it was determined that two bullets were better, one on each side. That way the bite was more even."

We moved on to the medicines. "The biggest killer in the Civil War wasn't the rifle but the microbe," he said. "These medicines killed a lot, too." He ticked off the potions and tinctures in the medical wagon of a Civil War physician, including silver nitrate, castor oil, turpentine, belladonna, opium, brandy, and quinine. "Only one came close to curing anything, which was quinine for malaria." He showed me a bottle with a skull and crossbones. "This is carbolic acid, used to clean wounds. But what it mostly did was eat tissue." Gerache shook his head. "If they'd known to dilute it a hundred or so times, they'd have had Lysol, a perfect antiseptic."

Gerache ended with a brief lecture on dysentery, which disabled men of both armies by the thousands. "The South could have won the War if it had found a cure for the flux," he said. "Instead, they handed out medicines which only made things worse. Here, let me show you some of my purgatives."

When the grisly tour was done, Gerache told me how he'd started collecting old weapons and other artifacts as a child. "When I was coming up, no one was interested in this stuff, so people would give me things that had been sitting in their attics and basements. They'd say 'Take it, we're glad to get it out of the house.'" He chuckled. "My parents were worried. They thought minié balls would lead to cannonballs or worse, the way parents worry now about marijuana leading to hard drugs."

During World War II, Gerache served in the Pacific with a MASH-style unit, evacuating wounded from the battlefield. Returning home, he thought about going to medical school, but after years overseas "I felt like life was passing me by." So he opened this pharmacy instead, in an old building that had served as a saloon during the siege. Collecting Civil War medicines and instruments had become an outlet for the career he sometimes wished he'd pursued in real life.

Gerache often shared his collection with school groups, and also performed mock amputations at reenactments. Mostly, though, he displayed his wares for his own personal pleasure. "I have my collectibles at the store because I'm here twice as much as I'm at home. So why not have them to look at?"

Gerache had also confirmed his parents' fears. For years he'd heard rumors about a huge Confederate gun buried on the edge of town. "I got to thinking, bullets and pistols are nice. But maybe I ought to have a cannon." He'd found what looked like the edge of a cannon barrel poking from an old woman's flower garden. The woman didn't want her yard torn up, so Gerache purchased the land, still unsure what lay beneath. "I bought a pig in a poke," he said.

The pig turned out to be a 9,000-pound Parrott Gun, one of the Confederacy's huge riverside cannons. Gerache pointed out the store window at a traffic circle across the street. In the middle squatted the Parrott, its ten-foot barrel pointing toward the water. The cannon was worth at least $60,000 to collectors, but Gerache didn't worry about security. "Nobody will move that, unless they've got a construction crane," he said. "It's been hit by cars a few times but that's it."

Someone rapped on the pharmacy door. Gerache looked up as if to wish them away. "Come by my house after work," he said, "and I'll show you a few more of my favorite things."

Retreating down the hill to the air-conditioned casino, I sat at the bar and scanned the tourist literature Lenore had given me, as well as newspaper clips I'd collected on Vicksburg. "If all that comes to mind when you think of our town is Civil War battle scenes, you're not even getting half the picture," the promotional literature began. "Don't get us wrong. Vicksburg's place in history is permanent. But Vicksburg **today** is much, much more. It's a place where old and new blend in delightful combination like nowhere else in America."

Actually, old and new weren't blending too well, and history was proving anything but permanent. Frenzied construction along the waterfront had changed drainage patterns and cut into the loose, silty soil of Vicksburg's fragile bluffs, hastening their erosion. The Park Service had recently been forced to close a blufftop gun battery because it had buckled following construction of a casino access road at the base of the hill. The massive cannon, which had once helped repel the Union fleet, now pointed impotently at a casino parking lot into which the gun battery now threatened to slide.

Another casino, ignoring the warnings of the Park Service and local historians, had bulldozed near a nineteenth-century black grave-

yard that held the remains of U.S. Colored Troops. Construction at
the site halted when the dozers turned up bones. "I just want to get
my deceased out of there," the graveyard's overseer told the local
paper, sounding like a general requesting a ceasefire to collect his
casualties.

Vicksburg's battlefield, or the portion of it preserved by the Park
Service, formed a crescent arcing across hills and ravines a mile or so
behind the waterfront. Touring it by foot and car, I found the battle
much harder to grasp than Shiloh. For starters, Vicksburg wasn't a
single, momentous clash between armies meeting on a defined patch
of ground. Instead, Vicksburg became a months-long campaign embracing several mini-battles and the forty-seven-day siege. Much of
the fighting occurred far from Vicksburg, as Grant drove inland to
encircle the city.

Vicksburg differed from Shiloh in other essential ways. By mid-
1863, generals had overcome their earlier disdain for digging in.
Shovels proved as crucial as guns, with the two sides gouging 60,000
feet of zigzag trenches. Also, civilians suffered alongside soldiers,
enduring heavy bombardment and near-starvation during the siege.
Vicksburg, in sum, offered a preview of the sort of grinding, total
warfare that Grant and Sherman would later wage in the East—and
that European armies would pursue with even greater savagery in
the twentieth century.

The battlefield park's most conspicuous feature was its "monument overload," as one ranger put it. The plaques and memorials
totaled 1,323, and that was after a significant subtraction; during
a 1942 metal drive, half the cast-iron tablets were donated to the
World War II effort. One monument stood out. Modeled on the Pantheon in Rome, it was inscribed with the names of 36,000 Illinois
soldiers, including an extraordinary private named Albert D. J.
Cashire.

"In handling a musket in battle," a comrade recalled, "he was the
equal of any in the company." Cashire also "seemed specially adept at
those tasks so despised by the infantryman," such as sewing and
washing clothes. Cashire fought in forty skirmishes and battles and
became active in veterans' affairs, marching in parades for decades
after the War.

Then, in 1911, while working as a handyman in Illinois, Cashire was hit by an automobile and taken to the hospital with a leg broken close to the hip. The doctor who examined Cashire discovered what the Illinois veteran had so long concealed; Cashire was a woman, an Irish immigrant née Jennie Hodgers. Hodgers was eventually sent to an insane asylum and forced to wear women's clothing until her death in 1915.

"I left Cashier [sic], the fearless boy of twenty-two at the end of the Vicksburg campaign," one former comrade wrote after visiting her at the asylum. "I found a frail woman of seventy, broken, because on discovery she was compelled to put on skirts. They told me she was as awkward as could be in them. One day she tripped and fell, hurting her hip. She never recovered."

A former sergeant said that Hodgers told him, "The country needed me, and I wanted excitement." Money may have tempted her as well; for a poor Irish immigrant, the soldier's pay of $13 a month represented a stable if modest income. Vicksburg's battlefield museum displayed a picture of Hodgers in uniform, a mannish figure with short hair who stood conspicuously shorter than her comrades (she was barely five feet tall). The museum also told of 400 other women who went to war disguised as men. One, Sarah Emma Edmonds, chose to reveal her sex in 1884, when she appeared for a reunion of the 2nd Michigan Infantry as a woman.

Hodgers's secret, at least, lived after her, with her assumed name etched on the Illinois monument at Vicksburg, and on a veterans' headstone the War Department placed by her grave. Decades later, another stone was added that read:

ALBERT D. J. CASHIRE
CO. G, 95 ILL INF CIVIL WAR
BORN
JENNIE HODGERS
IN CLOGHER HEAD, IRELAND
1843–1915

The Vicksburg siege produced other oddities. The Confederacy experimented with camels, and one colonel used a dromedary to carry his personal baggage—until a Union sharpshooter killed the animal. There were also Vicksburg's famed caves, dug by civilians as protection against the Union bombardment. Some of these burrows became elaborate affairs, furnished with carpets and beds and serviced by slaves. But most were crude, crowded dugouts that one resident described as "rat-holes." Like the soldiers, civilians also saw food supplies dwindle to a meager daily ration. When beef ran out, they ate mule meat, frogs and rats. Flour was replaced by a blend of cornmeal and ground peas. "It made a nauseous composition, as the cornmeal cooked in half the time the pea-meal did, so this stuff was half raw," one Southerner wrote. "It had the properties of india-rubber and was worse than leather to digest."

By early July, both soldiers and civilians were on the brink of starvation, and surrender became inevitable. The Confederate commander, an émigré from Pennsylvania named John Pemberton, told his officers: "I know their peculiar weaknesses and their national vanity. I know we can get better terms from them on the Fourth of July than on any other day of the year." He was right. Grant generously agreed to parole the 30,000 Confederate troops within the Vicksburg defenses.

Even so, the fierce and protracted fighting in Vicksburg left the community deeply embittered. Though the city and its surrounding county had been one of only two in Mississippi to vote against secession (Natchez was the other), post-War Vicksburg hallowed the Cause and disdained the national battlefield as a "Yankee park." Mississippians initially refused to erect a state monument there, and never put up a memorial to Pemberton, the Northern-born rebel commander. As late as the 1950s, Joe Gerache had told me, "folks didn't talk about the surrender here. It was a 'cessation of hostilities.' The people of Vicksburg never gave up, it was only that Yankee general Pemberton who lost the city."

As elsewhere, a great deal of myth underlay this romance. Just before the surrender, Confederates petitioned Pemberton in a letter signed "Many Soldiers," telling him: "If you can't feed us, you had better surrender, horrible as the idea is, than suffer this noble army to disgrace themselves by desertion." Nor were cruel modern tactics

limited to the Northern side. The Confederates placed Union prisoners in Vicksburg's courthouse as a human shield to deter Northern
gunners from firing on the building.

The courthouse survived with only one hit, and now housed
Vicksburg's city museum. It was the most eccentric—and politically
incorrect—collection I'd yet visited in the South. In the "Confederate
Room," alongside a piece of orginal hardtack and a copy of the *Vicksburg Citizen* printed on wallpaper because newsprint ran out, I found
a pair of Confederate trousers "made by a plantation mammy" and a
photograph of a Southern matron with "her slaves who refused to accept freedom." An exhibit on Jefferson Davis, who delivered his first
public speech on the courthouse grounds, stated: "There was a very
special relationship between Jefferson Davis and his slaves. He was
not only their master but also their friend." Another display pointed
out: "Ironically, Gen. U.S. Grant was a slave owner while Gen. Robert E. Lee freed his slaves."

This last was a hoary bit of Southern propaganda. Grant's in-laws
were Missourians who owned slaves before the War, though Grant
himself never did. As for Lee, the slaves in question were those his
wife inherited in October 1857, with the stipulation that Lee, as ex-
ecutor, emancipate them within five years. Lee missed the deadline
and didn't free the slaves until December 29, 1863.

In another room, I found a Ku Klux Klan hood with eye holes
and a red tassel. "The Klan's purpose was to rid the South of the
carpetbag-scalawag-black governments, which were often corrupt,"
the accompanying text said. "Atrocities were sometimes attributed
to the Klan by unscrupulous individuals."

But the most striking exhibit of all was titled "The Minié Ball
Pregnancy." It featured a Civil War bullet and a picture of a Vicksburg doctor whose medical feat was described as follows:

> During the battle of Raymond, Miss. in 1863 a minié ball re-
> portedly passed through the reproductive organs of a young rebel
> soldier and a few seconds later penetrated a young lady who was
> standing on the porch of her nearby home. The story was written
> later by Dr. Le Grand G. Capers of Vicksburg for the American

Medical Weekly. Capers claimed that he tended their wounds, that the girl became pregnant from the fertile minié ball, that he delivered the baby, introduced her to the soldier, that the two were married and had two more children by the conventional method.

I realized with a start that I'd heard a bowdlerized version of this tale on my elementary school playground. Was it possible that this proto-urban legend had some basis in fact?

I found the museum's curator, Gordon Cotton, sifting papers in a backroom. Cotton was a striking Shelby Foote look-and-sound-alike, a kinship partly explained by the two men having grown up in the same part of the Mississippi Delta. "I heard someone laughing out loud and knew you must be reading about the Minié Ball Pregnancy," he said.

I asked if he thought the story could possibly be true.

"The girl's mother believed it, and nothing else matters," he replied. "I guess you could say that baby was the original son-of-a-gun."

Part of the story was indeed factual. Dr. Le Grand Capers was the real name of a Confederate surgeon who wrote about the minié ball pregnancy in the *American Medical Weekly* in 1874, under the headline: "Attention Gynaecologists! Notes from the Diary of a Field and Hospital Surgeon CSA." However, Capers intended the article as a spoof of the wildly inflated stories of medical prowess reported by other doctors in the War. Not everyone got the joke and Capers's medical reputation never recovered.

"I decided to just present the story as Capers did, " Cotton said with a shrug. "History shouldn't be dull." The same attitude extended to the other exhibits, which Cotton himself had arranged with what he freely admitted was a strong Southern bias. "This is Vicksburg's attic," he said. "Our story is the story of Vicksburg, not somewhere in Pennsylvania. People might say, 'that's a Southern view,' but this is a Southern town."

Most of the items came from local households. The Klan hood had literally come from an attic, stowed in a trunk by a relative of Cotton's. The outfit originally belonged to Cotton's great-grandfather, a Confederate private. "The Klan's part of our history, good or bad," he said. "People often ask me if my great-grandfather hated blacks.

No, I tell them. He hated Yankees. Anyway, if it hadn't been for the Yankee occupation, we wouldn't have any good stories to tell."

Cotton lived in the same 1840s farmhouse where he, his father, grandfather and great-grandfather had all been born. One of Cotton's cousins still slept in a bed riddled by bullets when Yankees killed her great-great-grandmother during a plantation raid. "Her killers were tried upstairs in this courthouse," Cotton said. "So you see, we're never far from our history. I'm not going to go through this museum rewriting the past just to please someone in the present."

Anyway, the present wasn't very pleasing to Cotton, particularly the casinos. "I'm still of that old Protestant work ethic, you work for what you get. I don't believe in ill-gotten gains and games of chance." Not that he was a prude. "We had a wonderful whorehouse district," he said. "It's gone." He acknowledged, too, that the casinos had created thousands of jobs and pumped millions of dollars in tax revenues into a state that had long been the poorest in the nation.

But Cotton felt the casinos were spoiling the town's historic atmosphere and peddling a false version of the past. It was true that antebellum Vicksburg, like many river towns, was a rough place renowned for its vice and violence. But the riverboats themselves were usually tame commercial vessels that frowned on gambling. "If steamboats caught a professional gambler on board, they'd put him off at the next stop," Cotton said.

Vicksburg also had fought to rid its streets of vice. Its namesake, Reverend Newitt Vick, was a stern evangelical Methodist who founded the town as a model outpost of Christianity. When it became a den of iniquity instead, citizens organized to chase the gamblers out. One notorious gambling den called the Kangaroo refused to close. So in 1835, vigilantes led by a doctor named Hugh Bodley armed themselves and marched on the Kangaroo. As they approached, someone shot through the door, killing Bodley. The crowd then burned roulette and faro wheels in the streets and lynched several gamblers. "Some of the others ended up as catfish food," Cotton said, gazing out at the water.

A few blocks from the courthouse stood a small obelisk that read: "Erected by a grateful community to the memory of Dr. Hugh Bodley Murdered by the Gamblers July 5, 1835 while defending the morals of Vicksburg." When the new casinos arrived in Vicksburg, representatives of Harrah's came to Cotton for advice about pretty-ing the shore and integrating the city's history into their design. He showed them a picture of the Bodley monument, though not its in-scription. Harrah's asked if the memorial could be moved down by the water, close to the casinos.

"I think that would be ideal," Cotton told them. Then he showed them the monument's words. He chuckled. "They were not amused," he said.

FROM HIS OLIVE SKIN and unusual surname, I'd guessed that the pharmacist Joe Gerache was of southern European extraction. But when I arrived at his home in suburban Vicksburg, I noticed a Jewish menorah perched on the living room mantel. Then, as we began chat-ting, he referred to Vicksburg's *schvartze*. He caught himself and said, "That's Yiddish for black people."

"I know. My grandfather used that word all the time."

"You're Jewish?" he asked.

When I nodded, Gerache yelled to his wife in the kitchen. "Ann, you know what? Tony's an M.O.T.!" Then to me: "That's 'member of tribe.'" Before I could say pastrami on rye, I'd been invited—commanded—to attend synagogue the next night and hustled into the living room to watch a documentary Ann had taped about Jewish life in Mississippi. By the time I'd finished, dinner was ready and I found myself at the kitchen table as Joe intoned the Hebrew prayers for food and wine.

"Actually, I'm Catholic," Joe said, noshing on a dill pickle. "My grandparents came from Italy. But I go to Ann's services and she comes to mass with me."

Southern Jewry often made for this sort of colorful intermingling. When I'd lived in Mississippi, a Jewish co-worker and I were fre-quently asked by a small synagogue in Meridian to help make *minyan*, the quorum of ten worshipers needed for a Jewish prayer service. The Friday phone calls were always the same: "Y'all gonna come make *minyan* at church tonight? We'll be playing poker after the service." Jewish-Southern culture had also bred the ultimate in fusion food: a place in Alabama called Gershon Weinberg's Real Pork Barbecue.

At Vicksburg's synagogue, the *minyan* often included three non-Jewish women who sang in the temple's choir, and several black custodians as well. A visiting rabbi came only on High Holidays, so on other occasions the congregants took turns acting as lay reader. On the Friday night I attended, an insurance salesman in a seersucker suit read the Sabbath service in Southern-accented English. Few among the dozen worshipers appeared to be under sixty. "We haven't had a bar mitzvah here in ten years," the insurance salesman said when the short service ended.

As in Meridian, the congregation in Vicksburg kept a curious post-synagogue ritual. Usually, the entire group drove across the bridge to Louisiana to a crawfish joint called Po Boys. On the night I visited, Po Boys was closed, so we went instead to a local restaurant and dined on fried chicken, pork loin and hush puppies. For most of the meal, a woman named Betty Sue held court, quizzing everyone for family gossip, as Southerners were so fond of doing. "What was her maiden name? . . . Is he Earl's cousin? . . . Did he marry that gal from Memphis?"

But there wasn't much family to talk about, at least not locally. As in many Southern towns, Jews first came to Vicksburg in the nineteenth century as peddlers. Working their way up the Mississippi, they settled down and opened businesses. But in this century, young Jews began leaving for the city. This migration was hastened by Jewish boys going off to fight in World War II, and later by the civil rights movement, which brought a temporary influx of Northern Jews. Their long hair and liberal views unsettled the local community. "They lived in black areas and related to people differently than we did," Ann Gerache said, echoing what Shelby Foote had told me. "We didn't know how our Christian neighbors would treat us after that."

In several Southern cities, white supremacists fire-bombed synagogues. While there was no such violence in Vicksburg, the Jewish community continued to dwindle and now numbered only about seventy. "That's including folks who don't live here anymore but plan to be buried in Vicksburg," Ann said.

The next day, I visited the Jewish cemetery, wedged between a Pizza Hut and the battlefield park. The fighting at Vicksburg had spilled across the cemetery grounds, and gravestones marked Levy and Metzger mingled weirdly with historic plaques to the Mississippi Light Artillery and the Green Brigade of Texas.

About 20,000 Jews lived in the Confederate states at the start of the Civil War. In some ways, the mid-nineteenth-century South had been more welcoming to Jews than the North, where anti-immigrant sentiment reached fever pitch in the 1850s. Grant, while fighting in Mississippi, often railed against Jewish "speculators" and issued orders proscribing their movements, at one point terming them "an intolerable nuisance" and demanding that army railroad conductors stop Jews from traveling south of Jackson.

But viewed from Vicksburg's synagogue and graveyard, there was a sad, end-of-the-line feel to Southern Jewry, at least that portion of it living outside Florida and a few big cities. In another decade or two, it seemed likely that all trace of rural and small-town Jewish life would be gone, except for graveyards like this, and the Semitic names—Cohen, Kaufman, Lowenstein—still dimly visible on the front of abandoned shoe shops and department stores across the backcountry South.

My second week in Vicksburg, I was evicted from Harrah's. I hadn't bothered to book ahead to Memorial Day, naively supposing that no sane person would celebrate the start of summer here, in a town already so heat-struck that every time I stepped outside my glasses fogged and slid down my nose. But gamblers knew no seasons; what better way to while away the 100-degree days than in a climate-controlled casino? Every other hotel in town was also booked. So I cashed my few chips and headed for the Natchez Trace, as flatboatsmen and busted gamblers had so often done in the nineteenth century.

Driving out of town, I decided to make one last stop at the battlefield. The morning paper had mentioned a noonday wreath-laying at the cemetery. Like many Americans, I'd almost forgotten that Memorial Day meant something more than a three-day weekend at the beach or blackjack table. It was, in fact, the mass slaughter of the Civil War that had led to the holiday's creation. Vicksburg seemed an appropriate place to see how Southerners honored their war dead.

The ceremony's site was a shady corner of the sprawling Union cemetery, near a plaque that read: "Forty Four Known By Name, Others Known Only to God." Of the 17,000 soldiers buried at Vicksburg, only 4,000 were known by name. A motorcade pulled up trailing streamers and flags. Forty people climbed out, mostly graying men wearing army caps and medals. It looked at first glance like any veterans' gathering, except that all but one of the participants was black.

The group filtered in among the small stumps marking Vicksburg's nameless dead. Someone laid a wreath and said a brief prayer. Then soldiers fired a 21-gun salute and a bugler played Taps. As the crowd fled the midday sun, I chatted with the ceremony's organizer, a man named Willie Glasper. He said that Memorial Day observances in Vicksburg had stopped altogether in the 1970s. It had been his decision to revive the holiday with the wreath-laying and a short parade through town.

"I'm a mailman, not a veteran, but I played here as a boy and used to study these graves," he said. "I look at the War from a freedom standpoint. One side won, the other lost, and we became free as a result." He paused. "Maybe that's why the white folks don't come."

Like July 4th, Memorial Day had a tortured history in Vicksburg, as it did across much of the South. It was Southern women who pioneered the spring custom of decorating soldiers' graves (Columbus, Georgia, had perhaps the strongest claims to the first Memorial Day in 1866). But the ritual quickly caught on in both North and South. In 1868, the main Northern veterans' group, the Grand Army of the Republic, designated May 30th as the date when all veterans' posts should decorate Union graves. The South, characteristically, went its own way. Southern states declared their own "Confederate Memorial Day," varying from state to state and timed, in part, to correspond with the peak of the spring blossom season. It was only in this century, as sectional bitterness waned and new wars produced a fresh crop of dead, that the late-May Memorial Day became a truly national holiday.

But old habits died hard. Glasper said there had long been two American Legion posts in Vicksburg, one all-white, the other all-black. "Their attitude is, 'You do Memorial Day, we'll do Veterans Day,'" he said. Each year, Glasper went through the ritual of inviting the white Legion post to the wreath-laying. But the only white in attendance this year was a non-veteran: Vicksburg's mayor. The white Legion post didn't even open on Memorial Day. And its own observance, on Veterans Day, was held at a downtown median strip decorated with monuments from this century's wars, rather than at the Civil War cemetery.

"It's that way with a lot of things here," Glasper said. "If blacks put something on, whites don't come. And too often when whites put something on, we don't go. We're self-conscious around each other."

Glasper invited me to a reception at the American Legion post, a small building on the back street of a black neighborhood. En route, he pointed out a new museum he and several others were setting up to honor black Vicksburgers (whose ranks include Sarah Breedlove Walker, America's first black woman millionaire). I asked why the group didn't try instead to include its exhibits at the city museum I'd visited at the Old Courthouse. Glasper looked at me strangely. "That's theirs," he said. Even the YMCA in Vicksburg had two branches: one white, one black.

At the Legion hall, veterans and their families sat beneath balloons and bunting, slathering hot dogs with relish. The mayor circulated through the small crowd, glad-handing veterans and droning on about his achievements ("Reduced taxes, paved fifty-eight streets, built a new swimming pool and ballpark, halved unemployment, put in an eleven-million-dollar sewer system . . .").

I found a seat beside a woman who had been teaching at Vicksburg's schools for twenty-five years. She said school integration occurred without incident and blacks were now well represented politically. But socially, the color line remained intact. "You'd think veterans, of all people, could cross the line. They have so much in common," she said. "But then, most of these men fought in all-black units, even in Korea. So I guess they just never reached out to each other."

Across from me sat an eighty-year-old named Laura Jones, who served as president of the Legion's women's auxiliary. She was the granddaughter of a black soldier who had served at Vicksburg; his name was etched on the Illinois monument. When she was a girl, her family would visit the battlefield park every weekend. "It was free, we could play on the monuments, pick pecans and walnuts and plums, and look for Grandaddy's name." She shared two other vivid girlhood memories. "The Klan hanged a boy on Grove Street. I remember the tree. And I saw a woman with tar all over her. She washed clothes for white folks and some white man had taken a liking to her. That made it her fault, of course. Luckily, someone stopped the Klan before they put the feathers on her, so she just got the tar."

Laura Jones had seen that sort of terrorism vanish in her lifetime. But she despaired of ever seeing true racial amity in Vicksburg. "Instead of ironing out our differences everyone wants to go their own way." She'd asked the local high school if its band might participate in the Memorial Day parade. "They said, 'School got out a few days ago and the uniforms have been washed and put away.' Well, we can wash them again. The cleaners aren't leaving town. But that's their excuse. There's a Miss Mississippi pageant in July. I bet you the school band comes out for that. And they come for the Christmas parade, when school's out." In the end, the Legion hall had paid for several black bands to come from out of state.

I was surprised to learn that the racial divide ran so deep. Vicksburg had largely escaped the civil rights violence that wracked so many Mississippi communities. And, like river towns everywhere, it seemed more open and cosmopolitan than inland communities. The Vicksburg economy was now strong, thanks to gambling, and blacks I'd spoken to over the past week had praised the casinos for their equitable hiring practices. Nor had I seen the sort of inflammatory displays of rebel emblems common to Todd County, Kentucky, and other places I'd visited.

But Laura Jones said I shouldn't be fooled by Vicksburg's veneer of geniality. "Things haven't changed because deep down people's hearts haven't changed. No law, no government, no corporation is going to make you do the right thing. That comes from inside." She swatted a fly on the relish jar. "The outside's changed," she said, "but the inside's the same."

I finished my hot dog and drove out of town in a tropical down-pour; even the weather had conspired to rain on the Memorial Day parade. Vicksburg confirmed the dispiriting pattern I'd seen else-where in the South, beginning in North Carolina. Everywhere, it seemed, I had to explore two pasts and two presents; one white, one black, separate and unreconcilable. The past had poisoned the pres-ent and the present, in turn, now poisoned remembrance of things past. So there needed to be a black Memorial Day and a white Veter-ans Day. A black city museum and a white one. A black history month and a white calendar of remembrance. The best that could be hoped for was a grudging toleration of each other's historical mem-ory. You Wear Your X, I'll Wear Mine.

10

Virginia and Beyond

THE CIVIL WARGASM

War is the congress of adolescents.
—JOHN BERRYMAN, "Boston Common"

We were hurtling down the interstate somewhere near Richmond when Robert Lee Hodge poked me hard in the ribs.

"Don't farb out!" he bellowed. "You think the Yankees got any sleep at Gettysburg? On Burnside's mud march? Wake the fuck up!"

Rob clutched the wheel with one hand, wrestling a windblown roadmap with the other. Tobacco juice had dribbled down his beard and stained the collar of his butternut jacket. He'd taken off his brogans; I could smell putrid sock wool. Or maybe it was me. I groped in my sweaty blue pantaloons and pulled out a pocket watch. Ten o'clock; must be spring, 1864.

"Yellow Tavern's this exit," Rob said, tossing aside the map and swerving across two lanes of traffic. "If we don't get lost, we can see where Jeb Stuart got popped and still make Cold Harbor by lunchtime."

I'D RETURNED FROM Mississippi to a phone call from Rob, announcing that the time for our "Gasm" had come. It was June, the days were long, and Rob had a brief window between a modeling date for a Civil War painter and a major reenactment at Gettysburg. "Are you ready to power-tour?" he'd asked.

In truth, I wasn't sure. I'd first heard about the Gasm while spooning with the Southern Guard months before. Rob and Joel Bohy, the wasp-waisted construction worker, told me how they'd first met several years ago at a Gettysburg reenactment. Striking up an instant kinship, the two decided to take a spontaneous tour of the War's eastern theater. They drew up a list of must-see sites; it ran to over thirty, many of them several hundred miles apart. Joel only had a week before returning to work in New England.

Where others might have seen a logistical nightmare, Rob glimpsed opportunity. "Everybody does the Civil War in a controlled way," he said. "We wanted something crazy." So the two set off on a high-speed trek from Gettysburg to Antietam to the Shenandoah Valley and dozens of battlefields in between. They traveled as hardcores, of course: clad in their fetid uniforms and camping on whatever battleground they happened to be near at dark. The one major concession to modernity was the car in which they raced between stops.

"We only had an hour or so at major sites and a few minutes at minor ones," Rob said. "So the whole War just washed over us at warp-speed." Fatigue heightened the thrill. "It was dreamy, religious, a holy trek." He and Joel read liturgically from soldiers' diaries and memoirs; at some battlegrounds, they scooped up clods of sacred dirt. It was Joel who had dubbed their ecstatic pilgrimage the "Civil Wargasm."

The two had vowed to repeat their hajj each summer. But after their second trip, Joel returned to Massachusetts, got a girlfriend, drifted away from the Civil War. So the next year Rob did the Gasm with another buddy. Now it was my turn. I was flattered that he regarded me as a suitable partner. But I was also apprehensive. My previous brushes with Rob's hardcore life had lasted only a day. This would last a week and come freighted with expectations. Could I measure up to the Gasm's transcendent standards? More worrisome, could I hack a week of sleeplessness and scratchy wool in Virginia's summer heat—not to mention the twenty-four-hour companionship of Robert Lee Hodge?

◦ ◦ ◦

On the Monday morning we'd chosen to begin our trip, I headed to Rob's apartment. He lived in the basement of his brother's place, a suburban town house beside Washington, D.C.'s beltway. Civil War gear lay strewn across the garage floor. "His brother doesn't like this stuff all over the house," Rob's girlfriend, Caroline, explained. It was easy to see why. The unwashed clothes and utensils were so rank that I was surprised his brother hadn't called an exterminator.

Rob had run off to do a last-minute errand, so Caroline offered me a cup of coffee. A comely twenty-three-year-old with oversized glasses and brilliant red fingernails, she seemed as remote from the nineteenth century as the IdentiKit town house in which we sat drinking mugs of Mr. Coffee. "I think Rob likes that his girlfriend isn't into the Civil War," she said, "because all the rest of his life is."

Caroline had first met Rob at a restaurant where he waited on her table. His long, pointed beard struck her as odd, but it wasn't until he turned up for their first date—clad in a Confederate jacket—that Caroline realized what she was in for. "I thought, 'Oh no, he's a complete dweeb,'" she recalled. "I told him, 'The Civil War may be cool to you, but for me it's, like, lots of names and dates and so what?'"

But Rob hadn't pressed his obsession on her, and gradually she came to enjoy his company—even to appreciate the Civil War. "Before, these people in the past seemed, like, not human. Something else. Now I realize they were the same as us, just in a different time." She'd gone to a few reenactments and had even sewed a rough cotton shirt for Rob. But Caroline drew the line at watching the interminable movie *Gettysburg*, in which Rob appeared as one of Pickett's men. "Anyone who just went to see it as a movie and wasn't into the Civil War, they'd like die," she said.

Rob's car pulled into the driveway. Caroline drained her coffee. "I tell friends, 'He's not as weird as he sounds,'" she said. "You just have to try hard to understand him."

"Do you?"

"A bit." She smiled. "But maybe that's because I'm a counselor for the mentally retarded."

Rob burst through the door, smiling triumphantly. "I scored some

sowbelly," he said. "This pork's so salty it'll bring tears to your eyes."
He tossed the slab bacon in my lap, along with a potato and a wilted
onion. "I didn't have time to make any hardtack," he added, apologetically.

I'd told Rob I wanted to go Federal this time, so he'd set aside pale-
blue trousers, a checked shirt, a scrunched forage cap, and a navy-
colored sack coat with a flaky yellow stain. "Some candles melted in
the pocket," Rob explained. "Nice accident." Otherwise, I wasn't quite
as disreputable as before, though no more comfortable. The pants
were gargantuan, the jacket puny, and by the time Rob strapped on
my bedroll, canteen, knapsack, tin cup and cartridge box, I felt like a
snail toting an ill-fitting shell.

"I got this one in '81 and this one in '84," Rob said, tossing me
brogans with huge holes in the soles. "It's peak tick season, and
Lyme disease is a big problem this year. So keep an eye out."

"What about bugs?" I asked. "Have we got a tent, or a mosquito
net?"

Rob frowned. "This is the Gasm, Tony. The holy of holies. Bug
bites are spiritual. You're lying there listening to mosquitoes buzz in
your ear, trying to sleep, and thinking, 'This is what They experienced. This is the real deal.'"

When I'd finally put on all the gear, Rob stepped back and nodded
approvingly at my Union impression. "You look ready for Andersonville," he said.

Rob donned his customary Confederate rags. We made a strange
pair: Johnny Reb and Billy Yank, stuffed into the front seat of my
cramped sedan as we pulled into rush-hour traffic on the beltway.
Glancing at the commuters in adjoining lanes, with their ties and
jackets and stuporous expressions of Monday morning malaise, I
felt suddenly giddy and burst out laughing.

Rob smiled, obviously feeling the same absurdist glee. "This is my
true calling—a Civil War bum," he said, biting into the day's first
plug of tobacco. "The Gasm's a Bohemian thing, like a Ken Kesey bus
tour, except that we're tripping on the 1860s instead of the 1960s."

Actually, the Gasm struck me as a fusion of the two decades: a
weird brew of road culture, rancid pork, and the quest for the elusive
"period rush," the phrase hardcores used to describe the druglike high

of traveling through time. "This is day one, so I wouldn't expect too much," Rob cautioned. "But wait till we've driven a thousand or so miles with no sleep and not much to eat. Then it's goose-bump city."

For now it was mostly just city. We turned off the beltway and crawled along Route 29, known in the 1860s as the Warrenton Turnpike. Federal troops traveled this same route to Manassas in July 1861. They were trailed by politicians and picnickers who expected to see a festive afternoon spectacle that would quickly snuff the South's rebellion. Also along was William Howard Russell, a London *Times* correspondent, whose diary we'd chosen for our inaugural reading.

Russell traveled in better style than we did. Setting off from Washington in a horse-drawn carriage, he put "tea into a bottle, got a flask of light Bordeaux, a bottle of water, a paper of sandwiches, and replenished my small flask with brandy." Crossing the Potomac, Russell entered what he called "a densely wooded, undulating country" interspersed with fields of Indian corn and wooden homes skirted by slave shacks.

Today, the same route was studded with stoplights and franchise outlets: Staples, Subway, Blockbuster. Russell described our first stop, Fairfax Courthouse, as a village of forty houses girdled by gardens and fields. It now lay near the center of a suburban county of 900,000 people. Rob pulled off the road beside a few cannon aimed out at the swirling traffic. A plaque by the guns read: "This stone marks the scene of the opening conflict of the war of 1861–65, when John Quincy Marr, Captain of the Warrenton Rifles, who was the first soldier killed in Action fell 800 feet S 46 degrees W (Mac) of this spot."

Rob explained that Marr fell seven weeks before First Manassas, when his rebel riflemen encountered Union scouts. Some Southerners therefore regarded Marr as "the first Virginia martyr." But for Rob, the real significance of the site was sartorial. "We'll see Marr's uniform later on in the Gasm," he said. "His coat's olive-brown. That's because the Confederacy had weak vegetable dyes that oxidized quickly."

As we left Fairfax, Rob took out a notebook and pen, scribbling, "GASM, Day One. 10:00 A.M. John Quincy Marr memorial." Book-keeping was a feature of the trip he hadn't told me about. "By the second or third day it all starts to blur, so you have to keep a tight record before you get totally tapped," he said.

A little later, we paused again, at a roadside plaque stating that Clara Barton "ministered to the suffering" at a hospital near this spot, now a clotted intersection. Rob scribbled in his notebook again. "Two hits in half an hour, not bad," he said. "That's why Northern Virginia's great Gasm territory. It's high density."

Since moving to Virginia, I'd often glimpsed similar markers in roadside weeds or beside petunia-prettified malls, recalling minor engagements and forgotten figures from the War: ACTION AT DRANESVILLE, THE GALLANT PELHAM, STONEWALL JACKSON'S MOTHER. It was nice to finally have an excuse to pull out of traffic and read the details. But I couldn't help wondering if we were the first in years to stop and read these signs—or at least since Rob had last passed this way on an earlier Gasm.

In late morning, we crested a low ridge and spilled into the "plain of Manassas," a broad basin whose western lip was formed by the Bull Run Mountains. At roughly the same spot, the *Times* reporter, William Howard Russell, described a landscape "enclosed in a framework of blue and purple hills, softened into violet in the extreme distance." To the Englishman, the view "presented one of the most agreeable displays of simple pastoral woodland scenery that could be conceived." These days, the view of the Bull Run Mountains was shrouded by smog and the plain had filled with one of the most disagreeable displays of suburban sprawl anyone could conceive.

Modern Manassas, a fast-growing bedroom community for Washington, was so hideous that some locals called it "Manasshole." The town had gained modern renown as the place where Lorena Bobbitt hacked off her husband's penis and tossed it in the grass outside a 7-Eleven. The town's historic railroad junction, which had caused North and South to clash here twice in the space of thirteen months, was now swaddled by miles of housing tracts, fast-food joints and car dealerships. Civil War entrenchments had been bulldozed to make way for bowling alleys, shops, offices and access roads, many of them named for the history they'd obliterated: Confederate Trail, Dixie Pawn, Battlefield Ford, Reb Yank Shopping Center.

We ran a four-mile gauntlet of neon before finally glimpsing a split-rail fence that enclosed a small sanctuary of trees and grass. This was the battlefield park, about the size of a suburban golf course. Parking at the visitors' center, we were instantly mobbed by youngsters gawking at our uniforms. "Cool," one boy exclaimed. "I didn't know you guys knew how to drive."

Rob fixed the boy with a stony rebel stare. "Didn't we drive them blue-bellies off this field, boy?" he growled. "Not oncet but twice?" The boy squealed with delight, then turned to me. I shrugged, tongue-tied, realizing what a long week it would be playing Yankee Doodle to Rob's fierce Dixie.

The boy and five others trailed us to the crest of a small knoll at the center of the park. It was here that the beleaguered Confederate, General Barnard Bee, famously declared to his broken troops, "Look men, there is Jackson standing like a stone wall!" Bee died of his wounds before anyone could ask if he meant this as praise or derision; after all, Bee's troops were fighting hard while Thomas Jackson's lay prone behind the hill's crest, holding their fire. But Jackson's men soon proved steadfast, the nickname stuck, and an equestrian statue of the famed Virginian now towered over Manassas.

"This is Arnold Schwarzenegger doing Stonewall," Rob quipped to his youthful audience, pointing to the rippling musculature of both Jackson and his steed. In real life, Rob explained, Jackson was a college professor of average stature. His horse, Little Sorrel, was described by one of Jackson's aides as "a plebian-looking little beast" whose gait was "always the same, an amble." Rob turned to me and whispered enigmatically: "We'll see Little Sorrel later in the Gasm."

From the statue we strolled to the farmhouse where a bedridden eighty-five-year-old widow, Judith Henry, became the first civilian casualty of the War when an artillery shell crashed through the roof. Beside the Henry house stood a small mound of bricks and artillery shells, dedicated in 1865, "In Memory of the Patriots who fell at Bull Run." This was believed to be the nation's first monument to Union soldiers.

First Manassas was littered with firsts, which explained why it was better known than Second Manassas, a far bloodier battle fought on roughly the same ground in 1862. First Manassas was, first of all,

the first major engagement of the War, which prompted one of the
first great quotes of the conflict. When General Irvin McDowell
warned Lincoln that his troops were raw and unready for battle, the
president replied: "You are green, it is true. But they are green, also.
You are all green alike." Northern troops proved not only green but
yellow, fleeing toward Washington in a panicked retreat that William
Howard Russell dubbed "the Bull Run races." To Southerners it became known as "The Great Skedaddle."

First Manassas was also the first battle where North and South
adopted the annoying habit of calling the same engagement by
different names. Southerners tended to name battles after nearby
towns—hence, Manassas—while Northerners chose geographic
features, usually a body of water: hence Bull Run, the stream on
whose banks the fight began. This rule also prevailed at Sharpsburg
(known to Northerners as Antietam, after a creek near the town)
and Murfreesboro (Stones River), though not at Shiloh, which the
South named for a log church, while Northerners originally referred
to the battle as Pittsburg Landing, after a nearby docking place. Go
figure.

First Manassas also marked the first use of the railroad to deploy
troops for battle. Confederate reinforcements arrived in "the cars," as
they were then called, just in time for the fight. And First Manassas
was the first time the keening "rebel yell" was heard as Confederates
burst from the woods. Rob walked our juvenile coterie to the spot
where this occurred. "Since they didn't have tape recorders back
then," he said, "no one knows for sure what the yell sounded like.
There's at least three different versions."

"Let's hear them all!" several boys shouted.

Rob perched one foot on a cannon wheel and cleared his throat.
Then he let loose a blood-curdling, full-throated caterwaul. The
boys giggled and hunched their shoulders, as if spooked by a Hal-
loween ghost. "That's one," Rob said. The second was a quick succession of high-pitched yelps, like a foxhunter's call. The third was a
peculiar, apelike grunt that rose gradually into a piercing howl. "A
mating call," Rob joked.

By now our small audience had swelled to a crowd, with kids imi-
tating Rob in an unruly chorus of grunts, yips and shrieks while

their parents lobbed questions about Civil War arcana. As Rob patiently answered each query and voice-coached the children, I could see in their rapt, youthful faces a platoon of future hardcore reenactors.

It took an hour for Rob to finally break free. So we made quick work of Second Manassas, sprinting along the unfinished railroad bed where Stonewall Jackson's men threw rocks at oncoming Yankees when they ran out of bullets. We also visited a nearby field where musket fire had been so intense that lead residue still lingered in the soil. Second Manassas claimed 25,000 casualties, five times the toll at First Manassas. By the late summer of 1862, such slaughter had become almost routine.

There was a later battle of Manassas that I'd witnessed myself. A few months after my return to the United States, the Walt Disney Company unveiled plans for "Disney's America," an historic theme park within cannon-shot of the battlefield. Disney's "imagineers" concocted a fantasy Civil War fort, complete with pyrotechnic displays, "Disney's circle-vision technology," and daily reruns of the *Monitor* dueling the *Merrimack*. "It is going to be fun with a capital F!" a company spokesman exulted.

Disney's plans provoked immediate protest. Manassas lay along the *axis mundi* of Civil War remembrance, within an hour's drive of sixteen battlefields. Critics warned that the theme park would ravage this "hallowed ground" and substitute McHistory for the brutal reality of the Civil War. In the end, the park's foes prevailed in a rare triumph of high culture over low.

But as Rob and I sat in gridlocked traffic just outside the national park, the victory looked hollow; like the rebels at Manassas, preservationists had won the battle but seemed doomed to lose the war. Virtually every inch of the park we'd just visited lay within earshot of heavy traffic. At nearby Chantilly, scene of a bloody fight the day after Second Manassas, the battlefield had vanished beneath tract housing. A short way to the southwest, at Brandy Station, site of the largest cavalry battle in American history, developers planned to build a Formula One racetrack.

I felt relieved when we finally broke free from the sprawl around Manassas and drove west through Thoroughfare Gap, into the rolling farmland of the Virginia Piedmont. As the azure Blue Ridge loomed before us, I dug into my pack for the second reading we'd chosen for our Gasm: Ambrose Bierce's first impression of Virginia as a young Union private in 1861. "Nine in ten of us had never seen a mountain, nor a hill as high as a church spire," Bierce wrote of his Midwestern regiment. "To a member of a plains-tribe, born and reared on the flats of Ohio or Indiana, a mountain region was a perpetual miracle. Space seemed to have taken on a new dimension; areas to have not only length and breadth, but thickness."

Rob had been raised in Ohio and shared Bierce's wonder at the scenery, though not Bierce's vocabulary. "I'm peaking," he said, gazing at the rolling hills and pastures verged by dry-stone walls. "It TKOs you, this one-two punch of history and landscape. You don't get that in Ohio, or almost anyplace outside Virginia."

For a while we drove in silence along the Snickersville Turnpike, a narrow road along which troops of both armies had marched. At one point I instinctively reached for the radio dial to hear the news; then, after a few headlines—Bosnia, the budget deficit, presidential politics—I turned it off. Our Gasm wasn't yet a day old but already I resented the intrusion of current events.

The day so far had also made me curious about Rob. I'd been struck by his rapport with the kids at Manassas and wondered who or what had sparked his own Civil War obsession as a boy in Medina, Ohio, a day's drive from anything connected to the conflict.

"Well, my name sort of marked me," Rob said. His father came from Alabama and a vague allegiance to the Confederacy had migrated with him to Ohio. So when Rob was born on Stonewall Jackson's birthday, an older brother suggested the name Robert Lee, apparently confusing the two commanders' close-by birthdays.

Rob's siblings also handed down their Sears Blue and Gray set, a collection of plastic soldiers. "They were about two inches tall," Rob recalled, "but the clothing really got me, particularly the rebels with their slouch hats and bedrolls. I used to talk to them." For his first-grade picture, Rob wore a Confederate kepi. "It was cheap," Rob said. "I was a farb back then."

Rob cut short his autobiography as we crossed the Shenandoah

River and rolled into Harpers Ferry, the scene of John Brown's famous raid on a federal arsenal in 1859. Brown hoped to arm slaves with pikes and guns and ignite a black rebellion across the South. Instead, he managed only to spark a local firefight which claimed as its first casualty a free black baggage-master, shot dead by Brown's men. Vengeful Virginians mutilated the corpses of insurrectionists killed in the raid, then tried and hanged Brown and six other survivors. It was on the gallows that Brown sealed his fame by handing a prophetic note to one of the guards: "I, John Brown, am now quite *certain* that the crimes of this *guilty* land will never be purged *away* but with Blood."

Brown, with his shovel-shaped beard and blazing eyes, had always seemed a spooky figure, and Harpers Ferry struck me as a spooky town. The main street pitched down an impossibly steep hill, dead-ending at a peninsula shadowed by sheer bluffs. An ancient, white-wash advertisment for Mennen's talcum blanched the rocky crags on one cliff, with only the gigantic word POWDER still legible.

The town's cramped streets bore the seedy cast of an unprosperous tourist trap, which Harpers Ferry had in fact been for 135 years. Merchants began hawking relics within weeks of John Brown's raid, even manufacturing pikes and selling bits of rope and pieces of wood allegedly taken from the gallows. Post-War speculators bought the engine house in which Brown and his men holed up during the raid, and carted it off to the World's Columbian Exposition in Chicago in 1893. Later, the engine house returned to Harpers Ferry, eventually coming to rest near its original location by the river.

Rob and I stood for a few minutes gazing at the peripatetic structure, a small brick oblong with stable-style doors and an empty cupola (Union troops swiped the bell during the War). It was dusk and the engine house and other sites were closed. We walked along the vacant streets and pressed our faces to the window of the John Brown Wax Museum: "88 Life Size Figures & Scenes. Life Story of John Brown Youth to Gallows." As we wandered back to the car, I felt oddly as though we'd broken into a museum after hours.

Driving up the hill to the modern part of town, Rob pulled over to pick up two hitchhikers with long hair, backpacks and walking sticks. They'd just wandered off the Appalachian Trail, which snaked through the hills nearby, and were searching for a store to stock up on supplies. "It's like the Dead Zone, eh?" one of them said. As he and his friend clambered into the backseat, which was cluttered with gear—Rob's musket, sowbelly wrapped in a bandanna, a half-drained six-pack of beer—I noticed the two exchanging glances. Then one of them leaned forward and asked, "You guys part of the living history demonstrations here?"

"No," Rob said, flashing the hitchhiker one of his patented thousand-yard stares. "We're just living it."

The hiker glanced at his buddy again. "That's cool," he said.

When we'd gone less than a mile, one of the hikers announced, "You know, it's a nice evening. I think we'll hop out at that stoplight and walk it from there."

The two men dragged their backpacks from the car with a hurried "Thanks a lot, man," and sprinted down an empty side street. I recognized their paranoia from my own summers hitching around America, climbing into strangers' cars alert for any flicker of weirdness or trouble. Rob gave more than a flicker; he fairly broadcast wacko.

"What was wrong with those guys, anyway?" Rob asked, popping a beer and speeding out through the darkening town.

We crossed the Potomac into Maryland, as Lee's army had done after routing the Federals at Second Manassas. By carrying the War north, Lee hoped to demoralize the Union and convince Britain and France to recognize the Confederacy. He also wanted to steer the fighting away from Virginia's war-ravaged farms during harvest. But Lee's detour from his Virginia supply base forced rebel soldiers to live off the land. The Confederates who straggled through Maryland in September 1862 were as ragged as the Southern army would ever be until the last, desperate days before Appomattox.

"When I say they were hungry, I convey no impression of the gaunt starvation that looked from their cavernous eyes," Rob read from a Maryland woman's diary, as we sat by the river. "All day they crowded to the doors of our houses, with always the same drawling complaint: 'I've been a-marchin' and a-fightin' for six weeks stiddy, and I ain't had n-a-r-thin' to eat 'cept green apples an' green cawn.'"

Unripe apples and corn caused diarrhea, draining the men still more. Many rebels also went barefoot. One Marylander described passing Confederates as a "ragged, lean and hungry set of wolves. Yet there was a dash about them that the Northern men lacked. They rode like circus riders." Rob became even more animated than usual as he read these accounts, which described the exact image of the Confederacy he sought so hard to capture in his reenacting: threadbare, famished, lice- and dysentery-ridden, yet for all that romantic.

It was ten o'clock when we reached Sharpsburg, the small Maryland town where Lee's northern push ended beside Antietam Creek, on September 17, the bloodiest day of the Civil War. Sharpsburg didn't appear much bigger now than it had been in 1862. Modest storefronts and shallow-porched houses clung to the main street. The only sign of life was an old tavern called Pete's, with a neon Coors sign flickering in the window and a Union and Confederate soldier posted on a placard by the door.

As soon as we stepped inside, I wondered if we'd made a mistake. The entire bar crowd turned to stare at us, and their gaze wasn't altogether friendly. Most of the patrons were young men with unkempt beards, cut-off T-shirts, menacing tattoos, and eyes red from hours of assault drinking and smoking. One of the men looked up from the pool table and mumbled, "Looks like we've got some Civil War boys here."

Ignoring their stares, I headed straight to the bar and studied a handwritten menu listing pickled eggs and something called a Jell-O Shooter. "What's that?" I asked the barmaid.

"A Jell-O and vodka slush," she said.

"Try one, Yank," the man beside me said. "It'll fuck you up good."

I ordered beer instead and slipped, reflexively, into the gee-whiz reporter mode I often adopted in awkward spots. "What do folks do here in Sharpsburg?" I asked my neighbor.

"Drink," he said.

"What else?"

"Fish."

I turned to the man on my other side and asked the same question. He, too, was cross-eyed from alcohol. "We fish," he said blearily. "And drink. I drank my breakfast. Lunch, too."

Rob stood a few feet away, listening to a long-haired man who wore leather chaps and a black T-shirt decorated with a skull and crossbones. The man spoke in a drunken stage whisper. "Well, Johnnie," he told Rob, "*you* can stay, but your Yankee friend has got to go." He sounded like he was teasing, but I couldn't tell for sure.

"Round here," another man barked, "we don't like the Feds."

Rob nodded approvingly. "If the government doesn't stop telling people how to live," he bellowed like a rebel of old, "there just might be another Civil War."

"Damn right! The government isn't going to take away my guns!"

"Nossir!" Rob said, slapping the man's shoulder. "Once we lose those guns, no telling what goes next."

At this point one of the bikers offered to buy us a round. Another man wanted to put us up for the night. We politely declined both offers, drained our beers, and slipped back into the Maryland night.

Relieved, I complimented Rob on his performance. He smiled and hummed "My Maryland," the wartime song that began "The despot's heel is on thy shore!" and ended "She breathes! She burns! She'll come! She'll come!" Maryland never did come—into the Confederacy, that is. But the sympathies of many of her citizens remained strongly Southern. It was a Marylander, John Wilkes Booth, who leapt onto the stage of Ford's Theater shouting *"Sic semper tyrannis!"* after having put a bullet in Lincoln's head. For the crowd at Pete's Bar, at least, sentiments hadn't changed all that much in the 130 years since.

As we drove to the edge of the battlefield park, Rob disclosed our plan of attack. We'd hike under cover of darkness to our camping spot in Bloody Lane, the sunken road where the South lost several thousand men in the space of three hours. It was a loony scheme, not to mention illegal. I knew from my visit to Shiloh that darkness didn't protect us from park rangers trolling with night-vision gog-

gles. Anyway, sleeping in a ditch that had once brimmed with Confederate dead struck me as vaguely necrophiliac.

"Don't worry, I went there with Joel," Rob said, raising the ghost
of Gasms past. "I bloated in the Lane and had my picture taken, but
I felt bad about it and tore the picture up. This time we'll just sleep
there." As for trespassing after dark, Rob said we were actually pro-
tecting the park. "If I ever catch a vandal touching a monument or
cannon, they'll wish for a ranger to come save their ass from me."

So we suited up, with our haversacks and canteens and blankets
rolled and tied like sausage and slung across our chests. Rob poured
a last bottle of ale into a wicker jug. "It looks so much better that
way," he explained, leaving me to wonder who would appreciate this
touch of authenticity as we crept through the dark.

As we set off down a road skirting the park, lightning began to
flash, illuminating our path. There was also occasional traffic. Each
time headlights approached, we sprinted off the road and flung ourselves in the tall wet grass, lest the passing car belonged to a park
ranger or policeman or local citizen who might choose to report a
Confederate and a Union soldier sneaking onto the battlefield at
night. After ten minutes we were soaked and exhausted from this
ludicrous exercise, which reminded me of a wretched high school
football drill: running full tilt in pads and helmet and then sprawling
on the fifty-yard line.

A half-mile down the road, we climbed awkwardly over a split-rail
fence and bushwhacked in what Rob guessed was the direction of
Bloody Lane. Night-blind, he led us straight into a tangle of bram-
bles and barbed wire. Scratched and bleeding, we pushed on, through
woods and fields and woods again. At one point, crunching through
chest-high thorns and listening for Rob's tramp in the dark ahead, I
began to appreciate the utter misery of marching. In some memoirs,
soldiers told of welcoming battle simply as an end to the agony and
boredom of another day's march. I also felt the reckless urge that
soldiers so often succumbed to, shedding their gear and staggering
on unburdened. And we'd only been walking an hour; in the summer
of 1862, many of Lee's men marched over 1,000 miles.

"At least we're losing some weight," Rob said, dripping with sweat. "I need to drop five pounds if I'm going to look good at Gettysburg next weekend."

We glimpsed the outline of a building that Rob recognized as Piper's Farm, a bed-and-breakfast that had served as James Longstreet's headquarters during the battle. A light still glowed inside, so we slipped through the garden and into the cornfields beyond, hoping no one would hear us or decide to let fly a barrel of buckshot.

By then, the moon had risen. As we hiked between the tall rows of corn the view opened up, with mountains silhouetted on all sides. The moon was bright enough to read by. Loose clouds and distant flashes of lightning flitted across the night sky, matching the ground-level flicker of fireflies. Rob's scarecrow frame formed a clear outline just ahead of me, with his slouch hat and pointed beard and bedroll humpbacked on his shoulder. He looked less like a Confederate than a freight-jumping hobo.

Swigging from his jug of ale, Rob turned and said, in a giddy stage whisper, "This sure as shit ain't normal." Meaning us, trespassing in the dark, searching for a corpse-haunted ditch to spend the night in. I felt the same surge of Dharma Bum glee I'd experienced that morning as we set off on the Gasm; as though I'd crawled out my bedroom window for a lark with some dissolute buddy my parents didn't approve of.

Our spirits deflated a moment later when we spotted, at what seemed an impossible distance, the observation tower that marked one end of Bloody Lane. "We've been walking the wrong way for an hour," Rob confessed. Using the tower as a guidon, we turned and marched through yet more fields and woods and over fences, stopping every few hundred yards to make sure we could still see the tower through the trees.

It was 2 A.M. when we reached Bloody Lane. The sunken road was much deeper than Shiloh's, a full man-height below ground level and fronted by a snake-rail fence. In 1862, this made it a natural trench from which the Confederates could repel wave after wave of Federal infantryman charging across an adjoining field. Eventually, the Federals seized one end of the Lane, allowing the Northerners to fire down and along its length. "We were shooting them like sheep in a pen," a New Yorker recalled. The bodies lay so thick, another soldier wrote, that "they formed a line which one might have walked upon" without touching the ground.

This "ghastly flooring" was now covered in low grass and we unfurled our gum blankets, heavy tarps made of vulcanized rubber. I looked quizzically at Rob. "Charles Goodyear, patented 1844," he assured me. Then, lighting candles, we read aloud from our final selection for the day: the memoir of John Brown Gordon, who commanded an Alabama regiment defending Bloody Lane.

"With all my lung power I shouted 'Fire!' Our rifles flamed and roared in the Federals' faces like a blinding blaze of lightning. The effect was appalling. The entire front line, with few exceptions, went down." Gordon was shot five times at Bloody Lane, with one bullet shattering his cheek. "Mars," he later observed, "is not an aesthetic God."

Rob closed the book and snuffed out the candles. We lay on our tarps, still soaked with sweat from our long hike. A breeze came up and the sweat turned cool. Ground moisture began to leach through our tarps. The damp—and our body funk—began to attract mosquitoes. Then, around 3 A.M., came the coup de grâce: a low-lying fog from the nearby Potomac, rolling through the swales and valleys and into the Sunken Road. The temperature dropped precipitously, making it unseasonably cold, like San Francisco on a foggy summer's day.

I tossed and turned in my sodden clothes, vainly searching for a position that might afford some warmth. Spooning seemed the only hope for sleep, except that Rob—wet, wretched and writhing—looked about as comforting to hug as a sick walrus.

"This kind of night will give you a good phlegm roll, like they had in the War," he groaned.

"What's that?" I asked, not really wanting to hear the answer.

"It's when you're so congested with phlegm that you can't cough it out and it just sort of rolls around in your chest and throat. There's a guy who writes in his diary that 'when one hundred thousand men began to stir at reveille, the sound of their coughing would drown that of the beating drums.'"

Rob coughed a bit and went on, "There's also stuff in the pension rolls about pneumonia and bronchitis that made these guys miserable for the rest of their lives. And if your feet don't dry well after a night like this, you'll have horrible blisters. The wet skin just tears right off when you march."

At least no one was shooting at us. "I was at the National Archives the other day," Rob said, "reading about this guy who got popped in the balls and the bullet came out his sphincter. Had to wear diapers the rest of his life."

Rob droned on in this vein until he talked himself to sleep. I lay awake, afflicted by the creeping paranoia known only to 4 A.M. insomniacs—especially those camped illegally in a foggy ditch where the dead once lay in heaps. Something rustled on the grassy bank above our heads. A park ranger with infrared goggles? Why was my breath suddenly so raspy? And who was that huge white figure standing down the Lane, pointing straight at us?

I finally managed a shallow doze until dawn. Opening my eyes and peering through the still-dense fog, I realized that the specter eyeing me in the night was a tall stone soldier clutching a stone flag. Rob lay in a fetal curl and looked at me with what seemed a rare flash of hardcore self-doubt. "Sometimes I wonder how I ended up here," he moaned. "I tend to blame that Blue and Gray set from Sears."

Not wanting to compound our crime by starting a fire on the battlefield, we decided to seek breakfast in town. The fog covered our movements as we crept back to the road, which lay only a few hundred yards from Bloody Lane, a distance we'd stretched into five miles or so during our circuitous night hike. Finding a diner that opened at 6 A.M., we perched at the counter and devoured our eggs and home-fried potatoes while studying a photographic book filled with pictures of the Antietam dead.

"These are some of the best shots you'll ever see of bloated people," Rob said. "See this guy with the puffy eyelids and the mouth all puckered? Classic bloating. The lips can't close, so they swell outward, in an O. Or they can curl in. See, here's an innie, there's an outie."

Rob soaked up some yolk with his toast and turned the page. "Look at the legs on that guy, real thick, no wrinkles in the fabric. And the pants are pinched around the groin. He wasn't that thick in real life." The man beside us glanced up from his sports page and paid his bill. "I guess I'm intrigued by these pictures," Rob went on, "because I haven't seen corpses in real life."

The photos also offered clinical evidence Rob could use to refine his Confederate impression, live as well as dead. "The pictures are close-ups and they aren't staged, so you can study the belt buckles, the piping on their trousers, the bits of carpet that Confederates sometimes used as bedrolls. See that dead guy's canteen with the corrugated tin? It's captured Federal issue. That's the sort of solid documentary evidence of what rebels wore that you can't get anywhere else."

Mathew Brady's display of these pictures at his New York studio soon after the battle proved a pivotal event in the history of both war and photography. Visitors to Brady's gallery confronted a reality they'd often seen represented in art and print but rarely if ever in photographs. "With the aid of the magnifying glass, the very features of the slain may be distinguished," reported the *New York Times*, which likened Brady's exhibit to "a few dripping bodies, fresh from the field, laid along the pavement."

Oliver Wendell Holmes Sr., who had traveled to Antietam in search of his wounded son, glimpsed the pacifist message inherent in Brady's stark portraits of the dead. "The sight of these pictures is a commentary on civilization such as the savage might well triumph to show its missionaries," he wrote. For the first time, Holmes realized, mankind possessed images that stripped war of its romance and revealed combat for what it really was: "a repulsive, brutal, sickening hideous thing."

The military certainly understood this; after the Civil War, it censored photographs of American battle dead for almost eighty years. Not until the 1960s would the public routinely see vivid images of their own sons at war. In that sense, the TV-fueled opposition to Vietnam wound back to the pictures of the Antietam dead that Rob and I studied over coffee and eggs.

As we returned to the battlefield, I was also struck by how closely the landscape still resembled the one shown in the 1862 photographs. It was easy to align each grim portrait with the bucolic farmland across which the soldiers fell: flung promiscuously along a split-rail fence by the Hagerstown Turnpike, surrounding artillery caissons near the Dunker church, sprawled across a cornfield where advancing troops had been exposed by the glint of their bayonets above the man-high stalks. Over 130 years later, the corn was still there, tended by descendants of the German-American family that had sown the same field in 1862.

There was one photograph in particular Rob wanted to revisit. Enlarged to wall size and hanging inside the Antietam visitors' center, it showed Confederates marching through the streets of Frederick on their way to the battle. The image was believed to be the only photograph from the entire war showing rebels on the move (rather than in camp, dead on the field, captured, or posing stiffly for a studio portrait). Though blurred and faded, the photograph—crowded with lean jaunty men in slouch hats—perfectly captured the ragged panache of the rebel army.

The photograph had inspired Rob and his fellow Southern Guardsmen to concoct a peculiar fantasy. They wanted to stage precisely the same scene, with hardcores filling the role of each Confederate pictured, right down to their equipment, expression and stance. Then, they'd position an old camera in a window and take the exact picture all over again. "That's about as close as you could ever get to Being There," Rob said.

Our own time-travel was drifting off course. We'd lingered around the battlefield for twelve hours, a veritable epoch by Gasm standards. And Antietam was what Rob called "early war"; we still had the rest of '62 and the first half of '63 to tour in what remained of the day. This meant speeding several hours south to central Virginia, where most of the action occurred in the eight months following Antietam.

As we drove back across the Potomac, Rob took out his notebook and updated the list of stops we'd made so far. "We're up to ten, if we count First and Second Manassas as separate hits," he said. "Not too bad for the first twenty-four hours."

MIDWAY THROUGH the long morning drive, Rob twiddled the radio dial until he found a rock 'n' roll station to keep us awake. Then, shouting over the music, he previewed the next phase of the

War, between Lee's retreat from Maryland in September 1862, and his ruinous march to Gettysburg the following June.

"These were the South's Glory Days," he said, borrowing from Bruce Springsteen. At Fredericksburg in late 1862, Lee repelled a Union invasion in one of the most lopsided slaughters of the War. Then, the next May at Chancellorsville, Lee crushed "Fighting Joe" Hooker and his 134,000 Federals, the largest army ever assembled on American soil and a force twice the size of Lee's.

Chancellorsville proved Lee's greatest triumph and also sealed the sainthood of Stonewall Jackson, who was mortally wounded while flanking the Federals—the apogee of his brief military career and ultimately that of the Confederacy's. "Stonewall was a lot like Jimi Hendrix and Jim Morrison," Rob said. "They were all peaking when they died and didn't stick around to become has-beens."

The analogy wasn't airtight. Morrison and Hendrix were sex-crazed hippies who OD'd on drugs; Stonewall was a Bible-thumping teetotaler who sucked on lemons and sipped warm water because he thought the human body should avoid extremes. But Rob was onto something. If Jackson had survived, and failed to change the course of the War, his luster might have been dulled by the South's eventual defeat. "Better to burn out than to fade away," Rob wailed, echoing Neil Young.

We were doing both by the time we reached the outskirts of Fredericksburg, which bore a depressing resemblance to Manassas. Developers had achieved what several Union generals never could, conquering Fredericksburg and littering the elegant colonial town with acres of modern crud. As we crawled along Jeff Davis Highway, past a shopping mall called Lee's Plaza, Rob scanned the ranks of franchise restaurants. "Fast food's one of the compromises you make on the Gasm, in the interest of speed," he said. "When you power tour, sometimes you have to power lunch." Rob ticked off our options, slotting in his own tags for all the familiar names. "Toxic Hell," he said, pointing at a Taco Bell. Then came "Pizza Slut." Arby's, inevitably, became "Farby's." We settled for the drive-thru window at Hardee's, which at least bore the name of a rebel general in the Army of Tennessee.

Lunch made us even drowsier, so we decided to do what Rob

called "a drive-by hit" on Fredericksburg (appropriately, an urban battle fought partly at night). Then we headed to Chancellorsville, ten miles west of town. In 1863, Chancellorsville wasn't a ville at all, just an inn called the Chancellor House located at the intersection of the Orange Turnpike and a plank road (literally, wooden planks nailed to logs laid over the mud). The battle also formed the unnamed backdrop to *The Red Badge of Courage*, in which Stephen Crane described a landscape of "little fields girted and squeezed by a forest."

Now, Chancellorsville was slowly being sucked into the maw of greater Fredericksburg, with subdivisions and faux plantation houses poking through the trees at every turn. The Park Service oversaw only a fraction of the vast battleground; earlier in the century, the government had been slow to acquire land near Chancellorsville, arousing suspicions that it wasn't eager to commemorate the most resounding of Southern triumphs.

Now, every inch not formally protected by law appeared slated for ruin. The local paper reported that a company called Fas Mart planned to build a gas station and convenience store on the spot where Stonewall Jackson turned the Confederate army in the famous flanking maneuver that won the day for the South. The irony was unintended—a Fas Mart supplanting Jackson's fast march—but the neglect of history was not. "It's just a handful of people concerned about the battlefields," the county supervisor told the newspaper, defending Fas Mart in the name of "property rights."

Near the center of the sprawl-pocked battlefield, we turned in at the small visitors' center. Rob told the ranger behind the desk, "We want to see everything relating to Stonewall Jackson's getting popped." The ranger interpreted Rob's question in narrowly anatomical terms. "All we have here is Stonewall's arm," he said. "The rest of him's in Lexington, along with his horse."

I caught Rob's eye. *Stonewall's arm?* We knew, of course, that surgeons amputated Jackson's shattered arm near Chancellorsville. But nowhere in the visitors' guide was there any hint that the sacred limb still resided on the premises.

"We don't really tell people about it," the ranger explained, "unless they specifically ask." Then he pulled a map from beneath the desk and showed us how to reach the arm's burial ground, on private property a short drive west. "You may find some lemons lying around," the ranger added.

Just outside the visitors' center stood a monument marking the site of Jackson's wounding, at the climax of his triumph on May 2. After a day-long march around Hooker's huge force, Jackson's men crashed out of the woods shortly before sunset and demolished the Union flank. At nightfall, as the Union fell back in disarray, Jackson galloped ahead of his lines to reconnoiter the enemy and judge whether to press the attack by moonlight. He was riding back through the dark woods when North Carolina pickets mistook his entourage for Union cavalry. "Pour it to them, boys!" an officer shouted. The volley struck Jackson three times in the hand and arm and killed four of his fellow riders. Jackson, ever the dour drillmaster, allegedly declared to an aide, "Wild fire, that."

A few yards from the monument lay a large quartz boulder dragged to the site by oxen soon after the War. The lump of stone, known simply as "the Jackson rock," was somehow more eloquent than the fine Victorian statuary that usually adorned such spots. A teenager stood reverentially studying the stone. He had spiked hair, earrings in every orifice, black combat boots, cutoff camouflage shorts and a T-shirt that read: "Sex Pistols. Pretty Vacant." He looked up and nodded at Rob, and said, Punk to Grunge: "Nice threads. Where can I get some of those?" Rob gave the teenager his address and promised to send a copy of the hardcore "vendors' list" he'd mailed me when I first expressed interest in reenacting. As the teenager wandered off, Rob said he often recruited people this way. "The uniform's like a worm, it's bait on your hook. Once they nibble at it, all you've got to do is reel them in."

From the site of Jackson's wounding, we worked our way backwards in time to the pine grove where Jackson met Lee on the night before Stonewall's final march. The two generals sat on hardtack boxes beside a campfire, plotting their bold scheme to split the Southern army and send Jackson around the Union flank. Their parting the next morning, known as the "Last Meeting," was the

most sanctified of all the Lost Cause's hallowed moments, reproduced in countless prints and paintings that once adorned the homes
of many Southern whites.

"We'll do all the art and mythology stuff tomorrow in Richmond,"
Rob said. Today's lesson was anatomy. So we drove on, stalking
Stonewall's arm. Probably no limb in history was so heavily signposted. We passed an historical marker by the road titled "Wounding
of Jackson" and another labeled "Jackson's Amputation." After Jackson's wounding, litter-bearers carried him off the field under heavy
fire, twice spilling the general on the ground. Then came chloroform
and the surgeon's scalpel; a tiny stump was all that could be saved of
Jackson's left arm. Stonewall, characteristically, took the loss in
stride. Awakening from his drugged sleep, he declared that the doctor's bone-saw had sounded "the most delightful music."

The next day, Jackson was loaded on an ambulance and taken to a
farm well behind the lines. An aide, meanwhile, bundled up the severed arm and carried it to his own brother's house for burial in the
family graveyard. We parked on the quiet country lane leading to
the spot. Rob dug two Ambulance Corps armbands from his haversack—"to get us in the right spirit"—and we slipped them on before
walking solemnly toward the burial ground, which lay at the center
of a just-tilled cornfield, ringed by a small iron fence and a perimeter
of gopher holes.

The graveyard was unremarkable, except for one lumpy stone
with an inscription that read: "Arm of Stonewall Jackson May 3
1863." No birth or death dates, no list of accomplishments. Just date
of severance. It got stranger than that. A nearby marker stated:
"During a mock battle attended by President Warren Harding in
1921, Marine Corps General Smedley D. Butler exhumed the arm
and reburied it in a metal box." Butler, I later learned, had heard
from a local man that Jackson's arm lay buried there, and arrogantly
declared, "Bosh! I will take a squad of marines and dig up that spot to
prove you wrong!" He found the arm bone in a box several feet beneath the surface and repented by reburying it and erecting a bronze
plaque, which had since disappeared.

It was midafternoon, we were dazed and spent, and the graveyard
seemed as good a place as any to rest for a while. Rob lay with his

eyes closed while I read aloud from the books we'd picked up at the visitors' center. Amidst hagiographic retellings of Stonewall's triumphs I caught glimpses of Jackson's famed idiosyncrasy. This was a man who was fearless in battle, but so hypochondriacal that he believed eating a single grain of black pepper was enough for him to "lose all strength in my right leg." He was a stern Presbyterian who frowned on public dancing, yet loved doing the polka with his wife in their parlor. A Virginian who owned six slaves, he broke state law by teaching blacks at Sunday school. He was also a merciless taskmaster who pushed his men ceaselessly and shot deserters without remorse, yet succumbed himself to battle fatigue during the Seven Days campaign and napped catatonically through much of the fray.

"He wasn't stable. That's attractive to me," Rob said. "Plus the fact that he always won. I may be a loser but at least I was born on the same day as a winner."

The identification went deeper than that. Jackson and the "foot cavalry" he led were mostly men of humble background from the Shenandoah Valley. Jackson grew up in the hill country of what was now West Virginia and spent his youth Huck Finn-ishly; orphaned at seven, he later rode a raft down the Ohio to the Mississippi, selling firewood to passing steamers.

Rob's own family came from the same sort of modest, upcountry Southern stock. His father was born in a log house in hardscrabble hill country near Rock Creek, Alabama. A mule-trader's son, he quit school after the eighth grade and at sixteen caught a ride to Cleveland, where he arrived with $15 in his pocket. While boarding with a Southern family, he met Rob's mother, whose clan came from Tennessee. Nine days after they married, Rob's father shipped out to fight the Japanese and returned thirty months later, shell-shocked, one of only seven men in his unit of fifty-seven to survive.

Rob's father had recently retired from selling used cars and moved with his wife to the log homestead in Alabama that his forebears had lived in for generations. "Even though I was raised in the North I feel strong ties to the South, or at least the poor part of it my family came from," Rob said. He'd been gratified to discover at the Archives that his ancestors were common farmers who owned no slaves. Such yeoman often resented the plantation gentry, who could be exempted from military service if they owned twenty or more slaves, a loop-hole that prompted the famous Southern gripe: "a rich man's war and a poor man's fight."

Rob clearly cast his lot with the latter. "I like to think of myself as the average grunt," he said, peeling off his filthy socks and draping them over a gravestone to air.

We snoozed beside Stonewall's arm until the cool of the day, then trudged back to the car. The land all around us was actually twice-fought ground. Almost a year to the day after Stonewall's wounding, the North fought Lee's army again in the dense thicket just west of Chancellorsville, known as the Wilderness. In some spots, soldiers stumbled on bones of men left unburied from fighting the year before.

The Wilderness wasn't so wild anymore; apart from a few road-side exhibits, stray cannons, and trails winding into the woods, much of the battlefield had been lost to development. We followed one line of trenches until it ended abruptly at a vast, brick-walled compound with a sign that said: "Fawn Lake, An NTS Club Community."

Curious, we followed a shaded entrance road into the community, which was bordered by signs warning "security patrols in effect." Then came a guard booth. The sentry said only residents were allowed beyond this point, but he let us drive just far enough to glimpse the golf course, artificial lake and wooded homesites that lay beyond. The development was laid out along streets and cul-de-sacs named for Longstreet, Jackson, Burnside, Appomattox—the only hint that minié balls, rather than golf balls, had once sliced through the air all around here.

As we wound back out of the development, Rob pointed to rifle pits still dimly visible in the road's median strip. "I should go bloat in one of those trenches," he fumed. "I'd like these rich fucks to have to look at me every time they tee off."

I had never seen Rob so angry. He'd told me before we set off that every Gasm finds its own theme; the dispiriting leitmotif of ours, at least so far, was the devastation of Virginia's historic landscape. The Wilderness a golfers' rough; Stonewall's flank march a Fas Mart; Jackson and Lee and Longstreet now names of shopping malls and streets built on the ground over which they'd once fought.

Rob and his fellow hardcores often staged marches to raise money for the preservation of battlefields and the landscape surrounding them. But sometimes Rob thought more radical action was required. "I fantasize a lot about my buddy who has a twelve-pound Napoleon firing some solid shot at this shit," he said, as we drove past a housing development called Lee-Jackson Estates.

We pushed on, past historic markers and realtors' signs, until we reached Spotsylvania Courthouse, where Grant battled Lee a few days after the Wilderness. By May 1864, both armies had learned the grim lesson of Bloody Lane; here, the trenches twisted and turned so the defenders could "enfilade" attackers, or fire on them from several sides. The rebels also axed trees from in front of their breastworks to create a clear kill zone. Then they sharpened the felled trees and deployed them as pikelike obstacles called abatis, bristling in front of their trenches. Spotsylvania was a long way from Shiloh, where generals regarded trench digging as unmanly and demoralizing, and a short way from the Western Front in World War I.

It was also here, at a salient called Bloody Angle, that some of the most intimate and fevered killing of the entire War occurred. At dawn on May 12, Grant threw 20,000 men at the rebel line; for eighteen hours, often in heavy rain, the two sides engaged in a rare instance of prolonged hand-to-hand combat as they hacked, bludgeoned, bayonetted and blasted away at point-blank range. The attack achieved little, except some 14,000 casualties. Corpses packed the muddy trenches so densely that burial parties simply collapsed the breastworks to cover the dead.

For half an hour I listened to Rob read aloud from accounts of the carnage: "The writhing of the wounded and dying who lay beneath the dead bodies moved the whole mass. . . . Troops were killed by thrusts and stabs through chinks in the log barricade, while others were harpooned by bayonetted rifles flung javelin-style across it . . . I never expect to be fully believed when I tell what I saw of the horrors of Spotsylvania." The horrors of it all were starting to numb me. Chancellorsville, Spotsylvania, and the Wilderness ranked three, four, and six in the list of bloodiest Civil War battles; Fredericksburg rounded out the top ten. All told, the ten-mile-square territory we'd traversed that afternoon claimed 100,000 casualties. The writer Bob Schacochis called Civil War Virginia "the abattoir of the South." At Bloody Angle, I felt as though we lay near the center of that slaughterhouse.

Butchery on the scale that occurred around Spotsylvania was hard to grasp, even for those who committed it. Curiously, many of the soldiers' accounts described a single oak tree, almost two feet in diameter, felled in the hail of small-arms fire. After the battle, the bullet-riddled stump was featured at the Centennial Exposition in Philadelphia and later installed at the Smithsonian. "The death of this single tree," one historian observed, "was a way of measuring the scale of combat that surpassed understanding."

The death of a single man was also easier to grasp than the massacre of thousands, particularly if that man happened to be Stonewall Jackson. Even the nonpartisan Park Service literature referred to his death site by the name Southerners gave it: the "Jackson Shrine." As shrines went, it was modest: a small frame cottage at a sleepy rail spur called Guinea Station, where doctors sent Jackson to recover after the amputation of his arm. During the twenty-seven-mile ambulance ride, civilians lined the route, offering the wounded general fried chicken, biscuits and buttermilk.

We waited until full dark, then crept along a half-mile gravel road leading from the old railroad station to the Shrine. Except for a caretaker's house and a few dogs howling in the dark, there wasn't much to worry about. It was a fine, starry night and the A-frame cottage stood clearly silhouetted in a small clearing not far from the railroad tracks. Unfurling our bedrolls on the building's front porch, we took turns reading aloud about Jackson's final days.

At first, Jackson seemed headed for a brisk recovery. But after a few days, nausea and fever set in. Doctors diagnosed this as pneumonia, though modern physicians suspected that Jackson's falls from his stretcher at Chancellorsville may have caused internal bleeding as well. Doctors treated the pneumonia with crude measures common in that day, such as bleeding Jackson and cupping his chest with hot glass to raise a blister and draw out ill humors. But on the morn-

ing of May 10th the general's doctor informed Jackson's wife that
her husband would not last the day. When she told her husband,
Jackson asked the doctor for confirmation, then announced: "My
wish is fulfilled. I have always desired to die on Sunday."

The scene recalled an interview with Shelby Foote I'd read, in
which he talked about the deathbed rituals of the mid-nineteenth
century. "When you are dying, the doctor says you're dying," Foote
said. "You assemble your family around you and sing hymns and you
are brave and stalwart and tell the little woman that she has been
good to you and not to cry. And you tell the children to be good and
mind their mother, Daddy's fixing to go away. That was called making a good death, and it was very important."

Jackson's death wasn't just good, it was sublime. After consoling
his distraught wife and cuddling his newborn daughter, he declined
the doctor's offer of brandy, declaring, "I want to preserve my mind,
if possible, to the end." Then, as Foote told it in his narrative of the
War, Jackson slipped into a deathbed delirium, "alternately praying
and giving commands, all of which had to do with the offensive.
Shortly after 3 o'clock, a few minutes before he died, he called out:
'Order A. P. Hill to prepare for action! Pass the infantry to the front.
Tell Major Hawks—' He left the sentence unfinished, seeming thus
to have put the war behind him: for he smiled as he spoke his last
words, in a tone of calm relief. 'Let us cross over the river,' he said,
'and rest under the shade of the trees.'"

Bizarrely, legend held that Robert E. Lee also ordered A. P. Hill
into battle from his deathbed. "Tell Hill he *must* come up," Lee said,
before making his own good death by uttering, "Strike the tent."
A. P. Hill was a hot-tempered, gonorrhea-wracked commander who
wore a red shirt into battle and feuded with his superiors. Judging
from Lee's and Jackson's last words, Hill obviously got under their
skins. I wondered whether Hill reciprocated by mentioning either
commander on his own deathbed.

"Don't know, but I doubt it," Rob mumbled sleepily. "Hill got
waxed at Petersburg, near where Pickett was getting loaded at a fish
fry while losing the Battle of Five Forks."

"Hunh?"

"We'll see it all later in the Gasm," Rob said, drifting off to sleep.

I lay awake for a while. Night erased all sign of the twentieth century, as it had at Antietam, and lying there on the wood-slat porch, a few feet from where Jackson died, I felt the mournfulness of our campsite. Eight weeks after Jackson's death, Lee's army self-destructed at Gettysburg. Southerners and Civil War buffs had speculated ever since that Gettysburg—and, consequently, the whole course of the War—might have gone differently had Jackson been there. "That old house," the English prime minister David Lloyd George observed on visiting the Jackson shrine in 1923, "witnessed the downfall of the Southern Confederacy."

Guinea Station also possessed a spare dignity that suited the man it enshrined. The cottage bore little resemblance to the grand manses of the plantation South, just as Jackson had little in common with patricians such as Lee, who hailed from one of Virginia's leading families, married into another, and spent his adult life shuttling between vast estates. Jackson, by contrast, married a minister's daughter and when she died in childbirth he married another, honeymooning each time at Niagara Falls. He settled in a modest town house near the Virginia Military Institute, where he taught until the War broke out. His professor's salary didn't allow for much extravagance, even if his Presbyterian temperament had permitted it.

My musings were interrupted by Rob, who rolled over and mumbled, "Forgot something." Then he pulled out his notebook and scribbled: "Gasm, Day Two."

5:30	wake up, Bloody Lane
6:00	breakfast at diner, look at bloaters
7–9:30	antietam: cornfield, dunker church, museum
12–1	fredericksburg (drive-by)
2–5	chancellorsville, wilderness, stonewall's arm
6–8	spotsylvania
10–1	jackson shrine. cosmic. read about death

We were only to May 1863, the midpoint of the War. "Get some rest," Rob said, pulling a blanket over his head. "Tomorrow we've got to do Jeb Stuart's death, plus Richmond and the rest of '64."

Tomorrow arrived a few hours later when a freight train roared past, just fifty or so yards from our campsite. In the dim predawn light I peered through the windows of the cottage, which revealed itself now as a handsome weatherboard structure with a shingle roof, wide pine floors, white walls and a stark Shaker beauty. In one room stood the bed in which Jackson died, a four-poster with ropes beneath the mattress and a jack to tighten the hemp before bed (hence the phrase "sleep tight"). A clock sat on the mantel, the same one that had ticked away the last minutes of Stonewall's life. It was set to 3:15, the exact time of Jackson's death.

A year and a day after Stonewall's death, Lee's army lost its most renowned cavalryman. The site of Jeb Stuart's mortal wounding, Yellow Tavern, sounded appropriately romantic: the sort of rustic saloon where Stuart might have danced in his spurs on the night before battle. Though a teetotaler and devout Christian, like Stonewall, Stuart cultivated the image of a wanton Cavalier, with his extravagantly coiffed beard, silken yellow sash, crimson-lined cape and ostrich plume poking up from his slouch hat. Stuart spoke of his daring rides around the Union army as if they were fox chases; after one narrow escape, he declared he'd rather "die game" than accept surrender.

Stuart fell gamely enough, shot off his horse while emptying a pistol at George Custer's cavalry just north of Richmond. Only thirty-one, he quickly joined Stonewall in the pantheon of Confederate gods. But the site of Stuart's last battle seemed as elusive as the fleet horseman had been in life. The crossroads where the eponymous Yellow Tavern once stood now featured a car lot, a body shop, and a Go-Kart store. Even the name had vanished from the map. The commercial sprawl surrounding the crossroads now belonged to a Richmond suburb called Glen Allen. Apart from a roadside historical marker—perched beside the Cavalier Motel—there was no hint of the fight that claimed one of the War's most colorful and courageous figures.

Finally, after wandering a maze of cul-de-sacs and housing tracts—Jeb Stuart Parkway, Stonewall Glen, Lee's Crossing—we found an obelisk within earshot of the interstate. Erected in 1888 by Stuart's men, the monument bore a classic paeon to Southern manhood: "He was Fearless and Faithful, Pure and Powerful, Tender and True." We stood there for a few minutes, trying to conjure the gallant Cavalier over the roar of truck traffic on I-95 and the insistent pock-pock of a tennis ball from a nearby court. *Sic transit* Yellow Tavern.

Later, after talking to historians and touring other lost corners of the Civil War landscape, I began to grasp the melancholy logic of Yellow Tavern's demise and that of so many other sites. While other wars on American soil occurred largely along the frontier, the major clashes of the Civil War were mostly fought for control of rail junctions, crossroads, and river or sea ports: Manassas, Atlanta, Charleston, Chattanooga, Fredericksburg, Petersburg, and so on. During America's rapid industrialization in the fifty years after the War, many of these transportation hubs naturally grew into commercial and manufacturing centers. What highways and office blocks hadn't yet claimed, suburbs were now devouring. Only at isolated battlegrounds such as Antietam and Shiloh was there much hope of the historic landscape remaining relatively pristine.

LEAVING YELLOW TAVERN, we sidled around Richmond, as Lee and Grant had done in 1864. Once again, the armies met on ground they'd fought over before: the gentle hills and swampy streams east of Richmond, where Lee drove back George McClellan in 1862. We decided to tour only the latter campaign and headed for Cold Harbor, where the fighting climaxed in early June of 1864.

Cold Harbor wasn't actually a port and it certainly wasn't cold; on the day we visited the temperature soared to 95. Harbor was believed to be an archaic English term for a tavern, and Cold a reference to the food served there. Either that, or Cold was a corruption of coal. Or, possibly, the whole name referred to a pleasant rest stop originally known as Cool Arbor. Whatever.

The tavern had vanished along with much of the battleground, covered now in suburban homes, including one tract incongruously named Strawberry Fields. What remained was a small, peaceful glen with Union and Confederate trenches separated by a few hundred yards of flat, almost open ground. After the Wilderness and Spotsylvania, Grant believed Lee's army was exhausted. So he ordered a Somme-style assault that he thought would crush his well-entrenched but badly outmanned foe.

His soldiers knew better. On the night before the dawn attack, one of Grant's staff officers observed: "Many of the soldiers had taken off their coats, and seemed to be engaged in sewing up rents in them. This exhibition of tailoring seemed rather peculiar at such a moment, but upon closer examination it was found that the men were calmly writing their names and home addresses on slips of paper, and pinning them on the backs of their coats, so that their dead bodies might be recognized upon the field, and their fate made known to their families at home."

At 4:40 A.M. on June 3rd, 60,000 Federals poured out of their trenches along a front of seven miles. The waiting Confederates replied with a fusillade so fierce that windows rattled in Richmond, twelve miles away. "The division in front seemed to melt away like snow falling on moist ground," a Union soldier later wrote. In a matter of minutes the Federals lost over 6,000 men. "When I got by myself where I would not be ashamed of it," a Vermont soldier wrote home after the failed charge, "I cried like a whipped spanniel [sic]."

Grant later acknowledged that the assault was the worst blunder of his military career. But he compounded the slaughter by leaving hundreds of wounded men howling in the hot June sun. In one of the most callous episodes of this or any other war, Grant and Lee dickered for days over the terms of gathering the wounded from between their lines. Grant didn't want to lose face by requesting a formal truce; Lee, who had none of his own troops in the no-man's-land, saw little reason to give in. As the haggling went on, Shelby Foote wrote, "The cries of the injured, who now had been three days without water or relief from pain, sank to a mewling."

Grant finally caved and called for a cease-fire. When Union litter-bearers climbed out of their trenches, four days after the assault, they found only two men still alive amongst the piles of stinking corpses. One burial party discovered a dead Yankee with a diary in his pocket, the last entry of which read: "June 3. Cold Harbor. I was killed."

o o o

From Cold Harbor we crawled through dense traffic into downtown Richmond. The former capital of the Confederacy was now a bustling urban center of 750,000 and the tail of a megalopolis whose head lay at abolitionist Boston. But Richmond's integration into the extended "Bos-Wash" corridor was relatively recent, and the city seemed somehow more Southern than I'd expected. There was a geniality and leisure in the way people spoke and smiled at each other that resonated much more of Memphis or Charleston, a day's drive away, than of Virginia cities just a short distance north. At a diner, the waitress addressed me as "honey" and drawled the daily special: chicken and dumplings, buttermilk biscuits, fried squash. Somewhere on the stretch of I-95 we'd driven earlier in the day, we'd crossed the invisible line that still separated North from South.

Southernness branded Richmond in another, spookier way. The city was a vast cenotaph of secession, with tens of thousands of rebel graves, countless monuments, and the remains of Confederate bulwarks, armories, hospitals, prisons, old soldiers' homes. Confederate history formed such a rich humus beneath modern Richmond that the past sprouted in odd, forgotten spots, the way glimpses of pharaonic grandeur could suddenly appear amidst the chaos of twentieth-century Egypt. On a dead-end street in Richmond's predominantly black East End, we found a towering shaft modeled on Pompey's Pillar in Alexandria; a rebel perched on top, gazing out at abandoned factories, highway flyovers and downtown office towers (in one of which Jeb Stuart IV now labored as a stockbroker). At Hollywood Cemetery, Richmond's answer to Cairo's City of the Dead, a rough granite pyramid inscribed with the words "Alumni et Patriae Asto" (In Eternal Memory of Those Who Stood for Their Country) overlooked the graves of 18,000 Confederates.

In a less classical vein, a plaque on a concrete floodwall by the James River stated: "On this site stood Libby Prison C.S.A." The location of another infamous dungeon, Castle Thunder, was now a parking lot. Jeff Davis's misnamed executive mansion, the pale-gray "White House of the Confederacy," now sat in the shadow of a huge hospital complex. We skipped a tour of the house and headed instead for the much greater treasure adjoining it: The Museum of the Con-

federacy, finest of the Lost Cause's many reliquaries and the reposi-
tory of captured rebel flags returned to the South by an act of Congress forty years after Appomattox.

Rob said we had time for only a fraction of the museum's exhibit.
Predictably, he made a beeline for glass cases containing clothes,
mostly those of the men whose lives we'd spent the past few days
touring. We began by inspecting the bullet-riddled overcoat worn by
John Quincy Marr, whose death site at Fairfax had been the first
stop of our Gasm. "This was probably a sumac dye, light purplish
gray in the original," Rob said of the coat's muddy olive hue. "Oxygen and sunlight dulled its color."

We moved to a case displaying Jeb Stuart's thigh-high boots,
plumed hat, white gloves and a portrait of the general that he'd
signed, characteristically, "J.E.B. Stuart/Warpath Sept. 3d, 63." Another glass box held the amputation kit used to sever Stonewall's
arm, as well as an aide's jacket stained with the great man's blood.
"We're starting to make those Gasm connections," Rob said reverentially. "That jacket probably passed along the porch we slept on last
night. And that Black and Decker set touched the arm we napped on
top of yesterday afternoon."

But Rob reserved his deepest awe for the costumes of ordinary
foot soldiers: crumpled kepis, tattered brogans and pants made of
homespun jean cloth. "It was basically a twilled blend of cotton and
wool," Rob said, expertly studying the trouser fabric. There was also
a sewing kit, called a "housewife," used by soldiers to repair their
garments.

After racing through the other two floors of the museum, we sped
across town to a cluster of buildings that had once comprised a
Confederate Vatican: a city within a city devoted to a single faith.
The enclave, spanning several blocks, embraced a former Confeder-
ate soldiers' home and veterans' hospital, the Confederate Memorial
Chapel and the Confederate Memorial Institute, better known as the
"Battle Abbey of the South" (an allusion to the shrine William the
Conqueror built to honor the noblemen who fought with him at
Hastings). The Abbey contained the most famous artistic tribute to
the Lost Cause, a set of murals that mirrored the Bayeux Tapestry's
telling of William's conquest of England.

Painted in the grand style by a Frenchman trained at the École des Beaux-Arts, the murals followed a classical conceit, equating the seasons with the brief life-cycle of the Confederacy. "Spring" celebrated the South's early successes. Stonewall sat astride Little Sorrel as soldiers marched past, waving caps and leaning forward, as though eager to do battle. "The colors are strong but Jackson's off," Rob opined.

"Summer" showed the full Confederate pantheon: Lee, Jackson, Stuart, Longstreet and a half-dozen other generals. "These guys were never all together at once in real life," Rob said. "Anyway, they look too rigid."

"Autumn," the best of the murals, featured Jeb Stuart leading a charge in full Cavalier regalia. "The total Three Musketeers look," Rob quipped. "Fluid motion, very nice." The last mural, "Winter" depicted a collapsed artillery battery with dead horses and gaunt, retreating rebels. "A bit too sentimental," Rob judged, returning to "Spring" and doing the cycle all over again.

Rob's stylistic critique surprised me. "You do any painting?" I asked him.

"It's a long story," he said. I coaxed the short version. Rob, like me, had spent his childhood doodling Civil War scenes. Unlike me, he showed real talent. In high school, he won a statewide art contest with a painting of two rebels on a covered bridge. The prize was a trip to Washington for both Rob and the painting, which went on display at the Capitol for a year. This spurred Rob to major in studio art at Kent State.

"I wanted to keep doing naturalistic Civil War scenes," he said. "My teachers wanted me to go back to finger painting. Abstract expressionism, that sort of thing. One teacher called my stuff 'cornball illustrative bullshit.' He told me I should get out of art and into something else." Rob laughed. "I took his advice. Dropped out of college and became a Civil War bum, which is more or less what I've been ever since."

Painting was a side of Rob I'd known nothing about. A more familiar talent—his flair for drama—emerged a few minutes later, when we crossed the street to the magnolia-girdled headquarters of the United Daughters of the Confederacy. The building was a mausoleum-like hulk with small windows, a locked front door and a side entrance protected by bulletproof glass, a security camera and a tiny speaker box. Rob pressed a button and asked to come inside. A woman's voice responded that the building was open only for members.

Rob stepped back so the camera could take in his gray uniform and the outraged expression on his face. "I'm a Sons of Confederate Veterans member," he bellowed. "You're saying that just because I'm a man you can't let me in?"

A young woman in a long dress appeared at the door. "I don't want a scene here," she sighed, agreeing to give us a brief tour. She led us briskly through hushed hallways lined with glass cases. I glimpsed a soldier's Bible that deflected a bullet at First Manassas, a replica of Varina Davis's engagement ring, and a framed picture of Lee's family tree. In a side office, our guide pointed out a large doll made in the image of the UDC's founder. Then, passing a closed door, she said, "That's the room for the Children of the Confederacy."

"Is that where they cook up the questions for the catechism quiz?" I asked, recalling the contest I'd seen in North Carolina.

"I'm not allowed to say," she said. Rob also tried to engage her in conversation, with equally little success. But then, we'd been on the road for three days without a shower or a change of clothes. The few people we passed gave us a wide berth. I couldn't blame our guide for whisking us through.

At the door, I tried one last question: Was it strange, in this day and age, to be sequestered inside a shrine to the 1860s? The woman glanced over her shoulder and whispered, "Strange isn't the word. Time warp's more like it." A recent migrant from New England, the woman had answered an ad in the paper for museum work. There was no mention of the UDC. "I think the only reason they hired me is because my family's Southern Baptist." She'd been in culture shock ever since. "Up North the War's over. Not like here." She smiled thinly, shut the heavy glass door, and withdrew into her cloister.

As we sprawled beneath the shade of a magnolia tree, I complimented Rob on his acting job at the door. Rob looked at me quizzically. It turned out he *was* a Sons of Confederate Veterans member and frequently attended the group's meetings. Somehow, I'd assumed Rob's allegiance to the Confederacy didn't go beyond the sartorial and sentimental. Many SCV members I'd met were rabid defenders of the rebel flag and reactionaries when it came to contemporary politics. As an Ohio-born art student whose personal philosophy seemed, if anything, anarchistic, Rob didn't quite fit the mold.

"I think of myself as a liberal Confederate," he said. "I want the history preserved, and I think the Confederacy's a great story about men who did incredible things. But I don't subscribe to a lot of the politics that comes with it."

"Like what?"

"Like race. I don't give a shit if my sister marries a black guy. Unless he's a farb."

Rob's comments raised a question I'd been chewing on since the start of my trip. Was there such a thing as politically correct remembrance of the Confederacy? Or was any attempt to honor the Cause inevitably tainted by what Southerners once delicately referred to as their "peculiar institution"?

The question loomed again—massively so—a few minutes later as we strolled down Richmond's most famous, or infamous, street: Monument Avenue. The boulevard was lined with statues of the Confederacy's Holy Trinity—Davis, Lee and Jackson—and of two of their ablest lieutenants, Jeb Stuart and Matthew Fontaine Maury, a naval commander and brilliant oceanographer.

Having grown up near Washington, where most residents remained oblivious to ubiquitous pigeon-spattered statues of Union generals, I'd never really understood why people made such a fuss over Monument Avenue. But as we peered up at Robert E. Lee astride a rippling steed, I was taken aback. Lee's white granite statue stood sixty-one feet. The sculptor had substituted a French hunting horse for Lee's wartime mount; Traveller was judged too slender a model for such a titanic equestrian. The other monuments were almost as imposing. And their placement on a tree-lined boulevard more than fifty yards wide gave the statues a dominating presence in what was otherwise a low-roofed residential district.

The scale of Monument Avenue also amplified the weirdness of the whole enterprise. After all, Davis and Lee and Jackson and Stuart weren't national heroes. In the view of many Americans, they were precisely the opposite: leaders of a rebellion against the nation—separatists at best, traitors at worst. None of those honored were native Richmonders. And their mission failed. They didn't call it the Lost Cause for nothing. I couldn't think of another city in the world that lined its streets with stone leviathans honoring failed rebels against the state.

I wasn't alone in harboring such thoughts. We'd arrived in Richmond amidst a fierce debate about the first proposed addition to Monument Avenue in over sixty-five years. Arthur Ashe, the black tennis star and Richmond native, had recently died, and the city planned to honor him with a statue a few blocks from Lee and his fellow Confederates (in statue-studded Richmond, only one monument currently honored a black—Bojangles).

We learned all this from the local papers while sipping iced tea at a sidewalk cafe. "Thought I felt a tick digging into me," Rob said, groping in his trousers. With his other hand he slapped the back of his neck. "These flies seem to like me now. I must be pretty ripe." Two women at the next table got up and moved inside.

As Rob hunted parasites, I read that plans to place Ashe's statue on Monument Avenue had aroused so much opposition from both blacks and whites that city officials had backed off. They now favored several alternatives, such as putting the statue in a black neighborhood, or near a park where the young Ashe had watched whites play tennis on courts from which he was excluded. A public hearing on the issue was scheduled for later in the day.

I glanced at Rob, who was now gouging behind his ears. "Would it be correct, Gasm-wise I mean, to go to the meeting?" I asked.

Rob stroked his beard rabbinically. "I think it's kosher," he said. "As long as there's some Confederate content." The only question was what to do until the late-afternoon meeting. Rob studied our map of Richmond and circled several spots we hadn't yet toured. "More dead rebs," he said.

Hollywood Cemetery, the largest and most illustrious collection of Confederate dead anywhere in the South, was remarkably hard to find. We circled a run-down neighborhood several times before spotting an oddly juxtaposed sign on the side of a building: an arrow pointing to both "Victory Rug Cleaning" and to the losers' boneyard.

The hilly burial ground held over 18,000 Confederates, many of whom had perished at Richmond's wartime hospitals. The remains of 3,000 men killed at Gettysburg were later disinterred and brought here for reburial. We found George Pickett's urn-capped grave near a weedy field filled with his men. Their graves were marked by crude stone stumps bearing only numbers and the letters CSA. "That's how they were regarded in life, too," Rob said. "'How many men can you bring up?' 'Fifteen thousand.' Guys like Pickett spoke that way." The crowded field of anonymous stumps reminded me of a John Berryman poem about a Civil War monument. The dead, he wrote, were "Misled blood-red statistical men."

We drove past the modest obelisk marking Jeb Stuart's grave and then to a life-sized bronze of Jefferson Davis overlooking the James River. The monument's inscription encapsulated the militant victimology that prevailed in the post-War South: "Blessed are they which are persecuted for righteousness' sake, for theirs is the kingdom of heaven." Davis was bizarrely persecuted in death as well; his poorly embalmed body began to deteriorate before the eyes of thousands of mourners while it lay in state. At Hollywood Cemetery, Davis endured one final indignity. The bronze statue above his grave gazed for eternity directly at a memorial emblazoned with the surname of one of his foremost antagonists: GRANT (one Thomas E., not Ulysses S.).

From Hollywood we sped through another "Confederate Rest" with 17,000 graves, then to Shockoe Hill cemetery in a decayed neighborhood tucked beneath a tangle of interstates. At the graveyard's entrance stood a wrought-iron enclosure with a pattern of entwined muskets, rebel flags, kepis, and sabers. A plaque with a Jewish star stated: "To the Glory of God and In Memory of the Hebrew Confederate Soldiers Resting in this Hallowed Spot. Erected by Hebrew Ladies Memorial Association organized 1866."

The Hebrew Confederates were listed alphabetically, from M. Aaron to Julius Zark. One carried a curious addendum: "H. Gersh-

berg should correctly read Henry Gintberger." Had one of Henry's
Gentile comrades got his surname wrong? Another grave was listed
as anonymous. How was the man's religion known, but not his
name? And why were the Hebrew Confederates buried here instead
of at Richmond's other rebel graveyards?

There was no one to answer these questions, at least not in the
abandoned environs of Shockoe Hill. I got the distinct sense that
Rob and I were the first visitors to pass this way in months. Nor
were our various city tourist guides any help. Like Charleston, Richmond seemed ambivalent about its Confederate history. Both cities paid lip service to their most prominent Civil War sites—Fort
Sumter, Monument Avenue, the Museum of the Confederacy—but
clearly preferred to highlight other, less controversial attractions:
the arts, dining, shopping. In Richmond, this New South gloss partly
reflected the city's demographics. After several decades of white
flight, the city proper was now mostly black. On many of the streets
we'd toured during the day, we hadn't seen a single white.

This metamorphosis, and the ambivalence I'd sensed, became even
more obvious at the public hearing about Monument Avenue. A
black protester stood outside City Hall with a sign saying "White
Racism Lives" and a red rag tied around his leg representing "blood
from centuries of oppression." Inside, Richmond's black mayor and
majority-black city council sat facing some 400 residents, ranging
from blacks in African dashikis to whites in blue jeans and rebel-
flag ties.

I'd expected to see an urban version of the angry meeting I'd attended in Todd County, Kentucky, where white parents vented their
rage over plans to change the school's rebel mascot. What I witnessed instead was a thoughtful discourse on public art, the potency
of historic symbols, racial healing, and affirmative action—albeit for
a deceased black male who had fled Richmond at eighteen to escape
what he later called "its segregation, its conservatism, its parochial
thinking."

An elderly white man in a seersucker suit and a red bow tie was
one of the first to speak. His appearance and courtly drawl fit my
stereotype of a stuffy Richmonder—an image that his words quickly

contradicted. "We have Monument Avenue, not Confederate War Monument Avenue," he said. "Let's change it from a fantasy to a true Monument Avenue. If we don't, we'll be saying to the world that Arthur Ashe was not good enough to be on that street."

He was followed by a retired black foreman who expressed a similar view. "We've got to do something now to get over that fight back then," he said, referring obliquely to the Civil War. "That's the only way we'll finally sort out this black/white thing."

Other blacks could barely contain the rage they felt about Monument Avenue and the decades of Confederacy-worship they'd suffered through before the civil rights struggle. For them, putting Ashe on Monument Avenue represented emotional payback, an in-your-face gesture that would salve some of the insult blacks had so long endured. "I want my hero's statue as tall as Lee's," one man shouted. "I want Ashe to be as big as all outdoors. Arthur Ashe is bigger than Lee!"

But other blacks believed Ashe would be diminished rather than exalted on Monument Avenue. "The other guys on that Avenue would have enslaved him if they could," a college student said. "Why place Ashe among men who in the 1990s would be judged nothing more than criminals?" Another man was blunter still. "Why would I want my hero on a promenade of losers?" he asked.

As the debate went on, I felt my own opinions see-saw, as the city council's obviously had since the monument was first proposed. I sympathized with those speakers who felt Richmond needed to make a symbolic break with its past by integrating Monument Avenue. But I also found myself applauding an elderly black man who proposed putting the statue in a place that might inspire black youths today, rather than in a mostly white neighborhood, haunted by Confederate ghosts, where Ashe himself would have feared walking as a child. The next speaker, though, made an equally valid point: putting Ashe's statue in a black district would perpetuate the segregation the tennis star endured in life.

Equally compelling were the arguments of several speakers who opposed the statue's placement on aesthetic and historic grounds. Ashe's twenty-four-foot likeness would be dwarfed by the sixty-one-foot-tall Lee. Also, a modern statue of a twentieth-century athlete, clad in tennis sweats and clutching a racket, would appear informal and incongruous on a boulevard lined with nineteenth-century military men. Whatever one felt about the Confederates, their enshrinement on Monument Avenue was historic in its own right, a unique museum piece of the Lost Cause mentality.

Still others gave this rationale a political twist. "Ashe isn't a soldier and his statue will barely reach Lee's saddle," said Wayne Byrd, who headed a chapter of the Heritage Preservation Association, a pro–rebel flag group I'd encountered elsewhere in the South. "This statue will trivialize Ashe and be disrespectful of Confederate-Americans who hallow the other men on that street."

In the name of inclusiveness and sensitivity—both to Ashe's memory and to "Confederate-Americans," a heretofore neglected minority—Byrd proposed memorializing still another ignored group: black Confederates. Recent scholarship suggested that some slaves and free blacks fought in the rebel ranks, though their numbers and motivation were unclear. In effect, the Heritage Preservation Association, one of America's most politically incorrect groups, was trying to claim politically correct motives while making a gesture that was precisely the opposite. By honoring blacks who took up arms in defense of their white masters, the group had found a sly way to disassociate the Cause from slavery.

During a break, I approached Byrd in the hall and asked what he meant by the term Confederate-American. "A Confederate-American—then and now—is simply anyone who's against big government," he said. "We as Southern Americans just want to be left alone."

"Yeah, the South wanted to be left alone—to oppress people!" a long-haired man shouted.

"It was not about slavery!" a man with a rebel-flag T-shirt barked back. "It was states' rights!"

"Exactly. The right to own slaves. Tear the statues and plantations down!"

"Should we tear down the Pyramids because they were built by slaves? And what about Washington and Jefferson? They owned slaves. Should we tear down memorials to them?"

I noticed a white man in jeans and duckbill cap standing off to the side, smoking a cigarette and shaking his head as the others shouted. Wallace Faison was a peanut farmer from a small town near the North Carolina line. "For me it's not political at all," he said quietly. "The South—we lost. I feel like I lost, too. Monument Avenue is like that last Valhalla, that spiritual place I can go. It's crazy, I can't explain it, but that's how I feel."

Back in the council chamber, we stayed to hear one more speaker, an accountant in thick glasses and a dark charcoal suit. Jim Slicer was a native of Washington, D.C., where Civil War statues were what he called "just men on horses" that no one cared about. "I've been here in Richmond for six years and I still don't get it," he said. "To me, having the principal Richmond monuments dedicated to the Lost Cause is like saying we're dedicated to no hope, no future. It's like having a monument to unrequited love."

The question for Slicer wasn't whether Ashe belonged on a pedestal beside Davis, Lee and Jackson, but rather, "Do *they* belong? Does Monument Avenue?"

As Slicer headed out of the chamber, I asked what alternative he'd propose. "I'd do the same thing with Lee and Davis that the Russians did with statues of Stalin and Lenin," he said. "Take them down or at least don't add to their ranks. Stop honoring wrong." As for Ashe, he'd propose a whole new street to celebrate the tennis star and other modern Richmonders. "Make it an avenue of the future, not the past."

He chuckled, adding, "Of course, it will never happen. This town can't shake its past. I've learned that much from my six years in Richmond."

Slicer was right. In the end, the city council reversed itself and voted unanimously to put the Ashe statue on Monument Avenue. A councilwoman explained that the gesture was a necessary evil, to exorcise Richmond's historic demons. "Ghosts still haunt us, and we haven't resolved that," she said.

FROM RICHMOND Rob and I headed to another haunted place: Petersburg, twenty-three miles south of the capital and scene of the Civil War's endgame in 1864 and 1865. It was here, after the debacle at Cold Harbor, that Grant laid siege for nine months, finally breaking the Confederate defenses a week before Lee's surrender at Appomattox. By then, Lee's once-proud army had atrophied to a scarecrow band of men and boys beset by hunger, disease and desertion. Photographs of the rebel dead at Petersburg showed smooth-cheeked, shoeless youths of fourteen or fifteen, half-sunk in trench mud, among the last and certainly the most pointless casualties of a cause that would be truly lost a few days later.

At twilight, Petersburg seemed destitute and semi-abandoned. Black families crowded on the rickety porches of once-elegant ante-bellum homes whose original owners had likely been slaveholding whites. Parking at what we took to be downtown, Rob and I wandered past vacant factories and peanut warehouses until we came to a sign saying "Old Towne" and a few faint stirrings of commercial life. Stepping inside a New Orleans–theme restaurant, we were immediately accosted by six men seated on stools by the bar.

"Hi, I'm Jim!"

"You guys reenactors?"

"Need a beer?"

This was more than the usual Southern hospitality, particularly given our appearance and stench after three days' hard touring. We settled in beside a young, balding man named Steve. "The social life in Petersburg is so limited that it's a relief to see a face you don't recognize," he said. Steve, the city's only legal aid attorney, also explained why Petersburg seemed so derelict.

"Desegregation," he said. "The day they integrated the schools was the day a lot of whites called U-Haul." Before the civil rights movement, Petersburg was so segregated that blacks and whites swore to tell the truth in court while placing their hands on separate Bibles. Following turbulent, court-ordered school integration in 1970, whites fled en masse to a suburb called Colonial Heights —or "Colonial Whites," as Steve called it. The suburb was now bigger than Petersburg and attracted almost all the area's new development.

Left behind was a struggling city of 38,000 people, three-quarters of them black and a quarter in poverty. Petersburg's apartheid was so profound that graduates of the first integrated class at the city's main public high school had recently held two twenty-fifth reunions: one for whites, one for blacks. Steve, who had moved to Petersburg straight after law school, planned to flee as soon as he could land a job elsewhere.

"This is the anus of the South," he said. Then, realizing he'd talked for twenty minutes straight, he asked, "What brings you guys to town?"

"Just passing through," Rob said. "We'll hit the battlefield tomorrow. Anything else to do?"

Steve drained his beer and cast a melancholy eye around the bar. "You're looking at it," he said.

Five other men looked back at us, waiting their turn to buy us a beer and cry into theirs. Rob glanced at me and tilted his head, as if to say "outta here." So we thanked Steve and headed back into the empty streets. "They should hire that guy at the local tourist bureau," Rob said.

Returning to the car, we drove past pawn shops, wig shops, and a used-car lot ("Rebates are Here. Turn Tax Refunds into Wheels!") until we reached the farmland just beyond. Rob had chosen as our campsite a small battleground named Five Forks. It was here that Phil Sheridan's cavalry broke one flank of Petersburg's rebel defenses, opening the way for an all-out Northern assault that forced Lee to abandon the city. Five Forks was also notorious as the battle during which George Pickett and his cavalry commander, Fitzhugh Lee, gorged themselves on fish and bourbon while their troops faced disaster a short distance away.

We parked by a marker for the battlefield and threw down groundsheets twenty yards off the road. Rob lit a candle and read about the battle, with emphasis on the fish lunch. "Pickett joined me about two o'clock. We lunched together on some fine shad which Dearing and I had caught in the Nottoway [River] two days before," recalled General Thomas Rosser, who hosted the meal. Another rebel officer told of finding Pickett prone under a tent, "with a bottle of whiskey or Brandy, I don't know which for I was not invited to partake of it."

Pickett finally stirred himself to join his embattled troops, but the fight was soon lost and so was Pickett's already wobbly reputation.

The incident still rankled twenty-four years later; Jefferson Davis, just before his death, wrote of "that fatal lunch as the ruin of the Confederacy."

Rob snuffed the candle and we lay in the tall grass, bone-weary from another long day of touring. Five Forks got its name from the starfish of roads that converged there in Civil War days. Unfortunately, they still did. Each time I started to drift off, headlights flickered through the trees and another car hurtled down one of the roads, usually with the windows open and radio blaring. I felt like getting up and waving a checkered flag.

After an hour, we decamped and trudged into the woods, well away from the road. As we settled gratefully onto a bed of pine needles, rain began to sprinkle down. After a few minutes it began to pour. We broke camp again and hiked deeper into the woods until we found an abandoned cabin with mud chinking and an overhanging porch with support beams that had long since rotted away. The place looked unsteady, but we were too wet and exhausted to care and huddled beneath the leaky roof until the storm ended.

"Hallelujah," Rob said, throwing down his groundcloth again. His elation lasted thirty seconds. It was a hot, steamy night and we lay in thick summer woods in wet, stinking clothes. Rob rested his head on a haversack filled with three-day-old sowbelly. Our campsite was a virtual real-estate ad for mosquitoes: STILL WATER! HUMID AIR! ROTTING MEAT! RANK SKIN!

They came in ones and twos at first, like reconaissance aircraft, then buzzed us in swarms, dive-bombing our eyes, ears, nostrils, lips. I threw a blanket over my head but was soon so hot I had to throw it off again. Bugs instantly assaulted every inch of exposed skin. Beside me, Rob thrashed and swatted and cursed. "Fuck George Pickett and fuck his goddamn fucking shad bake!"

There was nothing to do but wait the night out, which I did with weary, circular thoughts, interrupted by moans and howls from Rob. I tried lying perfectly still, thinking about baseball, Buddhism, the names of presidents, the names of Civil War generals, the names of the last fifty movies I'd seen. I looked at my pocket watch. It was still only 2 A.M.

At some point apathy or blood loss eased me off to sleep. Waking at dawn, I found ticks in my scalp and chigger bites lining my wrists. Rob lay with a blanket wrapped tightly around his head, his palms over his ears like the woman in Edvard Munch's *The Scream.* Momentarily deranged, I wondered if Rob might have died from his wounds. But then his muffled voice came from under the blanket. "Every time I slipped off I was in the movie *Midway,*" he moaned, "with Japanese and American propellor planes taking off over and over again. I kept thinking there must be an aircraft carrier nearby." Rob threw the blanket off; his eyelids and cheeks were swollen with bites. "That was the worst night of my life," he declared. For Rob Hodge, that was saying quite a lot.

We sat silently for a while, scratching. For the first time on the Gasm we'd camped well away from humanity. The morning was misty; smoke seemed unlikely to attract attention. So we decided to risk a fire. "Anyway," Rob said, "if we don't eat this salt pork today, it'll be lethal." As opposed to merely toxic, which it no doubt was after three days in Rob's haversack. "If we cook the crap out of it," Rob assured me, "it probably won't kill us."

So I gathered sodden twigs and managed to start a smoldering fire. Rob deftly peeled away the pork's whitish skin, then cut the meat in cubes and tossed it in the half-canteen he used as a fry pan. "Sometimes you find a pig's nipple," he said, poking at the sowbelly.

Rob guessed it would take forty-five minutes to cook. I didn't feel like staring at pig meat simmering in its own grease on the off chance that a nipple might appear. So I decided to forage, as the Confederates here might have done, and hiked back out to the car. Driving down one of the five roads, I came to a village called Dinwiddie and a restaurant with a huge sign saying "That's A Burger!" I wondered, sleepily, if the food was so bad that it might be mistaken for something else.

The place was shut but a newspaper box offered the *Dinwiddie Monitor,* whose banner proclaimed: "The only newspaper that gives a hoot about Dinwiddie County." I returned to our campsite and read Rob the list of arrests in the Sheriff's Log—public drunkenness, writing a bad check, "three counts of curse & abuse"—and reports on tent revivals and family reunions, summer staples in small Southern towns.

This passed the time until Rob announced that breakfast was done. The fry pan now held a puddle of bubbling black grease with fatty chunks bobbing atop the scum. Rob poked his knife into the murk, insisting, "There's lean meat in there somewhere." Then he skewered a chunk of charred gristle and dangled it just beneath my nose. *"Bon appétit,"* he said.

I peered dubiously through my spectacles and shook my head. Rob wiggled the knife. "C'mon," he coaxed, "just think of it as blackened country ham." I closed my eyes and bit. Rob stabbed another piece and popped it in his mouth. We gasped, eyes filling with tears. The meat didn't resemble meat at all; it tasted like a soggy cube of salt, soaked in grease. Rob tried a second piece but quickly spat it out.

"I bet this stuff killed more rebs than Yankee bullets ever did," he groaned. By now we'd lost all appetite for a planned second course of potatoes and onions. So Rob emptied the pan, making sure to spill grease onto his trousers and dab a bit in his beard.

THUS REFRESHED, we headed off to tour the Petersburg defenses, or what we could find of them. Fort Sedgwick, dubbed "Fort Hell" because of the constant mortar and sniper fire aimed at it, now lay beneath the franchise hell skirting town. When we stopped to ask directions, a policeman said, "Where the Kmart is, that's the approximate location." Fort Mahone, another famous rampart, had been leveled, too, and now lay beneath a Pizza Hut parking lot.

What remained of the battlefield offered an even starker preview of World War I than had Spotsylvania or Cold Harbor. During the 292-day stalemate here (roughly a quarter of the entire War), the armies constructed sandbagged bombproofs, chevaux-de-frise (porcupine-like obstacles bristling with spikes) and trip lines of telegraph wire strung between tree stumps. The Union even experimented with a precursor of the machine gun known as the Gatling gun, a multi-barreled weapon that spat out bullets with the aid of a hand crank (this was also the origin of the gangster slang "gat").

It was here, too, that the Union pulled off the boldest engineering feat of the War. Seeking to break the deadlock, Pennsylvania coal miners burrowed a 500-foot tunnel beneath a rebel salient. Then they detonated four tons of gunpowder, literally blowing the defenders sky-high. But the Union assault that followed quickly degenerated into a gruesome folly. Advancing troops plunged straight into the huge pit the blast had created, allowing Confederates to gather round the rim and fire down at the helpless, close-packed Federals. The Union force lost 4,000 men before retreating.

The Battle of the Crater, as it became known, left a hole 170 feet across and 30 feet deep that remained clearly visible today. Before the Park Service took control of the site in the late 1960s, the depression formed part of the Crater Golf Course, with fairways and putting greens laid out across the battleground and holes named for figures from the Petersburg campaign.

Walking through the woods, we found a monument to the 1st Maine, which suffered the worst regimental loss in one action of any Federal unit in the Civil War; 632 of the 850 Maine men became casualties during a brief, futile charge. Broken beer bottles, used condoms and small glass vials now ringed the monument. A nearby plaque with a map of the charge was obscured by graffiti that said, CRACK HOUSE! Petersburg's battlefield evidently doubled as an urban park after dark.

Depressed by the scene, we headed to the visitors' center to gather intelligence about where to go next. A ranger told us that Virginia had just opened "Lee's Retreat Route," a self-guided driving tour of the rebels' 100-mile flight from Petersburg to Appomattox. At each stop along the way, roadside transmitters broadcast historical reports, which tourists could tune in on their car radios. "You just park, listen and drive on to the next stop," the ranger explained, handing us a map and guidebook.

Rob was ecstatic. "It's Gasm heaven," he crowed. "We'll score twenty hits without getting out of the car."

The first stop was a crossroads west of Petersburg called Sutherland Station. As we sat with the motor running, listening on the radio to a report about the skirmish there in 1865, a line in the guidebook caught my eye. "For a down-home experience, visit the rather eclectic museum at Olgers Store if Jimmy is around."

Olgers Store perched just across the road. At first glance, it looked typical of the dwindling stock of country stores that once dotted rural crossroads across the South: a low-slung weatherboard building with a ramshackle verandah and the words "Olgers Gro" printed on an old Pepsi sign. Just inside the screen door stood a large statue of Robert E. Lee, spray-painted a brilliant gold. A sign around its neck said, "Come on In. Everything Else has gone wrong."

We were about to do just that when a giant appeared from around the corner of the store. He toted a machete and the largest watermelon I'd ever seen. "I unveiled that statue the day the retreat route opened," he said. "You shoulda been here. Confederate blood hasn't run so high since the Battle of the Crater."

He raised his machete and hacked the huge melon into three meal-sized slices. Handing us each a piece, he settled onto the porch's sagging top step. "Hope you're not rushing off anywhere. You know what they say, 'Two weeks at Olgers Store equals any college education.'"

Jimmy Olgers was the rare person who could be called, without hyperbole, larger than life. He was, first of all, extraordinarily large: six feet six and 320 pounds, poured into gym shorts and a sleeveless T-shirt from which his arms and legs poked like huge pink tree limbs. This towering physique was matched, incongruously, with the head of a 1950s science teacher—buzzcut, square head, black-framed glasses—and the syrupy, almost purring drawl of a Southern funeral director.

Olgers did in fact work at a funeral parlor—when he wasn't preaching, composing poetry, writing a column for the *Dinwiddie Monitor,* or serving as unofficial mayor of Sutherland Station, population 1,000. But his true avocation was minding the store, which his grandfather built at the turn of the century and where Olgers himself was born. However, "storekeeper" didn't quite fit, either. Olgers Store wasn't a store anymore and to call it "a rather eclectic museum," as our guidebook had, was a bit like calling the Grand Canyon a rather big hole in the ground.

"He's exactly life-sized and made from a junk heap," Olgers said, leading us inside to look at the Goldfinger Lee. The general's sword grip was actually a hoe handle, the hilt made from roof shingle, the scabbard a piece of muffler—all of it covered with sheet rock. Strangest of all, the statue's creator—a dissolute-looking man named Frank—suddenly materialized from behind Lee's broad-shouldered figure.

"I make everything," Frank said, "I made my teeth too." He yanked out his irregular bridgework and handed it to me as proof.

"You shoulda seen Frank the day that statue was unveiled," Olgers said. "He was so proud his head was bigger than a washtub."

I handed Frank his teeth and asked Olgers about an enormous cotton garment dangling from the rafters behind Lee's head. "Largest pair of bloomers in the world, worn by Bertha Magoo, a 749-pound lady," Olgers said. Before I could inquire further about Bertha, Olgers plunged deeper into the room to show us an old ham boiler, a whale vertebra, a section of tree limb labeled "largest pine in the world," a colonial suit and horsehair wig belonging to a signer of the Declaration of Independence, and a photograph of an extremely hideous woman.

"Juanita, my first wife," Olgers said. "She was crazy about collards, which cause gas, you know. She ate a whole pot one day. I heard the explosion in the field, but by the time I got to the house it was too late. Nothing left." He shook his head. "God I miss that woman."

Olgers started his collection as a boy, first with arrowheads and minié balls he dug up himself, then with stray items that neighbors brought by the shop. So when the store closed in 1988, Olgers turned it into a display case for all the junk he'd gathered over the years. Now, every inch of floor, wall and ceiling was festooned with bric-a-brac. "I was born here the night Hitler sent a thousand bombers against London, and slept for many a year in that corner," Olgers said, pointing at a pile of rusted tools and a bone I couldn't identify. "Jawbone of an ass," he said, moving to an adjoining room, cluttered with old lunchboxes. "Mom and Dad slept here," he said.

Olgers's parents had recently died, a month apart. "When they ran this place, it was the hub of the community," he said softly. "My momma was a doctor, not one that had gone to medical school but one that people brought sick babies to. Folks back then didn't go to a doctor unless they were really sick. My daddy pulled teeth—I pulled a few, too. And my mother would write letters for people who couldn't write themselves."

The store had also been general in the true sense of the word, living up to its advertising sign outside: "You Name It! We Got It!" A stain on the floor marked where a fifty-gallon barrel of molasses had sat for years, beside drums of kerosene-lamp oil, tins of lard, and tubs of hogs' feet and heads. Hog parts also had hung from the walls: hog shoulders, hog jowls, hog ears.

The house specialty was souse, a concoction of congealed pig's ear and foot, shaped into a loaf and sliced like bread. "Nearest thing to God's manna on earth," Olgers said, smacking his lips. His mother also made chitlins (pork entrails, battered and fried), scrapple (a fried mush of hog scraps I'd gagged on once at a backroads diner), and a nameless mix of pigs' digits and other bits: cooked, rolled in flour, and fried with sweet marjoram.

"Whoooo Lord, it makes me squeal just to think of it," Olgers said. "The new generation, they don't know real eating, just hamburgers and pizzas." They didn't know real shopping, either. "Wal-Mart, Kmart, whatever-Mart. They and the car killed the country store. People would come here and sit and talk like they always did, but they didn't buy anything." Finally, after his family had operated the store for eighty years, Olgers was forced to shut the place down and go work at a funeral home. "The day that store closed," he said, "a whole way of life went with it."

We sat on the porch, spitting watermelon seeds and watching traffic pass on the busy new highway bypassing town. I told Olgers about my journey and asked why Southerners like himself revered the past. "Child, that's an easy question," he said. "A Southerner—a true Southerner, of which there aren't many left—is more related to the land, to the home place. Northerners just don't have that attachment. Maybe that means they don't have as much depth." He paused, then added, "I feel sorry for folks from the North, or anyone who hasn't had that bond with the land. You can't miss something you never had and if you never had it, you don't know what it's all about."

I'd heard Southerners say this sort of thing a hundred times before, usually without irony while driving a Jeep Cherokee through
traffic-choked suburban streets or watching TV in a ranch-style
home that could be Anywhere, America. But Olgers had lived the life
he praised. He'd rarely strayed more than a few miles from Sutherland until going off to college at William and Mary, an hour's drive
east, and then only for three months. "I was so homesick I couldn't
bear it," he said. "The food was worse than awful, the professors
were atheists, and my roomate was an animal."

"What do you mean?" Rob asked, obviously intrigued.

"He took me to a Viking Party. There were men wearing hats
with horns, throwing women in sheets over their shoulders. They
brought a girl in to sacrifice, and by the time they were done with
her she wished she had been." Olgers shook his head. "This wasn't
any panty raid, child." Soon after, Olgers retreated to Sutherland. "I
feel honored because I wasn't stained by college. Education isn't
everything, at least not the formal kind."

In the thirty-five years since, Olgers had left Sutherland only
twice: to honeymoon in Washington, D.C., and to see the ocean in
North Carolina. "I'm a homebody, a home soul," he said. "Olgers
Store has been my domain."

Reaching for his walking stick—a ski pole—he led us through the
95-degree heat to what he called the "home place," a stagecoach inn
across the road where some part of his family had lived for umpteen
generations. Then, leaning against the ski pole, he gave his own rendition of the fight that occurred in the inn's front yard in April 1865.
"Only four thousand Confederates faced twenty-three thousand Yankees, but Lee told them to hold the railroad line at all costs. So they
dug in along a line of giant cedars that stood just so, and the North
charged three times, at nine in the morning, at one in the afternoon
and at five. The last time they broke through. One of those cedars
had a cannonball in it for a hundred years."

At the turn of the century, Olgers's grandfather replaced the inn's
heart-pine siding. "When he pulled it off, minié balls just came
rolling out, there were that many of them." Leading us inside, past
a deaf eighty-year-old aunt who sat bottling pickles in the kitchen,

Olgers pulled back the living-room carpet to reveal a splotch on the wood beneath. "Southern blood," he said. "They dragged the wounded in here." One of Olgers's ancestors had fought near the inn and died of his wounds a few days before the War's end.

To me, it seemed sad and pointless for men to have fought and died at that late date, rather than surrender. But Olgers didn't see it that way. He thought the South's leaders were wrong—"if they'd won, we would have been a divided country and had slavery for a few decades more"—but he identified with the individual soldier's allegiance to home. "A man has to make a stand in his life, at least once," he said. "That's what happened here. They knew they'd lose but they were going down defiant, right here on the land where they lived."

He walked us to a family graveyard and strolled between the headstones. The cemetery held enough Gothic characters to fill a Flannery O'Connor story, at least the way Olgers described them. There was a great-grandfather shot through the wrist in the War who was later hospitalized "for itch," Olgers claimed. "The hole in his arm was so big that my daddy used to stick his finger in it as a child." Another veteran swore that he'd never shave again if the South lost the War. "When I was a kid, he had a beard hanging like Spanish moss all the way down to his knees." Olgers also pointed out the graves of a dozen aunts and great-aunts, all of them spinsters. "So many of the boys were dead in the War that for a while there was no one to marry," he said. "Then it sort of became a family habit."

Olgers showed us his own plot, beside his parents, and said he had only one fear about meeting his maker. He was the first in a long line of yellow-dog Democrats to vote for the party of Lincoln. "When I meet up with my grandpappy at the Pearly Gates, I hope he doesn't find out." But in other respects Olgers remained true to his rebel forebears. He refused to travel the rest of the retreat route, and had never visited Appomattox, just a short drive down the road. "That way," he explained, "it can always be early April in 1865 and we haven't yet lost the War."

We wandered back to the store. Olgers had to close up and go to work at the funeral parlor. But he offered us a parting gift: a Mason jar filled with murky turtle soup he'd cooked the day before. "I've got to get all the Yankees my grandpappy missed," he said, slapping the back of my Federal uniform. Then, heading for his car, he broke into song:

> *They killed half a million Yankees with Southern steel and shot,*
> *Wish it was a million more instead of what they got.*

Olgers waved and drove off, leaving us with our turtle soup and a bushel of homespun wisdom to digest. We peered through the store window and snapped a last mental snapshot. "That's the epitome of the Gasm," Rob said, shaking his head. "So much stuff that you can't possibly take it all in, and you don't know what to do with it anyway. So you just let it wash over you."

THE SAME WAS TRUE of Lee's retreat route. We wound west from Sutherland Station, over narrow bridges and past forgotten towns where the Confederates skirmished with pursuing Federals. We paused at a wood-frame church with a floor still bloodstained from bodies laid out there 130 years before; at a tiny museum with a silver tray on which a local slave served lunch to Robert E. Lee; at the Amelia County courthouse, where the Confederate monument read, "O comrades, wheresoe'er ye rest apart, Amelia shrines you here within her heart." The rest was a blur of rolling farmland and deserted railroad spurs with names like Deatonville, Jeterville, Farmville, Rice's Depot.

This was "Southside" Virginia, a rural enclave between the state's flat Tidewater and the rolling hills of the Piedmont. Like Jimmy Olgers's domain, Southside seemed to have largely escaped the modern era. Amelia County, through which we traveled for most of the day, had half its 1865 population. One of the retreat route's stops was an extinct village called Jamestown, of which our guidebook said, "The town died around 1920."

This pastoral, unprosperous landscape came as a shock after all the sprawl we'd passed through elsewhere in Virginia. The scenery also formed an appropriately wistful backdrop to the narrative unfolding on our car radio. Marching day and night for a week, Lee's scarecrow army was stalked as much by hunger as by Union cavalry, and the rebels spent precious hours foraging for food or waiting at railroad junctions for rations that never came.

By the end, Lee's men quaffed creek water and ate parched corn intended for their horses; 500 of the rebel mounts died of starvation during the army's last three days in the field. And all the while, Phil Sheridan's and George Custer's well-fed cavalry kept closing in, hunting down the Confederates as they would the Plains Indians after the Civil War. But there would be no Little Bighorn here, only a rearguard battle at Sayler's Creek at which five Southern generals and almost a quarter of Lee's soldiers surrendered, prompting Lee to exclaim, "My God! Has the army been dissolved?"

One of the tour stops near Sayler's Creek occupied the parking lot of another general store. Unlike Olgers's, this shop was still in business and displayed oddly paired signs in the window: "Game Checking Station: Bear—Deer—Turkey" and "Current Jackpot 3 Million." Inside, we found the store deserted, except for a young black man shooting pool by himself at a ragged, ill-lit table. He wore sunglasses, a Simpsons' T-shirt and an Atlanta Braves baseball cap. "You all must be doing that reenact thing," he said, looking up at us with a bemused grin.

Rob sighed and explained for the fiftieth time what the Civil Wargasm was all about. The man listened patiently, put down his pool stick and said, "I been waiting for somebody like you to answer a question about that War."

"Fire away," Rob said.

"Let's roll the clock back. It's 1861. You two be first cousins, really. You both white, right? One North, one South, but it's just a mind thing. Why you got to kill six hundred thousand cousins? Can't you work it out?"

Rob looked at me. I looked back at him. The man walked to the window and pointed down the road. "I grew up down that way, feeding cattle by Sayler's Creek," he said. "Six thousand dudes got hurt or killed, three days before the War be finished. For what?"

As the Gasm's Union representative, I felt obliged to speak up. "At least some Northerners," I offered, "thought they were fighting to free the slaves."

The man lowered his sunglasses and looked me straight in the eye. "You shittin' me, right? I fought in the Gulf War. Nobody be getting their butt shot off for no freedom thing." Then he rolled the clock back again. Pointing at Rob, he said to me, "Say your mother's sister's son, he's got slaves. You gonna say to him, 'Let's fight over it'? C'mon now, no way. What you really gonna say is this." He paused for a moment, then continued in a perfect-pitch parody of redneck dialect: "Hey, Billy Joe, whatever you want to do with those niggers is okay by me. Keep 'em in chains, what the fuck. Your momma is my momma's sister."

He returned to his normal voice. "It's a big lie, this slave war thing. It don't matter really, except that whites today still like to say, 'Damn, my ancestors died for those niggers, they should be thankful.' What I seen in the Gulf War, it made me realize war is useless. The main man, Saddam, he still be there. It was politics and greed. Same as in your war. Seems to me y'all could'a worked it out." With that, he slapped a dollar on the counter, took a lottery ticket from beside the cash register and stalked out the door, leaving us alone in the deserted shop.

AN HOUR LATER we reached Appomattox Court House, where North and South did finally work it out, in the parlor of Wilmer McLean's farmhouse. There was a classical symmetry to Lee's surrender, as there was to so much about the War. The Army of Northern Virginia stacked its arms four years to the day after the South fired the War's first shot on Fort Sumter. And the surrender was signed in the home of a woebegone farmer who had moved to Appomattox after fleeing his former house at Manassas, site of the War's first land battle. "I was the alpha and omega of this contest," McLean told a Northern visitor a few months after the surrender.

At least that's how the story went. Even Ken Burns highlighted the coincidence in his documentary, which he opened with the tale of farmer McLean, the "aging Virginian" who "had had enough" after the Manassas battle and moved his family to the safety of Appomattox only to have the War follow him there.

The truth, according to park rangers at Appomattox, was a good deal more complicated and less romantic. For one, McLean wasn't a farmer; he was an entrepreneur who rented his in-laws' plantation house to the rebels during First Manassas. Nor did he quickly flee Manassas in search of a safe haven for his family. He stuck around for two years, then realized that Southside Virginia was a more convenient headquarters for his main business: war profiteering. Among other things, McLean speculated in sugar, which he acquired through a brother in Cuba and sold at inflated prices to the Confederate government.

After the War, McLean used his brief acquaintance with Grant to secure a job as a tax collector at the port in Alexandria. He was also, at various times in his life, a bankrupt, a deadbeat, and a man so distrusted by his wife (a wealthy widow) that she made him sign a prenuptial agreement. "Vistors always come in here talking about 'poor Wilmer,'" said Patricia Schuppin, the ranger showing tourists through McLean's restored home. "I have to break the bad news that he was a pretty unscrupulous fellow."

After the surrender, McLean's house had quickly fallen prey to tourists and profiteers, including McLean himself. He sold the furniture from the parlor where Lee and Grant met, and charged soldiers a gold coin to visit the room. Speculators later bought and disassembled the farmhouse in hopes of shipping it to Washington as a tourist attraction. The scheme failed and the ruined house sat for decades, a pile of lumber and mortar that locals often raided for "surrender bricks" to sell the occasional tourist. Appomattox Court House remained a virtual ghost town until the Park Service restored the village after World War II.

The rebuilt McLean parlor, a formal room with heavy curtains, seemed claustrophobic and somehow too small for the momentous history it encompassed. On April 9, 1865, Lee and Grant chatted about their service together in the Mexican War, then wrote out the terms of surrender. One of Grant's aides, a Seneca Indian named Eli Parker, penned the formal document (and apparently pocketed Grant's original draft, which he later sold). There were no theatrics or handing over of swords, though one aide was so overcome with emotion that someone else had to take over for him.

The ranger, Patricia Schuppin, said visitors often responded with similar emotion, particularly Southerners. "I had a lady here yesterday who started weeping, and when she found out I was from Mississippi she asked me, 'How can you work in this terrible place?' I told her I didn't think it's terrible. Reuniting was the only way the South could survive, and we merged back in while keeping our essential culture."

Schuppin saw another positive result to the conflict. "The War did a lot to launch the women's rights movement," she said. Before 1860, women in most parts of the country couldn't own or run businesses, unless they were widowed or let a man manage their property. "But during the War you had women working as nurses and clerks and factory laborers, and running businesses and plantations. After the War they started to sue for the right to keep doing so." The War also boosted the suffragette movement, with women like Susan B. Anthony forming political groups to support Lincoln, abolition, and, by extension, the right of women to vote.

I wanted to hear more, but a crowd of tourists arrived and Schuppin apologetically returned to her post. "Someone's sure to ask about poor Wilmer," she sighed.

We wandered over to a restored tavern where the Union army had printed passes so Confederates could return to their homes unhindered. Here, talking to another ranger, I learned of one more myth about Appomattox. I'd often heard Southerners speak sentimentally of rebel ancestors who arrived home starved and spent after walking all the way from Virginia. While some soldiers may have done so, the parole passes entitled Confederates to travel free on any Union-controlled ship or railroad, and to draw rations from Union troops they met along the way. The South also had hundreds of thousands of rations stockpiled at major cities and rail junctions.

"Any Confederate who walked home to Alabama without a crust in his pocket probably did so out of pride rather than necessity," the ranger explained.

As so often on my journey, I was reminded that what I thought I knew about the War was based more on romance than on fact. Fables about Appomattox were so rife that a former park ranger had written a book called *Thirty Myths About Lee's Surrender*, and a sequel offering twenty-one more. One of the most enduring misconceptions was that

Lee's surrender marked the end of the Confederacy. In fact, Lee surrendered only the 28,000 men under his command, leaving another 150,000 or so rebels in the field. The last land battle didn't occur until a month later, at Palmito Ranch in Texas; it resulted, ironically, in a Southern victory. The last Confederate general to capitulate was Stand Watie, a Cherokee who surrendered his Indian troops on June 23rd. Meanwhile, a Confederate cruiser called the *Shenandoah* kept seizing Union whalers in the Bering Sea until late June and remained on the loose until docking at Liverpool on November 6, 1865, a full seven months after Lee's surrender.

Once we'd toured the few restored buildings, there wasn't much else to see. Appomattox Court House remained a tiny village verged by rolling woods and pastures. This spareness amplified the eloquence of what happened there. In contrast to so many sites we'd toured, battlefield heroism didn't figure much in the picture. Instead, Appomattox honored a much rarer, less heralded virtue in America: reconciliation, mixed with what might be called sportsmanship. Grant frowned on celebration by his troops, and confessed to feeling sad and depressed "at the downfall of a foe who had fought so long and valiantly, and had suffered so much for a cause, though that cause was, I believe, one of the worst for which people ever fought."

Lee, for his part, proved equally graceful in defeat. He struck a rancorous passage from the draft of his farewell address, which an aide had prepared. Instead, Lee simply thanked his men for "four years of arduous service, marked by unsurpassed courage and fortitude." He later urged his fellow Southerners to accept defeat and serve the reunited nation. "True patriotism sometimes requires of men to act contrary at one period to that which it does at another," he wrote after the War to P. G. T Beauregard. "The motive that impels them—the desire to do right—is precisely the same."

At the formal stacking of arms, the oft-wounded hero of Gettysburg, Joshua Chamberlain, ordered his men to honor their foes with silence and a chivalrous gesture called "shoulder arms." His Confederate counterpart, John Brown Gordon—whose battle scars numbered thirteen—responded with a flourish that Chamberlain described in his memoir. Gordon, Chamberlain wrote, wheeled his horse to face the Union general, touched the mount "gently with the spur so that the animal slightly reared, and as he wheeled, horse and rider made one motion, the horse's head swung down with a graceful bow, and General Gordon dropped his sword-point to his toe in salutation." It was hard to imagine modern Americans ending any contest with such grace, much less one that lasted four years and claimed over a million casualties.

Leaving the park, we stopped at a small graveyard established in 1866 by local women. It contained the graves of nineteen men who died in a brief fight at Appomattox just before the surrender. Eighteen of the graves were Confederates, but one had a headstone that read: "USA UNKNOWN Union Patriot." It seemed remarkable, only a year after the War, that women who had seen their own husbands and sons march off to fight were willing to lay a Yankee to rest here, alongside Confederates.

But the graveyard also bore signs of the prideful defiance that quickly resurfaced in the post-War South, undoing so much of the reconciliation attempted at Appomattox. A plaque erected by the United Daughters of the Confederacy listed the number of Lee's men at 9,000, less than a third of the true total, thus making the odds faced by the rebels even more overwhelming. The inscription read: "After four years of heroic struggle, in defense of principles believed fundamental, Lee surrendered the remnant of an army still unconquered in spirit."

AFTER FOUR DAYS of arduous touring, I too felt ready to surrender and trudge home. But Rob insisted we press sixty miles west to Lexington, in the Shenandoah Valley. Lexington was the second city of Confederate remembrance: Medina to Richmond's Mecca. Stonewall Jackson taught college in Lexington before the War and Robert E. Lee after it. Both men lay buried there. So did their horses. "Well, not exactly buried," Rob said, offering no details.

So we wound out of Appomattox, past a billboard for "Bruce and Stiff Funeral Home" and into the Appalachian foothills. Driving at sunset through one of the loveliest stretches of Virginia, I found myself humming "The Night They Drove Old Dixie Down," and feeling oddly melancholy, as Grant had at Appomattox. We'd reached the

War's traditional end point, its period, and the darkening hills under-scored the South's hard-fought demise. "It's views like this," Rob said, as we crested the Blue Ridge and rolled into the Shenandoah Valley, "that make you appreciate what Jimmy Olgers said about people fight-ing for their land."

We reached Lexington at first dark. Navigating past a strip mall called Stonewall Square and into a gracious quarter of antebellum homes, we spotted a shop-window poster for a musical called *Stone-wall Country* playing that night at an outdoor theater. The show seemed a fitting way to conclude a Gasm that had taken as one of its principal themes the mercurial career of Stonewall Jackson.

At the start of the musical the director welcomed the audience, then glanced at us and said, "I'd be particularly interested to know what you two think of the show." I'd become so accustomed to trav-eling in uniform that at first I didn't know what he meant. The di-rector needn't have worried; the costumes looked fine and the show offered an irreverent tour of the landscape we'd just explored. There was Jeb Stuart, in silk sash and thigh-high boots, singing "I'm a day-light earthshaker, I'm a midnight merrymaker." Then came "A. P. Hill's Blues," a mournful recap of the rash general's clashes with his superiors. And throughout there was Stonewall, a cartoonishly stern figure, sucking on lemons as a choir mocked his catatonia during the Seven Days battle with a tune called "Seven Day Freak-Out."

Rob became enamored with one of the hoop-skirted actresses, so we lingered after the show to pay our respects. Then Rob spotted her leaving with an actor whose uniform Rob regarded as the worst in the show. "Fucking typical," he moaned. "Chicks always dig farbs. You'll see flamers in purple jackets who look like Barney and they're the ones getting all the chicks."

I gently observed that the hardcore look had its drawbacks in the chick department. Rob glared at me. "What are you saying? I should stop washing my beard in bacon grease?"

It was late. A cold rain lashed the theater's circus-like tent. Even Rob wasn't keen to sleep in a torrent beside Stonewall's grave, as we'd originally planned. So we tossed our bedrolls on the boards where we'd just watched *Stonewall Country* performed. Rob dutifully re-corded all the hits we'd made that day, then scribbled evasively, "Midnight. Camp in Stonewall Country." He snuffed the candle and said, "I don't want a written record of farbing out."

FARBS GOT CHICKS; they also got sleep. For the first time all week we managed more than a wretched doze. It was a good thing we'd found cover; over breakfast, we learned from a waitress that flash-flooding had washed out roads and drowned several people.

As rain kept pelting down, we toured the Virginia Military In-stitute, where Stonewall taught Artillery Tactics and Natural and Experimental Philosophy (this academic combo wasn't as strange as it sounded; in the 1850s, natural philosophy was akin to physics). Stonewall's name and a Horatio Alger-ish quote attributed to him adorned VMI's barracks: "You May Be Whatever You Resolve To Be." A statue of Stonewall overlooked the parade ground, beside the cannons used by his troops at Manassas.

Stonewall also held sway at Jackson Memorial Hall, a chapel that doubled as a museum filled with relics of the martyred professor, including the india-rubber slicker he wore at Chancellorsville and a copy of *Bartlett's Spherical Astronomy* that Stonewall used in classes. Inside the textbook, a cadet had scribbled of Jackson: "The Major skinned me this morning by asking extra questions on Venus. I wish he would leave me and Venus be." Other students found Jackson so stiff and stultifying that they dubbed him "Tom Fool," "Square Box," and "Old Jack," though he was only in his thirties at the time. Like Ulysses Grant, a failure at a succession of jobs in the 1850s, Stonewall Jackson found success in war that he never enjoyed in civilian life.

The museum's prized exhibit was Jackson's war-horse, Little Sor-rel—or what remained of him. The gelding's tattered hide had been stretched over a plaster of Paris body and mounted on a diorama-like platform scattered with dirt and leaves. The dumpy, dull-brown horse stood stiffly, as though at attention, still wearing a saddle and bridle that Jackson used in the War.

For Little Sorrel, this was the end of a long, strange ride that began in 1861, when Jackson procured the horse from a captured

Union train. Jackson, an awkward rider, liked the gelding's gentle gait ("as easy as the rocking of a cradle," he wrote his wife). Mount suited master in another way; both were unimpressive physical specimens whose attributes only became obvious in battle. Though described by one of Jackson's comrades as "a dun cob of very sorry appearance," Little Sorrel proved tireless on the march and calm under fire. The horse survived a bullet wound at Manassas and bolted only once, when Jackson was shot while riding him at Chancellorsville.

Captured by Union forces, then recaptured by the rebels, Little Sorrel spent his post-War years touring county fairs and Confederate fetes. Souvenir hunters clipped so many hairs from Little Sorrel's mane and tail that the horse eventually required guards. Nor did the horse's death at the age of thirty-six end the indignity. The horse's hide went on display in a caged exhibit at VMI's library, while his bones were used in biology class.

Now, finally, Little Sorrel had come to rest in the school's museum, where he had only to endure gawking tourists and occasional visits by a Smithsonian taxidermist who patched tears in the horse's flanks and cracks on his face. "If he'd got popped with Stonewall at Chancellorsville," Rob said, gazing into Little Sorrel's glass eye, "he never would have had to go through all this."

From VMI we strolled to Washington and Lee University. Here it was Robert E. Lee who reigned supreme. Lee Chapel, where the general worshiped and worked as the school's president, offered a startling illustration of Lee's Christ-like stature in the post-War South. Filling the altar was a life-sized sculpture of Lee, crafted from measurements of his face and physique made by the sculptor just before the general's death. Even the thickness of Lee's lips and the width of his ears were made to measure. Lee lay on a field cot, in full uniform, as though cat-napping between battlefield maneuvers. His recumbent form reminded me of Norman knights lying atop their tombs in Westminster Abbey.

"Square-toed boots, just like the originals," Rob said.

"Size seven," the chapel's guide added. "Just like Lee's."

Rob nodded. "Lee had small feet and was short in the legs but long in the torso, so he seemed bigger in the saddle than on the ground."

"Did you know Lee liked to have his feet tickled?" the guide countered.

As she and Rob swapped anatomical trivia, I wandered outside to view the grave of Lee's mount, Traveller, who died nine months after her master when she stepped on a rusty nail and contracted lockjaw. Like Little Sorrel's, Traveller's bones had endured endless shifting about. Buried beneath the same blanket that had covered her in the War, Traveller was soon disinterred, only to sit around a taxidermist's shop for forty years. The skeleton was later displayed at the college, where students scribbled their initials on the horse's bones. When the skeleton began to deteriorate, Traveller was reburied beside the Lee Chapel's back door, beneath a simple granite slab. Visitors had left carrots there as a token of respect.

We completed our morbid tour at the cemetery where Stonewall lay buried—twice. There was a statue of Jackson clutching field glasses, and a nearby headstone that stated, "The remains of Stonewall Jackson have been removed from this spot and now repose under the monument." Rob chuckled, recalling the bizarre, twice-dug grave of Stonewall's amputated limb near Chancellorsville. "Smedley Butler must have got here, too," he said.

We stood for a while in the rain by Stonewall's graves, then climbed back in the car and drove through the Shenandoah Valley, which Stonewall and his men fought so hard to defend. Though traveling north, we were headed "down the Valley," in local parlance, from the high ground around Lexington toward the valley's floor near Winchester.

As we sped through the rain, Rob begged me to make a few last hits. "We could do Cross Keys and Port Republic at the same exit," he said, gazing wistfully out the window as we approached the turnoff for two of Stonewall's hard-fought battles.

But I kept my foot to the accelerator, eager now for a hot shower and a reunion with my wife. Rob, meanwhile, had a date with his hardcore mates at Gettysburg, where a string of reenactments would begin the following day. As we reached the beltway ringing Washington, Rob opened his notebook and recapped the day's dozen or so hits. Then, gazing pensively out at the traffic, he scribbled a few concluding thoughts on our Gasm:

"Very productive. New dimensions. Holy. Spiritual. Humorous. Educational. Maximizing time. Intense. Peaked many times!"

Five days later, Rob called collect from a phone booth in Gettysburg. The reenactments were done, but he'd stuck around with a few fellow hardcores. Now, he'd decided to end his long Civil War sojourn with a flourish. "Tomorrow's the anniversary of Pickett's Charge," he said. "We're gonna do it at the exact time and on the exact ground that Pickett's men did. Wanna come?"

My chigger bites and poison-ivy rash were just starting to subside. But I was curious to see how Rob's time-travel fantasy played out. So donning my wire-rims and the filthy brogans I'd left airing on the porch, I drove to our rendezvous point by General Pickett's Buffet, part of the modern sprawl of fast-food joints, wax museums and cheap motels that encroached on the Gettysburg battlefield.

Rob wasn't there, but his three companions were easy to spot. They looked like Rob clones: lean men with chin beards, tattered butternut uniforms, sunburned faces and the thousand-yard stare bred of too many nights spooning by campfires. I was a little jarred, though, when all three introduced themselves with Northern accents. Don and Johann came from New York, Bob from Ohio. They'd first met Rob while filming a movie on Andersonville, in which all four played half-starved Union prisoners. "We saw this ad in the *Civil War News*," explained Johann, a tall handsome man of Scandinavian descent who looked like a young Max von Sydow. "It said a film company was looking for 'thin males aged eighteen to thirty-five.' Guess we fit the bill."

Rob appeared, clutching a spare rebel uniform for me and a book he called "the bible"—the Army War College's minutely detailed guide to Gettysburg. "We're going to follow the exact path of the 24th Virginia," he announced, brandishing a map of the unit's route during Pickett's Charge.

It was high season at Gettysburg and tourists swarmed across the battlefield. But we managed to find a quiet spot in the woods bordering Seminary Ridge and huddled in the shade, as Confederates had done during the long wait for the assault to begin. "After a noonday lull," Rob said, consulting the bible, "the Confederates opened up for over an hour with 140 cannon, the largest concentration of artillery in American history to that point." The cannons' blast carried to Pennsylvania towns 150 miles away.

Rob had brought along several other books and we took turns reading aloud, waiting for the midafternoon moment when the Confederates "stepped off" from the woods and into the open ground lying between the rebels and the Union line on Cemetery Ridge. "There were fifty thousand horses at the battle," Rob said, gnawing on a piece of hardtack. "Can you imagine the manure?" We also learned that the temperature reached 87 degrees on the day of the Charge; that Pickett graduated last in his class at West Point; that the general oiled his long ringlets with scented balm; and that Rob wrote his senior paper in high school on Pickett's Charge and got a C-minus.

Probably no half-hour in American history had been more closely scrutinized than Pickett's Charge. Yet hard facts about the assault remained remarkably scarce. No one knew for sure how many men participated, which units breached the stone wall marking the main Union line, or what time the charge began and ended. The assault was also fogged by more myth and misconception than just about any episode of the War. Even the name was a misnomer; Pickett's men formed only a third of the Southern force and James Longstreet, not Pickett, commanded the assault. Nor could anyone say for certain what Pickett did during the charge. Some sources even placed him near the rear, gulping "Confederate chloroform"—a.k.a. whiskey—certainly not in the lead with saber raised, as I'd shown him in my childhood mural.

Gazing out at the open valley the Confederates crossed, we tried to imagine what the rebels must have felt as they waited for the order to advance. This gave me an excuse to read my favorite passage on the Civil War, from Faulkner's novel *Intruder in the Dust*. In one impossibly long sentence, Faulkner captured both the drama of the stepping-off and the nostalgic might-have-been that had lingered in Southern imagination ever since.

> For every Southern boy fourteen years old, not once but whenever he wants it, there is the instant when it's still not yet two o'clock on that July afternoon in 1863, the brigades are in position behind the rail fence, the guns are loaded and ready in the woods and the furled flags are already loosened to break out and Pickett himself with his long oiled ringlets and his hat in one hand probably and his sword in the other looking up the hill waiting for Longstreet to give the word and it's all in the balance, it hasn't happened yet, it hasn't even begun yet, it not only hasn't begun yet but there is still time for it not to begin against that position and those circumstances. . . . yet it's going to begin, we all know that, we have come too far with too much at stake and that moment doesn't need even a fourteen-year-old boy to think *This time. Maybe this time* with all this much to lose and all this much to gain: Pennsylvania, Maryland, the world, the golden dome of Washington itself to crown with desperate and unbelievable victory the desperate gamble, the cast made two years ago; or to anyone who ever sailed even a skiff under a quilt sail, the moment in 1492 when somebody thought *This is it*: the absolute edge of no return, to turn back now and make home or sail irrevocably on and either find land or plunge over the world's roaring rim.

When I finished the passage—which required several gulps of air to read aloud—Johann shook his head. "Guy could fuckin' write," he said. One of the other men checked his pocket watch and nodded at Rob: the moment of no return had arrived. Rob stood up and pointed at the copse of trees on Cemetery Ridge, which the Army of Northern Virginia had used as its guidon. "Men," he said, mimicking Pickett's speech in the movie version of Gettysburg, "today you fight for old Virginia!"

We took swigs from a pocket flask and solemnly shook hands, saying, "See you at the top." Then Rob led us out of the woods. "Dress ranks," he shouted. "Shoulder to shoulder. Forward, march!"

As we left the shaded woods, the midafternoon sun felt blindingly hot and bright. Cemetery Ridge shimmered in the distance, about a mile away across an undulating field that tilted gently upward. As we marched silently through the tall grass, I could feel the ground crunching beneath my cracked boots. The haversack rubbed uncomfortably through the wool shoulder of my butternut jacket. I felt a band of sweat forming beneath my slouch hat. My heart began thudding, more from excitement than exertion. I felt suddenly light-headed. *This is it. Plunging over the world's roaring rim.* Were these the first stirrings of a "period rush"?

My reverie was broken by something bright in the grass. I reached down to find a gaudy plastic sword some child must have lost. Then I heard whirrs and clicks just off to our left. A skirmish line of tourists had formed about fifty yards off, aiming cameras and binoculars at us. Several others approached from our right flank.

"Let's pick it up, boys," Rob said, stepping faster. But there was no escape. Within minutes we'd been swamped by people in shorts and T-shirts who bombarded us with questions and camera flashes.

"Are you guys reactors?"

"Which one of you's Pickett?"

"You gonna win it for us this time?"

We ignored them as best we could and marched quickly on, eyes trained to the ground. But a few followers still clung to either side of our line. A lobster-red woman in a halter top matched Rob stride for stride, carefully studying his uniform.

"What are you guys?" she asked.

"Confederates," Rob mumbled.

"Ferrets?"

"Confederates," Rob repeated.

"Oh," the woman said, looking underwhelmed.

When we'd finally sloughed off our entourage, Rob paused to consult his battlefield guide and angled us slightly to the left, toward the inaptly named Bliss Farm. Suddenly, drums began banging to our rear. I turned and saw about a hundred tourists marching behind us, evidently inspired by our example. Most of the men in the front rank wore duckbill caps advertising ball teams and cattle-feed brands. One carried a drum, another played "Dixie" on a fife, a third waved a rebel battle flag.

"Sir," Johann said to Rob, "the Tourists of Northern Virginia are close on our rear."

Rob glanced over his shoulder. A man waved his fist and shouted, "Give 'em hell, boys!"

Rob ordered, "Route step, 110 paces a minute!" and we quickened our march until we'd left the shadow army behind. We entered a field covered with chest-high corn. Cemetery Ridge loomed just above the stalks. "Dress ranks," Rob shouted, and we moved closer together, our shoulders almost touching, as the Confederates had done each time an artillery shell tore a hole in the their line.

We reached the Emmitsburg Road, which ran roughly parallel to Cemetery Ridge and marked the starting point of the rebels' final dash for the Union line. It was here that Union guns opened in earnest with close-range canister and rifle shot, ripping into the rebels as they swarmed over a plank fence bordering the road. One board of the fence was later found shredded with 836 bullet holes.

We faced no such firestorm, only a heavy line of skirmishers: campers, RVs, pickups. As we clambered over the fence, cameras and videos poked out windows and sunroofs, aimed at us like roadside deer. "Could you guys do that again?" a man called out, reloading his camera.

We snaked between the vehicles and rushed onto the gentle slope on the far side of the road. Rob shouted, "Double quick!" and we formed a flying wedge, as the Confederates had done, sprinting across the last hundred yards of open ground. One rebel later described this stretch as "covered with clover as soft as a Turkish carpet." Whether the clover was still there I couldn't tell; the ground was too thickly strewn with bodies, kneeling or lying prone, their cameras poking through the grass for a dramatic action snapshot. The crowd was so dense that I had to shoulder aside several people as I loped behind Rob toward the stone wall at the top of the slope.

"Home, boys, home!" Rob shouted, waving his slouch hat. "Home is over beyond those hills!"

We reached the stone wall amidst a final hail of snapping shutters, then slumped on the ground, hot and exhausted. The charge had taken us twenty-five minutes, about the same as the original. We'd lost only one man, left behind at the Emmitsburg Road nursing his blisters. This was a far better ratio than the actual Confederates, almost two-thirds of whom were killed, wounded or captured in the assault. One Mississippi company lost every man. All told, the Confederacy took 28,000 casualties at Gettysburg, including thirty-one of the thirty-two senior officers who led Pickett's division during the charge.

"What were you guys trying to prove?" asked a man in a Hard Rock Cafe T-shirt. "The rebels I mean."

"You boys prisoners now?"

"Did it really happen like in the movie?"

After catching his breath, Rob began patiently answering each question in turn, as I'd seen him do at Manassas. Watching the rapt crowd, I began to feel less resentful of the gawkers we'd attracted all along the charge. From their questions, it was clear that Rob's interrogators felt deeply drawn to Gettysburg. But visiting the place, on a July day thick with gnats and tour buses, they seemed vaguely disappointed and didn't know quite what to do with the empty fields, the silent cannons, the mute blocks of marble. By charging across the landscape in our rebel uniforms, we'd given a flesh-and-blood boost to their imagination, a way into the battle that the modern landscape didn't easily provide. For one of the few times during my brief reenacting career, I felt I'd done something worthwhile by putting on a uniform.

Still, it was hard to avoid feeling like a creature at the zoo. When I wandered inside to use the visitors' center bathroom, the man at the next urinal looked at me and said, "Do they let you guys piss inside?" Buttoning up my fly, I heard a familiar click behind me and turned to find a boy smiling over his camera. "Gotcha," he said.

Returning outside, I found Rob and his friends hoisting their gear. They had a date with a photographer who wanted to duplicate the most famous picture of the entire War: three lean Confederate prisoners standing proudly beside a snake-rail fence at Gettysburg. The photographer was also putting together a Civil War calendar and planned to use a portrait of Rob as the accompaniment for one of the months. "Poster boy for the Confederacy," Rob said with a grin. "Next thing you know I'll be doing centerfolds."

Still, Rob confessed to feeling a bit depressed. Tomorrow, his ex-tended escape from the twentieth century would end, and he'd go back to waiting on tables to pay the rent.

"I've had this uniform on for ten days straight," he said, wistfully fingering a sleeve starched with grime. "It'll feel like farbing out when I finally get in the shower."

11

Georgia
GONE WITH THE WINDOW

*You drive through Atlanta . . . and take a look around,
and up, and you wonder, what is this place? Is this a place?*
—WALKER PERCY, *Going Back to Georgia*, 1978

etreating south to Virginia, like the ferrets after Pickett's Charge, I plotted my campaign through the crucial stretch of Civil War real estate I'd so far skirted. In the year following Gettysburg, while Lee locked the Federals in a bloody stalemate in Virginia, the Union army out "West" battled its way into the Confederate heartland of Georgia and Alabama. "I begin to regard the death and mangling of a couple of thousand men as a small affair, a kind of morning dash," William Tecumseh Sherman wrote to his wife in July 1864, after a bloody repulse in north Georgia. Five weeks later, Sherman tersely telegraphed his superiors, "Atlanta is ours, and fairly won"—a victory that saved Lincoln from defeat in the fall elections and helped seal the doom of the Southern Confederacy.

Reaching Atlanta was far easier now than in Sherman's day. Fueled by Georgia's 97-cents-a-gallon gas and unenforced speed limits, I bombed down an interstate that spilled straight into Peachtree Street, the city's main drag. Unlike Sherman, I approached

Atlanta with trepidation. Though I'd never visited the city proper, it was impossible to travel the South without getting trapped in Atlanta's tentacled airport, or being blitzed by TV images of the city's bland skyline, its relentless boosterism, its bloodlessly efficient baseball team. Atlanta loomed in my imagination like a blimp-sized smile button.

I'd also absorbed the prejudices of non-Atlantans I'd met in my travels (admittedly, mostly folks of a traditional bent). To Southrons, as true sons and daughters of Dixie liked to call themselves, Atlanta was the anti-South: a crass, brash city built in the image of the Chamber of Commerce and overrun by carpetbaggers, corporate climbers and conventioneers. "Every time I look at Atlanta," quipped John Shelton Reed, the South's wittiest observer, "I see what a quarter million Confederate soldiers died to prevent."

Atlanta-bashers had even made a science of the city's disloyalty to Dixie. Reed, a sociologist by trade, cited surveys showing that Atlanta's "pace of life"—as measured by walking speed, length of bank transactions, per capita wristwatch-wearing—*exceeded* the national average. Even worse, Atlantans ranked below average in their hospitality to strangers (i.e., making change or helping a blind person across the street). "The only thing remarkable about Atlanta," Reed opined, "is the number and variety of table-dancing establishments."

Arriving in Atlanta at dusk, I was mostly struck by the number and blandness of its malls and shops. The interstate deposited me in Buckhead, an upscale district that an Atlantan had recommended as "colorful" and "close in." Cruising slowly down Peachtree, I passed Lenox Square (America's first suburban mall), a restaurant with a sign that said "A Buckhead Tradition since February," and countless "detail salons," a hardcore breed of car wash where attendants cleaned vehicles with tweezers and Q-Tips. Every ten blocks or so stood a chain restaurant called Mick's; the road map I'd picked up at a gas station labeled every Mick's, posted like mileage markers all across town.

It was several Mick's and six miles from Buckhead to Atlanta's compact downtown. Whatever peach trees once bloomed here were gone, supplanted by a forest of office towers bearing corporate names: Coca-Cola, Delta, Georgia-Pacific, CNN. Climbing out of my car, I toured the only visible nineteenth-century survival: Underground Atlanta, a commercial district that remained below street level as the modern city grew up around it. Underground originally served as a railroad-side market where slaves and other "wares" were unloaded and sold. Now, its quaint gaslights illuminated renovated shopfronts: Victoria's Secret, Sam Goody, Foot Locker, Hooter's, The Gap.

Like most newcomers, bred on *Gone With the Wind*, I assumed that Sherman and his torch-wielding soldiers bore the principal blame for Atlanta's arid modernity. This notion was also ingrained in the city's self-image. Atlanta took the phoenix as its symbol; its motto was *Resurgens*. But the next day, at the Atlanta History Center, I learned that the modern city hadn't exactly risen from Civil War ashes. "Atlantans leveled much more of Atlanta than Sherman did," said Franklin Garrett, the city's leading historian.

At eighty-nine, Garrett's memory was so encyclopedic that the History Center held an annual trivia contest called "Stump Franklin." He'd last been stumped several years before, when he failed to recall the name of a doorman at a 1920s department store. But he remembered the building. "Gone. Same as the whole block," he said, consulting a map and ticking off the structures like so many extinct species.

Evanescence had always come with the territory in Atlanta. While most antebellum Southern cities—Savannah, Charleston, Mobile, New Orleans—grew up around colonial ports, Atlanta began only twenty-four years before the Civil War as a railroad end point called Terminus. Showing an early talent for reinvention, Terminus quickly shed its funereal name and became a bustling rail and munitions center during the Civil War. Retreating Confederates torched much of the city before Sherman's men added to the bonfire. Even so, Garrett said, about a quarter of the city, including some 400 homes and buildings, survived the flames.

What old Atlanta couldn't survive was the city's ceaseless remaking of itself after the War. The devastation was so complete, Garrett said, that not a single antebellum building now remained. The city's battlefields had fared just as badly. Peachtree Battle Shopping Center was virtually all that recalled the rebels' rearguard assault at

Peachtree Creek in July 1864. Even the name Peachtree had lost its historic cachet. Peachtree was such a desirable business address that hustling Atlantans had simply cloned it; there were now thirty-two streets with the fruit tree as part of their name.

While Garrett mourned the loss of so much history, he felt this devastation reflected the city's essential character. "Atlanta's always been on the go," he said. "Never was a moonlight-and-magnolia city like Savannah or Charleston. It always had more of a Rhett Butler attitude than an Ashley Wilkes one."

This go-go attitude had a progressive side, of course. It was an Atlanta newspaper editor, Henry Grady, who popularized the phrase "New South" in 1886 to describe a region ready to reconcile with the North—and ready for Northern investment. Atlanta was the first Southern city to abolish the poll tax and integrated far more easily than most urban centers. The city also began electing black mayors in the 1970s and had become a Mecca for middle-class blacks from across the nation. The Chamber of Commerce got in on the act, too, once taking as its slogan, "A City Too Busy to Hate."

Like so much about Atlanta, this hype had a way of clouding reality. Atlanta's inner city remained among the poorest and most crime-ridden in America, and urban blight was matched by frenzied white flight. Even so, it was impossible to wander downtown Atlanta without being struck by the profusion of black professionals and interracial couples, and by the casual mingling of blacks and whites at bars, lunch counters and offices.

But Atlanta's comparative racial amity—and ceaseless peddling of its progressive image—abetted the city's neglect of its past. Whatever history Atlanta couldn't tear down, it bobbed around, lest any ugly blot from the past mar the city's reputation. During the run-up to the 1996 Olympics, this sanitizing of the past became downright Orwellian. A suburb called Roswell, under pressure from corporate sponsors, deleted "antebellum" from the title of its annual historical festival (it also tried to bar Confederate reenactors from participating). Roswell's Historic Preservation Commission also removed a marker pointing out slave quarters beside an antebellum home. "We'll just put it right back out after the Olympics are over," a local official said. "This is history."

At day's end, as glass towers emptied downtown, I saw another side of Atlanta that boosters preferred not to advertise. While blacks headed home to urban neighborhoods or close-in suburbs south of downtown, whites streamed onto freeways toward distant enclaves, mostly north of the city. Atlantans referred to the beltway ringing the city as the "perimeter," as though it represented a real frontier between the majority-black city and the overwhelmingly white suburbs. There was even a corporate outpost oxymoronically called "Perimeter Center."

Atlantans also spoke of their beltway-ringed city as a doughnut. There were now two telephone area codes, one for "inside the doughnut," the other for outside. And while the population of the city proper had dwindled since 1970, dipping below 500,000, the metro area had doubled in size to over three million people, mostly living outside the doughnut.

Joining a twelve-lane highway, I lost myself in the tangle of interstates leading out of the city. Despite its rapid growth, north Georgia remained remarkably pastoral. Greater Atlanta didn't so much sprawl as metastasize, with exurban nodes appearing suddenly amidst piney woods, rolling hills and red-clay fields. Greater Atlanta had also sprouted an astonishing crop of gated communities. One, called Sweetbottom Plantation, offered upscale homes modeled on those in Charleston's Battery and New Orlean's Garden District: a bit of Old South grace transplanted to New South suburbs, with security gates and private roads.

I ended my drive at Stone Mountain, just east of the city. Reputedly the largest hunk of exposed granite in the world, the dome-shaped mountain poked up from Atlanta's wooded perimeter like a very tall, very bald man in a crowd. Chiseled on its face was the world's largest bas-relief sculpture, a three-acre carving of the Confederate trinity—Lee, Jackson and Davis—riding horses and holding hats over their hearts. Lee alone stood nine stories tall.

Commissioned by the United Daughters of the Confederacy in 1915, and begun by the same artist who crafted Mount Rushmore, Stone Mountain was intended as the South's foremost Confederate shrine. It also became a rallying place for the Ku Klux Klan, which was reborn there in 1915 and later declared Atlanta its Imperial City. But eighty years later, when the park at Stone Mountain's base was named an Olympic venue, the Invisible Empire became, well, invisible. A museum exhibit on Stone Mountain, opening just before the Games, omitted any mention of the Klan. "I think some chapters are just better left to the historians," Atlanta's mayor told the local press.

The park's management had also chosen to soften the Confederate content of a popular laser show that used the sculpture as a backdrop. Curious to see the result, I joined several thousand people strewn on blankets and banana chairs at the mountain's base. As the lights came up, I was struck by how different Stone Mountain was from Mount Rushmore. Here, the figures were shown in profile, in relatively shallow relief, as though a huge Confederate coin had left a fossil-like print in the mountain's face.

This impression lasted about ten seconds, the time it took for the sound track to kick on, playing as overture a familiar soft-drink jingle: "There's always Coca-Cola!" Laser beams created a Coke bottle dancing across the mounted Confederates. This was followed by a cartoon strip featuring a good ol' boy named Buford, traveling through a time tunnel—though not very far. Animated rock guitarists flashed onto the mountain to the strains of ZZ Top and the Beatles. This segued into the theme song from *Beverly Hills Cop*, accompanied by abstract images: trapezoids, stars, clusters.

No musical riff or laser image lasted more than a few seconds. I caught snatches of the B-52s singing "Heading down the Atlanta Highway" and Alabama doing "Forty Hour Week." Charlie Daniels's "The Devil Went Down to Georgia" collided with Ed Sullivan introducing the Beatles as airplanes landed to the strains of "Back in the U.S.S.R." Then came sports iconography—the Braves, the Falcons, the Hawks—before Elvis appeared, thrusting his pelvis across Traveller's rippling flank. At this point, I felt sure I could hear Robby Lee and his famous mount rolling over in their graves up in Lexington.

The show concluded in a blur of cliches: Scarlett O'Hara, peaches, plantations, and the mascots of various Georgia universities. Then Elvis appeared again, singing "Dixie" in a slow, sensual drawl as the lasers outlined Lee, Jackson and Davis. The crowd began to cheer. But as the mounted men sprang to life and galloped across Stone Mountain, "Dixie" segued into the "Battle Hymn of the Republic" and Lee broke his sword across his leg. The two halves of the blade quickly transmogrified into a map of North and South, merging together as the sound track belted, "His truth is marching on." Finally, to expunge any last hint of the Cause, the sound track played "God Bless the U.S.A." amidst images of the Lincoln Memorial, JFK's grave, Martin Luther King Jr., and a ballot box. Fireworks exploded and the mountain became, in turn, an immense American flag, the Statue of Liberty and Mount Rushmore. The music and lasers abruptly cut off and the three horsemen of the Confederacy melted into the night.

I sat there for a while, letting "Dixie" and the "Battle Hymn" and Lee and Lincoln and Elvis all jangle around in my head. The show was a puddle of political correctness. The message seemed to be that there was no message—no real content to any of the divisive figures or songs or historic episodes the laser show depicted in its fast-paced cartoon. Why debate who should or shouldn't be remembered and revered when you could just stuff the whole lot in a blender and spew it across the world's biggest rock?

Like so much in Atlanta, Stone Mountain had become a bland and inoffensive consumable: the Confederacy as hood ornament. Not for the first time, though more deeply than ever before, I felt a twinge of affinity for the neo-Confederates I'd met in my travels. Better to remember Dixie and debate its philosophy than to have its largest shrine hijacked for Coca-Cola ads and MTV songs.

BUT THEN, even neo-Confederates in Atlanta were different. While traveling the South, I'd often encountered representatives of the Heritage Preservation Association, an Atlanta-based group renowned for its attack-dog tactics in defense of the rebel flag. So I made a lunch date with the group's president, Lee Collins. I expected to encounter a gaunt, fiery-eyed man with a rebel-flag pin and nineteenth-century hair—the sort of figure I'd often met at neo-Confederate gatherings. Instead, I was greeted at my hotel by a groomed, thirty-something preppy who wore a button-down shirt, a designer tie and horn-rimmed glasses.

"We can eat Southern," Lee Collins said as we climbed into his minivan, "or we can go further South than that." Intrigued, I chose the latter. Collins picked up his car phone and began chatting in Spanish. Then to me: "My wife's Colombian and I've been itching to try this place." Collins turned up Buford Highway, the main thoroughfare of immigrant Atlanta, and drove past Asian noodle bars and Muslim butchers before pulling into a hole-in-the-wall cantina. Collins ordered off the menu, again in fluent Spanish.

"We have a culture—Southern culture—that's been bleached from the fabric of America," Collins said, slathering tortilla chips with hot sauce. "My children are half-Hispanic and I'm proud of that. But they're also half-Southern. I want them to be proud of that, too."

Collins had met his wife through a Colombian folklore and dance group. Since then, he'd made a number of Hispanic contacts, which had helped expand his non-Confederate livelihood: a computer-consulting business. "My background is engineering," he said. "I'm trained to identify problems, implement and monitor a solution, then move on to the next problem. We don't get wrapped up in emotion. The same goes for the Heritage Preservation Association."

The HPA had a computer bulletin board and a toll-free hot line (1-800-MY DIXIE) so members could report "heritage violations," such as a hotel chain's decision to stop displaying the Georgia state banner, which incorporated the rebel flag. The HPA ran ads, directed letter-writing campaigns, lobbied the state legislature during debates over the flag. The HPA even had a political action committee, or PAC, to funnel money to sympathetic candidates.

"The heritage movement is a brand-new industry," Collins said, hoeing into rice and beans. "It's like Lotus was ten years ago, producing spread sheets while others produced software. Now, Lotus will sell you a database. We've created a niche, too. A niche of the civil rights industry. Our niche is Southern heritage."

Collins also had learned to appropriate the idiom of civil rights and of liberal groups combating discrimination. "We're chosen people, surviving many atrocities," he said, sounding like a spokesman for the Anti-Defamation League. Mimicking the NAACP, the HPA had created a legal-defense team to assist victims of bias, such as a textile worker who was fired for pasting a battle flag to his toolbox.

"The main thing I've learned from the civil rights movement is the power of perseverance," Collins said. "It took fifteen years to get the Martin Luther King holiday. We're in this for the long haul."

Most other neo-Confederates I'd met were romantics. The South they revered was hot-blooded, Celtic, heedlessly courageous; their poster boy was the Scottish clansman played by Mel Gibson in the splatterfest *Braveheart*. In their view, rationalism and technological efficiency were suspect Yankee traits, derived from a mercantile English empire that had put down the Scots and Irish.

Collins was well acquainted with this philosophy, but he didn't subscribe to it as an organizing tool for today's struggle. "Nostalgia's not a powerful enough force," he said. "If it were, the Sons of Confederate Veterans would have ten million members and the Christian Coalition would have a thousand."

Even so, Collins wasn't immune to certain strains of neo-Confederate ideology. In his view, Atlanta's New South trappings were simply an extension of the Civil War and the North's efforts to mold Dixie in its own image. "The New South breaks the back of the agrarian economy and promotes an industrial South," he said. "That's succeeded. But it hasn't captured the hearts and minds of the people."

To Collins, this helped explain Atlanta's suburban sprawl. "People here still have a rural mentality. They want space," he said. "Southerners may work in a factory but they still dream of owning a farm." No matter how many Northerners flocked to Atlanta, an essential Southernness would endure. "We have an extra layer of armor. Our culture."

Collins's armor deflected every arrow I tried to fling at his arguments. The heritage movement wasn't backward-looking, he said; it was tuned precisely to the times. "We're anti-federal. Con-federal, if you like. I'd rather that Georgia not get one federal dollar." He believed this same independent streak had sparked the Civil War, which in his view was fought over economic issues and constitutional sovereignty. "If all the South wanted to do was maintain slavery, the easiest way was to stay in the Union, where slavery was legal." Nor did the rebel flag symbolize the oppression of blacks; after all, the Stars and Stripes flew over slavery for eighty years, which the battle flag of the South never did. "The Confederacy was an attempt to institute a strict interpretation of the Constitution. Period."

I'd heard most of this before, but never so slickly presented—and never over plantains and chile verde. Collins even offered an entrepreneurial critique of Atlanta's failure to exploit Confederate history. "We have a natural resource, it's inexhaustible. That resource is Southern heritage. Stone Mountain—people don't come there to ski, they come because it's a Confederate memorial. It makes me sick, the lost opportunity to capitalize on something we have. It's bigger than oil because it's inexhaustible and it doesn't pollute the atmosphere."

Collins was a busy man. He tossed down a cup of café con leche and handed me a business card and a copy of the HPA's "mission statement." One thing he wouldn't share, though, was the size of his organization. "In keeping with the strategy of Lee at Appomattox," he said, "I don't release numbers. The element of uncertainty has been good for us."

BACK AT MY MOTEL, flipping through the HPA's literature, I noticed an ad for another enterprise I'd often wondered about while traveling the South: a north Georgia business called the Ruffin Flag Company. I'd seen Ruffin wares advertised in dozens of Southern publications, and for sale at shops and reenactments across the region. It struck me that Ruffin Flag might be a good place to take the commercial pulse of the neo-Confederacy, and to get a better sense of the movement's size and shape than Lee Collins was willing to give me. Also, the name of the company's owner intrigued me. Soren Dresch didn't sound like the usual Celtic-blooded descendant of Confederate soldiers.

Ruffin Flag was based east of Atlanta in a small town whose loquacious sign—"A Dixie Welcome to Crawfordville, Ga. Homes, Stores, Schools, Churches, Factories and Business Locations"—announced a depleted downtown where many of the homes, factories and businesses were now abandoned. Main Street, lined with de-cayed storefronts and fading "Soda Malt" signs, had the picturesque seediness of a Deep South movie set, which it frequently had been.

Crawfordville also was the hometown of the Confederacy's asth-matic and ascerbic vice president, Alexander Hamilton Stephens. In refreshing contrast to modern vice presidents, Stephens didn't hesitate to bad-mouth his boss, once calling Jeff Davis "weak and vacillating, petulant, peevish, obstinate but not firm." His mansion, Liberty Hall, still perched at the edge of town, its slave quarters in-tact. Just across the street stood a wood bungalow with a rebel flag flying out front. This was the headquarters of the Ruffin Flag Com-pany, quite literally a cottage industry.

Just inside the bungalow's front door, I found Ruffin's owner punching holes in leather belts decorated with the rebel banner. Soren Dresch was a doughy, balding man of thirty-one. He wore khakis, docksiders and a polo shirt, and spoke with a Northern ac-cent. At first glance, he could have passed for the slightly rumpled manager of a Cape Cod yacht club.

This wasn't too far off the mark. When I asked about Dresch's name, he explained that his father was a philosophy major and Yale Ph.D. with a fondness for the gloomy Dane, Sören Kierkegaard. "My full name's Soren K. Dresch," he said, "but the K's just a K. Dad liked Kafka, too, I guess."

Raised in New Haven, Connecticut, Dresch had displayed Copper-head tendencies from an early age. "I had a shrine to the Confederacy in my room. Rebel flags, license plates, things I'd gotten through the mail." Dresch wasn't sure where this allegiance came from. His fa-ther's family hailed from Kansas, his mother's from Ohio. "My dad was a liberal sixties-type, he rebelled against the system," Dresch said. "Maybe I was rebelling against him. He hated all my stuff and once tried to throw it out."

But Dresch remained a rebel, seceding to the University of Ala-bama after high school. It was there that he'd discovered a flair for commerce. His first enterprise: importing cheap rebel flags and sell-ing them to students. This was the mid-1980s, when attacks on the flag by the NAACP and other groups helped spark a renascence of passion for the flag, particularly at Deep South universities. Then, like Lee Collins, Dresch found a niche he could fill. "There was this void at the quality end of the market," he said.

Dresch took me into his showroom, in what had once been the parlor of the modest cottage. He pointed to a rack of license plates, including one sold by a competitor: "Save Yo' Confederate Money Boys—the South's Gonna Rise Again." Dresch grimaced with distaste. "When I started, that was the only sort of stuff on the market. Rebel-flag bug screens, bumper stickers, and tacky T-shirts. Rednecky stuff." One entrepreneur even marketed a rebel-flag bandanna that doubled as a diaper.

Dresch showed me one of his own license plates, bearing the Confederate seal: George Washington and the motto *Deo Vindice*. Another plate displayed the Alabama state flag: a red Saint Andrew's Cross set on a white field. "Quality," Dresch said. "Taste. When I started in business I thought the cheapest stuff would sell best. But the opposite is true because the Confederacy is dear to people's hearts. I've sold forty thousand license plates since 1992."

He led me into another room, where a computer glowed in one corner beside a telephone answering machine. Dresch picked up an afghan decorated with the rebel flag. "Hand-loomed Carolina cloth," he said, stroking the dense fabric. Quality Confederama didn't come cheap. Some of Dresch's wares sold for $100 apiece. "Customized flags are even more," he said. For instance, a flag specially designed for draping a casket.

Dresch also sold smaller items: beer coolers, belts, dog collars. "But nothing racist," he assured me. His bumper stickers stuck to innocuous slogans, such as, "Dixie: Old Times There Are Not Forgotten." And his T-shirts tended toward black-and-white images of renowned Confederates, including one depicting a man with a long mane of white hair and a rifle perched against his knee. This was Edmund Ruffin, for whom Dresch's company was named. A prominent antebellum agronomist who authored a ground-breaking treatise called "An Essay on Calcareous Manures," Ruffin became a fanatical secessionist and allegedly fired the first shot at Fort Sumter.

Four years later, depressed by the South's defeat, Ruffin wrapped himself in a rebel flag and wrote a final diatribe in his diary, which Dresch had printed on the back of the T-shirt: "And now with my latest writing and utterance, and with what will be near my last breath, I here repeat and would willingly proclaim my unmitigated hatred to Yankee rule—to all political, social and business connections with Yankees, and the perfidious, malignant and vile Yankee race." Ruffin then fired his last shot through his own brain.

Dresch smiled. "I move a lot of Ruffins," he said. But his best seller by far was a T-shirt emblazoned with another fierce Confederate: Nathan Bedford Forrest, the "Wizard of the Saddle" and first Imperial Wizard of the Klan. "Lee, of course, used to be our best seller," Dresch said. "But Forrest has eclipsed Lee fivefold in the last few years."

Dresch's success in selling Forrest T-shirts gave commercial confirmation to the trend I'd sensed across the South: a hardening, ideological edge to Confederate remembrance. As Dresch put it, "Southerners are getting tired of taking it on the chin. They're getting more aggressive. Lee's the Southern gentleman who represents reconciliation with the Union. Forrest represents the spirit of going after them with everything you've got."

As I'd learned from Shelby Foote, Forrest differed from Lee in another way, which helped explain his special appeal to working-class Southerners. Born to poverty and possessing little formal education, Forrest was a self-made man who became a wealthy slave trader before the War and rose from private to lieutenant-general during the conflict. "Come on boys," Forrest once wrote in a recruiting ad, "if you want a heap of fun and to kill some Yankees."

I continued my chat with Dresch at a local diner, over cornbread, turnip greens, and ham. Dresch confessed that he'd added some padding during his years in Dixie, and also adopted a slight Southern inflection. "Subconsciously, I've probably worked on that," he admitted. But Dresch maintained one curious tie to the North. His flags were made, not by diehard Southern seamstresses, but by a sect of Apostolic Lutheran women in the upper peninsula of Michigan, one of the most northerly reaches of the continental United States. Dresch had met a few of the women during a visit to Michigan and was impressed by their work ethic and attention to detail. Sewing from their homes, these Northern women now earned $6 an hour making flags from a pattern book called *Emblems of Southern Valor*.

"One of the ladies quit because she thought the flag represented opposition to the U.S.," Dresch said. "But most of them don't have much idea what this is all about."

I asked Dresch what Edmund Ruffin might think of a company bearing the firebrand's name that nonetheless maintained business ties to the perfidious Yankee race. Dresch shrugged. "He'd probably put a bullet through my head." For a man named after the author of "Fear and Loathing Unto Death," Soren Dresch seemed remarkably unperturbed by the contradictions of his peculiar livelihood.

After lunch, Dresch reached into his pickup and selected a Ruffin T-shirt and several other items for me to take home. "Let me know how they play up in Virginia," he said, heading back to his office. "I haven't got much market penetration up there."

M Y SECOND WEEK in Atlanta, I stopped at the city's main tourist office and chatted with a genial redhead named Mary Ann. I told her I'd visited Stone Mountain and a few other War-related sites, and wondered if I'd missed anything.

"Not much," she said. Then, digging through a drawer, she pulled out a brochure in rather the manner of a convenience store clerk reaching for a plastic-covered *Hustler.* "We don't display this one because it wouldn't be P.C. and someone might be offended," she explained. The pamphlet, compiled by a local Daughter of the Confederacy named Izabell Buzzett, offered a brief guide to rebel monuments scattered around Atlanta. I told Mary Ann I'd collected dozens of similar brochures across the South. She nodded, adding sotto voce: "In most other cities, this would be out front and Mrs. Buzzett would be standing here behind the counter, not me."

But this was Atlanta. Nor was there much demand for traditional Confederate history from the tourists who came into Mary Ann's office. "Where's Tara? That's always their first question," she said. "Then, 'Where are Scarlett and Rhett buried, and are they next to each other?'"

"What do you tell them?"

Mary Ann smiled. "I try to break the news gently. 'Honey, you know it's a movie, don't you?' Then I have to explain that the whole thing was filmed in California. Not one scene in Georgia." Tara's fields were actually a patch of the San Fernando Valley, tinted red to look like Georgia. Even the oak trees around Tara were fake, crafted from telephone poles.

"It's sad to shatter people's illusions," Mary Ann said. "They expect Tara to be right here by the Civic Center." As consolation, she pointed them to a collection of movie memorabilia at the Road To Tara Museum and a reproduction plantation at Stone Mountain.

One group, though, always wanted more. "The Japanese worship Scarlett," Mary Ann said. "They always come in here and say, 'I am searching for Gone With the Window.'"

I lolled outside for a while, thumbing through the brochures Mary Ann had given me. I could of course follow the trail Mrs. Buzzett laid out, and search for obscure Confederate obelisks. But I'd been there, done that. I was also intrigued by Mary Ann's comments, which confirmed something I'd sensed throughout my travels: *Gone With the Wind* had done more to keep the Civil War alive, and to mold its memory, than any history book or event since Appomattox. Anyway, Atlanta begged for a different approach. Why dig for the real and unremembered past when I could search like the Japanese for the fictional one instead?

THE INTERSTATE EXIT for Jonesboro, half an hour south of Atlanta, spilled onto Tara Boulevard. The road led past Tara Auto World, Tara Mobile Home Park, Tara Hardware, Tara Baptist Church and the usual offerings of fast food, fast gas and fast cash. I turned off Tara Boulevard, past Tara Music, Tara Trophies, Tara Florist and entered downtown Jonesboro, a pleasant row of brick storefronts facing a railroad depot with a sign that said, "Home of Gone With the Wind." At the Clayton County Chamber of Commerce, a picture of Tara hung behind the front desk. Lee Davis, the chamber's vice president for marketing, reached for my copy of the novel. "Clayton County—we're mentioned right there on page six," she said. "That's the world's best marketing program."

Davis had one problem, though; there wasn't anything in Jonesboro or Clayton County to market. In the phone book, there were forty-seven listings under Tara, including Tara Billiards, Tara Church of Christ, Tara Dermatology Center, Tara Sanitation. The only thing missing was Tara.

"Margaret Mitchell's great-grandparents, the Fitzgeralds, had a place near here," Davis said. "But that's it." Nor did modern Clayton County much resemble the countryside Mitchell described in her novel as a "pleasant land of white houses, peaceful plowed fields and sluggish yellow rivers." Now a fast-growing bedroom suburb of Atlanta, Clayton County's "savagely red land" had been plowed under for subdivisions and shopping malls. Also, like Peachtree Street, the setting for *Gone With the Wind* was no longer an exclusive address. "Just about every county in Georgia already tries to cash in on the whole hoop-skirt thing," Davis said.

On the way out, we paused at a lobby exhibit of *Gone With the Wind* memorabilia. Beside a movie still of Vivien Leigh I noticed a picture of a woman who looked remarkably like her. "Who's that?" I asked.

"Oh, that's Scarlett O'Hara," Davis said. "The professional one, I mean. She won some pageant a few years back and she's pretty much been Scarlett ever since."

Her real name was Melly Meadows—short for Melanie, just like Ashley Wilkes's wife—and she lived nearby. So I gave her a call and arranged to meet at her home office just off Jonesboro's main street. The young woman who greeted me on the porch wore tight blue jeans and a loose, open-necked blouse. But there was no mistaking her resemblance to Scarlett, at least as portrayed by Vivien Leigh: alabaster skin, slim waist, oval face, cupid-bow mouth and long dark hair tied back with an emerald-green ribbon.

"I'm so happy you came by," she said, gently shaking my hand. "Here, let me give you my brochure and business card."

Embossed on the card was her photograph in antebellum dress and Melly "Scarlett" Meadows printed in both English and Japanese. "Southern Belles & Gentlemen also available," the pamphlet said. Melly invited me to join her on the porch swing. "I've sort of become Scarlett O'Hara Incorporated," she sighed.

Melly Meadows was a self-made Southern belle. After years of being teased by classmates about her resemblance to Vivien Leigh, she entered a Scarlett look-alike contest at a local mall and beat forty other wannabes (her sister was runner-up). After that, she started donning her hoop skirt for local charity events. Before long, she'd been hired to appear at business breakfasts, ribbon cuttings and other promotional events around Atlanta. She'd gone on to promote everything from Vidalia onions to tourism in Atlanta to Coca-Cola in Japan. In a good year she cleared $50,000.

Now in her early twenties, Melly was planning for life after Scarlett, and had begun studying at a local college. "I want to be a Christian evangelist," she said. This seemed like quite a jump, from belle to Bible student. But Melly didn't think so. "I stick to best-selling books," she explained.

Actually, Melly hadn't read *Gone With the Wind* until recently. Nor did she study the book for beauty tips; apart from staying out of the sun to keep Scarlett's "magnolia-white skin," the look came naturally to Melly. But hoop skirts took some getting used to. Her antebellum attire weighed over twenty pounds and was hard to walk in. At first, Melly said, she often knocked over chairs and plants. And once, while sprinting across a rain-soaked plantation yard for a TV commercial, she'd run up her hoop and collapsed in the mud.

"You realize real quick that it wasn't all that glamorous back then," she said. "With all those hoops and crinolines and pantalets, women were probably sweaty and stinky most of the time."

Nor did the costume transform male admirers into bold Rhett Butlers. Melly noticed that men tended instead to become shy and respectful. "Anyway, it's hard to get very close to someone in a hoop skirt." Melly had also learned to deflect unwanted advances with Scarlett-like brass. "I just smile and say, 'You're a blackhearted varmint' or 'I should slap you in the face!'"

Melly kept an office in the modest brick bungalow where she still lived with her mother. She led me to a back room equipped with a fax, laser printer and five telephone lines. "With rollover and voice mail of course," she said. "I have a cellular phone when I'm on the road."

She booted up her computer and showed me a file called "Belles." It listed thirty-some women she'd trained as stand-ins. "If someone calls with a job and I can't do it," she explained, "I tell them, 'I can book you someone else.' I subcontract Rhetts, too." She even had a Mammy on tap. I asked if she felt any discomfort with this aspect of her Old South role. "Not really," she said. "Scarlett was disrespectful to everyone. She's often mean, a bit harsh. If anything, she was nicer to her slaves than she was to her children."

Melly, though, did find some qualities in Scarlett with which to identify. "I like her flair for business, that's a similarity. And I'm fairly feisty." Melly also shared Scarlett's fondness for shocking behavior. Once, at a formal event welcoming Japan's royalty to Atlanta, Melly fell to chatting with the Empress. "I thought to myself, gosh, their life is awfully structured," Melly recalled. "So when she asked me if I wore a corset, I said in a loud voice, 'Do you want to see my underwear?'" Then Melly lifted her skirt to reveal red pantalets. The gesture pleased the Empress and made Melly an instant celebrity in Japan.

Melly had since visited Tokyo several times and now spoke Japanese well enough to make small talk with admirers. "Once I was speaking Japanese to a tourist in Atlanta and a woman gasped, 'Oh my gosh, the Japanese have even bought Scarlett O'Hara!'"

Like Mary Ann, the woman I'd met at the tourist office, Melly sensed a special Japanese affinity for *Gone With the Wind*. "In some ways, their culture is similar to the Old South," she said. "Traditional women wear kimonos and are admired for their delicate nature, while men are tough and strong." Melly showed me a Japanese newspaper profile of her and translated the headline: "Miss Scarlett, A Traditional Japanese Girl."

Melly sensed another kinship between nineteenth-century Georgia and twentieth-century Japan; both rebuilt themselves after being ravaged by war. "Their symbol of royalty is the phoenix, just like Atlanta," she said.

It so happened that Melly had a date the next night with a Japanese tour group. So I caught up with her again at a Southern-themed restaurant in Atlanta. Melly stood in the parking lot wearing a hooped taffeta skirt, lace gloves, and emerald-colored earrings that matched her green velvet belt and purse. A bus pulled up and twenty-five Japanese surged toward her, talking excitedly, bowing and posing beside her for pictures. Melly pointed the toe of her white shoe and pulled up her skirts to reveal red pantalets. The tourists laughed and clapped. Then she turned around and looked seductively over her bare shoulder in an uncanny mimic of Vivien Leigh. For the moment at least, Melly Meadows seemed a very long way from Bible school.

The group moved inside to a formal dining room, and Melly sashayed between the tables, making chat in Japanese. I asked the group's tour guide, a man named Daijiro, to translate her banter.

"You are so handsome, you look like Clark Gable."

"What is your company?"

"I am very fond of your Emperor and Empress."

Daijiro said the group was composed of retired fruit and vegetable wholesalers on a week-long tour of America. They were visiting three places only: Niagara Falls, Las Vegas and Atlanta. "We want to see the history and beauty of America," Daijiro explained.

I asked him why *Gone With the Wind* had such strong appeal in Japan. "You must understand the times," he said. "In the 1930s we saw American movies, then during the war we didn't. These movies came back after the war and *Gone With the Wind* was the most popular. I think it gave people hope to see this woman fighting so hard to build her land back. Also, she stands by her family, which is something we admire."

He paused. "There is something else, but this is just my idea. I think people watched the movie and thought, 'This is the real America, a wonderful place, not the one we fought in war.'"

The food arrived and the tourists dipped tentatively into gumbo and cornbread. Daijiro watched Melly for a moment, then added, "Scarlett's strength fascinates us. But inside we feel more like Melanie Wilkes, who is polite and kind."

Listening to Daijiro, I sensed another kinship between Japanese and Southern culture; they shared a subtle, mannered code that often seemed contradictory and confusing to blunt, unmannerly outsiders like myself.

As the main course arrived, Melly waved good-bye. "Oh fiddle-dee-dee!" she sang out, swishing from the room and down the restaurant's grand staircase. Her mother waited out front in a minivan with the engine running. Melly had another appearance that evening and was already late.

I offered Melly my arm so she could hoist her hoop skirt into the van. "Why, you're a true gentleman, even if you are a Yankee," she drawled, swinging the van door shut. Her mother sped off, leaving me alone in the parking lot with the faint fragrance of verbena lingering in the warm Georgia night.

MELLY MEADOWS LEFT ME with something else: a curious tip. Despite what I'd heard at the Chamber of Commerce, Tara was still in Clayton County. Melly knew only vague details—"a big old house belonging to a crazy old lady"—but she passed on a name: Betty Talmadge, the elderly ex-wife of former Georgia governor and senator, Herman Talmadge.

Betty Talmadge lived seven miles west of Jonesboro on a narrow lane that dead-ended at a Greek Revival plantation house. By the entrance stood a precise miniature of the mansion, about the size of a doghouse. A sign on the front said "Rabbit E. Lee" and a bunny hopped out to sniff at me. Then a large, one-legged woman appeared across the lawn. "I'm Betty," she shouted. "Lost my leg a few years ago from a blood clot. Let me show you my house."

Betty sprinted across the lawn on her crutches, leading me onto the mansion's verandah. "I'm told they hid grain in here so the Yankees wouldn't steal it during the War," she said, tapping one of the columns with her crutch. "Good story. Who knows."

Betty clumped inside, across wide pine boards covered with a needlepoint rug. "I quit smoking on June 8th, 1970, at 8 P.M.," she said, admiring the carpet. "My needlework took off after that." She also showed me a glass case filled with flowers sent to her by Pat Nixon as thanks for a luncheon Betty hosted for the First Lady after her husband's resignation. "Pat was nice. I liked Dick, too. He got caught, that's all."

This casual view of political scandal had family roots. Betty's father-in-law, Eugene Talmadge, was a long-time Georgia governor who once told voters, "Sure I stole, but I stole it for you." He also liked to warn political foes, "I'm just as mean as cat shit." Southern

politics didn't produce characters like that anymore, least of all in
Georgia, whose most recent governor of note was a pious peanut
farmer from Plains.

Betty led me into another room, adorned with paintings of herself
as a young Washington hostess. "Done yesterday, as you can tell," she
dryly observed. "Washington was fun back then. People had wild parties. Drank too much and fooled around." She shook her head. "Those
days are gone. Gone with the wind, you could say."

Grateful for an opening, I nudged the conversation around to my
literary search. Betty laughed. "Oh, this isn't Tara, it's Twelve Oaks.
I've got Tara, too, but that's another story." The story of Twelve
Oaks (the Wilkes family estate) began with a 1973 *New York Times*
piece, which Betty had carefully preserved in plastic sheeting. It reported that the Talmadge estate was "believed to have been Margaret Mitchell's model for Twelve Oaks." The reporter offered no
further details. Nor did Betty.

"Margaret Mitchell, like all writers, may have pushed it or pulled it
a bit," she said. "But this is the house. Or that's what I tell people."
She smiled and put the newspaper clip back in its folio. "The *New
York Times* is the paper of record. If it prints something, it must be
true." I couldn't help wondering if Betty herself had been the unnamed source of the *Times* anecdote, but it seemed rude to ask.

Betty had turned the story to good use. In 1975, without warning,
her husband filed for divorce. Then he was reprimanded by the Senate for financial misconduct and voted out of office. Returning to
Georgia, Betty found herself a downwardly mobile divorcee rattling
around an eleven-room mansion in the countryside. Echoes of Scarlett again.

"I was a small-town girl who married at eighteen," she said. "You
were considered an old maid if you got to twenty-two without a husband. The only advice my mother had was this: 'You just be a lovely
complement to your husband.'" She laughed. "I swallowed all that.
But my mother never told me what you do when you're fifty-three
and your husband takes off."

What Talmadge had done was become a hostess again, this time
for pay, feting businessmen and foreign tourists with dinners at her
alleged Twelve Oaks. Her set-menu "Magnolia Supper" included

Scarlett Carrots, Rhett Butler biscuits and abra-Ham Lincoln. "The social secretary for Ladybird Johnson taught me to name dishes," Betty said. "It's a conversation starter. You'd be surprised, but a lot of prominent people are ill at ease socially. It loosens them up."

This cutesy habit extended to her animals; hence Rabbit E. Lee, whom I'd met at the door. Talmadge took me out back and introduced her other farm creatures: Ulysses S. Grunt, Clark Gobble, Scarlett O'Hen, the Honorable John C. Cowhoun. "I'll do anything to make my Yankee friends smile," Betty said.

I steered the conversation back to Tara. Betty said that fifteen years ago, she'd learned that the farmhouse owned by Margaret Mitchell's great-grandparents, the Fitzgeralds, had become vacant and fallen prey to vandals. "I decided as long as I had Twelve Oaks, I might as well have Tara, too." She bought the derelict house over the telephone for $1,000.

Betty pointed across a field at what looked like a pioneer cabin, perched at the fringe of pine woods. This was the Fitzgerald place, or all of it that Betty had salvaged; she kept what remained of the house's grander Victorian addition in storage. I gazed at the building and felt a twinge of disappointment. Betty's home at least was an antebellum mansion, Twelve Oaks or not. But this weatherboard shack looked like it might once have belonged to the Slatterys, the "swamp trash" who lived down the hill from Tara, not to the O'Haras.

But the story didn't end there. Soon after buying the Fitzgerald place, Betty heard that the facade of the Hollywood Tara was for sale. Its aged owner, Julian Foster, had purchased the movie set twenty years before in hopes of creating an antebellum Disneyland in Georgia. His dream never materialized and the rotting facade had become an albatross. But Foster, a paranoid man, refused to disclose Tara's location. "He kept saying, 'I'm the only person who knows where it is. That's my insurance,'" Betty said.

In the end, Foster took Betty on a circuitous drive that ended at a barn in the north Georgia hills. She bought the set for $5,000, one-fiftieth the cost of Tara's construction in 1930s Hollywood. But before she could take possession, Foster died. "I contacted his widow," Betty said. "She said the sale was still on, but I was now the only person who knew where to find Tara."

Betty had a poor sense of direction, and after a week-long search by car and small airplane she still couldn't find the barn. It was only through a canceled rent check for the shelter that she finally tracked Tara down. "I got it," she said, "or it's got me, I'm not sure which."

The set was built of plywood, composition board, and papier-mâché (supplies "you could get at Sears," one of the set's creators confessed in an interview after the movie's release). Nonetheless, an appraiser hired by Betty had compared the set to other Hollywood props—the tail from the lion costume in the *Wizard of Oz*, the piano in *Casablanca*, the HMS *Bounty*—and set Tara's value at $1.2 million. "I guess I should feel rich, but I don't," Talmadge said. "At least not yet."

Betty hoped to peddle Tara, the Fitzgerald House and Twelve Oaks as a package, forming the core of a theme park like the one Julian Foster had dreamed of creating. But she hadn't found any takers. So Tara remained in storage—where, exactly, Betty wouldn't disclose. "I'm like Foster," she said. "I don't tell anyone where it is. That's my insurance."

But she agreed to show me pictures of the set, which was now in pieces: a door, a few columns, a papier-mâché brick. It looked the way Tara might have if Sherman's men had burned the place down after all. Betty, though, hadn't surrendered all hope. Seeing me to the door, she smiled defiantly. "Tomorrow, as they say, is another day."

TOMORROW FOUND ME IN Jonesboro again, still on Tara's trail. I'd learned that a retired mailman named Herb Bridges had amassed the world's largest collection of *Gone With the Wind* ephemera. He was also reputed to know everything about the novel's fictional and historic landscape—including the true location of the O'Hara estate.

Bridges was a small, gentle man of sixty-five who lived in a brick ranch house along the rural mail route he'd worked for thirty years. His former job was one reason he knew the local landscape so well. Working for the post office had also led to his trove of memorabilia, which he'd begun collecting years ago when he'd spotted a first edition of the novel at a used bookshop. "I don't know why I bought it," he said. "It cost twenty-five dollars, which in those days seemed like an awful lot of money." The book was now worth about $10,000.

Then one day, Bridges visited a library in Atlanta and a strange urge overcame him again. "There was a copy of the book in Czech," he said. "And I thought to myself, wouldn't it be nice to own one?"

Bridges didn't know much about publishing, but he knew how to work the postal system and managed to have a Czech edition sent through the Iron Curtain. "Then I got to thinking, what does it look like in Bulgaria?" So he wrote to Sofia. Gradually, as his modest budget allowed, Bridges acquired copies from Vietnam, Ethiopia, and dozens of other countries. "It became a joke at the post office," he said. "Here I was, a mailman in rural Georgia, getting all these packages from these Communist countries. I think some people thought I was a spy." He'd even located a copy from Latvia, published in 1938—shortly before the small Baltic state vanished as an independent country for fifty years.

Bridges also began sending away for movie posters and scripts, and kept an eye out for kitsch at flea markets: Scarlett-shaped perfume bottles, plates painted with Ashley's face, assorted dolls, puzzles, matchbooks, and other tchotchkes. "People think this sort of promotional junk started with *Star Wars* and *Batman*," he said, showing me several rooms cluttered with the stuff. "As you can see, it didn't."

Unfortunately, Bridges's children didn't share his obsession, and he didn't want to sell his collection piece by piece. So, like Betty Talmadge, Bridges kept waiting for a wealthy "Windie," as cultish fans of the book and movie were known, to buy his possessions and put them on permanent display. "I'll probably be buried in a vault with this stuff, like one of those pharaohs," he said. "Then a few centuries from now they'll dig me up, along with all these Scarlett and Rhett and Mammy dolls, and wonder, 'What weird, idol-worshiping religion did this man belong to?'"

Bridges had also picked up an impressive trove of trivia about the book and movie, which he shared at local colleges and adult-ed programs. So later that week, I went to hear him lecture at an Elderhostel in Jonesboro. Fifty people listened raptly as Bridges exhibited his trinkets and an equally colorful array of anecdotes. Margaret Mitchell was a five-foot-tall, 100-pound flapper who once declared, "Being one of those short-haired, short-skirted, hard-boiled young women who preachers said would go to hell or be hanged before they were thirty, I am naturally a little embarrassed at finding myself the incarnate spirit of the Old South!" She titled her first draft "Tote the Weary Load" and originally named her heroine Pansy, not Scarlett. And she was only forty-eight when an off-duty taxi driver ran her down as she crossed Peachtree Street to watch a movie. I also learned that the actress who played Prissy ended up on welfare in Harlem; that Nazi Germany banned the film because it romanticized resistance to occupation; and that Clark Gable had false teeth and breath so malodorous that some actresses resisted kissing him.

After the talk, a small white-haired woman with a name tag that said "Peggy Root. Magnolia, Ark." stared intently at Bridges's movie posters. "You can't imagine what *Gone With the Wind* meant to my generation," she said in a gentle drawl.

When I asked why this was so, her eyes misted over. "Poverty," she said. "Ours, I mean. When I was coming up in Arkansas, we didn't have chairs in both the kitchen and setting room. So the adults dragged chairs from one room to the other while the kids sat on the floor. Life was that bare. Then this book comes out about a rich South we never knew. It was escapism, I guess."

A small, bald man appeared at her shoulder. This was Peggy's brother, Ray. "Our father was a sharecropper," he said. "He had to do a half-dozen other jobs to get by. Cut railroad ties. Kill possums and sell their skins. Pick pecans. And he'd go around to all the sharecroppers who had less than a bale of cotton, put their shares together to make a bale, and take it to market to sell."

"Remember the man Daddy cut ties with?" Peggy said.

Ray smiled. "Daddy had a partner who would pull off his clothes and cut railroad ties in the nude. He told everyone it was because the mosquitoes made him work harder. But the real reason was that he only had one pair of clothes and didn't want to ruin them in the woods."

As children, Ray and Peggy worked six days a week in the fields. On Sundays they went to church. The only entertainment they recalled was listening to the *Grand Ole Opry* on a neighbor's radio. "I was in the eighth grade when I first read *Gone With the Wind*," Peggy said. "But I hid it from my mother. She was Assembly of God, very fundamentalist. She didn't approve of risqué literature." Then came the movie, which was even more romantic. "It was like visiting another planet," Peggy said. "And to think our ancestors lived like that. The only one of ours we'd heard about was a grandfather who went broke and lost his mind over the Civil War. He papered his living room with Confederate dollars."

She went quiet for a moment. "I was a good student, the first woman in my family to finish high school. Sometimes I wonder if there hadn't been a Civil War, maybe I could have been a Margaret Mitchell." Instead, Peggy had worked as a telephone operator and rarely traveled beyond rural Arkansas. "This is my first vacation in years," she said of the Elderhostel program.

Ray glanced at his watch. "One o'clock," he said, studying the class schedule. "Laughter Therapy."

Herb Bridges finished gathering his things. "I should have told these folks about the real Tara and Twelve Oaks," he said. "Or where they would have been." Caught up like the others in the book's romance, I'd almost forgotten that this was why I'd sought Bridges out in the first place.

Bridges offered to show me the sites, which he'd found by matching the geography described in the novel with Margaret Mitchell's own time in Clayton County. We turned down a wooded lane called Tara Road, then parked by a thicket of kudzu-draped cedars. This was the location, Bridges said, of the old Fitzgerald house that Betty Talmadge had moved fifteen years before, and that Margaret Mitchell often visited as a child. Bridges had learned from Mitchell's brother that the farmhouse was once surrounded by cotton fields. The site now faced a raw subdivision—"Andover at Hawthorne. A Swim/Tennis Community from $79,900"—with duplexes planted around cul-de-sacs so new they hadn't yet been named.

This spot wasn't mentioned in the novel, but it provided Bridges with the starting point for his sleuthing of Mitchell's imaginary landscape. "We know she liked to take long walks around here," he said. "If you look closely at what she might have seen, it matches awfully closely to the book."

We drove a mile or so to a fork in Tara Road. Bridges said, "Remember the first scene of the book, when the Tarleton twins leave Scarlett?"

I opened my paperback: "When they had rounded the curve of the dusty road that hid them from Tara, Brent drew his horse to a stop under a clump of dogwood." Bridges smiled. "This is the spot."

He'd based his calculation on the lay of the land and the site's distance from real coordinates in the book, such as Jonesboro and the Flint River. "Just to make sure, I talked to some old people around here," he said. "They all told me there was once a clump of dogwoods at exactly this spot."

The dogwoods had been supplanted by a copse of real estate signs—"FOR SALE TARA Realty Company"—and by a sign pointing to Tara Beach, a spit of sand beside a nearby artificial lake. Bridges continued slowly down Tara Road, referring me to the book's next scene, in which Scarlett waits for her father to return along the road from the Wilkes estate: "In her thoughts she traced its course down the hill to the sluggish Flint River, through the tangled swampy bottoms and up the next hill to Twelve Oaks where Ashley lived. That was all the road meant now—a road to Ashley and the beautiful white-columned house that crowned the hill like a Greek Temple. 'Oh Ashley! Ashley!' she thought, and her heart beat faster." The road reappeared a few chapters later, during the O'Haras' carriage ride to the Twelve Oaks party: a dusty trace bordered by wild violets, Cherokee roses, "savage red gulches" and cotton plantations.

Now, bulldozers pummeled the red land, sowing tract houses. But the topography matched the text, eerily so, with the road dipping down a gentle slope to the the sluggish brown Flint. It was easy to conjure the swamp bottom where the white-trash Slatterys clung to their three acres of land between the O'Haras' and Wilkeses' estates. On the opposite side of the river, the road rose toward a hill with a panoramic view of the surrounding landscape. "Twelve Oaks," Bridges said, pointing to the top of the hill.

There was no Greek Temple atop the rise, just woods and cows and undulating pasture. Bridges pointed at the dense woods skirting the meadow. "Mitchell writes about the 'soughing pines seeming to wait with an age-old patience' to reclaim the land," he said. "Well look. They have." I couldn't help wondering, though, how long it would be before the woods were claimed by another swim/tennis community.

We retraced our route, back across the Flint and up the hill on the other side. Bridges paused near the bygone dogwood clump. A long driveway wound up a small knoll. "Tara would be back there, no doubt in my mind," he said. "This has to be it."

A handwritten sign at the base of the driveway said For Sale By Owner. But Bridges wasn't keen to go any closer, and conceded he'd never done so. "You run into some ornery folk around here," he said. I reckoned Bridges, a former mailman, knew what he was talking about.

He dropped me back at my car, and I sat for a while flipping through the novel, rereading passages on Tara. "It was built by slave labor, a clumsy, sprawling building that crowned the rise of ground overlooking the green incline of pasture . . . 'Land is the only thing in the world that amounts to anything,' he shouted. ''Tis the only thing in the world that lasts, and don't you be forgetting it!'. . . 'Yes, yes! To Tara! Oh, Rhett, we must hurry!'"

I circled back along Tara Road and pulled up the driveway with the For Sale By Owner sign. The road ended at a low-slung weather-board house with a cinder-block foundation and a washing machine on the porch. Two bearded men stood leaning against pickup trucks, spitting tobacco juice.

"Excuse me," I said. "Did you know that this is where Tara was. I mean, would have been if it were real."

"No it ain't," said one of the men, who introduced himself as Cooper. "Tara's back down the road a mile. That's where that crazy old lady found it. Now there's a hundred fifty-five duplexes going in."

I realized he was talking about the old Fitzgerald house, and tried to explain what Herb Bridges had just told me. Cooper turned and glanced at his modest house. "Lived my whole damned life in Tara and never even knowed it." He shrugged. "My wife's crazy about all that *Gone With the Wind* stuff. But it just don't flip my boat." His eyes narrowed. "'Less there's money in it."

"What's it selling for?" I asked.

He thought a moment and said, "Fifty something." This was a ludicrous sum, given that modern split-levels with swimming and tennis privileges were selling down the road for seventy something. I confessed that I wasn't looking for property, just information. Cooper looked disappointed, but told me about a few Civil War graves nestled in the woods behind his house. "There's snakes back there as big as your arm, but you're welcome to poke around if you want."

Bushwhacking through the dense brush, I found a few stones almost buried by vines and pine needles. I could just barely make out the inscriptions. One, undated, said simply: "John M. Turner. Papa." But two others had the familiar, slightly pointed top of Confederate headstones I recognized from a dozen battlefields. ("They're shaped that way to keep the damn Yankees from sitting on them," a Sons of Confederate Veterans member had told me.) Brushing away vines, I found one marked "Elijah A. Mann Co. E 10th Ga. Inf. C.S.A." and another that said, "Lieut. Sidney D. Mann Co. D. 44th Ga. Inf. C.S.A." No O'Haras or Wilkeses or Tarletons. Still, I wondered if Margaret Mitchell might have tramped back here as a teenager and had her imagination stirred by these lonely Confederate graves.

Hiking back through the woods and into the yard, with its rusted bikes and battered pickup trucks, I climbed in my car and navigated slowly out toward the interstate, past red earth gashed with still more real-estate signs ("Ashley Woods," "Tara Pointe," "Grand Oaks at Tara New Homes from the 80s"), and then past Jonesboro, Tara Shopping Center, Tara Alternator and Starter, Tara Transmission, O'Hara's Food and Spirits. And I realized that it was probably a good thing that the Japanese never found Tara. It was gone. Gone With the Window.

BACK IN ATLANTA, I called the historian I'd visited, Franklin Garrett, to corroborate what I'd seen and heard in Jonesboro. He laughed hoarsely, then told me that Margaret Mitchell had phoned him in the 1930s, before finishing her novel. She wanted to check if any of the names she planned to use corresponded with families in the 1860 city directory. "She didn't want to embarrass anyone by using that name and attaching it, say, to the owner of a lewd house in her novel."

Later, after the movie's release, Garrett helped the city plan a tourist route past the approximate locations of Miss Pittypat's house and other spots in Atlanta mentioned in the book. He quickly received a long, angry letter from Mitchell. "Franklin," she wrote of the sites, "they weren't anywhere except in my mind."

"What about Tara and Twelve Oaks?" I asked.

Garrett chuckled again and mentioned several letters that Mitchell penned when fans of *Gone With the Wind* began trekking to Georgia in search of the famed plantations. I found one of the letters quoted in an old newspaper story. Mitchell told how she'd scoured the backroads of Clayton County while researching her novel to make sure that the scenery she described was indeed fictional. She even jumbled the county's geography and checked that there were no Tara-like homes with tree-lined avenues. She did this so that no one might think their own grandmother was the model for Scarlett O'Hara. Mitchell was miffed that people were nonetheless determined to pin her fictional creations to firm ground.

"My trouble," she concluded, "seems to have been all for nothing."

So, apparently, had mine.

12

Georgia
STILL PRISONERS
OF THE WAR

The time is not come for impartial history.
If the truth were told just now, it would not be credited.
—ROBERT E. LEE, 1868

Heading east from Atlanta, I shadowed Sherman's route as he rampaged toward the sea: reducing homes to charred chimneys known as "Sherman's sentinels," twisting railroad tracks into "Sherman's neckties," and sending parties of foragers, called "bummers," to pillage the countryside.

Or so I'd always imagined. Since arriving in Georgia, I'd been doing some reading. Once again, I learned that much of what I'd absorbed of the Civil War was more mythic than factual. Sherman talked a good game, pledging to "make Georgia howl," but the reality of his March rarely matched his words (at least in Georgia; he was harsher on the Carolinas). One Georgia geographer had painstakingly mapped the March route and found that many homes alleged to have been burned were still in fact standing. "The actual destruction of private dwellings," he concluded, "was rare indeed."

Nor was Sherman's March, which caused few civilian deaths, notably cruel by historic standards. As compared to the laying waste to Europe during the Thirty Years' War, the routine massacres of

Native Americans—or the murder and mayhem caused by Confederate guerrillas such as William Quantrill—Sherman's treatment of Georgia civilians was almost genteel.

His surrender terms certainly were. When Joseph Johnston yielded his forces soon after Appomattox, Sherman drafted an agreement so lenient that it provoked outrage in the North, compelling Sherman to match the terms Grant offered Lee. Sherman had lived in the South for twelve years before the War and shared many of its attitudes. All this helped to explain an odd circumstance; Sherman was much less reviled by Southerners a century ago than today. Georgians received Sherman courteously during a return visit to the state just fifteen years after his March. When he died in 1891 (having devoted his post-War years to Indian-fighting, memoir-writing and roller-skating), Sherman's pallbearers included his wartime foe Joseph Johnston. Eighteen years later, a reporter for *Harper's* magazine retraced Sherman's March and noted "a surprising absence of bitterness" among inhabitants along the route.

The same wasn't true now, at least in the town of Conyers, where I stopped to attend a Sons of Confederate Veterans meeting at the Masonic Hall. The session began with an SCV commander hurling firebolts at enemies of the South, most of whom seemed to reside in nearby Atlanta—or "the occupied city," as he called it. He griped about Atlanta's liberal newspaper, "The Journal and Constipation," and about Georgia's governor, who once called for changing the state flag. "We are a unique people," he concluded to loud applause, "and others are jealous because they don't have the heritage we have."

The night's main speaker, Mauriel Joslyn, was a Georgia author who had studied the wartime diaries and letters of Confederates captured in the War. A slim woman with a prim bun, octagonal glasses and a long dress topped by a frilly neckline, she looked rather like my image of Emily Dickinson. "I had twenty-five forebears who fought in the War," Joslyn began, warming up her audience. "We always say we gave a regiment." Then, as prelude to her talk, she performed a peculiar call-and-response. Mixing recent news stories about Bosnia with accounts of Sherman's March, she asked the audience to guess each time if the perpetrators were Serbs or Yankees.

"Her husband was a captain in the opposing army," Joslyn read. "She was sick in bed when two soldiers entered her room. They raped her and she later died in a mental hospital." Joslyn paused. "Yankees or Serbs?" (Yankees).

"Drunkenness is rampant. Many soldiers are drawn by the promise of pillage and roaming at will, and are responsible for many of the atrocities committed against civilians." Sherman's bummers or Serbian gunners? (Serbs).

This went on for fifteen minutes. Like most in the audience I guessed wrong half the time. "So you see," Joslyn concluded, "there isn't much difference between what Sarajevo and Georgia suffered."

The main subject of Joslyn's talk was an oddly gentle contrast to the atrocities she'd just catalogued. While researching a group of captured rebels, she'd found that the prisoners kept up a lively correspondence with Northern women. Many of the men had been injured and captured at Gettysburg. Recuperating in Pennsylvania, often for months, they were nursed by young women from Baltimore, Philadelphia and New York who stayed in touch after the men were shipped to Northern prison camps.

The correspondence became quite formalized. If a prisoner was released, he'd pass on the name of his pen pal to a fellow inmate. The women also swapped their correspondents' names. One Northern woman, jealous of her letter-writing friends, went to visit Fort Delaware (viewing rebel prisoners was a curiosity excursion for civilians) and tossed a cored apple to one of the Confederates. Inside the fruit was a $10 bill and her address. "He was cute—I have his picture," Joslyn said of the prisoner. The two corresponded for several years and married following the War.

Intrigued by Joslyn and by her unusual research, I went to visit her home the next day in a town called Sparta. "Excuse the mess—it's always 1860-something in this house," she said, leading me into a kitchen cluttered with reenactors' uniforms, Civil War calendars, and piles of books. Joslyn wrote for the local paper, and her husband worked as a soil scientist. But their true calling was the Civil War.

"Either we're reading something or we're getting ready for a reenactment," she said. "It's almost like we've adopted a different code of behavior. To me, the modern South is like a curtain I'm always trying to see through to what was there before."

Joslyn unearthed a sheaf of Confederate prisoners' letters to Northern women that she'd gathered at various archives. Many of the letters began "Dear Cousin" or "Dear Aunt"—a way to dodge prison-camp rules against writing to nonrelatives. The letters also steered clear of politics or details about the War. This, too, was a way to avoid censorship. But Joslyn suspected the correspondents also weren't keen to dwell on their regional differences.

"They had other things on their mind," she said. "Literature, art, and flirting like crazy." One suave Mississippian wrote wistfully to a Northern woman of missing "those endearing scenes, those enchanting beauties that give the youthful heart its buoyancy." He begged his pen pal to send him "a copy of Shakespeare or Byron," and enclosed locks of his golden hair. Joslyn sighed. "I'd like to have met him."

James Cobb, a dashing Texan, inherited a correspondent named Cora from a fellow prisoner. The two strangers exchanged photographs and quickly fell in love, writing at the same time each Sunday while gazing at each other's picture. "I walked in the (prison) yard until long after nightfall, with no companion save the invisible one which I felt to be near," Cobb wrote. "But oh, how unsatisfying is all this! There is still the restless longing for her actual presence." By late 1864, Cobb was addressing his pen pal as "my dear Cora" and telling her, "Think of all you would have me to say, & imagine it said."

For a time, Cobb also wrote to a friend of Cora's named Allison, a tease who enjoyed the tension her letters created on the homefront. When a suitor arrived as she was writing, Cora told the man to wait until she finished her letter—all of which she reported in delicious detail to Cobb. "If you were here and he could get hold of you, I would not answer for the consequences!" Allison's beau became so jealous that Cobb ended their correspondence, gallantly writing, "I do not desire to be the cause of a quarrel between lovers."

Joslyn said these letters had punctured her stereotypes about relations between the sexes in the 1860s. "There's a frankness and flirtatiousness that isn't what we think of as Victorian," she said. "And the men aren't talking down to these women at all. They write as equals." Perhaps, too, they felt liberated by their unusual circumstances. "They're probably much more intimate in these letters than if they'd been courting with all the formality that surrounded it in those days," Joslyn said.

The men also were tender with each other. Letters told of prisoners who washed clothes for fellow inmates, or taught them ballroom dance. "They even had exercise classes, sort of Jack LaLanne at Point Lookout," Joslyn said, referring to a Maryland prison. "And I've got letters the men later wrote to each other signed 'best love.' These guys obviously didn't have the stigma we have today about men showing affection for each other."

They'd also overcome the stigma of writing to civilians in enemy territory. If anything, the divide between North and South spiced the correspondence. "For the women, those 'awful rebs' were forbidden fruit," Joslyn said. The same was true for the men; Northern women were often stereotyped in the South as trollops or Puritans—or both, in the manner of Hester Prynne. "So this was all very titillating for both sides," Joslyn said.

The letter writing was also sustained by deprivation on the one hand and compassion on the other. One rebel thanked his pen pal for sending peaches, then asked haltingly for money. "It is something I never had to do before," he wrote, promising to repay the loan, "if I am permitted to live." His correspondent feared the money would be confiscated, but answered, "I pity you, being a stranger in a strange land, though you are a rebel and fighting against us."

Even more poignant than the letters were autograph albums the women sent for prisoners to sign. Often, the men put the words "unmarried" or "nairy wife, nairy child" beside their names. "There are three things I desire with an exceeding longing," one man wrote. "A Sword, a Wife and my Freedom." A Virginian wrote, "I am 22 and still single, but live in hopes." He died soon after from dysentery. Joslyn closed the album, teary-eyed. "My fellahs were always fishing," she said.

Few succeeded in catching anything. Those who didn't perish in prison returned to poverty-stricken homes and long-lost families. One destitute rebel waited six years after the War, scraping together money to set up a household before proposing to his pen pal. She accepted.

More typical, though, was the story of James and Cora, the couple who corresponded so passionately while gazing at each other's photographs. "I do earnestly hope," James wrote in December 1864, "that ere another Christmas shall have come, the longings of this one will have been displaced by full fruition!" Before the next Christmas he was indeed free and traveled to Philadelphia to meet Cora. But after a brief stay, James returned South and married a local woman. The two pen pals never saw each other again. When Cora married, she returned all James's letters. Then James's wife gave birth to a daughter, whom he named Cora. "I'd give my right arm," Joslyn said, "to know the rest of that story."

I was curious to hear more of Joslyn's. I wondered why she and other women I'd met, beginning with Sue Curtis in North Carolina, were so obsessed with the War's prisoners—a side of the conflict few men seemed passionate about. In fact, given that 400,000 men were captured during the War, almost twice the toll of combat dead, the fate of POWs was arguably the most neglected aspect of the conflict.

"This may sound sexist," Joslyn said, "but my theory is that men like the Civil War because it's an action story, they're caught up in the battlefield drama. The prisoners are an emotional side of the War. Women are attracted to all that raw feeling, we understand it better, it brings out a mothering instinct." She fingered the autograph album. "Remember, a lot of these soldiers were still boys, not yet twenty, starving in Northern prison camps, with no idea of when if ever they'd get home. More than anything, these guys desperately needed their mommies."

Joslyn's own love life had imitated her research. A tomboy who liked playing war as a child ("The boys were bullies, so they always played the Yankees"), she'd met her future husband while dating a cadet at the Virginia Military Institute. "My date said he had a roommate with a Civil War musket. That was Rick. I always say I married him for his gun."

Actually, they'd fallen in love later, while writing letters during Rick's air force service. There was another parallel; Rick's family came from up North. Luckily, he discovered he had a distant forebear who might have fought for the South. "It was almost a criterion of our getting married," Joslyn said. She'd saved all their letters, but planned to burn them someday. "I don't want anyone studying us the way I've been studying my fellahs."

Joslyn gave me a signed copy of the book she'd written about rebel prisoners. It had been published with little fanfare by a small press. "Almost a collector's item," she joked. I asked how she felt about laboring in relative obscurity.

Joslyn pondered this for a moment, squinting through her octagonal glasses. "I take the long view," she said. "People like me, we're the keepers of the past, like those monks with their Latin books back in the Dark Ages. Or maybe like the folks in Eastern Europe who kept their real history and religion alive after the Russian Revolution and all the attempts to purge the past. Now that Communism's gone, the truth is coming out of the archives."

I wasn't sure I caught the analogy. Leningrad seemed a long way from Point Lookout. But not to Joslyn. "To me, Civil War historians—Northern ones at least—are locking away the facts, too," she said. "So little people like me have to keep the true story alive. That way, when the Revolution ends, and people come looking for the history, we can say, 'Here it is. We kept it for you.'"

READING JOSLYN'S BOOK that night at a roadside motel, I better understood what she meant. Prisoners' love letters didn't figure much in her book, except to illustrate the horrors of Northern POW camps. This, in turn, was part of a broader mission: to redress the distorted picture most Americans had of Civil War POWs, derived from "myths" about Andersonville and its commander, Henry Wirz. In the view of Joslyn and the Southern historians she cited, rebel prisoners suffered far more than Union ones, and the North was responsible for the misery of both blue and gray inmates because of its cruel policies regarding prisoner exchange.

Most of this was news to me. Roughly 13,000 prisoners died from starvation and disease at Andersonville, and Henry Wirz went to the gallows as a war criminal, the only man so charged in American history. Refurbishing his reputation, and that of the prison camp he commanded, seemed an exceptionally quixotic mission, notwith-standing the South's passion for lost causes.

So I abandoned Sherman's March and headed instead for Ander-sonville, near Jimmy Carter's hometown of Plains in Georgia's rural southwest. Winding slowly out of upland Georgia and into the fer-tile prairie beyond, I felt as though I'd been here before. The crops might change, but the roadscape on small highways appeared much the same from southern Virginia to western Arkansas: single-wide trailers with satellite dishes, low brick ranches with home-based businesses (beauty parlor, blade-sharpening, fish taxidermy, towing and recovery), white-frame churches with exclamatory sermon signs ("Presenting Jesus!"), flyspeck settlements—"Welcome to Forkland. Town of Opportunities. Pop 764"—abandoned to time and kudzu vines and men in bib overalls loitering before a faded Gas and Gro ("Tank and Tummy—Fill Em Up"). Then a small town with a stone rebel on the square and a "family restaurant" serving plate lunches of chicken and dumplings, candied yams, turnip greens, pear salad and pecan pie. Then fields and woods again.

It was foolish to speak of "one South," just as it was to speak of one North. The former states of the Confederacy encompassed dozens of subcultures, from the Hispanic enclaves of Florida and Texas, to the Cajun country of south Louisiana, to the hardscrabble hills of Appalachia. Still, the geographic kinship between far-flung stretches of the backcountry South offered some clue to the cohesion and resilience the region displayed during the Civil War, and to the South's cherishing of Confederate memory ever since.

Nearing Andersonville, I was momentarily blinded by what looked like a snow flurry: bolls of cotton blowing across the road from a just-picked field. This, too, was a reminder of what had once bound the rural South together. Cotton was enjoying a comeback in the South and the crop always came as a small miracle to me. It seemed incredible that these perfect white blobs sprouted straight from nature, and that something so natural could at the same time seem so artificial.

My rural reverie ended abruptly at the gate to the national park at Andersonville. The entrance road ran straight into a sea of white gravestones packed so closely together that they almost touched, like

piano keys. Beneath lay the 13,000 Northern soldiers who died at Andersonville, a toll that roughly equalled the *combined* Union combat
deaths in the War's five bloodiest battles: Gettysburg, Chickamauga,
Chancellorsville, Spotsylvania, Antietam.

I'd arrived on a quiet weekday and a ranger named Fred Sanchez
agreed to show me around. Walking through the cemetery, he
pointed out that the headstones marking the camp's earliest casualties were better spaced than the graves of those who died later. Ini-
tially, he explained, prisoners were buried in simple pine coffins.
Then, as the death toll mounted, bodies were buried in trenches and
covered with pine planks. Before long, even this meager covering
was abandoned. "The gravediggers also started burying the corpses
on their sides so they could pack more in," Sanchez said.

A few graves stood out from the huddled rows of stone. One, inscribed "12196 L.S. Tuttle, Sgt., Me.," had a marble dove cemented
on top, facing north. Tuttle's widow, or one of his Maine comrades,
was believed to have added the dove decades after the War. Six other
graves lay to one side of the long tidy ranks. These belonged to the
so-called Raiders, camp ruffians who preyed on weaker prisoners.
Following a trial in which inmates acted as lawyers and jurors, the
Raiders were hanged and buried apart from their fellow prisoners.

The actual prison site lay a quarter-mile from the graveyard, on
what was now an undulating field. It was here, over the course of
fourteen months in 1864 and 1865, that Confederate guards herded
41,000 Union prisoners into a log stockade unsheltered from Georgia's harsh sun and heavy rains. The pen was designed for a third
the number of men it eventually enclosed. This left prisoners in
the summer of 1864 with an average of twenty square feet of living
space on which to pitch their "shebangs," A-shaped hovels fashioned
from overcoats, blankets and whatever else the prisoners could
scrounge.

Running through the stockade yard was a stream, Andersonville's
only water supply and also the site of the camp's latrines, called "sinks."
The stream, a branch of the inaptly named Sweetwater Creek, quickly
backed up in 1864 and flooded much of the camp. "You can see from
wartime photographs that it was basically a swamp crusted with
human waste," Sanchez said. On windy days, the stench carried all the

way to Americus, ten miles away. During storms, shebangs toppled and the stockade yard became a slurry of mud, feces and vermin. One survivor wrote: "We had to strain the water through our teeth to keep the maggots out."

Nothing remained of the original stockade, though a few log walls had been reconstructed by the Park Service. There were also posts delineating the "deadline," a perimeter inside the stockade that no prisoner could cross without risking gunfire from the guard towers (this was also the origin of the modern newspaper phrase). Other markers showed where prisoners dug molelike holes in a frantic search for clean water, shade, and, in some instances, escape tunnels.

At its peak squalor, Andersonville claimed the lives of 127 men in a single day. Many died from typhoid or gangrene, others from malnutrition. Vitamin deficiencies caused scurvy and scorbutus, painful diseases that rotted gums, loosened teeth, and ulcerated flesh. A small number of men were shot at the deadline or buried alive when their crude burrows caved in. Seven severely depressed prisoners were listed as having died of "nostalgia." Sanchez said some despairing prisoners intentionally crossed the deadline, or drank from the toxic swamp surrounding the sinks.

But the biggest killers by far were diarrhea and dysentery. This was due not only to the camp's lack of sanitation, but also to rations of rotted meat and coarse grain filled with shredded corncob, which irritated men's already weak intestines. There was a cruel irony to this. Pointing to several belching smokestacks in the distance, Sanchez said the surrounding landscape was now mined for kaolin, a chalky mineral used to make Kaopectate. "You had thousands of men dying of the runs right on top of one of the world's richest lodes of anti-diarrhea medicine," he said.

Sanchez's description of the handling of the dead evoked images of a plague-ridden medieval village. Each morning, prisoners hauled comrades who had died in the night to the camp's South Gate, where lumber wagons collected the corpses, twenty per load. Prisoners paid for the privilege of bringing out the dead, which gave them a few moments to forage for firewood. Prisoners also stripped the dead of clothes to use as patching for their shebangs.

Near the South Gate, signs now marked the location of vanished prison buildings, including the "Deadhouse" and "Dissecting House." The camp's commander, Henry Wirz, ordered doctors to examine corpses to determine what killed them—and to prevent any men from escaping by feigning death. The rebels also assigned most of the burial details and other labor outside the stockade to black prisoners, whose skin color made them more conspicuous in the event of escape. Ironically, this meant that black POWs fared much better than whites. Spending more time outside the fetid prison confines, blacks were able to forage, and also to get exercise and fresh air denied other prisoners.

As Sanchez grimly detailed all this, we strolled across the stockade yard, now a lush field blooming with goldenrod. Butterflies fluttered in the tall grass. On Civil War battlefields, there were always a few cannons and trenches to summon images of combat and bloodshed. Here, nothing. The only affliction that remained at all palpable was Andersonville's stifling climate. Even in autumn, the air felt suffocatingly humid, and mushrooms blanketed the boggy earth. The stream running through the camp was a brackish rivulet brimming with mosquitoes and gnats.

Andersonville differed from battlefields in another essential way. The suffering here was slow, undramatic, inglorious. For Sanchez, who had worked at the park for eighteen years, it was precisely this lack of drama that made Andersonville's horror so insidious. "We like to focus on the escapes, the shootings at the deadline, the extraordinary moments here," he said. "But in a way, the Andersonville story is very boring. It's a personal story of survival. Where will my next meal come from? Where can I find shade? Will my bowels hold out another day?"

This degrading struggle must have seemed doubly cruel to the battle veterans incarcerated at Andersonville. "Imagine surviving Gettysburg," Sanchez said, "only to end up here, wasting away from diarrhea."

Sanchez left me there to wander around for a while and also to visit a small building just beside the camp site, labeled Prisoner of War Museum. Inside, there was almost nothing of what Sanchez had just told me. Instead, a few items from Andersonville were displayed as part of a broad exhibit on American POWs from the Revolution to the Gulf War.

A larger museum, at the park entrance, offered videos of former World War II prisoners telling about their wretched treatment by the Germans and Japanese. A short, introductory video on Andersonville—with flabby reenactors farbishly cast as starving prisoners—explained that the South was unprepared for so many POWs, due to the North's refusal to exchange prisoners midway through the War. A wall exhibit gave the Andersonville tragedy a similar spin, noting that the North "realized it was to their advantage" to end exchanges because the South needed manpower more than the Union. Cited as evidence was a quote from Grant: "It is hard on our men held in Southern prisons not to exchange them, but it is humanity to those left in our ranks to fight our battles."

This was, at best, a selective and misleading version of events. No mention was made of another reason the North halted exchanges: to protest the South's refusal to trade the growing number of black soldiers in Union ranks. In May 1863, the Confederate Congress declared that the South would re-enslave captured blacks and execute their white officers. Grant, a grim purveyor of war by attrition, no doubt meant what he said. But he made his infamous statement more than a year after prisoner exchanges had already ended.

This Southernized presentation seemed odd at a park administered by the U.S. government. Nor did the inclusion of POW stories from other wars strike me as altogether benign. Its impact was to dilute the Andersonville tragedy, and also to sugar-coat its message for Americans; after all, the Confederates hadn't tortured their prisoners like the Japanese and the Viet Cong had. Unmentioned at either museum was what seemed a crucial distinction: Andersonville lay on American soil and saw the death of 13,000 Americans in American custody.

Heading over to the park office, I shared my reservations with Sanchez and two other rangers. The men shifted uncomfortably in their chairs. "You're not the first to come out of there pissed off," Sanchez said. "I've had to break up fights in that museum between Northerners and Southerners."

Controversy had dogged Andersonville ever since Clara Barton tried to establish it as a shrine to the dead immediately after the War. Southerners fiercely resisted any effort to memorialize the camp, fearing it would be used to demonize the region (or "wave the bloody shirt," as efforts to exploit sectional passions were known in the late nineteenth century). It wasn't until 1970 that a compromise was reached; Andersonville would become a national memorial, but only if it commemorated POWs from all American wars.

Even so, when the park set up its first museum, "we took a lot of flak," Sanchez said. "Southerners felt we were blaming them for what happened." The park softened its presentation, and later added the small POW museum I'd visited by the stockade. This had caused a different sort of controversy. One exhibit, which mentioned the large number of American POWs who collaborated with the North Koreans, had to be rewritten after complaints by Korean War veterans.

A new, much bigger POW museum was about to be built, and this had sparked yet another round of lobbying. An Alabama woman who headed a group called the Confederate POW Society demanded that half the new exhibits be devoted to Northern prison camps. "She came in here and started ranting about 'you-all's government,' as if the South wasn't yet part of the nation," one of the rangers said. The woman had since set up her own Confederate POW museum in the nearby hamlet of Andersonville. She and other diehards also gathered in Andersonville each year on the anniversary of Wirz's hanging, a week hence, to honor the captain's memory with song, speeches and prayer.

When I asked what the ceremony was like, one of the rangers chuckled uneasily. "Very weird," he said. "I have to live in this community so I shouldn't say any more."

As soon as I left the park and drove across the highway to the small community of Andersonville, I saw why the rangers remained so reticent. Andersonville had become a village-sized apologia for the prison camp that bore its name. The counteroffensive began with a roadside historical marker honoring Wirz, erected by the state of Georgia in 1956. It stated: "Had he been an angel from heaven he could not have changed the pitiful tale of privation and hunger unless he had possessed the power to repeat the miracle of the loaves and fishes."

Just beside the railroad tracks, where Union prisoners had disembarked, stood another marker, erected just a year before my arrival. Andersonville, it said, "honors both the memory of the Union soldiers who suffered and Confederate soldiers who did their duty while experiencing illness and death in numbers comparable to their unfortunate prisoners." This too, I'd later learn, was very misleading.

A rebuilt train depot beside the tracks had become a museum devoted to local history, and to Wirz, including pictures of the medal of honor awarded him by the Sons of Confederate Veterans in 1981 for "uncommon valor and bravery involving risk of life above and beyond the call of duty in defense of his homeland and its noble ideals." The SCV had also passed a resolution designating Wirz's hanging on November 10, 1865, at 10:32 A.M., "the moment of martyrdom," an occasion for annual remembrance of the "Confederate Hero-Martyr."

The rest of Andersonville's business district consisted of antique shops and a vegetable plant where many of the town's 247 inhabitants worked waxing and packing cucumbers and peppers. Towering over the main street was a granite shaft, inscribed WIRZ. Erected by the United Daughters of the Confederacy in 1909, its inscription said, "To rescue his name from the stigma attached to it by embittered prejudice." The obelisk also bore Grant's quote on prisoner exchanges, praise for Wirz's "humanity," and a line from Jeff Davis: "When time shall have softened passion and prejudice, when reason shall have stripped the mask of misrepresentation, then justice, holding even her scales, will require much of past censure and praise to change places."

I later learned that the UDC had originally composed an even more inflammatory message for the monument. It stated that the U.S. government, not Wirz, "is chargeable with the suffering at Andersonville" and listed doctored casualty rates at Civil War prisons. But outraged Northern veterans prevailed on Georgia officials to tone down the monument's language.

Still, local feelings about the camp and its memory remained fierce well into this century. At the town's bed-and-breakfast, I was escorted to my room by a New York native named Peggy Sheppard who had married a Georgian and lived here for fifty years. On her first visit, she said, her husband's friends took her for a drive through the prison camp. "They said, 'Here's where all the good Yankees are—under the ground.'"

That bothered her at the time, but not anymore. An amateur historian, she'd authored a small book sympathetic to Wirz. "The more I learned, the more I realized Northerners have been brainwashed about what really happened here," she said.

WONDERING IF I'D BEEN brainwashed, too, I decided to stay until the Wirz anniversary and spent the intervening days reading books, diaries and other records gleaned from the library and archives at the ranger's station. It was certainly true, as James McPherson observed in *Battle Cry of Freedom*, that "the victors wrote the history" of Andersonville, beginning with luridly embroidered diaries published by survivors who claimed that Wirz personally tortured and killed prisoners. This Wirz-as-Monster school culminated in MacKinlay Kantor's Pulitzer Prize–winning 1955 novel, *Andersonville*, and the movie based on it, starring William Shatner as the army prosecutor.

Recent scholarship painted a much grayer picture. By the time Andersonville opened in 1864, the Confederacy could barely feed and supply its own men, much less the flood of prisoners pouring into Andersonville during Grant's bloody campaign in Virginia. At its peak, Andersonville held a population larger than all but four Southern cities.

Most historians also judged Henry Wirz a bumbler rather than a brute. A Swiss-born émigré and homeopathic physician, he was ill equipped to deal with the Confederate bureaucracy or the South's collapsing infrastructure. He tried, for instance, to build a damming system that would flush the unsanitary sinks, but he never received the lumber and tools necessary to carry out his plan.

Wirz, an irascible and self-pitying man who spoke heavily accented English, also became an easy scapegoat at War's end. His trial was a sham. Wirz went to the gallows refusing to finger his superiors—one reason he was viewed as a hero-martyr by many Southerners—and none were ever prosecuted. Nor did anyone probe

the horrors of prison camps in the North, where supplies of food
and medicine were ample. At Elmira, regarded as the worst Union
camp, a quarter of inmates died, a rate only slightly lower than at
Andersonville. Had the South won the War, the commander of Elmira might well have hanged in Wirz's stead.

Yet if the traditional, Northern-slanted history of Andersonville
was filled with exaggerations and omissions, so too was the version
offered by Southern apologists. Wirz may have been a scapegoat but
he was hardly a war hero. He lied about his military record, claiming
to have been wounded at Seven Pines when he wasn't even present at
the battle—or, apparently, in any combat during the War.

Nor could the management of Andersonville be termed humane.
The prisoners lacked not only shelter and sanitation but also simple
utensils with which to collect and cook their rations. The clerk responsible for the cookhouse and other key duties was a corrupt profiteer who stole food and sold it on the black market. And when
sympathetic Georgians arrived at the camp with a wagon full of food
and clothing for the prisoners, they were turned away. The supplies
were given to rebel troops instead.

Bizarrely, one generous Georgian did later make it inside: a
woman named Ann Williams who stayed for one day and had sex
with seven inmates. After questioning her, Wirz reported that "on
every occasion (she had) refused to take money, saying to them that
she was a friend of theirs and had come for the purpose of seeing
how she could help them."

As for the Confederate guards, the notion that they suffered to the
same degree as prisoners was absurd. They could supplement their
rations by foraging and trading outside the camp, and also with supplies from home (most guards were teenagers and older men from
the surrounding countryside). They lived in tents upstream from the
unsheltered, latrine-flooded stockade. Over 200 guards died, about
10 percent of the total who served during the course of the camp's
existence. But this was hardly comparable to the 30–35 percent
death rate among prisoners.

Nor did the tragedy of Andersonville end with the camp's closing
in the spring of 1865. Almost three weeks after Appomattox, an

overloaded steamship called the *Sultana* blew its boilers on the Mississippi River, drowning or burning alive an estimated 2,000 passengers in the worst maritime disaster in American history. Most of the casualties were freed prisoners from Andersonville, on their way home at last.

THE ANNIVERSARY OF Wirz's hanging dawned gray and wet, so the ceremony in his honor was moved from the Wirz monument to a cramped log church on the main street. Forty people crowded inside, including several descendants of Andersonville guards, a dozen reenactors, and women in nineteenth-century mourning garb. I squeezed into a pew beside a man who introduced himself as Karl Hagmann, a representative of the Swiss consulate in Atlanta. "Each year someone comes to mark the Swiss presence, but this is my first time," he said. "Usually I go to commercial and cultural events in Atlanta." I asked what he thought of the Wirz controversy. "We, too, have a long history and are very patriotic," he said, adding diplomatically, "but I do not know so much about it. So I have no real opinion."

He was the only one in the room who didn't. "Almighty God, we remember before you this day, Henry Wirz," a minister intoned at the start of the ceremony. "Grant to us to be so faithful to the teachings of our Christian faith and our Southern cause that we will bring only honor to you, Holy Father, and to the memory of Henry Wirz and to all who suffered and died for the Confederacy. Amen."

He was followed by two medal-bedecked SCV officers who recapped efforts to rehabilitate Wirz's name. Their ultimate mission: a congressional pardon, like the one accorded Robert E. Lee in 1975. "We've got our guns loaded," one of the commanders shouted. "The South shall rise again. So hang in there!"

The keynote speaker was a publisher and editor of neo-Confederate books, including one called *Andersonville: The Southern Perspective.* "Some might say ours was, and is, a lost cause," Hank Segars said. "But it is only lost if we forget." He urged the audience to remember Wirz, then made what seemed a curious complaint for a book publisher. "MacKinlay Kantor's novel is still a best-seller at the Andersonville bookstore and many other places," he said, to loud groans from the audience. Decrying this and other Northern-biased accounts, Segars ended with a call to arms. Just as the rebels of old set off with guns and flags to fight the Yankees, Southerners today must do battle with the MacKinlay Kantors, the Ken Burnses, and all other propagandists defiling memory of the Confederacy and of hero-martyrs like Henry Wirz. "If our true history were known, we'd have four thousand people here today instead of forty!"

The service ended with a woman in a purple hoop skirt singing what I at first mistook for the "Star-Spangled Banner." The tune was the same and so were the first words, "Oh say, can you see." But the banner still waving in the dawn's early light wasn't the Stars and Stripes. "'Tis the Cross of the South, which shall ever remain, to light us to freedom and glory again." After several verses about defiance to tyrants and Spartans on shields, the song rousingly concluded: "As the Cross of the South shall triumphantly wave, the flag of the free or the pall of the brave."

Leaving the church, we followed a Confederate honor guard down the street to the Wirz memorial. The obelisk was now ringed by Confederate banners, as well as the Swiss flag. This seemed a bit strange, given the country's renowned neutrality. The Swiss diplomat I'd sat beside also looked rather bewildered as he helped lay a wreath by the monument. Then a band struck up "Dixie" and the crowd lustily sang "Look away! Look away!" with the Swiss consul lip-synching the words. Reenactors fired an honorary barrage into the drizzly sky and the ceremony ended.

The two medal-draped officers from the SCV, Jim Reynolds and Charlie Clements, lingered by the monument, exhorting a few remaining comrades to carry on the fight. Despite their martial bearing, neither man had a military background; Reynolds ran a legal research firm, Clements worked as a schoolteacher. As the crowd dispersed, I posed the question that had gnawed at me throughout my stay. Rather than proclaim Wirz a hero and blame Andersonville on the North, wouldn't it be more fruitful—and historically factual—to present Civil War prison camps as a dark chapter of our history that neither side should be proud of?

"That dog just won't hunt," Reynolds said. "Yankees started all this and we've got to resist with all available force, even if it seems one-sided."

"We don't want forgiveness," Clements added. "We want people to come over to our side."

"But why polarize the story?" I asked. "Aren't you swinging the pendulum to the opposite extreme?"

"Perhaps," Reynolds said. "But if we swing the pendulum all the way over to our side, maybe we'll nudge the accepted view over a bit closer to where it belongs."

This was history as Middle East rug barter. The seller names his price and the buyer makes an offer as low as the seller's is high. After a lot of haggling and cups of tea, they agree on a price. This was an entertaining if time-consuming way to shop. But it hardly seemed like a model for understanding our common history.

"Imagine a train running down a track," Reynolds went on. "A man from the North stands on one side and he says the train is moving left to right. A Southerner stands on the other and says it's moving right to left. They're looking at the same train and the same track and from where they're standing they're both correct. That's the way it is with Andersonville. We have a viewpoint that is just as valid, we would say more valid, but it's not being heard."

I suggested that he might be heard better if he offered a more balanced view.

"Perhaps," he said. "But we've been forced into an extreme position. It reflects our frustration over being blamed for every danged thing. We're tired of being put down and kicked around. We can point fingers, too, and in the case of Andersonville, we're pointing it right back at the North—at Grant, at Elmira, at all the other camps."

This frustration also bred fierce solidarity. As Clements put it, "When you're in a fight like this, you have to hang together. There's no room for dissent, even if we disagreed, which we don't. Wirz didn't compromise, he didn't betray his fellow Confederates. That's why he's a hero. We have to act the same."

Like so many neo-Confederates I'd met, the two men had walled themselves inside a stockade of their own creation and erected around it an ideological deadline. Anyone who made so much as a feint toward the opposite side had to be gunned down as a traitor to the Cause. As an outsider, I had even less hope of breaking through.

As the rain began pelting down in earnest, Reynolds clapped me on the back and urged me to return next year. "Maybe by then Wirz will have been exonerated," he said, "and we can hold hands and sing, 'Free at Last! Free at Last!'"

LEAVING ANDERSONVILLE, I felt ready to free myself from Georgia and head for Alabama, the one Confederate state east of the Mississippi that I hadn't yet explored. But thumbing through a Georgia tourist guide one last time, a brief entry caught my eye. "GEORGIA'S YANK-REB CITY: The small town of Fitzgerald is a living memorial to the nation's post–Civil War reconciliation."

Reconciliation? After Andersonville, the notion sounded refreshing. I checked my map. Fitzgerald lay an hour's drive southeast of Andersonville. Only a small detour.

At first glance, Fitzgerald resembled other Georgia towns I'd visited: a flat grid of wide streets girdled by small factories and franchise restaurants. Then I noticed the street signs: Grant Street, Sherman Street, Sheridan Street, and so on through the Union ranks. After that came a parade of Confederate generals: Lee, Johnston, Jackson, Longstreet, Gordon, Bragg.

Near the center of the grid stood a building labeled Blue & Gray Museum. Inside, I found the curator, an eighty-six-year-old named Beth Davis, tidying an exhibit of rebel slouch hats and Union kepis. "I try to make sure there's things from both sides in each display case," she said. Though I'd visited dozens of museums over the past year, this was the first where I'd seen any Union gear displayed, apart from items captured by the Confederacy or belonging to Northern prisoners like those at Andersonville.

The museum's evenhandedness mirrored Fitzgerald's extraordinary history. The town's namesake, Philander Fitzgerald, was a Civil War drummer who later became a pension attorney and publisher of a veterans' newspaper in Indiana. When a severe drought hit the Midwest in the early 1890s, Fitzgerald concocted a novel idea. "Why not start a soldiers' colony in the Southland and get all those old boys away from the bitter winters and drought?" Beth Davis explained.

As the farm crisis deepened, calls went out for help. The first to respond was the state of Georgia, which sent a trainload of food for both farmers and their livestock. Fitzgerald sensed an opening and wrote to Georgia's governor about his dream of a Southern colony. Though a rebel veteran, the governor wanted to develop his own state's underpopulated farmland. So he invited Fitzgerald for a visit. The two men settled on a turpentine camp in the virgin pine forests of south-central Georgia.

Fitzgerald promoted the colony in his newspaper, sold shares in the venture, and bought several thousand acres in Georgia. Then, in the summer of 1895, 2,700 Northern veterans and their families trekked South, many of them in wagon trains. At first, the pine barren to which they'd decamped seemed as bleak as the dustbowl farms they'd left behind. Nor were the natives uniformly friendly. One foe of the project blasted the colony as "a blot on the fair state of Georgia," and several landowners refused to sell the newcomers property. "Folks used to say there wasn't nothing of value down there, just pines, wiregrass, and Yankees," Davis said.

But the "pioneers" planted crops, established a settlement, and invited Georgians from the surrounding countryside to a festival celebrating the colony's first Southern harvest. "The organizers were worried about hotheads on both sides," Davis said, "so they planned two parades, one for Union veterans, the other for Confederates." But when the band began playing, veterans of the two armies spontaneously joined and marched through the town together. Thereafter, they merged to form Battalion One of the Blue and Gray and celebrated their reconciliation annually.

The timing of this embrace was remarkable. Two months before the town's first festival in 1896, Southerners met in Richmond to form the Sons of Confederate Veterans; the Daughters of the Confederacy had been founded in 1894. The last decade of the nineteenth century and first of the twentieth marked the high tide of Confederate remembrance, with communities across the South erecting monuments that defiantly proclaimed the righteousness of the Cause.

In Fitzgerald, though, Confederate veterans began settling beside their former foes. And reconciliation became etched on the town as indelibly as the sectional enmity chiseled on the stone warriors of other Southern communities. Fitzgerald built a huge wooden inn for tourists and prospective settlers. Pioneers planned to call it the Grant-Lee Hotel, but eager to placate their new neighbors, they reversed the generals' names. All streets east of the main street were named for Union generals, those to the west for their antagonists. One street bore the name of the Union ironclad, the *Monitor,* while another honored its rebel foe, the *Merrimack.* Lincoln Avenue and Appomattox Road skirted town.

By the time Beth Davis moved to Fitzgerald from Atlanta in 1942, soon after marrying a native of the town, the last of the veterans had died and blue and gray had become hard to distinguish. Even churches had merged, bringing together Southern Methodists with a group known originally to natives as "the Yankee Methodist Church."

Davis said her first inkling of the town's unusual lineage was the odd accent of elderly residents she met. "A lot of them didn't talk like we did," she said. Davis, whose grandfathers had fought for the Confederacy, also didn't know what to make of her husband's early-morning singing, which included the "Battle Hymn of the Republic." "He had a strong baritone and I was worried we were going to get evicted by our neighbors." Stranger still, her husband's family didn't celebrate Confederate Memorial Day on April 26, which remained an important holiday in Georgia. Instead, in late May, her husband announced that he was headed to the graveyard to play Taps on his cornet. She went along.

"There were men whose graves said 'He marched with Robert E. Lee' right next to a lot of dead Yankees," she recalled. "That's when my husband had to explain all about Yankee Memorial Day, that his father had fought for the Union, that half the town had fathers who did. I said to him, 'Martin Davis, you knew all this and didn't tell me? You think I wouldn't have come down here to live if you had?'" She laughed. "He said no, it was just that it had been drilled into him as a child not to discuss the Civil War with Southerners, including me." She smiled, adding, "That was the first I'd heard of Yankees with manners."

At first, Davis said, she found it discomfiting that her own grand-fathers once fought against her father-in-law. But gradually she became intrigued by Fitzgerald's history and wrote a play about the town's early settlers, called *Our Friends, the Enemy*. The play presented a casting problem, though. When it was staged locally during the Civil War centennial, the director couldn't find anyone left with a Northern accent. "I had to tell him we'd made Southerners of all of them," Davis said.

In a few ways, Fitzgerald had also turned the natives into North-erners. The United Daughters of the Confederacy still commemo-rated Confederate Memorial Day, but the group also showed up at the other Memorial Day, at which Davis herself laid a wreath honoring both blue and gray. The town's emblem bore an image of a Union and a Confederate soldier shaking hands across a map of Georgia, above the words: "Blood that mingled in bitter conflict was here united in brotherhood." When Davis opened the Blue & Gray Museum at the Lee-Grant Hotel, the offspring of soldiers from both sides donated heirlooms. Some residents—mutts descended from both Southern and Northern stock, or what Davis called "Yankee Rebels"—gave items from both armies.

The Lee-Grant hotel was gone now, and there was little apart from the town's street signs and Davis's small museum to recall Fitzgerald's remarkable history. "Folks joke about the fire depart-ment being on Sherman Street," Davis said. "But otherwise you don't hear much talk about the War."

In one sense, this seemed healthy. Though I'd often lamented the neglect of history in Atlanta and other places, I'd also seen how poisonous and polarized memory of the past could become. Still, it seemed sad that the story Davis had just told me wasn't widely known. However anomalous Fitzgerald might have been, it offered a glimpse of an alternative strain of post-War Southern history, akin to the many instances of racial progress and cooperation in the late nineteenth century that had been erased from modern memory by Southerners' demonization of Reconstruction, or by Northerners' smug stereotypes of a Klan-driven, Jim Crow South.

"History is lived forward but it is written in retrospect," the Eng-lish historian C. V. Wedgwood observed. "We know the end before we consider the beginning and we can never wholly recapture what it was to know the beginning only." Fitzgerald, for me, was a small reminder that the South's post-War history wasn't predestined to lead toward the strife and anger over the past I'd witnessed in so many other places across the South.

For Davis, Fitzgerald's story carried another, broader message for Americans. "If veterans could come together so soon after the War and forgive and forget, then surely we can overcome our differences," she said. "Old wounds were healed here, old barriers overcome. Seems like we should be able to do the same."

She shut off the museum lights and I offered to give her a ride home. Davis lived in one of the original frame houses built by the pioneers, on a cross street between two avenues named for Southern generals. "When we moved to this house, I said to my Yankee husband, bless his heart, 'Martin, if we've got to live in this nest of Yankees, I'm glad we're between Gordon and Bragg. I don't think I'd sleep as well between Sherman and Grant.'" She smiled, pausing at the door. "Funny, given all I know now, but sometimes I still feel that way."

13

Alabama

ONLY LIVING CONFEDERATE WIDOW TELLS SOME

I'm the last living veteran of the last living veteran of that war.
Probably a cheap kind of famous but, look, it's better than nothing.
—LUCY MARSDEN, in Allan Gurganus's
Oldest Living Confederate Widow Tells All

I plummeted down the Beeline Highway, past Pine Level, Orion, Needmore, and Jack. Cars swerved to the shoulder, hazard lights winking in the rain. A crackly voice on the radio warned of flash floods across Alabama. Pressing my face to the windshield, I finally spotted a small sign and careered into the parking lot of Elba General Hospital. Grabbing a pot of mums from the passenger seat, I splashed through ankle-high water, through the hospital's swishing doors, and skidded down the hall to the nurses' station. Then I blanked on her name, the name of a woman I'd never met, a woman who'd never heard of me.

"Where's the Confederate widow?" I blurted. "Is she all right?"

MY NIGHT RIDE TO ELBA had begun weeks before, in the northeast corner of Alabama. I was interviewing a neo-Confederate zealot when she said, off-handedly, "While you're in Alabama, you really should see the last Confederate widow."

"Last what?"

"Confederate widow," she repeated. "She lives in a nowhere town down by the Florida panhandle. Opp, I think." Then she resumed her rant about perfidious Yankees and the sanctity of the rebel flag.

I was titillated but dubious. Surviving offspring of Confederate soldiers, called "Real Sons" and "Real Daughters," were rare enough. Simple math seemed to rule out a surviving spouse. The last Alabama Confederate died in 1951 at the age of 104. So a Real Wife, if she existed, represented the spouse of a man who today would be pushing 150.

A news search on my computer wasn't encouraging, either. Amongst dozens of stories about Allan Gurganus's best-selling novel, *Oldest Living Confederate Widow Tells All*, I found an Associated Press item on the last nonfictional spouse: Daisy Cave of Sumter, South Carolina. She died in 1990, the A.P. reported, "closing yet another chapter in the Civil War story." No mention of Opp, Alabama.

Still, 1990 wasn't that long ago. Maybe this Alabama widow had slipped through the cracks. So I contacted a Daughter of the Confederacy in a town not far from Opp and asked if she'd heard of this legendary spouse. "Oh, you mean Miz Alberta Martin," Dorothy Raybon said. "Why of course. Her husband, William Jasper Martin, was a private in the 4th Alabama. I verified it myself."

When I asked why this widow had remained obscure, Raybon paused before responding. At the time of her marriage to eighty-five-year-old William Martin, Alberta Martin was a young farm woman with a small child. Later, only eight weeks after the old veteran's death, Alberta married again—to one of William Martin's grandsons.

Alberta now lived in a town called Elba (close to Opp) with a son she'd borne the veteran. I asked what they did down there. "Just sort of exist," Raybon said.

"What's Mrs. Martin like?"

"She's a real, sure-enough country lady," Raybon said. "She dips

snuff and keeps a little spittoon in her sweater pocket. And she tells
it like it is."

Early the next morning I called Alberta's home and got her son,
William. He said his mother had already gone out. She spent week-
days at the senior citizens' center, playing bingo and horseshoes. I
asked if I could come interview her. "Sure, anytime," William said.
"We don't go no place but Elba."

I studied the map. Elba lay deep in the south Alabama "Wiregrass," a rural territory with no feature more notable than its coarse,
spiky vegetation. The Wiregrass wasn't near anyplace I'd planned to
go. Anyway, I reckoned a few weeks' delay wouldn't ruin my scoop;
Alberta Martin had hung on for ninety years already and was still
spry enough to toss horseshoes. So I decided to tour the rest of Alabama, then stop off in Elba on my way to New Orleans, where I'd
vaguely planned some R and R in the French Quarter.

My wife, though, kept pestering me every night when we talked on
the telephone. "Have you seen that widow yet?" she'd ask, adding in
her inimitable Australian slang, "You'll hate yourself if she carks before you get there."

So one stormy afternoon I phoned Elba again to schedule a visit.
Alberta's son answered, but this time he was somber. "Momma woke
up real early this morning with gas pains something awful. I took
her to the emergency room and they say she's got to stay."

I felt a surge of panic. For a ninety-year-old, early morning "gas
pains" serious enough to require a hospital stay sounded ominously
like heart trouble. I asked William if I might visit her at Elba General. "She'd like that" he said, "so long's she's conscious."

So it was that I found myself speeding through high winds and
slanting rain and skidding down the hospital hallway. The nurse on
duty calmly glanced up from a paperback. "You mean Miz Martin?"
she said, smiling at my drenched mums and rain-plastered hair.
"Room 15."

The ward was small and silent. There appeared to be few patients
and no other visitors—unsurprising, given the tempest outside. The
door to room 15 stood ajar. No one answered my knock, so I stepped

just inside. Alberta Martin lay on her back with tubes running into her arms and bedsheets pulled up around her neck. The face poking up from the sheets looked as yellow and mottled as an apple-head doll. I'd arrived just in time.

Then Alberta opened her eyes. "You needn't a done that," she said, admiring the flowers. I set the mums on her night table, beside a glass filled with false teeth, and explained why I'd come. "Oh my," she said, gathering up her long white hair, which tumbled extravagantly across two pillows. Then she flashed me a warm, toothless smile and confirmed what had already become obvious—that I needn't have rushed. "I stay here so much it's almost like home," she said. The small, rural hospital was really a glorified doctor's office; anyone with serious problems, I now realized, would be transferred to a bigger facility.

But I was glad to be there and Alberta seemed glad to see me. Her son was what she called "high strung" and couldn't be counted on for company. "I made his bed 'fore I left this mornin'," she said. "Don't never leave the house till I done his and mine. Maybe you have to be carried away, somethin' wrong with you, and your bed will be unmade." Alberta settled comfortably onto her pillows. "Well, there's no bingo here," she said, "so I reckon we can talk all you want."

We talked for three hours, and could easily have talked for three more if a nurse hadn't kicked me out so Alberta could sleep. Like country folk across the South, Alberta liked to tell a story and take her time in the telling. So when I began by blurting out the obvious question—how had she come to marry a Confederate veteran?—Alberta smiled and said I couldn't understand that until I'd heard the whole story of "the hard way I come up in the world."

"I'se born just a piece from here, down yonder about five mile, in a little ol' no-house on the road to Opp," she began. I pulled my chair closer; her drawl and diction were the most foreign I'd heard since the Gullah-inflected speech of the Carolina Lowcountry. "My daddy and momma slept in one bed, my sister and me in t'other. In the next room was four brothers and five half-brothers and this that and t'other."

When Alberta was eleven, her mother died. Alberta left school and joined her father in the fields, sharecropping. "I hoed peanuts, picked peanuts, shook peanuts with a pitchfork to get the dirt off, stewed peanuts," she said. "And that was just the peanuts."

At fifteen, Alberta and her sister went to work spinning thread at a cotton mill, earning nine cents an hour. Soon after, she met a handsome young man with reddish blond hair. "He drove a taxi and drank and messed around," she said. "I was just young I guess and didn't have no sense. That was me. I got pregnant and then he just quit me and married 'nother girl he'd got pregnant."

Six months after Alberta gave birth, the taxi driver died in a car wreck. Alberta moved in with one of her half-brothers, who had four sons of his own. "When you stay in the country amongst your brothers and his boys and have to mind all of 'em," she said, "you get tired of it." So one evening, when an old man beckoned to her from across the fence, she went over to talk with him.

"I remember he had big ol' blue eyes, reddish skin and a mustache. Not bad for an old feller." That was William Jasper Martin, the Confederate veteran. He came up the road every day to buy tobacco at a nearby store, and each time he'd chat with Alberta over the fence. "We'd talk about nothin', what I call no sense, just talkin'," she said. "We didn't spark none." Sparking was old Southern slang for flirting.

But the talk soon turned serious. "He said he was huntin' him a wife and wondered if I'd be his," Alberta said. "I was tired of livin' in that house and needed somebody to help raise my boy. We'd knowed each other several months. So I told him, yeah, reckon so."

William was eighty-five, but he possessed one asset most younger men lacked: a decent, steady income. As a Confederate veteran, he drew a $50-a-month pension from the state, more than many sharecroppers earned in a year, particularly during the boll weevil-wracked years of the 1920s.

"We got married at the courthouse," Alberta said. "I wore a blue dress, wasn't no special dress. He wore common clothes, too. His friends serenaded us round and round with cowbells and made a racket hollerin' and hoopin'." But there was no further celebration. "Times was hard then, people didn't know what a honeymoon was."

The gap in their ages also made for a certain formality. "I called him Mister Martin," Alberta said. "I never did call him any other name because he was so old. He called me Sis, like my daddy. But I called that old man Mister Martin, even in bed."

I asked if she had any regrets about marrying a man sixty-five years her senior. Alberta smiled. "Better to be an old man's darlin' than a young man's slave," she said.

Ten months after their marriage, Alberta bore another son, William Jr., known as Willie. Her husband was generally kind to the children, she said. "But he was high strung, I can tell you that. He'd just as soon kill you as look at you."

He was also vague about his Civil War days. "He didn't talk much about it and I didn't ask much," Alberta said. "He said he went up to Virginny and was hungry. If they crossed a field, anythin' you could get to, potatoes or anythin' that a person could eat, they'd get it. He ended up in a hospital up there, pneumonia I think. He said he was reported dead but it was his little brother got kilt, not him. He never did say nothin' about the Yankees or shootin' anythin', 'cept a bobcat."

Even so, William attended veterans' conventions each year in Montgomery. Then, during a reunion in 1932, he fell ill and died a few days after his return home. "He's in a grave over in Opp. It's got a marker, says what war he was in." That was all the last Confederate widow knew about her husband's service to the Cause.

Alberta quickly remarried, to William's grandson Charlie, and more or less forgot what little she knew about her previous husband's military service. Then, sixty years after William's death, she saw a TV show at the seniors' center about the Daughters of the Confederacy. "They were goin' on and on about daughters and such, and here I'm a wife," she said. "Or was one oncet."

She also watched a TV adaption of Allan Gurganus's novel *Oldest Living Confederate Widow Tells All.* "It was a good picture all right, it played good, but none of it did resemble me," Alberta said. She broke into a self-satisfied smile. "Anyhow, I done her one better. I ain't the oldest livin' Confederate widow. I'm the onliest one. The last of the livin'."

Eventually, Alberta's daughter-in-law in Arkansas pointed this out in a letter to the governor of Alabama. The governor's office passed the letter to the UDC, and that was how Dorothy Raybon in Greenville had come to research and confirm the legitimacy of Alberta's claim. The UDC arranged for a Confederate marker to be put on William's grave, and the governor's office proclaimed Alberta an Honorary Lieutenant Colonel Aide-de-Camp in the state militia. A Sons of Confederate Veterans' camp even named her an honorary cannoneer. "And I ain't never shot a peashooter," Alberta said, shaking her head.

Southern heritage groups also began escorting Alberta and her son to reenactments and remembrances across Alabama. "I remember one party they took us to up near Tuscaloosey," Alberta said. "They shot some guns and I was too close and that made me deaf in my right ear." She also found herself at a demonstration in Montgomery in support of keeping the rebel battle flag flying from the statehouse. "I think it should be there," she said. "One flag can just as well fly as another. But it's not worth no fuss and fight. Blacks all hate it. And you know, there's lots of people that's colored that's better than any whites. Some of the whites are the sorriest you ever seen."

Life had quieted down over the past few years, except for local reporters stopping by for an occasional interview. Alberta liked the attention, but confessed she couldn't really understand what all the hoopla was about. And it irked her a little that the questions were always the same. "I lived with that old man for five years and six months," she said. "He's been dead forever. I was married to my next husband, Charlie, for fifty years and six months. Why don't nobody ever ask after him?"

THAT NIGHT, at a bed-and-breakfast called Aunt B's, I read through a pile of documents Dorothy Raybon had given me about William Martin's military service. They included a peculiar exchange of letters in the 1920s concerning William's belated request for a Confederate pension. One state official wrote, "This old man's memory is so bad he cannot recollect his Colonel's name or his Captain's name and but little of his service." Another reported that William Martin couldn't even recall the company he'd served in. "He has lost his parole, and all the witnesses that were with him, so far as he knows, are dead."

William's application form also raised questions—or rather, failed to answer them. Asked what date he'd enlisted, William put down, "During the latter part of the War." Each question about his actual time in the army prompted a "Don't Remember" or "Don't Know." As to why he'd never applied for a pension before, William stated: "Could not furnish evidence needed." Under income and assets, the document recorded "none." At the bottom of the document appeared an X beside the notation, "his mark."

Though William could offer no proof of military service, he later managed to produce two witnesses—one of them his brother—who signed a statement saying they'd seen William go off to war. So William Martin got his pension and went hunting a wife.

I phoned Alberta's oldest son, Harold Farrow, at his home in Arkansas and asked if he recalled any more details about William's wartime experience. No, he said. In fact, Harold recalled little at all about his stepfather. "He was old and cantankerous. Just an old man who set around in a rocking chair, did nothing," he said. "But my brother and me must have pestered him, because he'd shake his walking stick and say, 'I'll whup you!'"

"Did he?"

Harold chuckled. "We lived in a wooden house that sat on cedar blocks, about thirty inches off the ground. So when the old man would grab his walking stick and get after us with it, we'd crawl under the house and yell, 'You, old Martin. Wish you were dead!'"

Harold had one other vivid memory. "He was a jealous man, he was really jealous," he said. Once, when Harold was six or seven, William's grandson Charlie came to visit. "Old man Martin went out with a shotgun and said, 'If you open that gate it'll be the last gate you ever open.' The old man must have had reason to be so angry. Jealousy I reckon."

Charlie went away that day, though he returned to marry Alberta two months after his grandfather's death. The family, including Alberta and seven-year-old Harold, then went to work in the fields, "We were the poorest of the poor," he said. "Worked six in the morning until seven at night." Harold left home at sixteen, joined the military and never returned to Alabama, except to visit his mother. "I'm glad she's getting a little attention," he said. "She's had a hard life. Yes she has."

THE NEXT MORNING, I toured what little there was to see of Elba, a town of 4,000 perched beside the Pea River. I asked a Chamber of Commerce official if Elba had any historic sites I might visit. "There's that bug statue over in Enterprise," she said, handing me a pamphlet about the neighboring town. In a bizarre act of homage, Enterprise had erected a monument to the crablike pest that ravaged Alabama's cotton fields seventy years ago. "In profound appreciation of the boll weevil and what it has done as the herald of prosperity," the inscription read. The weevil had forced cotton farmers to diversify, and Enterprise was now a leading peanut-growing center.

Elba, however, lacked its neighbor's sense of humor and its, well, enterprise. Originally known as Bentonville, Elba had renamed itself after the desolate island where Napoleon went into exile. Even odder was the cover of the Chamber of Commerce's glossy new brochure. It showed the entire town deep under water, and the words, "Elba Flood March 17, 1990." This seemed a curious choice for a promotional tool.

"We're trying to come up with a new slogan," the Chamber official added. "Something like, 'A Small Town for a Big Family.'" She paused. "We're small. That's about all you can say about Elba. Except for the Pea River always flooding."

"How about 'Home of the Last Confederate Widow'?" I suggested.

The woman smiled politely and shook her head. "Who in the world would care about that, except for a Civil War wacko?"

Returning to Elba General, I found Alberta as chipper as she'd been the night before. So we picked up her life story more or less where we'd left off, with William's death and her marriage two months later to Charlie Martin, a man about her own age. "It's funny, but I used to say that if he was the last man in the world I'd never marry him," she said. "He drank too much and messed around. But they say love's like a potato, it sprouts from the eye. He was nice-lookin'."

He was also fun, at least compared to his grandfather. "We'd go to square dances, mostly old-timey stuff," Alberta said. Though she wasn't a drinker, Alberta recalled one night she'd had a few with Charlie. "I got sky high. We danced all night. That was the happiest time of my life."

Financially, though, life was harder than before. When William died, Alberta didn't realize she could collect a Confederate widow's pension—a stipend for which she became ineligible the moment she remarried. So the family had to get by on the $7.50 a month they earned in the fields. Alberta also had to endure gossip about her quick remarriage to her previous husband's grandson. "You know people had a lot to say about it, but it wasn't nothin' of other people's business," Alberta said. "I couldn't raise them boys by myself, times was so hard back then."

Times stayed hard for most of their marriage. When Charlie died in 1983, Alberta's son Willie moved in with her and the two got by on social security and pensions from Charlie's and Willie's military service. Still, Alberta hoped she might collect a little extra now that she'd been recognized as the last Confederate widow. The UDC maintained a small relief fund for elderly members in need. "But they say someone has to pass on to make space for me."

Around noon, Willie stopped by the hospital. A crew-cut man with a bulbous nose and badly shaven cheeks, he appeared much older than his sixty-seven years.

"Willie, you don't look too good," his mother said from the bed.

"Now Momma, I'm not the one we need be worrying about."

The two of them bantered until a nurse came in to escort Alberta off for tests. Alberta told Willie to show me some family mementos back at the house. "We're in the sticks," he said, guiding me down a road behind a lumber yard near the Pea River. The Martins' simple, one-story home wasn't much larger than a trailer. Inside, an old couch and easy chair faced the TV and a rebel flag draped across one wall. "Some big wheel with the Confederates gave us that," Willie said. "Don't mean nothing special to me, 'cept it covers some chips in the paneling."

He pulled a scrapbook off the shelf. It was stuffed with letters and certificates from Confederate groups, and requests for Alberta's signature. One letter, from an SCV camp in South Carolina, explained that the flag now hanging on the Martins' wall had flown briefly in her honor above the capitol dome in Columbia. It was signed, "I remain yours in the Cause for which they fought." Willie shrugged. "We didn't even know they had all these groups, sons and daughters and children and such. These people must be rich to go to all these meetings. Don't have to work, I guess."

The scrapbook also included a family tree, showing that William Jasper Martin had married his first wife in 1868 when she was only thirteen. They had ten children before she died. Then he married a second time and had five more children. Alberta was his third wife and Willie his sixteenth child. "That old man really got around," Willie said.

Willie went to dig out a photo of William Senior from one of Alberta's bedroom drawers. I stood in the hall while he sorted through the detritus of nine decades of living. "She keeps all kinds of junk," he said, returning with a dog-eared recipe for Sour Cream Drop Cookies, an old family Bible, and a long, lustrous braid of auburn hair. "That's Momma's, don't know why she kept it."

Pressed inside the Bible were two old photographs. One showed Alberta as a young woman with dark hair spilling around her shoulders. The other showed a man with high cheekbones, a drooping mustache and a jaunty expression. Beside him sat a large, square-jawed woman with a prim bun piled atop her head. This was William Martin and his second wife, photographed at the turn of the century.

I asked Willie what he remembered about his father. "They say he's my father, I don't know," he said. "I was only four when he died. Seems to me he used to sit me on his knee and feed me sweet potatoes." He lit a cigarette and studied the picture for a moment. "Want to see the old man's grave?" he asked.

WE DROVE PAST cotton fields and pecan groves and into Opp, a small town much like Elba. Before heading to the graveyard, Willie decided to visit Alberta's eighty-six-year-old sister, Lera, who lived in a public housing project behind the Piggly Wiggly. We found Lera putting a skillet of cornbread into the oven. With her long white hair and creased face, Lera looked just like her sister. Their personalities, though, were quite different. "Bert was always more tempered than me," Lera said.

I asked Lera what she remembered about her sister's marriage to the Confederate veteran. "I'd have married him, too," she replied. "Fifty dollars a month was a lot of money in them days." She sighed. "That was times back then. A woman didn't have no choices. First Bert and me worked here at the mill in Opp. Twelve-hour days, six days a week. It was like a fog in there from all the lint. But they fired you if you raised the window."

Lera said Alberta left the mill when she had her first child. But then she was stuck caring for her half-brother and his family. "Bert wanted so bad to get away from home," Lera said. "That veteran was all right by me. I was working at the cotton mill and would visit on my day off. They set around. Neither one of them worked. They had it good." Lera, meanwhile, stayed at the mill for twenty-eight years and never earned more than a dollar a day.

I asked if she remembered William saying anything about the Civil War. "No, he didn't talk about it," she said. "Seems strange, now that I think on it, but folks didn't go on about themselves then like they do now."

The room went silent. I could smell the cornbread cooking. Willie said we best be getting to the cemetery. Seeing us to the door, Lera told Willie, "You tell Bert I said to stop belly-achin' and get back to her bingo."

The graveyard occupied a small, weedy plot beside a potholed road running out of Opp. The first headstone I looked at said, "Infant babe of L. W. and S. M. Fuller Born and Died April 25, 1922." Several other stones marked the graves of both newborns and mothers who perished in childbirth. Some stones were made of cement and seemed to have been crudely inscribed with sticks. Even the names were plain. "Sarah Coon" or "Omer W. husband of Texie Martin" or given names I'd never heard before: Croyal, Malizie, Ardiller.

Willie led me to a long slab laid flat on the ground, its surface completely blank. At the top end, though, a fresh marble tablet read:

WILLIAM JASPER MARTIN
PVT 4 ALA INF
CONFEDERATE STATES ARMY

This was the stone the Daughters of the Confederacy had erected a few years back. "Before, it was just that slab, no writing at t'all," Willie said. He snapped a Polaroid and stood quietly for a moment. "I can't cry 'cause I don't really remember the man."

We wound back to Elba, pausing by the crossroads where Alberta was born and raised. "She lived back over there," Willie said, pointing across fields of peanut and cotton at several weatherbeaten cabins clinging to the edge of a pine wood. The landscape looked straight out of a Walker Evans photograph of Depression Alabama. I realized, too, that Alberta or Lera might easily have served as models for one of Evans's most famous portraits: a sharecropper's wife in a plain cotton dress, her prematurely worn features starkly framed against the rough wood siding of a tenant's shack.

Back in Elba, I dropped Willie at his home and returned to the hospital with a box of chocolates. Alberta looked tired and griped about the Jell-O, juice and congealed salad she'd been fed for lunch. "I like grits and sausage and cheese and butter and a bannaner for breakfast," she said. "And a good lunch, too. Don't eat too much anymore in the evenin'. All that food gets to workin' and it hurts."

Stomach trouble had also forced Alberta to give up her beloved snuff, which she'd first sampled at the age of five. "A long time ago, when a child looked pale or wouldn't eat like they should, people said 'Give em snuff.' People thought it'd keep you from eatin' cotton bolls and leaves and one thing or another." I asked her about the portable spittoon the UDC lady had told me about. "Just a glass jar with a lid on it," Alberta said. "Snuff glass, I called it."

I took out the mementos Willie had found in her bedroom. She studied the photograph of herself for a moment, then fondled the braid of hair. "I don't imagine I was purty, 'cept for my hair. This ain't quite the color it used to be, it was a little darker back then." Alberta's parents were devout members of the Church of Christ and frowned on women cutting their hair. So Alberta had kept hers long until she was about thirty. "Then one day, like everyone else, I wanted short hair," she said. "So I cut it off. But as soon as I did I wished it back on my head, long and brown like that. So I kept this braid to remember myself by."

Alberta's face softened and she began talking about a country custom called the box supper. "What you'd do, you'd make like a little shoebox with ribbons and bows around it, dress it up with purty paper," she said. "In the box is enough food for two. Two apples, two bannaners, cakes and sandwiches. You take it to church and fellers start biddin' on it. The boy that buys the box gets to eat it with you, and the girl who gets the highest bid wins a prize. I loved box suppers."

"Did you ever win?"

"I might've once," she said. Alberta had gone to a box supper with the old veteran soon after their marriage, and men began bidding for her box. "I wasn't but twenty, weighed a hundred fourteen pounds back then. I had that long hair. Boys were biddin' and biddin' on my box. But Mister Martin didn't like that. He thought they were making fun of him and he was jealous, thought they might spark with me or somethin'." So they took Alberta's box down from the table and put up someone else's. After that, she and William stopped going to box suppers.

"I did win one contest," Alberta added. "I was in a nursin' home for three months after Charlie died, had a nervous breakdown. I had to rock in a rocker and the one that rocked longest won. I went five hours rockin'. The prize was five dollars."

It was late afternoon and Alberta appeared tired. For the first time since my arrival the day before, I sensed she'd had enough of my questions about a time long ago. "Got a whole life to study over here in bed," she said. "But I done passed thinkin' about them days, I think about the future." Then she looked at me closely, as if for the first time. "You got quite a time to go, ain't you?"

"Yes, m'am. I hope so." I paused for a moment, then asked her what she thought the future would be like. Alberta sighed, closing her eyes. "If it's like it usually been bein', it won't be so good."

I laid her auburn braid by the bed and slipped quietly out of the room.

o o o

As it happened, Alberta's future wasn't at all like it had usually been being. Nine months after my visit, I picked up *USA Today* and saw Alberta's picture. A small story reported that she'd been awarded a Confederate widow's pension by the state of Alabama totaling $335 a month (some of this was back pay; she'd become eligible for a pension again when her husband Charlie died in 1983). Alberta told the paper she planned to use the money to buy an air conditioner, a hearing aid and a new set of false teeth.

Alberta had also caught the eye of heritage groups again. The Sons of Confederate Veterans flew Willie and her to Richmond for the group's 100th anniversary, Alberta's first plane flight. She was greeted by a standing ovation. "She's a living link to the Confederacy," the SCV's executive director declared. "That's the closest any of us will ever be to a real Confederate soldier."

William Jasper Martin also came in for some posthumous glory. The United Daughters of the Confederacy published a profile of Alberta in its magazine. It was filled with unsourced claims about her husband's wartime heroics; William was wounded in a bloody fight near Richmond, the article said, and he later recalled the screams of men "cut down as a scythe would cut down grain." The story also reported that he'd fought until the end and surrendered with Lee at Appomattox.

By then, I knew a bit more about William Jasper Martin's service to the Cause. The vagueness of the tales he'd told his family, and his amnesia while applying for a pension, had left me wondering. So I went to the National Archives with a researcher who specialized in Confederate war records. William Jasper Martin was there all right. Drafted in late May of 1864, he was sent the next month to Richmond and turned up almost immediately in hospital records, suffering from rubella. He was released in July on a sixty-day furlough. Then he went AWOL and never returned. On his company's muster roll, William's name appeared beside the word "deserter" for the remainder of the War.

William's name turned up again two months after Appomattox,

when he went to Montgomery for a formal parole by federal officials. The papers recorded that he was five-feet-ten with dark hair, blue eyes and a "fair complexion"—much as Alberta described him. We also found records for William's younger brother, who was mistakenly listed in one document under William's name. He died of battle wounds, with personal effects totaling $3.05.

William was lucky he hadn't been caught and shot for desertion by Confederate authorities, or exposed years later and denied a pension. But I was glad for Alberta, and for the false teeth and hearing aid, whatever her measles-ridden husband might have done 130 years before up in old Virginny.

14

Alabama

I HAD A DREAM

The past is never dead. It's not even past.
—WILLIAM FAULKNER, *Requiem for a Nun*

Approaching Montgomery, I was jolted from my interstate trance by two anomalous sights. The first was a long line of men in white uniforms, shackled at the ankle, swinging hoes and hauling brush as shotgun-toting guards kept watch. Alabama had recently brought back chain gangs and positioned them by major highways for maximum publicity.

The second sight was a huge Chamber of Commerce billboard welcoming visitors to Montgomery:

WE'RE HISTORY!
VISIT THE CIVIL RIGHTS MEMORIAL,
THE FIRST CONFEDERATE CAPITOL.

The irony of the first line, which consigned Montgomery to Trotsky's dustbin, was matched by the startling juxtaposition that followed. Civil Rights and Civil War—joint billing as Montgomery's premier tourist attractions.

At first glance, driving into Montgomery at dusk, I wondered if the "We're History" sign was meant to be read literally. The downtown office blocks had emptied for the day, leaving Montgomery a virtual ghost town. Birds twittering in the trees made more racket than passing traffic. Checking into a hotel by the grand but forsaken railroad station, I asked the receptionist where I might find something to eat. She directed me to a franchise-clogged highway several miles from downtown.

She also explained why the city seemed so dead. The interstate cleaved Montgomery in half in the 1960s. White flight and suburban strip malls had since sucked the life out of the old commercial district. Not that Montgomery had ever been renowned as a happening town. "I have rarely seen a more dull, lifeless place," the London *Times* correspondent, William Howard Russell, acidly observed in 1861, soon after the rebels set up government in Montgomery. "It looks like a small Russian town in the interior."

But touring the city on foot, I discovered one advantage that Montgomery had over other Southern capitals I'd visited. Unlike Columbia or Jackson or Atlanta, Montgomery's antebellum core hadn't been cauterized by Sherman or razed by developers. Topography also conspired to elevate the past. The city's historic center perched on high ground known in more rural days as "Goat Hill." Depending on your perspective, Goat Hill represented one of the most hallowed or haunted places in the entire South.

Crowning the knoll was Alabama's domed capitol, where Jeff Davis took the oath of office in 1861 (a few months later, the Confederate capital moved to Richmond). A brass star marked the marble on which Davis stood. A century later, George Wallace pointedly occupied the exact same spot to deliver his inaugural address as governor. "It is very appropriate that from this Cradle of the Confederacy, this very heart of the great Anglo-Saxon Southland, that today we sound the drum for freedom," he declared. "Segregation now, segregation tomorrow, segregation forever."

Stepping into the foyer, I found myself surrounded by a school group about to start a tour through the capitol. "I'm Sandy," said the statehouse guide, a young black woman in a white headband and

African-print dress. "And this is Lurleen Wallace." Sandy pointed at a bust of George Wallace's wife, adding, "She served sixteen months as governor before dying of cancer."

We moved down marble hallways lined with portraits of Alabama's governors, a 175-year procession of stern-looking white men, plus Lurleen. Sandy pointed out a portrait of George Wallace and also of the current governor, "Fob" James, who was painted clutching a tree. "That's to show his closeness to the roots of Alabama," Sandy explained. Fob's full name—Forrest Hood James— incorporated the surnames of two famous Confederate generals.

We climbed a spiral staircase to the capitol rotunda, adorned with vast murals of Alabama history. One, titled "Wealth and Leisure Produce the Golden Period: Antebellum Life in Alabama," showed an elegant couple on horseback in front of a grand plantation. A black mammy held a white child on the mansion's porch. "That was twenty years before the Civil War when cotton was king," Sandy said.

We moved down the hall to the former Senate chamber. "Boys and girls," Sandy said, "this is the very room where Jeff Davis was elected president of the Confederate States, restored to look the way it did in 1861."

"What are those?" a pony-tailed girl asked, pointing at what looked like flower pots near the back of the chamber.

"Spittoons," Sandy said. "For the juice from chewing tobacco."

"Oooh, yuk!"

As Sandy explained how the chamber's original carpeting was pulled up and sent to rebel soldiers for use as blankets, I realized that the entire tour had become a replay of Golden Southern Oldies: secession and segregation, from Jeff Davis to George Wallace. I also noticed something odd about the school group. The kids were all white, they ranged widely in age, and accompanying them was a crowd of teachers, about one for every two students. A number of the children wore T-shirts saying, "Jesus's Kids Totally His."

Chatting with a woman named Roxie, I learned that the group was composed of home-schoolers from south Alabama on a field trip to the capital. "Right now the fourth graders are studying the Civil War," Roxie said. "From a Christian perspective, of course."

I asked what she meant. "We start with a canned curriculum

we get from a Christian-based outfit in Florida," she said. "Then we supplement it with things out of the library. And my brother's a Civil War buff. That helps."

"How do you handle slavery?"

"Well, the kids always ask, 'Why did people do it?' We explain that not that many people owned slaves. I had three great-great-grand-fathers in the War. They weren't wealthy. They fought for the South because it was their way of life." She paused. "Of course, we're Chris-tians. Slavery wasn't right. But we teach that slavery wasn't that big a deal in terms of causing the War."

Roxie's husband, Doug, wore wire-rim glasses and a knapsack la-beled "Jesus Loves You." He worked as an engineer and taught the kids science. I asked why he and his wife had chosen to home-school their children. "Because if you want some choice in your kids' cur-riculum, they call you homophobic or racist or something," Doug said.

"What do you mean?"

"Like slavery. That was a period of history, that's all. You can't gloss it over. But teach the truth. Public schools won't do that."

Doug and Roxie paused politely as Sandy told the kids about the marble stairs, which were crafted by freed slaves. "Our kids are sort of secluded," Roxie whispered. "So this is nice, having a tour guide who's, you know, different."

The tour wound outside to a towering shaft ringed by the flags of the Confederacy, and by statues representing each branch of the mil-itary. "This is to honor the soldiers they sent the carpet to," Sandy said. I studied the inscription beneath a Cavalier with a plumed hat and extravagant mustache.

> THE KNIGHTLIEST OF THE KNIGHTLY RACE
> WHO SINCE THE DAYS OF OLD
> HAVE KEPT THE LAMP OF CHIVALRY
> ALIGHT IN HEARTS OF GOLD.

We ended our tour at the brass star marking the site of Jeff Davis's inaugural. The kids, wide-eyed, took turns jumping up and down on the spot.

As the group wandered off, I lingered to chat with Sandy and asked how she felt about guiding groups through this Old South shrine. "I never thought in my life I'd be doing this," she said. "And some of the people who visit here obviously feel the same. You know, diehard rebels. They look at you as if to say, 'How did your black face get here?'" She laughed. "But I have all the answers to their questions, so they go away happy. If anything, it's the black groups from up North that are unsettled. They want to know why this is on their tour in the first place, and what in the world I'm doing here."

"What do you tell them?"

"I say, 'Look here, honey, history's changed and I wouldn't be here if it hadn't. Folks here wouldn't have me, and I wouldn't have them. I see black faces going through these halls every day—black officials, understand, not janitors and maids. We don't have any black faces hanging on these walls yet, but it's just a matter of time.'"

In her own small way, Sandy felt she was hastening the change. "I like to think these dead white guys are looking back at me and rolling in their graves." She locked eyes with a wigged antebellum governor. "I'm here, honey. This is the 1990s. Understand?" With that, she smiled and hurried toward the door as another group of tourists wandered in.

Touring the rest of Goat Hill, I kept encountering the same, startling juxtapositions. A plaque beside the capitol identified the statehouse as both the home of the first Confederate Congress and the end point of the Selma-to-Montgomery civil rights march in 1965. Just a few paces away stood the Dexter Avenue Baptist Church, where Martin Luther King Jr. served as pastor in the 1950s and helped lead the Montgomery bus boycott. On the street outside stood two plaques. One noted that Dexter Avenue was the site of Jeff Davis's inaugural parade: "'Dixie' was played as a band arrangement for the first time on this occasion." The other plaque told of the Dexter Church and the bus boycott.

A block behind the church, on the same street as the First White House of the Confederacy, stood the Civil Rights Memorial I'd seen advertised on the billboard outside town. Designed by Maya Lin and closely resembling her Vietnam memorial in Washington, the monument's black granite slab was etched with the names of forty people who died in the civil rights struggle. A few doors away, in the corridors of the state archives, busts of Confederate generals nuzzled busts of Booker T. Washington and George Washington Carver. Portraits of Nat "King" Cole and bluesman W. C. Handy shared wall space with the "Alabama Troubador," Hank Williams. In a section devoted to religious leaders, a painting of Martin Luther King hung beside one of Bob Jones, founder of Bob Jones University in South Carolina, a bastion of the Christian Right that banned interracial dating.

At times, this proximity of black and white icons became a bit strange. In the faded downtown business district, I found a derelict building that had once housed the Empire movie theater. A plaque told how Rosa Parks, at a bus stop here in 1955, refused to give up her seat to a white man, sparking the Montgomery boycott. On the plaque's reverse side, I read that Hank Williams won a song contest at the Empire in 1938 before going on to write classics such as "Your Cheatin' Heart."

Montgomery's forthright treatment of its past was a refreshing contrast to the other Southern cities I'd visited. Genteel Charleston would have wrapped the same history in gauze, or discreetly averted its eyes; I couldn't imagine a painting of the black insurrectionist Denmark Vesey beside portraits of other "rebels," such as the Citadel cadets or P. G. T. Beauregard. Atlanta would have bulldozed Goat Hill, or rewritten the inscription on the Confederate monument and bounced holograph cartoons off the mustachioed visage of the Knightliest of the Knightly Race.

Alabama had even finessed controversy over the rebel battle flag, which flew for several decades above the capitol dome. While South Carolina and Georgia kept debating whether to keep the symbol aloft, Alabama had lowered its flag in 1993 and placed the banner beside the capitol's Confederate monument. A few agitators on both extremes objected to this compromise, but the fight over the flag had gradually faded from public consciousness.

o o o

Montgomery's equipoise about its past seemed almost too good to
be true, and in one sense it was. On my third day in town, I awoke
to a story in the local paper headlined: "Union General's Marker
Stolen." The marker commemorated James Wilson, a cavalry commander whose troops sacked the nearby city of Selma in 1865 before
peacefully capturing Montgomery three days after Appomattox. The
marker, recently erected beside the capitol, had mysteriously vanished in the night. An anonymous caller told the newspaper, "The
persons responsible for erecting the marker should be 'tarred and
feathered and ridden out of town on a rail.'"

The main person responsible for erecting the marker was Will
Hill Tankersley, an investment banker and former chairman of the
Chamber of Commerce. I found him studying a Quotron on the
seventh floor of a downtown bank building. A silver-haired man
of about seventy, with a red bow tie and carefully groomed beard,
Tankersley was baffled by the Wilson marker's theft. "This is an
aberration," he said. "I'd say 99.9 percent of Alabamans care more
about who's going to win the Alabama-Auburn football game than
they do about the Civil War."

Tankersley belonged to the .1 percent who cared passionately.
"I'm a West Point grad, a sixth-generation Alabaman, and I'm proud
as punch that one of my ancestors was a seventeen-year-old from
Pineapple, Alabama, who fought until the day Lee surrendered," he
said. "But history's history. We lost. And the only action here in
Montgomery was Wilson's raid. So why not remember it the same
way we remember all the rest of our history?"

Tankersley paused to take a phone call. "It's at fifteen and a quarter, down an eighth." Hanging up, he brushed aside a copy of *Standard
& Poor's* and unearthed *Co. Aytch*, the famous memoir of Tennessee
private Sam Watkins I'd read at Shiloh. "What comes through from
these memoirs is how brave these boys were," Tankersley said. "I
reckon the boys from up North were just as dedicated. We shouldn't
demonize one side and deify the other."

Many Alabamans evidently disagreed. When the Wilson marker
first went up, Tankersley received a torrent of angry letters and
phone calls. "One guy called and said, 'As soon as they put up a

Nathan Bedford Forrest monument in Cleveland, you can put one up to Wilson here.'" He chuckled. "I told him Forrest didn't make it to Cleveland." Another caller likened the Wilson marker to a monument honoring Benedict Arnold. A neo-Confederate publication even created a prize called "The Will Hill Tankersley Scalawag of the Year Award," awarded to Southerners who betrayed Confederate heritage.

This ire took Tankersley by surprise. As Chamber of Commerce chairman, he had also helped engineer the exhaustive marking of Montgomery's civil rights history, an effort that caused little controversy. "It's funny, isn't it," he said, "that people get more bent out of shape about a war they lost a hundred thirty years ago than about a struggle that occurred in their own lifetimes."

Tankersley's balanced approach to Montgomery's history wasn't just philosophical. It also made business sense. "There were two great cataclysms that started here—the Civil War and the civil rights movement," he said. "Tourists want to see that." Memorializing both events was also a way to burnish Alabama's battered reputation. "This state is overflowing with resources," he said. "It's got a heck of a work ethic. I want to bring jobs here. But we've still got an image problem. When you're sitting in a boardroom in New York and hear about Fruit Loops waving rebel flags down here, it's bad for business."

Tankersley glanced at his Quotron. The market had stopped trading for the day on an upward spike, as it had so often during the long bull market. "You'd think stocks never went down," he said, shaking his head. "When it comes to some things, people have very short memories."

FOLLOWING WILSON'S PATH in reverse, I headed for Selma, an hour's drive west. Selma lay near the buckle of Alabama's Black Belt, the band of dark, fecund soil that once undergirded the richest cotton land in Dixie. In 1860, Dallas County (of which Selma was now seat) ranked first in Alabama in cotton production, slaveholding, and per capita wealth. Selma also became a key Confederate arsenal and manufacturing center. In the War's waning days, Nathan Bedford Forrest fought a doomed battle to save the town. Wilson's cavalry captured most of Forrest's men and torched Selma's arsenal before riding on to Montgomery.

Almost a century to the day after Forrest's last battle, Selma became famous for another rearguard stand. Alabama troopers in gas masks and helmets, backed by a mounted posse of hastily deputized locals, blocked civil rights protestors from crossing Selma's Edmund Pettus Bridge for a march to Montgomery. Then the lawmen assaulted the peaceful demonstrators with billy clubs, bullwhips, cattle prods and tear gas. Television footage of the melee stunned the nation. A week after the clash, President Johnson pressed Congress to pass the Voting Rights Act, which ended literacy tests and other devices used for so long to deny blacks the vote. Before the law's passage, only 250 of Dallas County's 15,000 voting-age blacks had succeeded in registering. A year later, the number was 9,000. Thirty years after the Selma bridge incident, the Black Belt of Alabama and Mississippi had more black elected officials than any other part of the nation.

The Pettus Bridge clash—known as "Bloody Sunday"—made Selma synonymous in the national mind with bigotry and brutality. But, like Montgomery, Selma had recently turned its troubled history to tourist advantage. "From Civil War to Civil Rights," declared a billboard rising from the farmland bordering town. At Selma's small visitors' center, an elderly white man took out a street map and carefully marked a half-dozen historic sites: antebellum mansions, remnants of the 1865 battle, the Pettus Bridge, the Martin Luther King Historic Walking Tour, and the Voting Rights Museum. "We've always lived in the past in Selma, and we still do," he said. "But the past has changed on us. It includes a lot of stories it didn't used to."

As we chatted, the man said he'd served on Selma's segregationist city council during the civil rights violence of the 1960s. "I was born in 1921 and was raised up with segregation and separate water fountains," he said. "It was stupid now that I think of it. All these signs saying 'white' and 'colored' when most people couldn't even read."

I asked how he felt about the changes since. "You get older and you mellow, I guess," he said. "The marchers corrected an injustice." He felt the same about the Civil War. "I was raised when Confeder-

ates were gods and all Yankees were devils. But the Civil War had to
be fought, just like the civil rights thing." So here he was, an elderly
man, directing tourists to the ground where both he and his forebears had fought and lost in defense of the Southern "way of life."

As I toured Selma, though, it became obvious that the changes
only went so far. While the Black Belt's political and touristic landscape had been transformed, the social and economic picture remained much the same. Across the railroad tracks, in predominantly
black east Selma, sprawled a shantytown of tumbledown shacks
propped precariously on cement blocks. Just outside town, I drove
through an all-black housing project, wedged between a forlorn ball-
field and a Budweiser plant. A sign at the entrance said "Nathan B.
Forrest Homes"—an odd choice, given Forrest's notoriety as a slave
trader and Imperial Wizard of the KKK. Drab housing projects also
ringed the Brown Chapel, which served as the headquarters for the
civil rights movement in Selma. In front of the chapel stood a bust of
King, inscribed with the words: I HAD A DREAM.

The west side of Selma was mostly white and far more affluent.
But the sprinkling of old mansions seemed only to underscore
Selma's fall from antebellum bounty. A cemetery at the center of
west Selma added to the doleful atmosphere. Live oaks dripped
Spanish moss, shadowing a tall shaft marking the mass grave of 150
unknown rebels. "There is Grandeur in Graves, There is Glory in
Gloom," the inscription read.

I ended my melancholy tour at the Voting Rights Museum, beside
the Pettus Bridge. The walls were lined with photographs of white
troopers chasing black marchers through clouds of tear gas. There
was one other visitor, a graying black man in a kente-cloth robe
and cap. "That's me, right there," he said, pointing at a photograph
showing a young man in coat and tie, arms linked with other
marchers. "We were so young then."

Reverend Richard Boone was only twenty when he helped direct
the Selma Project, as that phase of the civil rights movement was
known. "We used to wear yarmulkes with our overalls," he said. "We
considered ourselves Baptist rabbis." Later, Boone was arrested
while trying to integrate Montgomery's Empire Theater, where

Rosa Parks began her bus protest. "The good old days," he said. "Everything was clear, black and white, like these pictures."

These days, Boone found himself embroiled in much murkier protests. He'd spent the past three months picketing a black radio station in Montgomery that had dropped several controversial programs, including a weekly address by the Nation of Islam leader, Reverend Louis Farrakhan. Ironically, the station's office stood directly across from the Empire Theater. "You've got black faces now doing the white massah's bidding," Boone said. "It's like slave days, with house niggers lording it over field niggers."

Some of his former white allies were also now in the enemy camp. Boone had recently gone to the Million Man March in Washington and resented charges of anti-Semitism leveled at its organizer, Reverend Farrakhan. "It's true what he says about the Jews," Boone said. "They used to be on our side. But now a lot of them are bloodsuckers."

I let this go. We drifted through the rest of the museum, past plaster casts of marchers' feet and a chapel-like "memorial room" honoring martyrs of the struggle. The museum also hosted frequent civil rights observances, including one that afternoon to honor a veteran Selma activist named Irma Jean Jackson. So I returned a few hours later and joined Boone and about fifty others, almost all of them elderly and late-middle-aged black women.

"This museum is a place where we honor the foot soldiers," the master of ceremonies began. "We were once children in the struggle and we must never forget the deeds of Irma Jean and other young fighters." Then Irma Jackson spoke, recalling her political awakening as a student in college. "The time had come to take a stand for our rights," she said, before telling the familiar story of the Selma struggle. "We got to the foot of the bridge, they charged and started beating people and throwing tear-gas bombs. The sun eclipsed, there was that much smoke. You could hear skulls cracking as the men opened up heads with their billy clubs. People screamed and splashed in puddles to get water in their stinging eyes."

As Jackson went on, a few people in the audience began softly weeping. Then she urged the audience to remember the martyrs and "the cause for which they fought." I realized I'd heard all this before. Honor the young foot soldiers. Take a stand for our rights. The litany of heroic deeds and fallen martyrs. It was the same mournful refrain that ran through dozens of Confederate observances I'd attended.

Almost every sentence began to carry familiar echoes. Irma Jackson told of "marching all day and sleeping in the fields" between Selma and Montgomery—just as rebel soldiers had done in Virginia. She recalled other hallowed fields of battle—Birmingham, Tuscaloosa, Little Rock—which resonated with her audience as powerfully as Sharpsburg and Shiloh did for many white Southerners. While working in small towns across the South, Jackson said, "We all suffered from nervous stomachs and sometimes went two days without eating because the restaurants weren't integrated"— recalling, for me, the tales of lean Confederates foraging for green corn and green apples on their hungry march through Maryland.

Jackson's speech ended with the invocation of the sainted leader, in this case Martin Luther King. "All are soldiers but only some are warriors," she said. "He was a warrior, a warrior for his people, who sacrificed all that they might live free." The same lines might have been spoken at a Sons of Confederate Veterans meeting about Stonewall Jackson or Robert E. Lee.

When she finished, Reverend Boone gave a short address that echoed the Civil War even more explicitly. "To quote our greatest president, 'We are met on a great battlefield. The brave men, living and dead, who struggled here, have consecrated it far above our power to add or detract.'" Boone lit candles to honor the civil rights dead and the audience began singing "Ain't Gonna Let Nobody Turn Me Around." It was a rousing tune, but I sensed a mournful cloud hanging over the room. The civil rights celebrants seemed caught in the same ghost dance as so many whites I'd met, conjuring spirits from an exalted past of heroic sacrifice, halo-crowned martyrs, and unfulfilled dreams.

After the ceremony, I chatted with the museum's director, Rose Mary Sanders, a striking woman with short-cropped hair who wore brilliant African robes and silver bands that ran halfway up each arm.

I asked her if I was wrong in sensing a plaintive nostalgia among others in the audience.

"You're right. It's depressing because so little has really changed," she said. "We still have the same mayor we had on Bloody Sunday. We don't worry about being shot by the Klan, but we worry about being shot by one another. We integrated the schools, so now all the whites go to their own. Whites here still make three times as much as blacks. What's to feel good about?"

Rose Sanders didn't look or talk like a Selma native, nor was she one. She and her husband, Hank, were Harvard-educated lawyers who worked in Africa before coming to Alabama in the 1970s. They'd since become Selma's leading—and most controversial—activists. Hank, elected Alabama's first black state senator since Reconstruction, had once been arrested while trying to take the battle flag down from the state capitol. Rose had spearheaded a black school boycott to protest the "tracking" of black students into slow classes. The 1990 protest ultimately led to racial brawls, the closure of Selma schools and the summoning of the National Guard—to protect white students. When schools reopened, the remaining whites fled en masse to private schools.

Sanders's latest cause was a petition to change the name of the Nathan Bedford Forrest housing project I'd passed outside town. "Can you imagine Jews living in some subdivision named for Himmler?" she asked. But so far, her efforts had met with indifference from blacks. "Most folks don't know their history enough to be insulted. They've never heard of Forrest, unless it's Forrest Gump. So they just take it. The whites make heroes of killers like Forrest and because of our own ignorance or internalized oppression, we let it happen."

Another of Sanders's causes was faring better. She'd begun an alternative school for black teenagers who had dropped out or been held back because of discipline or learning problems. The students were currently studying African empires, Sanders said, and would soon move on to modern black history in America. When I told her about my own research, Sanders's eyes lit up. "Why don't you come back tomorrow and tell my students about it?"

I agreed, on the condition I could quiz her students about their attitudes toward the Civil War. Sanders laughed. "You won't have to ask," she said. "They'll let you know, loud and clear."

THE NEXT DAY, before heading to Sanders's class, I stopped in to see Selma's long-time mayor. Joe Smitherman's career was a minor classic of Southern politics. A former appliance-store owner, Smitherman had risen through the political ranks as an avowed segregationist, served as mayor during the civil rights turmoil, and deftly tacked with the changing winds ever since. He was now in his eighth term as mayor in a city that was 60 percent black and had a black majority on its city council and school board.

"When running against other whites, I've gotten ninety percent of the black vote," he said. This seemed a curious boast from a man who had once opposed voting rights demonstrators, and who had also once stumbled at a press conference, referring to "Martin Luther Coon."

Now a graying man of sixty-four, Smitherman wore a Snoopy tie and sat chain-smoking amidst mementos that mirrored the curious twists during his three decades in office: a Confederate flag, a tommy gun, framed photographs of George Wallace, Lester Maddox, Jesse Jackson, and the black assistant police chief of Selma. He reached into his filing cabinet for a news clip about a recent visit by John Lewis, a civil rights leader who was hospitalized with a severe concussion after Bloody Sunday. "Lewis said the change in Selma is 'almost unbelievable,'" Smitherman said. "And he had his skull busted open here."

But Smitherman didn't want to dwell on his city's civil rights turmoil. "People say, 'Oh Selma, that's where they set the dogs on people.'" He groaned. "We didn't even have dogs here. The dogs were in Birmingham."

Smitherman, though, was more than happy to talk about Selma's recent decision to market its civil rights history. "The idea was, what happened at that bridge, we've been stigmatized because of it for so long, why don't we sell it, too?" It was only recently, too, that Selma had become broad-minded about its Civil War history. "You have to remember the Yankees won the battle here and burned the town. Older folks in Selma naturally don't like making a big deal out of that."

I asked Smitherman about his own attitude toward the Confederacy. He responded by telling me about his childhood in the Depression, as the son of sharecroppers. "We were dirt poor," he said. "My father died when I was a few months old and my mother raised the six of us on welfare. For us, the Civil War was pride. It was all we had to hold onto. The rich whites, they had ancestors who were colonel this or general that. But we didn't know anything about that. It was just pride in having once been something."

These days, the city helped sponsor an annual reenactment of the Yankee victory at Selma, and also supported an annual commemoration of Bloody Sunday. Smitherman had even joined returning marchers on the bridge and awarded a key to the city to Reverend Joseph Lowery, who co-founded the Southern Christian Leadership Conference with King.

Even so, fresh clashes over race kept cropping up, including Rose Sanders's recent demand that the name of Nathan Bedford Forrest Homes be changed. "Everyone just calls it N.B.F. for short," Smitherman said of the housing project. "If you live at 118 N.B.F., do you really want to change to 118 Magnolia Gardens? We've got a Lee Street, a Jeff Davis Avenue, a Martin Luther King Street. We should be beyond that sort of thing."

As Smitherman walked me to the door, I told him I'd send a copy of whatever I wrote about Selma. He chuckled. "I don't give a damn what you do. Y'all always do the same, come in here smiling and then go home and write a dig at us." He clapped me on the back, straightened his Snoopy tie, and headed back into his office.

Several months later, I received two newspaper clips in the mail from a friend in Alabama. One told of a vote by Selma officials, including the mayor, to rename the Nathan Bedford Forrest Homes after a local civil rights leader. The other story reported that Joe Smitherman had outpolled a black candidate by just 52 votes to win his ninth term in office as Selma's mayor.

Rose Sanders's classroom, adjoining the Voting Rights Museum, was decorated with pictures of Rosa Parks, W. E. B. Du Bois, Ralph Ellison, and a Klansman hunched over a bleeding black man. A large poster declared: "I Need Respect, I Want Respect, I Will Give Respect." Fifteen kids, most of them sixteen and seventeen, straddled chairs or sprawled across desks. I'd just begun telling them about my travels when a student named Jamal raised his hand. "You got a name for your book?"

"Not yet."

He went to the blackboard and wrote in large block letters, REDNECKS OF THE SOUTH. The others laughed and started shouting their own suggestions. "Crackers of the South!" "Bigots!" "Peckerwoods!"

I smiled and ran the eraser across the blackboard. "What's the Civil War mean to you?" I asked.

"Nothing," several students sang out in unison.

"It's *his*-tory," a teenager named Percy said. "As in *his* story, the white man's, not mine."

I pointed out this wasn't really so. "Blacks fought in the War and slavery ended because of it."

"No it didn't!" a girl named Ni'key declared. "We just don't call it slavery anymore."

I changed tacks. "When I say the words 'Abraham Lincoln,' what's the first thing that comes into your head?"

"Benevolent racist."

"Just racist."

"He had slaves."

"That's not true," I said.

"He was probably paying blacks so little that they might as well have been slaves!" Ni'key shouted. Several other students came over and gave her high fives.

"What about the Emancipation Proclamation?" I asked.

"What about it?" Jamal said. "These Southern crackers were farm boys and slave hunters, so of course they were whipping those nerds from up North. Lincoln had to free the slaves so he could use them as soldiers."

We went back and forth for half an hour. In essence, the students were saying that the Civil War had nothing to do with race or slavery—much the same argument made by neo-Confederates who saw the War through the prism of states' rights.

I asked if any of the students attended Selma's annual Civil War reenactment. Percy laughed. "We got some crazy rednecks here. They could use all that shooting as an excuse to shoot us and say it was an accident."

"Hypothetical question," I said. "My great-grandaddy was in the Civil War, fighting for the South. How should I remember him?"

"Forget him. He's all bad."

"Those crackers did wrong. Why honor them?"

"Rednecks!"

"Peckerwoods!"

Rose Sanders finally stepped in. "The Vietnam War was evil," she said, "but we don't feel everyone who fought in it was evil."

The students went silent for a moment. "You got a point," one student said. "My uncle fought over there."

Then Sanders banged a desk. "But no monuments! We're trying to change criminal behavior among our young people. You can't do that and at the same time honor Confederate criminals."

"Right on!"

"The Civil War is still going on," Sanders said. "The only difference is that the Union army has betrayed us, too. So we're fighting a confederacy up North and down South."

"Tell it!"

"And why should we go watch some reenactment that honors the Southern way of life?" Sanders said. "The money I pay for that just goes into a pot that continues to oppress us. Only a few whites come to our bridge reenactment. They're signaling that our history isn't important. So why should we join in theirs?"

I listened silently. Sanders's message was the same refrain I'd heard across the South. My history and *his*-story. You Wear Your X, I'll Wear Mine. Both races sealing themselves off from each other. I was relieved when the class finally ended.

"You can see for yourself now," Sanders said, leading me back to the museum, "that there's a lot of fear and anger in these kids about that whole Civil War crowd."

I suggested this might not be so if they had more contact with the "Civil War crowd," some of whom, like Will Hill Tankersley in Montgomery, regarded themselves as progressives when it came to race.

Sanders frowned. "I prefer to deal with someone who admits their racism than with white liberals who hide it." Then she launched into a tirade against white civil rights workers, black "sellouts" like Julian Bond, and "Jews who knock down men like Farrakhan."

"Jews don't like Farrakhan because he calls them bloodsuckers," I replied. "If you're fighting racism, you shouldn't have a leader who says racist things."

"Don't tell us who our leaders should be," Sanders snapped. "If you give up on a leader because of a few things he says, you can't follow anyone."

"A few things?" I snapped back. "He says Hitler's a great man. As a Jew, I've got a problem with that."

"Oh, here we go again. Jewish suffering. What about our suffering? Our holocaust? What about the holocaust of Indians?"

We argued for half an hour before shouting ourselves out. I glanced around. We were surrounded by photographs of Bloody Sunday and the Selma to Montgomery March. Looking at these same photos the day before, I'd wished myself there on the Pettus Bridge, or marching behind Martin Luther King. "The good old days," Reverend Boone had called them. In a way he was right.

Sanders's thoughts seemed to travel along a similar plane. She walked me to a window and looked out through the rain as traffic crawled over the Pettus Bridge. "I guess I wanted to have this museum to add some clarity to history, or at least to remember a time when there was some clarity," she said. "It's gotten so complicated ever since."

I DROVE OUT OF SELMA through the late-afternoon gloom, past King's "I Had a Dream" bust, feeling lower than at any time during my long Southern ramble. If the Civil War infused my boy-hood imagination, it was the racial dramas of the 1960s that had molded my political consciousness. I was five when King made his Dream speech a few miles from my home. The March on Washing-ton was my first political memory—mainly, I suspect, because my parents fought over whether my mother should go. My father, a lib-eral but cautious man, feared trouble. In the end my mother stayed home.

Five years later, I sat on a friend's rooftop and watched Washing-ton burn during the rioting sparked by King's murder. It was about this time that I began drifting away from the Civil War. Thinking back, I couldn't remember why. But perhaps it was my growing awareness of the race-charged city around me; at some point, cool-looking Confederates didn't seem so cool anymore. And Union sol-diers, to me, had always seemed like a bore.

Or maybe my focus just shifted. In college I studied black history, tutored inner-city kids, wrote a turgid senior thesis on Southern black workers. It was my thesis advisor, a civil rights scholar from a black college in Mississippi, who urged me to go South after gradu-ation to work as a union organizer. While in Mississippi, I wrote my first newspaper article, on a maimed black logger, and found I liked writing better than agitating. In a way, my childhood fixation on the Confederacy had mutated into an adult preoccupation with the South and with race—and led, in a roundabout fashion, to my choice of careers.

The past year's journey had given me ample chance to revisit all this. But the South had changed on me, or I'd changed on it. My pas-sion for Civil War history and the kinship I felt for Southerners who shared it kept bumping into racism and right-wing politics. And here I was in Selma, after holding my temper with countless white supremacists, losing it with a black woman whose passion I'd ini-tially admired. Months before, in Mississippi, I'd learned that the union I'd worked for, once militantly integrationist, was now all-black. It had little use anymore for white sympathizers from up North. Nor, evidently, did black activists like Rose Sanders and Richard Boone. To some degree, this was inevitable and healthy. People had to fight their own battles; outsiders tended to get in the way, particularly in the South. Still, it saddened me that I sometimes felt like an enemy on the premises, among both whites and blacks.

Dᴿɪᴠɪɴɢ ᴏᴜᴛ ᴏꜰ Sᴇʟᴍᴀ, I pondered something else. Rose Sanders's students had offered me a glimpse of what angry young blacks in Alabama learned about the Civil War. I'd also seen a bit of what conservative whites—namely, the home-schoolers I'd met at the state capitol—taught their kids about slavery and secession. I was curious to know what lay between these extremes.

Through the friend of a friend, I contacted a history teacher in Greenville, a town of 8,000 an hour's drive south of Montgomery. Billie Faulk was about to teach the Civil War to her high school students, and said I could listen in. But the offer came with a curious caveat: the Civil War wasn't part of the prescribed high school curriculum.

"Alabama's course of study is pitiful," Faulk said, sweeping the blackboard clean between classes. A slim, attractive woman in her early forties, Faulk had the frazzled intensity of a twenty-year classroom veteran. In elementary school, she said, students made a high-speed pass at slavery and secession during survey courses covering all of Alabama and U.S. history. They returned to the War in eighth grade, at the tail end of a class covering U.S. history to 1877. "But most teachers fall behind during the year and end up rushing through the War," Faulk said.

Officially, that was all they got. Alabama had recently changed its curriculum so that high-schoolers studied U.S. history only from 1877 onward. I later called a state official, who explained, "We wanted to adjust the frame to include time closer to the present that's more relevant to students." Texas and several other Southern states had done the same.

Faulk bent the rules as best she could, supplementing the textbooks with material of her own and including a review of slavery and the War. But it was Band-Aid work at best. "Most kids simply don't have a grasp of the basic facts," she said, "so it's hard to really probe the issues."

Her students filtered in. Five blacks sat in a clump by the door. Six white students camped by the window. I sat alone in a row that formed a sort of no-man's land between the two groups.

"Let's talk about Southern society," Faulk began. "What does it mean to be Southern?"

"Country accent," one boy said. "Country ways."

"Backwoods, like."

"We farm more than people up north."

"We talk different and eat funny foods. Like we have a rattlesnake rodeo and a watermelon jubilee."

This seemed a rather narrow and self-deprecatory notion of Southern identity. Still, it was refreshingly free of rebel flags. Unfortunately, as Faulk had warned, it was also almost free of facts.

"How long did slavery last?" she asked.

"Until the 1900s?" one boy ventured.

"1940," another said, with certainty.

Faulk frowned. "Is that what the rest of you think?" The others looked at her blankly. "Well, the answer is 1865." She paused, then asked, "When did the Civil War start?"

"1812!"

"1840!"

"1816!"

"1861," Faulk corrected. "How do we know about slavery? What are our sources?"

"Books, like, and movies," one boy called out. "The Autobiography of Scottie Pippen."

"Miss Jane Pittman, you dummy!" a friend yelled, thumping him on the back. "Scottie Pippen plays for the Bulls." The class erupted in laughter.

Faulk asked the student what came to mind when she said the words "Old South."

"Big Houses."

"Big dresses, too."

"Big parties, like in *Gone With the Wind* and *North and South*."

"Hard work, cotton, slaves," a black student said. He was the only black to speak up during the class.

Faulk explained that the Old South wasn't very old or very grand in most of Alabama. Less than 1 percent of whites owned 100 or more slaves, and some of Alabama's finest plantations grew from log cabins built just forty years before the Civil War.

"You mean the one Lincoln grew up in?"

"When they freed the slaves did they all go and kill their old masters?" another boy asked.

"There's something I don't get," a third boy said. "If slaves were so cruelly treated, why do they always have pretty teeth in the movies?"

Faulk lectured for the remaining twenty minutes until the bell rang. "As you can see," she said, smiling wearily, "I'm competing with Hollywood. It's almost a let-down when they learn that the antebellum South wasn't all Scarlett O'Hara and Ashley Wilkes."

The same mythic gauze overlaid their notions about the Civil War. "They think it's all glory," she said. Faulk tried to dispel this romance by talking about the horrors of the War. Her own forebears had fought for the South; one went to war at fourteen, another in his sixties. "They were poor men fighting a rich man's war," she said. "I don't think there was much glory in that."

We headed for the cafeteria and piled our trays with fried steak nuggets, turnip greens, pickled beets and cornbread. Again, the kids separated loosely along racial lines. The same was true of the break period that followed, during which students milled outside in neighboring clumps of white and black.

Faulk's next class was world history, so I went to the school library to look at the textbooks she'd given me. "Like most people in the South, Alabamans held a strong belief in states' rights. Alabama joined the secession movement and fought against the Union in the Civil War." Those two lines were all the ninth-grade primer had to say on the subject.

Still, this was better than the apologias of old, which I'd read at a Montgomery library. "It was only a question of time when the slaveholders would have freed their slaves," claimed a ninth-grade textbook from the 1940s. A 1961 textbook showed kindly mammies and obedient field hands flashing "bright rows of white teeth." The pages were also filled with wicked Yankees, vicious scalawags, and venal carpetbaggers.

I poked my head in another classroom and found Ruby Shambray,

a heavyset black woman who had taught history in Greenville for
thirty-five years. "When I started here, the Civil War was my favorite subject," she said. "You just taught what happened and kids were
interested."

Back then, her students were all black. Then, when schools integrated in 1969, many middle-class white parents began sending
their kids to new, all-white private schools—known colloquially
across the South as "seg academies." This drained energy and resources from Greenville High, which was now mostly black and
working-class, like many other public schools in the region. Shambray said the school's library was poorly stocked, its computers few,
its labs antiquated. Alabama spent less on public education than any
other state in the nation.

Integration had also turned the Civil War into a minefield. "Suddenly, whatever I said was wrong," Shambray said. Blacks accused
her of soft-pedaling slavery while whites thought she was vilifying
their ancestors. Shambray found herself dreading the subject. "For a
few years, I would take a running jump from about 1855 to Reconstruction," she said.

Then, from about the mid-1970s to the mid-1980s, the atmosphere improved and Shambray learned to ease her students into the
Civil War. "I'd preface the whole issue by saying that none of us here
today were responsible for what happened. It's history, and we need
to discuss things in an open, intelligent fashion."

But like others I'd spoken to across the South, Shambray sensed
a hardening of attitudes from about the mid-1980s onward. Both
blacks and whites became contentious and less interested in facts.
"I've taught two generations now, and this one is different," she said.
"They're much thinner-skinned than kids used to be, but at the same
time more insensitive to others."

Each year, she asked for a special report on an historical subject.
"There's always a white student now who wants to report on the
Klan. I've had a few claim they're members." Blacks, meanwhile,
seemed intent on tuning out the nineteenth century. "They feel like
it's someone else's war, history that belongs to someone else," she
said, echoing what I'd heard in Selma.

The split extended to school trips to Montgomery. Black kids perked up at the civil rights sites, whites at the capitol and White House of the Confederacy. They also kept their distance in the classroom. "I don't seat students. The classes just segregate themselves. They've all just got used to it this way."

Shambray had taken a step back as well, feeling queasy again about teaching the Civil War. The new curriculum let her off the hook, since she wasn't required to teach events before 1877. "I have to talk about slavery and the War—it's too important," she said. "But I don't dwell on it."

The bell rang and I returned to Faulk's classroom for her eleventh-grade advanced placement history class. These students, at least, had a basic grasp of the facts and the discussion quickly turned to the War's causes and legacy.

"The Civil War's relevant because the effects are still obvious," one student said. "A lot of people are still poor and prejudiced in the South, and that basically goes back to the War."

"I think the racism is worse now than then," another girl said. "Back then, blacks and whites both farmed and often worked close by, even if they weren't equal. Today, we're so much more separate."

Another student stroked his peach fuzz and said, "The North deserves some blame. They talked a lot about emancipation but didn't do much for blacks after the War. And when blacks started moving North, whites weren't much better than here in the South."

A black student blamed parents for the persistence of prejudice. "The racism, it's generational. It gets passed down," she said. "It's like church. You don't choose which one you go to. You just do what your parents did."

The conversation had become free-flowing and I raised my hand. Why, I asked from my lonely perch in the middle aisle, were all the whites sitting on one side of the room and blacks on the other?

"It's just always been that way," one of the whites said. A black student nodded. "When we were younger we were all friends," she said. "You didn't think about black and white. But you get older, you hear things on the news. You look around. You hear the little things people say. Things change. We're still friends but it's different."

There was no animosity to this observation. It was just the way things were. At least the students were occupying the same classroom and talking to each other, unlike Rose Sanders's students or the home-schoolers I'd met in Montgomery. Or, for that matter, most students in the North. Washington, D.C., where I'd been educated, now had a public school system that was 97 percent black.

After the day's last class, I asked Faulk about the school's informal apartheid and the fact that white students seemed far more outspoken and self-assured than blacks. "We had an exchange student from Macedonia," she said. "He told me, 'You know, blacks are in the majority here but they're afraid of you.' He was right. Blacks have grown up with whites being dominant and they seem to tolerate it."

Like Ruby Shambray, Faulk was also bewildered by what she called "a blip of good ol' boyism" in recent years. "Before, kids really wanted to get along and understand each other. Then the urge just withered." She paused. "I graduated from a segregated high school here. I knew black kids got educated somewhere, but I didn't really think about it or stand up for change. Somehow, I'd hoped these kids would think more about these things, but I'm not sure they do."

I SPENT TWO MORE DAYS at Greenville High and left with mixed emotions about what I'd seen and heard. Clearly, the Lost Cause was close to being truly lost in the minds of young Alabamans. Only the advanced students grasped even the dimmest outline of the War's history. Nor were these teenagers unusual. I later read a survey about Southerners' knowledge of the War; only half of those aged eighteen to twenty-four could name a single battle, and only one in eight knew if they had a Confederate ancestor.

This was a long way from the experience of earlier generations, smothered from birth in the thick gravy of Confederate culture and schooled on textbooks that were little more than Old South propaganda. In this sense, ignorance might prove a blessing. Knowing less about the past, kids seemed less attached to it. Maybe the South would finally exorcise its demons by simply forgetting the history that created them.

But Alabamans seemed to have also let go of the more recent and hopeful history embodied in Martin Luther King's famous speech. "I have a dream," he said, of an Alabama where "black boys and black girls will be able to join hands with white boys and white girls as sisters and brothers." Alabama, like Mississippi, appeared to have made much greater strides than places less seared by the civil rights struggle, such as southern Kentucky. Even so, the past-tense rendering of King's quote in Selma seemed a sadly apt commentary on most of the 1990s South I'd visited.

On my last evening in Greenville, I went to see a retired teacher named Bobbie Gamble who taught for many years both at the public high school and at one of Greenville's private academies. "We really believed that if you started kids together from first grade, the whole racial attitude would change," she said. Gamble recalled staging a production of *Hello Dolly!* in the early 1970s. She cast black kids in many of the white roles, and parents of both races mingled comfortably in the audience. "Given what it was like here before, that was a small revolution," she said.

But viewed with twenty-five years' hindsight, the revolution appeared limited, and seemed to have turned reactionary. "No one really talks about true integration now," Gamble said. "Now, the goal seems to be separatism with everything equal. Not just in terms of facilities, but in terms of how we present society. Black history and white history. Black culture and white culture. We should be teaching all this as *our* culture, *our* history. But no one's trying to do that anymore. It's *Plessy* vs. *Ferguson* extended to everything."

Nor was separate really equal when it came to education. At first, Gamble said, white parents who sent their kids to private academies "were people with money who didn't want their kids sitting next to blacks." But as public schools deteriorated, the academies began to attract middle-class families who simply wanted their kids to have a better chance. The academies cost $150 a month, straining budgets and deepening resentment of blacks, whom many whites blamed for the decline of public schools. "It's a vicious cycle and the whole South is caught in it, the whole nation, really," she said.

On my way out of town, I stopped at Fort Dale South Butler Academy, whose sign proclaimed, "established 1969"—the year Greenville's schools integrated. The trim brick building was ringed with trailers to accommodate the school's rapid growth. There wasn't a black face among the hundred or so kids I saw running to buses as school let out. I wandered past an outdoor play area and saw a large Confederate battle flag painted on the pavement. Like the rebels of old, the seg academies had effectively seceded from the changing society that surrounded them.

Leaving Greenville, shadowed by the same melancholic cloud that hung over my visit to Selma, I kept replaying Bobbie Gamble's parting comment. "Remember, Bloody Sunday was only thirty years ago and school integration's even younger than that. Maybe we're just asking too much. Revolutions don't happen overnight."

Winding out of Greenville behind a long line of school buses, I hoped she was right.

15

STRIKE THE TENT

The quickest way of ending a war is to lose it.
—GEORGE ORWELL

I was midway to Gettysburg with a live chicken slung over one shoulder when I realized my Civil War odyssey had come to an end.

Rob Hodge marched beside me through the tidy farmland of southern Pennsylvania. Not that we could see much scenery. It was 3 A.M. "This is it—Nirvana," Rob said, pointing at the silhouette of a barn dimly visible in the midsummer moonlight. "Not one sign of the twentieth century."

Rob had pomaded his long black curls and greased his mustache in an upward twirl. He looked like a downmarket Pickett, clad in the still-unlaundered butternut he'd worn during our Civil Wargasm the summer before. In the year since, Rob had sought out new frontiers of hardcore reenacting. Forty other rebels trudged behind us, some of them barefoot, recruited by Rob for a twelve-mile forced march to a battle reenactment at Gettysburg.

"Most of what real soldiers did was march, not fight," Rob said, explaining his rationale for the hike. The march was originally planned for dawn, but Rob had decided at midnight to suddenly change plans, as commanders often did in the Civil War.

For added authenticity, Rob had purchased a rooster and three live chickens from a Pennsylvania farmer the day before. "The rebs carried livestock with them, so why shouldn't we? We'll cook these birds up before the battle."

One of the chickens had been pecking and defecating on my shoulder for three hours now, and any squeamishness I'd felt about its fate had long since vanished. I was ready to wring the bird's neck if Rob gave the order. Over my other shoulder I toted a gunnysack filled with mail from the homefront. Rob had painstakingly addressed the letters by candlelight before our departure, using a period pen. "We'll do a mail call at dawn so you won't have to haul that bag all the way to the battle," he assured me.

Headlights flickered on a bend in the country lane, just ahead. Instinctively, I turned and shouted, "Wagon!" A sergeant ordered the men to "fall out" and they cleared the road as the car sped past. One soldier stumbled drunkenly into the grass and fell face-down, giggling hysterically. "Laudanum problem, sir," I said to Rob. "I'll report it to the medical officer at first light."

Rob smiled and punched my shoulder. "Super hardcore," he said.

IT WAS THE THIRD SUMMER since my return to America, since my return to the Civil War. I couldn't glance at the calendar anymore without attaching parallel dates from the 1860s. May meant Chancellorsville and Stonewall Jackson's arm resting in the shade of the trees. June 9th was my birthday, but also the cavalry battle at Brandy Station. July 4th, of course, marked the surrender at Vicksburg and Lee's retreat the day after Pickett's Charge.

August was special in a different way. Having seen through so many anniversaries and remembrances, I'd added one of my own: an annual conference on Civil War medicine in Frederick, Maryland, which I attended for the third straight year with my father. The conference had become a new father/son ritual—or rather, a reconstituted version of our old one. Where we'd once pored over volumes of Civil War photographs, we now sat in a darkened auditorium watching slides and listening to lectures titled "Confederate Pest Houses" or "Substance Abuse and Anesthesia During the Civil War."

My father had just retired from full-time neurosurgery and returned, like me, to the Civil War. When he wasn't seeing outpatients, he poked around medical archives and wrote scholarly articles about wartime surgeons who pioneered techniques for treating head wounds. "Most of what they did was experimental," he whispered during a gruesome lecture on penetrating wounds to the cerebellum. "Eighty-three percent of missile hits to the head ended in fatality in the Civil War."

I was the last of three children and the only family member who had ever shared his passion for the War. My mother spent the weekend of the medical conference browsing with my wife through Frederick's antiques stores. Over lunch, my mother confided that she *had* once visited a few battlefields—while being courted by my father forty-five years before.

"His idea of fun on a midsummer afternoon was going to Bull Run," she said. "It was hot as hell and I wasn't a bit interested. I thought it was weird."

AFTER MARCHING THROUGH the dark for several hours, Rob ordered us into an orchard to rest until dawn. The men stacked their muskets in a tepee-like cone and threw groundcloths onto the dewy grass. Several soldiers spooned in the predawn cool.

I tethered my chicken to a split-rail fence and volunteered for sentry duty with Rob. This meant standing by the road with a wicker jug of honey liqueur, a vile brew that Rob had picked up while provisioning his troops. Between gulps, Rob gazed proudly at his sleeping men. It was a long way from our four-man Pickett's Charge the year before. Since then, Rob had become a one-man lollapalooza, creating impromptu events that attracted a growing crowd of followers.

At first light a rooster crowed on a nearby farm. Our bird was still sleeping. "Wake up, you farb rooster," Rob yelled, nudging the fowl with his boot. The rooster managed a half-hearted squawk and the men sleepily mustered. Then Rob shouted "Mail call!" I opened the gunnysack and took out the dense wad of letters. Struggling to decipher the smudged scribbles on the envelopes—reproductions of nineteenth-century ones, which Rob had dabbed with sealing wax—I called out each soldier's name.

For a few minutes the men quietly read their mail. One soldier learned that Yankees had seized his farm; another that his father had died of typhoid. Rob pored over a small tintype of a severe-looking young woman that was enclosed with a missive he'd addressed to himself the night before. "She may not look like much," he said in a choked voice, wiping away tears, "but she's my sister."

ONE HOT AFTERNOON, my father took me for a sentimental drive around Washington. At Rock Creek Park, he pointed out the remains of Union breastworks he'd scrambled over as a child, and from which the Federals repelled a daring raid by rebels under Jubal Early. We also paused on Pennsylvania Avenue, where my father had watched Civil War veterans pass during military parades in the 1930s. "I used to stand and stare at these old men with long beards going by in open cars," he recalled.

We ended our tour at the National Museum of Health and Medicine, which I'd last visited thirty years earlier when my father and I plowed through the ten-volume *Photographic History of the Civil War*. The museum was established to collect surgical specimens from Civil War battlefields, and one artifact in particular had struck my morbid boyhood imagination. At Gettysburg, a cannonball shattered the leg of Union general Daniel Edgar Sickles. He survived amputation, donated the leg to the museum—accompanied by a note saying, "with the compliments of Major Gen. D.E.S."—and went to visit his severed limb each year on the anniversary of his wounding.

Unfortunately, the leg had been temporarily removed for conservation. As I studied the limb's ebony-wood coffin and a picture of the stump-legged Sickles—who lived to the ripe age of eighty-nine—my father drifted over to an exhibit on head wounds.

"See the brains extruding?" he said, pointing at one picture. "That's a cerebral hernia." Another photograph showed a soldier who died of a depressed skull fracture after being kicked by a horse.

"It was over a major vein, they should have left it alone," he diagnosed. "The patient probably thrombosed."

We moved to a display of a surgical kit from the War. "Bone saw, file, gouging chisel, trepan," my father said, ticking off the contents. "I used something called a Hudson drill with a crank mechanism that wasn't all that different from what these guys had."

Somehow, as a child, it had never dawned on me that my father saw some link between his own work, digging bullets from the heads of young men shot on the streets of Washington, and the labors of Civil War surgeons who trepanned the skulls of wounded soldiers—often in hospitals a few blocks from the operating tables where my father spent most of his career. Thinking back, I realized we'd spent an inordinate amount of time studying volume seven of the *Photographic History*, the one devoted to wartime hospitals.

NEARING THE GETTYSBURG BATTLE, Rob halted our troop by a red farmhouse and ordered one of the men to go ask for water. A white-haired woman came to the door. She seemed remarkably unfazed by the forty fetid rebels gathered in her yard. "You're not the first ones here, though it's been awhile," she said. "Jeb Stuart's cavalry came by in 1863. They slept in the grist mill over there."

The woman pointed us to a spigot and went inside, returning with homemade loaves of potato bread and jars of apple butter. We filled our canteens and flopped gratefully on the grass, munching the heavy food. For me, this was the principal joy of reenacting. It restored my appreciation of simple things: cold water, a crust of bread, a cool patch of shade.

One of the woman's children came out with a camera. She scanned the crowd and decided to photograph a cluster that included me. I smudged some gunpowder on my face and struck a fierce pose. As the camera snapped, I thought back to the morning when Rob and his fellow hardcores had first appeared on the road by my house. I'd brought out refreshments and gawked at the men, just as these farmers were now doing.

Before we left the farm, Rob asked an adjutant to pen a note saying, "Thank you most kindly for your generous hospitality." Then he slipped the letter in a period envelope, adding a five-dollar Confederate note, and left it by the farmhouse door. "We make war only upon armed men," Rob declared, echoing his namesake, who ordered rebel troops to pay for all provisions acquired from Northern farmers.

The last several miles of the march took us along an old railroad embankment covered in crushed stone. The rubble felt brutal against my tired, poorly shod feet. Bits of tar bubbled on the cross-ties and heat waves shimmered up ahead. The unshaded track seemed to go on forever.

Rob had planned it this way, of course. "It's the scenic route, boys," he called out to his groaning troops. As one man pulled off his boots to study his blisters, the chicken he'd been toting broke free and scampered off the embankment. "Shoot the deserter!" someone shouted. But no one had the energy to give chase and the bird escaped into the woods. Rob shook his head. "Hardcore chicken," he said.

ALL SUMMER LONG, I'd culled the notes gathered during my long Civil War ramble. The journey had leached into a second year and eventually carried me to fifteen states. But somewhere along the line, I'd realized that it would take several lifetimes to fully explore the South's obsession with the War. I'd managed only brief forays to the outriders of the old Confederacy—north Florida, Arkansas, Louisiana, east Texas—and failed to reach more far-flung outposts I'd dreamed of visiting, including Brazil, where a diehard band of rebels known as the "Irreconcilables" established a colony after the War. Their descendants still held an annual *confederado festa* to honor their rebel forebears.

In the end, my journey had centered on the core Confederate states. And from the Carolina Lowcountry to the Mississippi Delta to the Shenandoah Valley, I'd often heard the same sentiments expressed. Everywhere, people spoke of family and fortunes lost in the War; of their nostalgia for a time when the South seemed a cohesive region upholding Christian values and agrarian ways; and, most frequently, of their reverence for larger-than-life men like Stonewall

Jackson, Robert E. Lee and Nathan Bedford Forrest. "That was our Homeric period," Robert Penn Warren wrote of the Civil War, "and the figures loom up only a little less than gods."

In reality, they weren't gods at all, which only made them more intriguing. The more I read, the more I realized that the marble men of Southern myth were often prideful and petty figures who hurt their own Cause by bickering, even challenging each other to duels. Northern generals were often worse, on and off the battlefield. A few years before Daniel Sickles lost his leg at Gettysburg (in a stupid tactical move of his own devising), he shot his wife's lover dead on a Washington street. Sickles got off with the nation's first successful plea of "temporary insanity." Then he took his wife back. It was hard to imagine Sickles—or Grant (an alcoholic), or Sherman (suspected of insanity), or Stonewall (ditto)—rising to the top of today's luster-less military.

The Civil War, as I'd seen on countless battlefields, also marked the transition from the chivalric combat of old to the anonymous and industrial slaughter of modern times. It was, Walker Percy wrote, "the last of the wars of individuals, when a single man's in-genuity and pluck not only counted for something in itself but could conceivably affect the entire issue." This was true not only of gener-als, but also of men like Jedediah Hotchkiss, a geologist and map-maker who scaled mountains to survey enemy positions before plotting several of the South's most triumphant maneuvers. Today, the same task would be performed by spy satellites and drone air-craft.

The Civil War was human-scaled in another essential way. Most of the War was fought across a pastoral, preindustrial landscape. Entire campaigns hinged on how many miles soldiers could walk in a day, how much forage they could gather for their horses, how much heat or ice both man and animal could endure. Soldiers and leaders also framed their experience in vivid rural imagery. Jefferson Davis feared that lowering the draft age to seventeen would "grind the seed corn of the nation." In 1864, Grant ordered Sheridan to so despoil the Shenandoah Valley's farmland that "crows flying over it for the bal-ance of this season will have to carry their own provender."

And yet it was new technology that made the War's romance and rusticity so palpable. Without photographs, rebs and Yanks would seem as remote to modern Americans as Minutemen and Hessians. Surviving daguerrotypes from the 1840s and 1850s were mostly stiff studio portraits. So the Civil War was as far back as we could delve in our own history and bring back naturalistic images attuned to our modern way of seeing.

But time-travel and nostalgia, and what Robert Penn Warren called "armchair blood-lust," explained only so much. For many Southerners I'd met, remembrance of the War had become a talisman against modernity, an emotional lever for their reactionary politics. Neo-Confederates had even taken their culture war to the Internet, on Web pages called DixieNet, CSAnet ("the E-Voice of the South") and Prorebel (site of the "Cyber-Confederate Army").

While I felt almost no ideological kinship with these unreconstructed rebels, I'd come to recognize that in one sense they were right. The issues at stake in the Civil War—race in particular—remained raw and unresolved, as did the broad question the conflict posed: Would America remain one nation? In 1861, this was a regional dilemma, which it wasn't anymore. But socially and culturally, there were ample signs of separatism and disunion along class, race, ethnic and gender lines. The whole notion of a common people united by common principles—even a common language—seemed more open to question than at any period in my lifetime.

But while my travels had brought me to some understanding of others' obsession, I still felt strangely unable to explain my own. A psychoanalyst would no doubt tell me that I associated the Civil War with boyhood evenings spent with my father, a workaholic professional who was otherwise often absent from my life. Somehow, though, this didn't fully explain the deep, almost spiritual contentment that often washed over me during my travels: studying Confederate muster rolls in a Carolina library, running my hand along a snake-rail fence at Chickamauga, dipping my toes in the Rapidan. Occasionally, people had talked about their passion for the War in ways that illuminated some part of my own. I thought back to Mike Hawkins, the bookish textile worker in North Carolina, who felt as though he'd "been away for a while" when he read his history books. Or June Wells, the Confederate museum curator in Charleston, who saw in a dead drummer boy's sticks the whole unspeakable horror of war.

Then there was Jimmy Olgers, the Virginia storekeeper Rob and I met on the Gasm. "You can't miss something you never had," he'd said of his tie to the land. "And if you never had it, you don't know what it's all about." That was the way I often felt about my attachment to the Civil War. It was just something I "had," like myopia or male-pattern baldness, a congenital trait passed down from my father on one side and my maternal great-grandfather, Poppa Isaac, on the other. The pleasure the Civil War gave me was hard to put into words, at least words that made much sense to any one other than a fellow addict.

"You're talking about a period rush," Rob said, when I tried to explain all this during the final mile of our Gettysburg march. "You're having rushes all the time and you don't even realize it."

Maybe he was right. Then again, I'd rarely felt the sort of period rush that Rob and his friends described while spooning by campfires or shivering in a picket post by a frozen Virginia stream. In a way, I was jealous. As a child, the Civil War had formed a vivid fantasy world I could enter with the stroke of a paintbrush, or by clutching a stick and imagining it a musket. In part, my journey had been an attempt to rediscover that boyhood rapture. But childhood fantasy kept colliding with adult reality—the reality of my dulled adult imagination and of the discomfiting adult questions that remembrance kept raising.

Still, here I was, marching to Gettysburg with a live chicken slung over my shoulder. Rob, of course, had the fever much worse than I did. But when I asked about the source of his own obsession, he became uncharacteristically tongue-tied.

"I'm like you, I guess, I can't really explain it," he said, draining the wicker jug of honey liqueur. "I mean, I could care less what I wear in the rest of my life, but out here I'm obsessed with my clothes. It's like I'm searching for the Holy Grail, except it's not a cup, it's a bit of gray cloth with just the right amount of dye and the exact number of threads."

It was early afternoon when we reached the Gettysburg reenactment. Rob had arranged for a fife and drum corps to meet us, and we marched onto the battlefield to the sound of "Dixie," past dense crowds of spectators armed with videocams and Instamatics.

Cannons began firing and someone came on the loudspeaker to announce that combat was about to begin. This was the cue for us to exit the battlefield. Rob and his followers rarely fought anymore; battles without bullets necessarily lacked authenticity. Hardcores preferred the unsullied experience of marching in the dark and reading mail from the homefront.

So the men retired to a nearby field to set up camp. I handed over my chicken and told Rob I had to head home. "Come back tomorrow for the return march," he said, slumping to the ground and magnanimously liberating the chicken. "Hiking on day-old blisters takes you to a whole different level."

But I'd decided in the night that I wouldn't be coming back, at least not for a long time. I had a three-month-old baby waiting at home with Geraldine. Marching in the dark, I'd missed them and felt guilty for being away on a Civil War lark. It was time to put away childish things, at least until my own child was old enough to play with them, too.

I drove south along the spine of mountains that ran from southern Pennsylvania to my home in Virginia, paralleling the route Lee's army followed during the retreat after Gettysburg. Crossing the Potomac at sunset, imagining weary rebels splashing through the river, I felt the same dreamy contentment that had washed over me so often during the past several years.

A few nights before, while reading a Robert Penn Warren essay about the Civil War, I'd come across several lines that spoke to me. "A high proportion of our population was not even in this country when the War was being fought. Not that this disqualifies the grandson from experiencing to the full the imaginative appeal of the Civil War. To experience this appeal may be, in fact, the very ritual of being American."

Reading this, I'd wondered if "the ritual of being American" helped explain why my great-grandfather bought a Civil War book soon after arriving here in the 1880s. As a teenaged émigré without family in America, he must have felt profoundly adrift. He arrived here only seventeen years after Appomattox, when memories of the conflict remained vivid. Poppa Isaac came from learned, rabbinical stock. Maybe he sensed that Civil War history was an American Talmud that would unlock the secrets of his adopted land and make him feel a part of it.

Or perhaps, like young immigrants today who quickly latch on to sports teams and pop-culture stars, he was drawn to the Civil War as a badge of citizenship. Then again, maybe one of his co-workers at the sweatshop where he labored had fought in a New York regiment and intrigued Poppa Isaac with stories of the War.

But as I crossed the Potomac and rode into the Virginia hills, I sensed that Warren's words applied equally to me. Lacking deep family roots in America, I'd started sinking my own in the one part of the Continent that felt somehow like home. I hadn't planned it this way, at least not consciously. But there was a ritualistic quality, in Warren's phrase, to my relationship with the Civil War landscape, whether it was the fields of Gettysburg or Burnside's Bridge at Antietam or some bit of rustic scenery—a crooked stone wall, an old graveyard, a simple frame house—that I glimpsed along country roads. These were places I'd felt deeply connected to since childhood, first through the study of sacred texts with my father, and then through my own attempts to reproduce them, like a medieval illuminate, on the walls of my attic bedroom and in the pages of my crude Civil War history.

It turned out that my Australian wife had roots here, too. While doing some family research of her own, Geraldine found a family tree and a faded photograph of a great-great-grandfather from America wearing what looked like a Civil War forage cap. I went with Rob to the National Archives and discovered that Geraldine may have had several forebears who served with New England regiments that fought in Virginia.

This didn't kindle a sudden passion on Geraldine's part for weekend drives to Manassas. But she consented to naming our new dog "Shiloh" and didn't yawn quite so histrionically when I droned on about the Civil War. Geraldine drew the line, though, when our son was born on the anniversary of Jackson's mortal wounding at Chancellorsville. No son of ours would be named Stonewall, nor for any of the other Virginians that Rob suggested: Jubal, Mosby, Ashby, Armistead.

We opted instead for another romantic figure from the nineteenth century: James Fenimore Cooper's adventurer, Natty Bumppo. All summer, Geraldine nursed Natty while listening to the sound track from *Last of the Mohicans*, dreaming of the day he might run through the woods in moccasins and leather breeches, as his namesake had done.

Me, I harbored a different fantasy. The upstairs bedroom we'd set aside for our son had old wooden beams and a sloping ceiling. The walls badly needed paint. Perhaps when Natty got a little older he could decorate them himself. I had a few old books on the shelf that might give him some ideas.

ACKNOWLEDGMENTS

I WOULD LIKE TO THANK the following people, without whom this book would have been a lot harder to do, and a lot less fun. Sue and Ed Curtis, for introducing me to the Sons, Daughters, Children, and Cats of the Confederacy. John Shelton Reed, for his wit and wisdom about the South, from which I've borrowed liberally. John Coski, the most priceless treasure at the Museum of the Confederacy. David Goodwin, a brave soul and boon companion in southern Kentucky. Bruce and Laura Lee Dobie, hosts with the most in Tennessee. Robert Rosen, a gentleman and a scholar of the Carolina Lowcountry. Plus others too numerous to mention who demonstrated how amply the South deserves its reputation for hospitality.

I would also like to thank my e-mail pen pals—Crawfish, Peter Applebome, Wolfgang Hochbruck—who were generous beyond measure with their own research. And the best bunch of critics any writer could hope for: Geraldine Brooks, Elinor Horwitz, Josh Horwitz, Dan Frank, Kris Dahl, Brian Hall, Michael Lewis and Peter Glusker. All your time is not forgotten.

INDEX